THE COMPLETE GUIDE TO

FOUR SEASON
HOME MAINTENANCE

THE COMPLETE GUIDE TO

FOUR SEASON HOME MAINTENANCE

How to Prevent Costly Problems Before They Occur

Dave Herberle & Richard M. Scutella

BETTERWAY BOOKS
Cincinnati, Ohio

Cover photograph by Newlight Studio
Text illustrations by Jay Marcinowski
Typography by Park Lane Associates

97 96 95 94 93 5 4 3 2 1

Library of Congress Cataloging-in-Publication Data

Heberle, Dave.
    The complete guide to four season home maintenance : how to prevent costly problems before they occur / Dave Heberle and Richard M. Scutella.—1st ed.
       p. cm.
    Includes index.
    ISBN 1-55870-278-4 : $18.95
    1. Dwellings--Maintenance and repair--Amateurs' manuals.
I. Scutella, Richard M. II. Title.
TH4817.3.H42 1993
643'.7--dc20
                                      92-38665
                                        CIP

Contents

Introduction

For a lot of people, this book's title is scary. Because it contains the term "maintenance," mysterious things come to mind, such as "What's behind my kitchen walls?" or "Where do the sewer lines *really* go?" or "Will I ever learn the shocking truth about my electrical system?"

Because our world has become so specialized, we can no longer fix everything we own. Appliances and components have become so well engineered and so intricate that highly specialized knowledge, skills, and tools are often required for their repair. A few centuries ago things were different. People understood the workings of the few possessions they had, and they knew how to fix them when failures occurred.

Please relax. This book has not been written so you can *repair* all kinds of complex inner workings of furnaces or refrigerators or leaking foundations, although some instructions for simpler repairs are included as part of a maintenance program. This book was published to help *prevent* your furnace, your refrigerator, and your foundation from needing those major repairs in the first place. In fact, in many cases you don't even have to understand how something works to perform effective preventive maintenance on it.

This is not to discourage you from further study on how your home and its components are put together. The more knowledge you possess, the easier it will be for you to understand the whole picture. If you feel you need to know how everything works and how it all fits together, then by all means consult books about new construction and publications featuring more in-depth discussions of each component or appliance you are interested in.

Rest assured that to establish a healthy preventive maintenance program for your own household, as outlined in these pages, you won't need elaborate tool kits, technical expertise, lots of money, or hours and hours of spare time. Instead, you will be surprised at how little effort is required and how substantial the return will be.

PREVENTIVE MAINTENANCE— WHAT IS IT?

Simply put, preventive maintenance consists of activities designed to increase reliability and to extend useful life. For our purpose, it includes:

- Inspections to identify deteriorating conditions or deficiencies.
- Record keeping to tell when inspections were last done and when they are due again. Records feature pertinent backup materials such as operating manuals, parts lists, servicing and repair histories, warranty and cost information, and vendor names, phone numbers, and addresses.
- Routine servicing of equipment, including minor adjustments, parts replacements, and simple repairs. Cleaning, lubricating, and filter changing are all considered routine servicing.
- Identification and evaluation of major deficiencies that are considered major repairs, so those repairs can be planned and scheduled in advance.

PREVENTIVE MAINTENANCE— WHO IS IT FOR?

Preventive maintenance is for anyone who manages a household. For people who own or rent. For men and women. For young and old. For people who live in single-family dwellings or in upstairs flats. For high-rise apartment tenants. For condominium, cottage, or mobile home owners. For do-it-yourselfers. For rookie and veteran homeowners alike. In fact, because the condition of the household, of the home and its furnishings, contributes so substantially to the contentment of the inhabitants, preventive maintenance is for *everyone*.

THE ADVANTAGES OF PREVENTIVE MAINTENANCE

Some people, when faced with the concept of preventive maintenance, consider it to be "work that is not yet needed." Indeed, why not just wait until something breaks and then fix it? During these busy times when people are working several jobs, putting children through school, exercising at health clubs, and spending hours in front of televisions and computer monitors ... we are busier, it seems, than ever. Why saddle ourselves with yet something else to do? In fact, what if the thing never breaks or never would have broken? Then you would have spent time and effort fixing something you never had to repair.

On the surface that might sound like an enticing argument. And perhaps in some areas it applies. You replace a satisfactory window pane when it cracks or shatters, not before. But for the most part, household components are not as simple as a window pane. You can let things go and hope they won't deteriorate or abruptly fail, but there is an element of risk involved. You are betting that nothing will happen. You are betting your furnace will make it through every sub-zero Saturday and Sunday winter night without expiring because you haven't had it tuned up in three years.

In truth, benefits offered by even the most basic program of preventive maintenance in the home are many and far-reaching. The most important ones are:

- Everything will last longer and stay nicer, too. You will increase the useful life of equipment, components, accessories, furnishings, and appliances, plus you will reduce the need for unexpected cash outlays to replace prematurely worn-out items.
- Your home will be safer. Everything will function as it should — without plugging up, overheating, leaking, or gradually falling apart and causing consequential damages.
- You won't be as inconvenienced. By helping to prevent abrupt, surprise failures, you will greatly reduce the number of situations requiring immediate or emergency attention.
- You will protect your investments. Your home and belongings will be worth more if and when you decide to sell or bequeath them.
- You will enjoy greater peace of mind, with less psychological, financial, and physical stress just knowing that things are in good shape.

Unfortunately, even the most ambitious preventive maintenance program cannot guarantee you won't encounter an occasional "surprise" failure of some kind. But that should be the exception rather than the rule. With preventive maintenance you will certainly pay far less — in time, money, and worry — over the medium-to-long run.

PREVENTIVE MAINTENANCE— A FOUR-SEASON AFFAIR

Many inspections, cleanings, and repairs are associated with specific seasons, and with good reason. It would not make much sense to tackle fireplace inspection and maintenance during hot weather. Nor would it be a sound idea to PM (Preventive Maintenance) an outside vegetable garden in the dead of winter. Each season can be used to spread a number of inspections out over its three months, so no particular month's maintenance tasks become overwhelming. By using the year's entire twelve months to spread out your own custom preventive maintenance schedule, the inspections and related maintenance tasks will require only brief investments of time each week.

Of course, one person's summer is another's winter. People living in the western hemisphere sometimes forget that the months of December, January, and February bring warm weather to the other side of the globe, in Australia, say, or New Zealand. Although the sample checklists and schedules have been developed for western climates, when you put together your own schedule, take your local conditions into account. If you live in a place where it rarely rains, then you needn't inspect for rain-related problems as often. On the other hand, if year-round sun and dryness are the rule, customize your master schedule by giving more attention to possible wear and tear caused by those conditions.

HOW TO GET THE MOST FROM THIS BOOK

To get the most from this book, finish this Introduction and skim the Table of Contents to see what is covered. Then read one section after another—they are not difficult—at a leisurely pace. By the time you complete a first read, you will have a good understanding of what it takes to PM a household, and you will be ready to put your own custom preventive maintenance schedule together, as outlined in Part 10.

During your first read, mark the sections that apply to your situation for later reference. Use a red felt-tipped pen or some other easy-to-see writing implement. At any time, feel free to make notes in the book's margins, underline key passages, or fold the page corners as a reminder. This book is meant to be a working tool—one that gets handled a lot. It can't save you time, money, and worry by sitting idle on a bookshelf. The more you use it, the more familiar and attuned you will become to preventive maintenance, and the better off your household will be.

Also read the Quick Checklists at the end of each section. They are meant as a fast study or refresher to each respective section. If you don't have time to reread sections once their inspections are due, at least scan the quick checklists to remind yourself what needs to be looked at.

Since preventive maintenance works best when done in a methodical, routine manner, a few inexpensive items to keep things organized can help:

A 3-inch-thick three-ring looseleaf binder with about sixteen dividers. The dividers should be labeled:

PM MASTER SCHEDULE
JANUARY
FEBRUARY
MARCH
APRIL
MAY
JUNE
JULY
AUGUST
SEPTEMBER
OCTOBER
NOVEMBER
DECEMBER
MAJOR REPAIRS
YEARLY SUMMARIES
NAMES, ADDRESSES, PHONE NUMBERS

■ A copy of your own custom PM Master Schedule. Part 10 will explain how to prepare your PM Master Schedule in detail, including how to select the items to be inspected. You will need a pad of 8½" x 11" sheets of graph paper, some transparent tape to fasten several sheets of paper together, a straightedge, and a pencil.

■ Copies of the Monthly PM Schedules. For these, either cut out pages 279 and 280, or copy it from the book to use as a template. Make a few dozen photocopies of the template. Write the monthly headings (January, February, March ...) on the copies and insert them where they belong in your binder.

THIS BOOK'S ORGANIZATION

There is no doubt that a household is a complex structure. *The Complete Guide to Four Season Home Maintenance* tries to make sense of the big picture by breaking down the typical household residence into six parts:

Outdoor Features and Accessories
The Exterior Shell
The Interior Shell
Utility Spaces
Major Operating Systems
Home Appliances and Accessories

Then five additional parts build upon the first six, by discussing:

Housekeeping
Financial Matters
Home Safety
Preparing Your Own Custom PM Schedule
Keeping at It

The first part, Outdoor Features and Accessories, covers such things as driveways, sidewalks, patios, swimming pools, fences, landscaping, and related topics. Real estate agents are the first to admit that the condition of what can be seen from the outside of any home is an accurate indicator of what to expect inside. To maintain top value of any dwelling, the outside features need to be kept in good shape.

The second section, the Exterior Shell, focuses on items such as doors, windows, siding, roofs, and caulking—those all-important components that separate the home's interior spaces from the weather.

The third part highlights the Interior Shell: the walls, ceilings, flooring, and other inside components we all tend to think of when we discuss the condition of the living spaces.

Part 4 features Utility Spaces and their own special sets of items to be inspected routinely. Utility spaces include attics, garages, basements, laundry rooms, and workshop areas—those places that are frequently taken for granted, but play a considerable role in the livability of any household.

The fifth section is particularly important — the home's Major Operating Systems. The electrical, plumbing, heating, cooling, water, septic, and security systems can all pose big problems when abrupt, surprise failures occur.

The sixth section outlines the inspections needed for Home Appliances and Accessories, which, by all standards, can be the most annoying of components to fail without warning. Part 6 includes sections that discuss refrigerators and freezers, ovens, electronic equipment, televisions, fireplaces, and furnishings.

The seventh part gives the lowdown on Housekeeping, with topics about cleaning and equipment needed for cleaning. Good housekeeping might sound boring, but it's not. You will find out why later.

Part 8 discusses Financial Matters. These, like everything else, bear watching. Attention to basics such as insurance policies, record keeping, conservation of water and energy, plus a few pointers on service contracts, contractor selection, and finding a good all-round handy person can save a lot of money over short and long hauls.

Part 9 is about the often forgotten topic of Home Safety. Everyone is safe in his or her own home, right? Not quite. Here you will find sections on Fire Prevention; Slips, Trips, and Falls; Electrical Safety; Poisons; and Environmental Factors—all important to a family's maintenance.

Part 10 explains how to prepare your own custom preventive maintenance schedule, which is probably why you picked up this book in the first place.

Part 11, Keeping at It, consists of a brief pep talk on how you can motivate yourself to continue your inspections and maintenance tasks, plus how to enlist the aid of others—friends and family members.

ONE CAUTIONARY NOTE: Keep in mind that there is a lot of information in this book, and not all of it will apply to your particular situation. Not every kind of detail applies to each home. Obviously, if you don't have a swimming pool, you need not include such an inspection on your PM schedule. However, if you ever consider the addition of an in-ground pool, you will probably want to read the section on swimming pools to understand what to expect in the way of future maintenance. That's another way this book can be used — in planning additions, remodeling projects, or new construction with ease of maintenance in mind.

If you have never before been responsible for taking care of a household, keep in mind that you need not make any repair you feel uncomfortable with. Instead, have a friend, relative, or friend of a friend tackle the job. Or hire someone else to do it. The same goes for some of the inspections. If you don't want to crawl up on the roof to inspect the chimney flashing, arrange for someone else to do it. The important thing is that you realize the inspections and maintenance must be periodically undertaken to keep your home in good condition.

Now enough introduction, let's get on to Part 1.

PART 1

Outdoor Features & Accessories

Years ago, when compact building lots in cities spawned row after row of clapboard and brick-sided 2½-story dwellings, there wasn't much room for anything but the house on each lot.

If space existed for a narrow cinder driveway, the lot was considered extra wide. If anything, backyards were reserved for little patches of lawn surrounded by fences, which, in turn, were lined with tulips or tomato plants. The homes were so close to the street that showcase-style landscaping was all but unheard

of. Wood decks and concrete patios were few and far between. Swimming pools were found at YMCAs.

Today, almost every homeowner desires spacious "grounds" of his or her own. Now outdoor features play a major role in the value, convenience, and enjoyment provided by suburban and city properties. Homes are set back from the street behind picture-perfect half acres of lawn and precisely trimmed trees and shrubs. Privacy is valued, and so is plenty of room for backyard barbecues, sports, and parties.

Driveways

Driveways are usually constructed of the same materials that make up walkways: concrete, asphalt, gravel, or brick. Driveways, however, receive much rougher use. Cars, vans, light delivery trucks, and occasional heavy trucks that traverse the typical driveway carry considerably more weight than do most pedestrians. Vehicle tires spinning against grit, stones, and dirt can wear the surface of the sturdiest concrete or asphalt. Oil, gasoline, grease, and other petroleum derivatives from vehicles will stain, weaken, and create slippery driveway surfaces. Weed growth and frost wedging can do cumulative damages to concrete or asphalt.

THE FOUR TYPES OF DRIVEWAYS

Chances are that your driveway is or will be constructed of concrete, asphalt, gravel, or brick.

Concrete

Most people know what concrete is. It is that hard, strong, white-to-grayish building material from which driveways, sidewalks, patios, foundations, and basement floors are made. Sometimes, though, concrete gets confused with cement. They are not the same. Cement is a component of concrete. It is a construction material made by finely pulverizing a heated mixture of clay and limestone or similar ingredients. When mixed with other materials—sand and gravel and enough water—cement will set itself and its accompanying ingredients into the hard, strong substance we know of as concrete. Most concrete cement is called "portland" cement, named after the Isle of Portland, England, the place where this type of concrete ingredient was first used.

Concrete is strong, hard, and rigid. Because it is not very flexible, it will crack when subjected to pressures greater than its load limits. Concrete can also chip, flake or spall, erode, and absorb petroleum-based products, solvents, paints, and other agents of disintegration and discoloration. Due to its porous nature, unprotected concrete allows water to enter and seep through from top to bottom (or bottom to top, depending on where the water is coming from). If that is not enough, alternate freezing and thawing temperatures can cause frost wedging, which in turn creates large cracks out of small cracks and causes chips of concrete to break free from parent material.

Even with the above drawbacks, concrete is still the most popular material for driveways. It is pleasant to look at. It can be poured to almost any configuration, from the gentlest curve to the sharpest angle. It is useful on flat or steep surfaces. It will accept a variety of finishes to match appearances with sidewalk, steps, patios, and garage floors.

Asphalt

Most people recognize the common paving material known as asphalt; they know it when they see it. It is a brownish-to-black bituminous substance manufactured of petroleum industry derivatives or byproducts mixed with stone pieces or aggregates. The petroleum byproducts consist chiefly of hydrocarbons: mixtures of tar, stones, and related materials. Asphalt is laid hot and soft. It cools to form a hard, firm material in a matter of hours. Few people know that asphalt is also found naturally, in the ground. Indeed, "mined" asphalt similar to what is manufactured today was used thousands of years ago, in Asia Minor, as cement or mortar.

Asphalt is neither as hard as concrete nor as durable. It can crack or "dry out" as its petroleum-based ingredients evaporate, and if unprotected, will deteriorate through weathering, freezing and thawing, and plant-root incursions. Asphalt will also soften from contact with spilled gasoline, solvents, or other petroleum products. Its surface is especially vulnerable. During hot weather it softens and can be gouged, dented, or scraped.

Still, after concrete, asphalt is the next most popular driveway material. It is useful for long driveways and driveways where large amounts of square-yard coverage are needed. It is less costly to install than concrete, especially if the area is at least wide enough for an automatic asphalt paving machine. Homeowners in rural and suburban settings often prefer the black color of asphalt where a bright, white concrete might appear too startling for the surroundings. Asphalt can also be used for garage floors, if routine maintenance prevents drippings of vehicle oil and gasoline from doing damage.

Gravel

Gravel driveways can be found in a wide variety of locations, from city to country. Some gravel drives are installed at the time a house is built, with the intention of upgrading to asphalt or concrete once the gravel "wears in" or is pounded into a sturdy base. Well-maintained gravel drives can be attractive. They offer an interesting textured look as varied as the stones that are used in their makeup. But in the long run they can be just as expensive—even more so—than their concrete or asphalt cousins. Ideally, the gravel should not be larger than one inch in diameter. Pea-sized stones are a fine choice. Stones larger than 1-inch diameter are much too difficult to walk on.

The stones should be placed over a base where they won't sink out of sight during wet weather. While you might think "the thicker the layer of gravel, the better," that is not always the case. In fact, gravel shouldn't be laid too deep or a car's tires will sink into the stones and lose traction.

Brick

For a different look, some homeowners prefer driveways made of brick or flagstone or other masonry products carefully laid in patterns over a bed of sand. Although these driveways are aesthetically pleasing, they can also require a lot of maintenance unless constructed tightly. Weeds will sprout in the sand. Dirt can collect between individual bricks or stones. Sand may wash out. Ants and other insects can build homes between and beneath the bricks. Bricks and stones can crack or loosen, and portions of the driveway might sink or heave. Maturing tree roots can push bricks or stones out of place from below.

CONCRETE DRIVEWAY INSPECTIONS

- A dull, porous surface indicates that the concrete's pores are open and not sealed. Such a condition will allow water and other liquids to enter and even pass through the concrete. The accumulation of moisture in pavement is probably the greatest cause of deterioration.
- Oil, grease, and other stains are difficult to remove. They should be "taken up" almost as soon as they occur. Rain and groundwater can also

travel or leach through the concrete from the ground up, pulling calcium salts to the driveway's surface and leaving unattractive white deposits or stains.

- Cracks in the concrete can be tiny stress cracks— just cracks, with no openings — or they can be larger, open cracks, up to and wider than ¼ inch. (See Figure 1-1.)

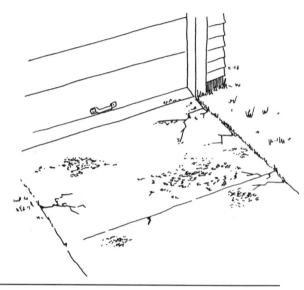

1-1. Cracks in concrete; spalling or flaking.

- "Spalled" or flaked, or chipped concrete may result from poor quality concrete or quality concrete subject to ice-melting rock salts or similar chemical agents. Once flaking starts, it will spread and go deeper with subsequent doses of ice melters and chemicals. (See Figure 1-1.)
- Heaved, sunken, or tilted block sections pose safety hazards, especially in winter and evening use of a driveway.
- Improper drainage can lead to pavement saturation with accompanying water damages.
- Erosion around and beneath the drive's perimeter can undermine a driveway's support or foundation.
- Encroachment by tree and shrub roots and foliage. In certain situations, unchecked root growth will crack the strongest concrete. (See Figure 1-2.) Foliage around the perimeter of a driveway, especially near the street end of the drive, can block the user's view of pedestrians, bicyclists, and oncoming traffic.
- Weed growth in expansion joints or other cracks look terrible and accelerate concrete disintegration. (See Figure 1-2.)

1-2. Tree-root encroachment.

CONCRETE DRIVEWAY REPAIRS

This section may be somewhat more than you expected in a book geared more to preventive maintenance than repairs. It is here to demonstrate that many components of the typical home can be worked on by the average head of a household or anyone else. Driveways are fairly forgiving components; they do not need to be fixed right now, like a plugged toilet or a blown electrical fuse. Driveway work can be planned for when you have time, when the weather conditions are right. While the remaining sections will not go as deeply into repairs as this section will, be aware that you can always research and develop the additional expertise needed to make repairs to other household components.

Crack Repairs

Crack repairs refer to cracks and holes that you can see into—where the concrete has actually moved or cracked apart greater than ¼ inch. These are not the hairline or stress cracks that frequently appear in concrete. There is nothing that can be done with hairline cracks. Cracks up to ¼ inch wide can be repaired simply by filling them with concrete caulk or filler from a tube or can.

For repairing cracks wider than ¼ inch:

1. Chisel out the crack or hole at an angle, making it wider beneath the surface. (See Figure 1-3.)
2. Clean the exposed concrete surfaces with a wire brush.
3. Vacuum or blow the dust and small pieces from the crack or hole.
4. Using a commercially available concrete stain remover or a weak solution of trisodium phosphate and hot water, scrub away any oil, grease, or related stains. Rinse with hot water.

5. Mix enough epoxy concrete to fill the prepared crack or hole.
6. Trowel the concrete mixture into the crack or hole. If repairing a full break all the way through the concrete, force the mixture to the bottom.
7. Using a flat 2" x 4" or other board, smooth the mixture even with the surrounding surfaces of the crack or hole. Remove all excess material.
8. Place a wet rag over the patch and keep it there for several days until the patching dries. Barricade the area so no one will drive or walk on the repairs until you are ready.
9. Clean all tools immediately with paint thinner or a similar cleaning agent.

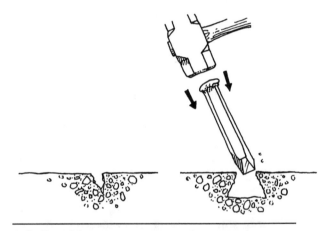

1-3. Repairing a concrete crack.

Surface Area Patching

Surface area patching is done on sections of concrete surfaces that are flaking or spalling, or are chipped, gouged, or otherwise damaged.

1. Chisel out all loose concrete.
2. Wire brush the affected areas.
3. Vacuum or blow the dust and small pieces from the brushed concrete.
4. Scrub the prepared areas with a weak solution of trisodium phosphate and hot water. Rinse with hot water.
5. Prepare enough patching material by mixing one part portland cement to three parts fine clean sand and enough water to yield a soft, smooth consistency. Add a small amount of concrete glue (follow package directions) to help "feather out" the edges of the patch and to help secure the patching material to the old concrete.
6. Trowel the patching mixture over the damaged sections.
7. With a 2" x 4" board or other straightedge, smooth mixture to meet the surrounding concrete evenly.

8. Place a wet rag over the patched sections. Keep the cloth wet for several days, until the patching sets. Barricade the area so no one will drive or walk on the repairs until you are ready.

9. Clean all tools immediately with paint thinner or a similar cleaning agent.

Notes

For concrete surfaces requiring very minor repairs, plastic or epoxy cement surfacing material is available at hardware and builder's supply stores. After the affected areas have been thoroughly prepared, smooth on the surfacing material according to the manufacturer's instructions. When mixing concrete patching material for repairs, do not mix more than you can use in an hour. Avoid working with concrete patching material when temperatures fall to or below freezing.

Heaved, Sunken, or Tilted Block Repairs

Sometimes an individual driveway panel or block will heave, sink, or tilt several inches out of line. It could be caused by the ground beneath settling or eroding. Problems of this nature have been traced to broken water lines, expanding tree roots, and even to burrowing animals. In any case, the offending piece may be realigned with a pry bar or lifting jack after the cause has been taken care of: a water line replacement, a tree root cut and removed, or a settled area filled in with soil and gravel. If a block must be sawn free from adjoining concrete, the job is best handled by a paving contractor.

Concrete Block or Panel Replacements

Concrete driveway blocks or panels that are beyond saving should be replaced. Once replacement of an individual piece or pieces has been decided upon, determine if the sight of new, "different" looking, usually whiter concrete will detract too much from the overall appearance of your driveway. If you feel the juxtaposition of dramatically different colors or shades of concrete within the driveway will ruin the look of your home's exterior, you may want to replace the entire driveway at the same time. Replacing the entire driveway will, of course, avoid the patchwork look of mixing new concrete with old. But really, it is a question of aesthetics rather than function.

CONCRETE DRIVEWAY MAINTENANCE

These are steps that can be taken to help maintain a concrete driveway. They don't *have* to be done if not needed. But the more closely they are followed, the better.

1. Remove all surface stains. Various concrete stain removers are available at hardware and builder's supply stores. Keep some on hand to remove stains periodically. The sooner a stain is addressed, the easier it will come out.

2. Correct inadequate drainage. Taking care of improper drainage can mean many things, from unplugging a leaf-filled gutter or drain to a full re-landscaping to prevent water from collecting against the driveway and saturating the surrounding ground. Simply put, a driveway's perimeter landscape should slope away from the drive. Sometimes adjacent grass sod will encroach and build up to a point where it is higher than the driveway surface and, consequently, will prevent water from running off the driveway. If this happens, just trim back and lower the adjoining sod by removing soil beneath the roots so rainwater and snow melt can run off again.

3. Correct erosion and encroaching tree/shrub roots and foliage. (See the section on landscaping.)

4. Seal the surface. No matter how hard and smooth concrete appears and feels, if unprotected, it is actually a porous material that can be penetrated by water. Every time temperatures drop below freezing, water present within the concrete will expand. When temperatures rise above freezing, the water contracts. Repeated freezing/thawing cycles can cause severe cracking and crumbling damage.

To protect against water and surface damage, concrete driveways should be periodically coated with a water repellent. The repellent, or sealer, penetrates the concrete's surface to form an effective moisture barrier. Before applying sealer, all other repairs should be completed, and the driveway should be cleaned with a concrete cleaner available in hardware and builder's supply stores.

You can determine if a concrete driveway needs to be resealed by its appearance. A dull porous surface means it is time to seal.

ASPHALT DRIVEWAY INSPECTIONS

The signs of asphalt deterioration are similar to those of concrete. Here's what to look for:

■ Bleached sections, places where the asphalt's dark black color has "bleached" or dried out by the sun's rays to a shade approaching a light gray. This drying out or oxidation accelerates "raveling"—the separation of the asphalt's ingredients—and erosion, and can literally reduce asphalt thickness by as much as half in five years.

- Stains from vehicle drippings where gasoline, oil, or other petroleum-based substances have stained and softened the asphalt. These appear usually where a car, truck, or motorcycle is parked. Grease, kerosene, anti-freeze, brake fluid, diesel fuel, salts, and a variety of de-icing chemicals can have similar effects.
- Small "spiderweb" cracks.
- Larger cracks and sections of crumbling pavement.
- Major undulations, ridges, or depressions in the asphalt.
- Improper drainage.
- Erosion around and beneath the drive's perimeter.
- Encroachment by tree and shrub roots and foliage.

ASPHALT DRIVEWAY REPAIRS

Crack Repairs

As an asphalt driveway ages, narrow cracks develop along the edges. Some spread to an inch or so in width and form alligator-skin patterns. To keep water, weather, and other agents of deterioration from ruining the asphalt, cracks should be filled shortly after they develop, weather permitting. Crack filling is a repair that should be made before resealing the surface of the driveway is attempted. Special tar-based asphalt crack fillers are available at hardware and builder's supply stores; most require an outdoor temperature of at least 50 degrees F. for successful use. On badly oxidized or dried-out cracked areas, an asphalt primer or tack coat should be applied before crack filling and resealing. The primer or tack coat will give the crack filler a stickier surface for adhesion.

Repairing Cracks

1. Clean the crack with a wire brush and vacuum or blow out the loose material.
2. Apply a thin coat of asphalt primer or tack, if needed.
3. Pour the crack-filler material into the crack until the crack is filled. If desired, sand can be sprinkled or swept over the filled cracks while the filler material is still tacky. The sand will help blend the crack into the surrounding asphalt and will also help to prevent shoe soles, car tires, and bicycle tires from sticking to the crack filler on hot summer days. If the surface will later be sealed, the sand will help a coat of sealer adhere to the crack filler.

4. Barricade the affected area so no one walks or drives on it until the filler material is sufficiently dried.
5. Inspect repaired areas the next day and add more filler if the initial material has settled.

NOTE: Fillers usually harden within 24 hours. Although the driveway can be used then, avoid parking directly on freshly filled areas for several days. When filling cracks, pay particular attention to the edges of the driveway where water can enter and do the most damage.

Patching Damaged Sections

Sometimes a section of asphalt will completely break up. In that case, the damaged paving should be completely removed and replaced. Here's how:

1. Asphalt patching compound is best applied when outdoor temperatures reach 70 degrees F. or warmer. If you must make repairs in colder weather, preheat the patching compound by leaving it indoors overnight. Never heat patching material with a propane torch or other open flame.
2. With a wide (about 3-inch) cold chisel, chisel out all damaged material by cutting down to the harder lower base asphalt level, if there is such a solid layer. You can end up with a hole that is quite a bit larger than the original. If you don't get all of the damaged material out, the patch will either pop out of the hole, or the surrounding asphalt will disintegrate while the patch stays in place.

   The same removal technique can be applied to asphalt ridges or sections of pavement that have raised. Ridges, however, have to be removed all the way to several inches below the desired paving surface. That makes for a very wide patch. Unless a ridge or raised area is so high as to be dangerous, it may be best just to leave it alone.
3. Clean out the hole with a stiff broom. If necessary, flush it with water from a garden hose, but let the prepared area dry completely before patching compound is applied.
4. Asphalt or blacktop patch can be purchased in various containers, most often in 60-pound bags at hardware or builder's supply stores. Position the patching compound in the hole, filling the area to slightly above the surrounding surfaces. Tamp the patching (tap it down) with the flat end of a 2" x 4" board. If the cavity is large, tamp the mixture as you fill the hole so the hole is filled in layers. Top off the patching by adding enough mixture so the surface is about an inch higher than the desired level.

5. Place a piece of sturdy scrap plywood over the patch and drive your car or truck over it. The vehicle's weight will help press the patch into the cavity, like a roller. If tight quarters prevent the use of your car or truck, you will have to settle for tamping the patch tight with the end of a board.

6. Freshly filled sections of asphalt should be left to cure about 90 days before they are coated with a protective asphalt sealer. That means you can patch in the spring and seal in late summer or early fall.

NOTE: If you have several holes and other small damaged areas that need to be replaced, call several paving contractors and find one who is receptive to the following scenario: whenever the contractor has a small amount of blacktop left over from another job in an area near your home, he could use it to make repairs in your driveway. Let him do it at his convenience, and you can probably get excellent repairs at little expense.

Driveway Resurfacing

If a driveway requires too many repairs to be practical, it may need a complete resurfacing. This should be done by a paving contractor. When getting quotes, ask the contractors if the use of a paving fabric, also called a geotextile, to strengthen the asphalt and to prevent old cracks from working their way through the new asphalt topping, is recommended.

ASPHALT DRIVEWAY MAINTENANCE

These concepts are similar to those mapped out for concrete driveways. The materials, though, are handled quite differently.

1. Correct improper drainage. See point #2 of Concrete Driveway Maintenance.
2. Correct erosion problems and tree/shrub roots and foliage encroachments. (See the section on landscaping.)
3. Seal the asphalt, if needed. Unless asphalt is protected by a layer of sealer on its surface, such a driveway will never reach its potential useful life. If left unsurfaced, asphalt will deteriorate from the weather and harmful chemicals such as deicers, oil drippings, and petroleum-based products. A blacktop sealer forms a waterproof coating that keeps harmful water, oil, and gasoline drippings from being absorbed by the paving. It also lessens the amount of asphalt ingredients that will otherwise evaporate out of the asphalt, leaving it dry, brittle, and subject to pulverization

when the elasticity is reduced.

The surface of an asphalt driveway should be resealed every year unless the drive is in a protected area and hardly ever used. There are three main types of sealer: asphalt base sealers, tar emulsion sealers, and aggregate sealers.

Asphalt base sealers are the most expensive. They should be used on new asphalt or on a surface that has been previously sealed with the same material.

Tar emulsion sealers are the least expensive and the most common. They are more popular than the others because they are available practically everywhere, are inexpensive, and seal well against gasoline and oil drippings.

Aggregate sealers, due to their extra body, are used to seal driveways full of large cracks and gaps. They also provide additional traction on steep grades.

NOTE: Do any crack filling or crack and hole patching that needs to be done *before* resealing a driveway.

Resealing an Asphalt Driveway

1. Driveway sealer comes in 1-gallon and 5-gallon containers. A 5-gallon container will usually cover about 350 square feet of driveway surface, depending on how thick you apply it, the condition of the asphalt, and the instructions. It is recommended you buy about 10 percent more than the product labels suggest in case you want to recoat a few spots after the sealer has dried. The condition of the asphalt can require more or less sealant. For example, a good grade of sealer will cover about 300 square feet of badly weathered asphalt, while the same amount will take care of almost 500 square feet of a driveway in excellent condition that had been resurfaced the previous year.

2. Hardware and builder's supply stores that sell the sealer will also sell applicators—disposable long-handled brushes with a squeegee attached to the back of the brush head.

3. Check the weather forecast before starting the job. Temperatures should be at least 60 degrees F., and no rain should fall for at least two hours after the sealer has been applied.

4. Cut away grass sod encroaching over the edges of the driveway so the sealer can be applied to the driveway edges as well. Sweep the driveway clean, concentrating on low or dished-in areas where rainwater and dirt collect. Put the debris in a wheelbarrow or bucket so it won't blow or scatter back onto the driveway. It is a good idea to sweep out the garage or carport at this time,

PART 1: OUTDOOR FEATURES & ACCESSORIES ▪ 19

too. Wind can whip into these areas as you apply fresh sealer and spread debris on renewed surfaces. Lift any encrusted deposits with a flat shovel. Then hose down the driveway. Mix and apply a household detergent cleaner to the asphalt surface for a still cleaner result. Use a stiff broom to scrub the asphalt. As you go, flush away the soiled water with clean water. A garden hose does a fine job of rinsing.

5. Inspect the driveway's surface after cleaning. Look for water beads that could indicate residues of oil or gasoline. Cracks should be repaired, with enough time for the fillers to dry. Badly softened, deteriorated sections of asphalt should be cut out and replaced with patching. You can work around any large sections of patching when you apply the sealer, to give those patches time to cure. If there is no softening, but the presence of oil and gasoline is apparent, use either a strong household detergent cleanser or a weak solution of trisodium phosphate and hot water to scrub away oil and gasoline residues, then rinse the area thoroughly and let dry. Another option would be to use an "oil seal" asphalt primer, which is then dusted with clean silica sand to encourage adhesion between repaired areas and the sealer. Remember that no sealer will adhere to oily surfaces.

6. If you use a more expensive asphalt sealer, make sure the pavement is dry before beginning the application. If you use the more popular tar-based sealer, the pavement should be completely dampened with water to achieve a better bond, or adhesion. The asphalt should have a slightly moist appearance, without any puddles of water present. Of course, it is important to follow the manufacturer's instructions, including all those designed for safety.

7. Apply a thin layer of asphalt primer or tack-coat material on badly oxidized or dried-out paving that will be receiving a tar-based sealer. Sprinkle clean silica sand over the primer or tack coat so the sealer will achieve proper adhesion.

8. Apply the sealer by pouring it directly onto the asphalt in manageable portions, covering up to 35 square feet of area at a time. Pouring it from the container is a lot easier than trying to dip the applicator into the bucket. Spread the mixture evenly, using the applicator brush. Work the sealer into the asphalt, making sure tiny cracks and holes get filled and the sealer covers the surface in a smooth layer.

9. With the squeegee side of the applicator, level the sealer on the surface with light, even strokes that travel in the same direction. The trick is not to leave any puddles of sealer on the driveway while applying an even coat. However, don't skimp on the sealer. If you press down too hard with the squeegee, you will scrape the original asphalt surface, and no sealer will be left as protection. You are shooting for a layer of sealer that is fairly even across the driveway's surface. Don't apply all the sealer at once. Two thin coats, with enough drying time in between, offer better protection than does a single coat of the same thickness.

10. Complete the entire driveway surface. Cover the edges, too. Wait 24 hours or until the sealer is dry to the touch. Look for missed spots. If you see patches of driveway that look extra dry, or places you missed completely, go back over those areas with more sealer. If most of the surface looks even and dry, give the entire driveway another coat. Always apply the second coat at right angles to whatever direction the first coat was applied, for better coverage.

11. Sand can be added to the sealer to give improved traction to the driveway surface. It can be mixed in with the sealer at a proportion of 2 to 3 pounds of clean sand per gallon of undiluted sealer and enough clean, cool water to achieve a smooth, creamy consistency. Or sand can be sprinkled onto the sealer after the sealer is applied but before it dries.

12. Barricade or tape off the driveway so no one walks or rides on it for at least 36 hours—longer during times of humid or wet weather.

GRAVEL DRIVEWAY MAINTENANCE

Springtime repairs allow a gravel driveway to be compacted firmly by use during the summer, which will minimize the amount of loose surface material that snow shovels and plows scrape away during winter.

1. Rake gravel from high spots to fill in holes, ruts, and depressions.

2. Rake back any gravel that was thrown into the lawn from winter snow removal.

3. The street end of a gravel driveway is critical to the drive's appearance and function. It should be kept sufficiently wide enough for cars to turn in and out.

4. Even driveways with garden-tie or other borders will gradually lose their gravel. Children will throw it around. Some stones will adhere to car tires and get tracked out. Snow shovels will remove a certain amount. Some will get pulverized or pushed into the sub-base. From time to time, the gravel will have to be replenished.

5. Keep weeds under control. If left alone, they will gradually encroach through the stones from the edges.

BRICK AND FLAGSTONE DRIVEWAY MAINTENANCE

Brick and flagstone driveways will literally fall apart if not maintained properly.

1. Tree and shrub roots around the driveway perimeter must be kept under control or they will push up the bricks or stones and ruin the driveway's integrity.
2. Keep the sand or mortar between the bricks or stones in good condition, and replenish it when necessary.
3. Don't let grass, weeds, or other plants grow between the bricks and stones.
4. Replace cracked bricks and stones as needed.

GENERAL DRIVEWAY MAINTENANCE

Certain points can apply to driveways of all construction types. Here are the most important ones:

1-4. Driveway visibility obstructions.

To maintain a safe exit at the street end of your driveway, make sure you inspect the trees, shrubs, bushes, flowers, and weeds that may be growing there. Is there adequate visibility for anyone turning into the driveway? (See Figure 1-4.) Could hedges be blocking a driver's view of a small child playing in the end of the driveway? Could an evergreen tree's lower branches obscure a driver's view of oncoming traffic as the driver is backing or pulling out into the street? Offending vegetation should be trimmed or removed.

If your driveway slopes downward toward a garage, periodically inspect the area during rainstorms to see if a drain/catch basin outside the garage is working properly. Clean out leaves, dirt, or other debris that may be clogging it. If no such drain is present outside the garage, and water is regularly running in beneath garage doors, check for water damage at the base of the garage doors and along the lower door frame. A drain/catch basin should be installed to prevent future problems.

Unless there is a border of some kind (such as a rubber border or garden ties) that separates your driveway from adjacent grass sod, periodically cut all grass and other vegetation that "grows over" onto the driveway edges, as you would trim along the edges of a sidewalk.

Many driveways, especially those located in country settings, have culverts or drain pipes for rainwater to flow beneath their surface along the roadway. (See Figure 1-5.) Culvert pipes should be inspected and cleaned out if needed.

Poke around inside a driveway culvert pipe with a shovel from time to time. Although these pipes are made to last, they eventually rust out. It is better to schedule a replacement to suit your timetable than to have your driveway suddenly collapse because a culvert pipe has given way. If a culvert pipe needs re-

1-5. Driveway culvert.

placing, make sure you choose a replacement of the same diameter.

Inspect for water problems on either side of the drive. Water may be saturating the ground against one side of a driveway, causing hazardous surface ice on the driveway or "block heaving" during winter. If this is the case, place a length of drainage pipe beneath the driveway, running from a small rock basin at the lowest collection point of the problem side to a screen-covered outlet on the other side of the drive.

The supporting ground on both sides of a driveway should be maintained to prevent erosion that could undermine the structural soundness of the entire driveway. Repair eroded areas by replacing missing soil and seeding affected areas. (See Figure 1-6.)

If you live in an area where snow plowing is needed, place stakes or snow fences to mark the edges of the driveway to guide snow plows as well as any visitors arriving by car. Lawns or flower beds lining the driveway can be hidden by heavy snowfalls and accidentally damaged by vehicles.

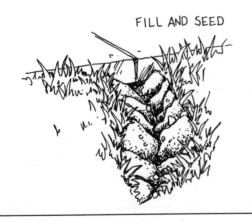

FILL AND SEED

1-6. Repairing driveway erosion.

DRIVEWAY SAFETY

When performing driveway maintenance and repair tasks, there are a number of safety precautions to consider:

- Avoid heat stress and heat illness by doing most work during early morning hours. Get help for the longer and more difficult tasks, such as resealing. Drink plenty of fluids and rest often.
- Bags of sand and containers of sealer and patching can be heavy. Use proper lifting techniques. Get help when needed.
- When working with chipping and hammering tools, wear gloves and goggles. Watch those fingers. Keep children away from the work area.
- When working with petroleum-based liquids, and emulsions and cleaners, see that there is adequate ventilation. Wear goggles. Use rubber gloves. Wear work boots, long pants, and shirts with sleeves.
- Wear goggles and dust masks for work in dusty conditions.

DRIVEWAY QUICK CHECKLIST

- ❑ Provide unobstructed incoming and outgoing visibility to drivers and pedestrians at the street end of the driveway.
- ❑ Repair cracks and holes.
- ❑ Repair flaking or crumbling sections.
- ❑ Repair heaved, sunken, or tilted sections.
- ❑ The drive should drain away from itself and the home, with no standing water after a rain. If it must slope toward the home or garage, the water should be routed to a storm drain.
- ❑ Seal the surface against weather, water, and other elements of discoloration and disintegration.
- ❑ Remove encroaching tree and shrub roots and foliage.
- ❑ Check for and eliminate erosion around and beneath the perimeter.
- ❑ Culvert pipes should be sturdy and kept free of debris.
- ❑ Eliminate weed growth in expansion joints and cracks.

Walkways

From a maintenance perspective, walkways can be thought of as tiny, lightweight driveways. Walkways are constructed of the same materials: usually concrete, but you will also find some made of asphalt, brick, stone, and gravel. Most maintenance and repair guidelines already covered in the section on driveways can be applied to walkways, but some differences do exist.

WALKWAY INSPECTIONS

- A dull, porous surface.
- Oil, grease, and other stains.
- Cracks in concrete or asphalt.
- "Spalled" or flaked, or chipped concrete; crumbling asphalt.
- Heaved, sunken, or tilted sections. These pose serious tripping hazards in walkways, and should be corrected for safety reasons. (See Figure 2-1.)
- Encroachment by tree and shrub roots and foliage. This can be another serious safety hazard if foliage blocks a driver's or pedestrian's view from or of the walk.
- Erosion around and beneath the walkway.
- Weed growth in expansion joints or cracks.

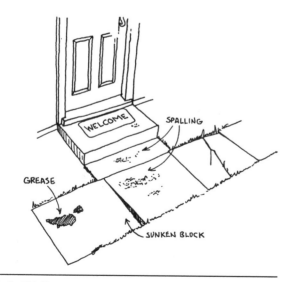

2-1. Walkway defects.

WALKWAY REPAIRS

Except for the repairs listed below, walkway repairs are almost identical to repairs outlined in the previous section on driveways.

Broken Step and Walkway Edges and Corners

1. While wearing leather gloves and safety goggles, use a stiff wire brush to clean off damaged sections.
2. Wash the cleaned sections with water from a garden hose.
3. While wearing goggles, use a carbide-tipped masonry bit in an electric drill to make ¼-inch wide holes about 2 inches deep into the edge of the concrete, perpendicular to the damaged areas. Space the holes about 2 inches apart, if possible. This will help give the repair something to anchor it quickly.
4. Prepare a small amount of mortar so the mix is slightly softer than the directions recommend. Force the mixture into the holes.
5. Drive lag screws or carriage bolts into the holes, leaving the heads protruding 2 to 3 inches if possible, but so they are not too close to where the finished edge or corner will be. (See Figure 2-2.)
6. Using plywood or scrap lumber, build a wood

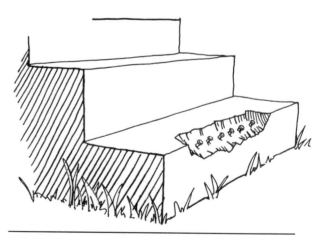

2-2. Step edge repair, step 1.

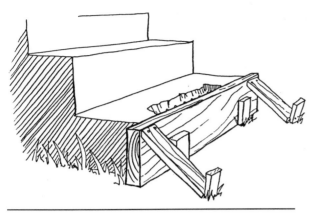

2-3. Step edge repair, step 2.

form to "box in" a new corner or edge. (See Figure 2-3.)

7. Remove all dust and debris, then hose down the working surfaces with water.

8. Prepare enough pre-mixed concrete patching to fill the wood forms.

9. Place the patching in the forms and tamp it firmly. Level off excess material with a 2" x 4" board or other straightedge.

10. Let the patch set for about 30 minutes. Trowel or finish off the new patch to match the original finish of the step or sidewalk block.

11. Small chips — if you still have them — can be glued back into place with a latex-based cement available at hardware or builder's supply stores.

Leveling a Heaved or Settled Walkway Block

Walkway blocks can heave or settle for a variety of reasons. Once they are out of line, they become safety hazards for bikers and walkers. Heaved or settled blocks can either be repaired or replaced. If more than one slab or block is affected, start with the one nearest the good section of walkway, then repair one slab at a time.

1. The block will usually be heaved or settled at one of the control grooves that had been cut into the walkway surface during installation. If it isn't cracked at a groove, use a masonry chisel and a small sledgehammer to crack it along that area. This will provide you with smaller sections that will be easier to handle. As always, make sure you wear safety goggles and use leather gloves when handling the hammer and chisel.

2. Lay a straight edge of a 2" x 4" board alongside and parallel to the walk, as a guide to indicate where you want the top surface of the walk to be. Use lifting jacks or steel pry bars to tilt or lift the lowest end of the slab into a correct position. You

will probably need a helper.

3. Prop up the slab with pieces of wood, bricks, or rocks. Use a helper. Be careful not to let the block down on your fingers. (See Figure 2-4.)

4. If there are roots growing beneath the slab, cut them out or they will continue to grow and push the block out of line again.

5. Measure the height to which the slab should be brought. Make sure it gets propped a little higher than the finished height should be, to allow for settling. Position stones or bricks under the slab to support it at that height. Then place pea-size gravel around the stones or bricks for additional support. If desired, concrete mix can be poured beneath the slab, around the stones or bricks.

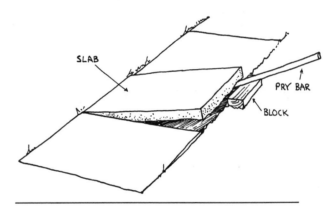

2-4. Leveling a block.

WALKWAY MAINTENANCE

Again, depending on which material a walkway is constructed of, maintenance is almost the same as for driveways.

- Remove surface stains.
- Maintain proper drainage.
- Prevent erosion from undermining the ground supporting the walkway. Replace eroded soil and reseed it.
- If needed, waterproof the surface with concrete or asphalt sealer.
- In order to have safe walkways, evaluate the places a walk intersects with streets, driveways, and other walks. You want pedestrians to have good visibility looking into traffic lanes. Trees, shrubs, and other vegetation blocking those views should be trimmed or removed.
- Vegetation growing between blocks or bricks should be eliminated.
- Replace cracked blocks, bricks, or stones as needed, or replenish gravel in walkways made of gravel or crushed stone.

WALKWAY QUICK CHECKLIST

- ❑ Provide unobstructed visibility to drivers and pedestrians at intersections with streets, driveways, and other walkways.
- ❑ Repair cracks and holes.
- ❑ Repair flaking or crumbling sections.
- ❑ Repair or replace heaved, sunken, or tilted sections.
- ❑ A walk should drain away from itself and the home, with no standing water after a rain.
- ❑ Seal walkway surfaces against weather, water, and other elements of discoloration and disintegration.
- ❑ Remove encroaching tree and shrub roots and foliage.
- ❑ Eliminate erosion along or beneath a walkway.
- ❑ Eliminate weed growth in expansion joints and cracks.

WALKWAY SAFETY

See the safety material in the driveways section.

Concrete Patios

A concrete patio, as a rule, is not a high-maintenance feature. If properly constructed with a good mix of concrete over a sturdy well-drained base, a patio will provide year after year of trouble-free service.

Some patios are installed low, so their surface is almost at ground level. Others jut a foot or two into the air, to meet a set of sliding glass doors or other entrance. Some patios have awnings or similar overhead protection (see Figure 3-1), while others are fully screened or glassed in. But many have no protection at all, and are exposed to weather year round. Fancier patios can have surfaces of flagstone, brick, or tile. Most patios, however, are plain, with nothing more than a concrete "swirl" or other patterned finish.

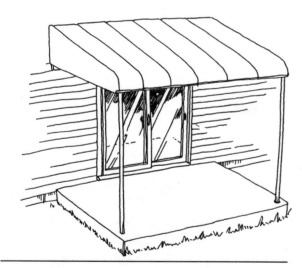

3-1. Covered patio.

CONCRETE PATIO INSPECTIONS

- Loose or missing safety rails or similar attachments.
- A dull, porous surface.
- Cracks or holes in the concrete.
- Spalled, or flaked, or chipped concrete.
- Loose flagstones, bricks, or tiles.
- Heaved or sunken sections.
- Improper drainage.
- Erosion around and beneath the perimeter.
- Encroachment by tree and shrub roots and foliage.
- Level of patio.
- Separation from house.

CONCRETE PATIO MAINTENANCE

1. After necessary repairs, if needed, are made to cracks and chipped or flaking areas (see section on driveway repairs), apply a good water sealant to the patio surface.
2. Trim back encroaching vegetation.
3. See maintenance portions of the sections on windows, doors, and exteriors if applicable, and follow recommendations for the equipment or accessories your patio has. For example: clean out sliding door tracks and make sure weep holes are open. Caulk areas where different construction materials exist. "Tune" gutters and downspouts. Tighten safety rails. In short, check the patio and its enclosure at the same time.
4. To check alignment of a patio, use a carpenter's level. A little slope or fall away from the house is desirable. But a patio that is cockeyed to one side or the other, or is slanting downward toward the house, should be evaluated and corrected if necessary by a contractor specializing in structural repairs.
5. Even if it stays fairly level, a patio may drift away from the house in equal proportions. If a patio is slowly disconnecting from the house, a contractor should be called in to provide qualified advice.

CONCRETE PATIO SAFETY

See the safety section for concrete driveways.

CONCRETE PATIO QUICK CHECKLIST

❑ Tighten existing safety rails or attachments. Or install new safety railings or
similar attachments where needed to
prevent children or visitors from falling
off a steep patio side.
❑ Repair cracks and holes.
❑ Repair flaking or crumbling sections.
❑ Have heaved, sunken, or tilted sections
evaluated by a contractor and repaired.
❑ Make sure the patio drains away from itself and the home, with no standing water puddles after a rain.
❑ If exposed to the outdoors, seal the surface against weather, water, and other
elements of discoloration and disintegration.
❑ Remove encroaching tree and shrub
roots and foliage.
❑ Eliminate erosion around or beneath the
patio.

Masonry Walls

Masonry walls can be functional. They can hold back something such as soil to prevent a driveway from washing out, or the side of a hill from sliding against a foundation. They can provide privacy. Or they can be decorative, used as a landscaping tool in a manner similar to that of a fence or hedgerow.

MASONRY WALL INSPECTIONS

As might be expected, this means looking for cracks, flaking, chipping, heaving, tilting, and water damage. You can use what you have already learned in the previous three sections, plus the following:

- Examine the wall's mortar. Cracks in the joints should be repaired before major damage occurs. Use an old screwdriver to scrape the joints. Sandy, crumbling mortar is a sign that deterioration has set in and should be repaired if the wall's strength and appearance are to be maintained.
- Look for crumbling, cracking, separation of surfaces, settling, or the appearance of moisture over a significant area. Any of these conditions demonstrates that the wall is going through some changes and should be investigated further. When in doubt, consult a masonry contractor, especially if the wall is an important part of your property.
- Look for buckling. Pressure against the back side of a wall can slowly push the masonry out of line. Such pressure should be relieved before further damage is done.
- Pay special attention to top courses on a stone wall. Look for loose stones. A good mason uses the largest, flattest stones on top for stability and to help repel water.
- Is moss or lichen growing on the wall? Either growth can cause children who are attracted to climbing masonry walls to slip and injure themselves. Ivy and other clinging vines may look attractive and quaint, but tentacle-like roots will work their way into tiny masonry cracks and slowly promote deterioration. The foliage can shelter an assortment of unwanted insects and small mammals.
- Is there a pattern of cracks, not just miscellaneous

bits of missing mortar? Fissures suggest a parting of one portion of the wall from another. Usually such cracks will zigzag like a staircase from one horizontal row of bricks or stones to the next. Wide, serious cracking generally means a shifting of the foundation beneath and time to call for expert help.
- Is any efflorescence present? Masonry is commonly afflicted with a condition called efflorescence. It appears as a whitish powder on the surface of a wall—a result of water-soluble salts that migrate to the surface of the wall's bricks or stones. When it appears in brickwork that has been standing for several years, it usually means that water is getting inside the wall. The source could be water entering through the top course of the wall. Or it could be from water building up behind a wall and exerting pressure through cracks and weak spots.

MASONRY WALL REPAIRS

Repairing Weakened Joints

1. Crumbling mortar can be removed with either a masonry chisel and hammer or a mortar tool that you can make: simply hammer a sturdy nail through a block of wood until the nail point extends ½ inch through the other side of the wood. Slide this extending nail point along and inside weakened mortar joints. In this manner, you can work out most of the disintegrated mortar, and you won't dig in too deep. Use water from a garden hose to flush out the loosened material.
2. Mix enough new mortar to replace the mortar you removed.
3. Wet the masonry thoroughly before you begin to replace the mortar, and keep the working area wet.
4. Apply the mortar with a small pointing trowel. Press the mortar firmly into the joint or crack, displacing all air pockets and making sure the joint or crack is full.
5. Remove excess mortar with the trowel edge. Finish off the mortar to match the existing joints by

pushing the tip of the trowel into the joint and then firmly moving the trowel along the joint at the correct angle to achieve the desired results. You will have to experiment at first to find what works. Good results can usually be had by placing the trowel tip first into a joint and holding the trowel lengthwise while firmly pressing the tip to form a concave shape.

6. Keep the newly filled joints damp for 2 or 3 days by wetting them frequently with a fine spray of water from a garden hose, or by fastening damp rags, or at the very least, plastic, against the wall.

Again, if the wall is solid concrete, a sizable crack should be undercut, cleaned out, moistened, and patched. The purpose of the undercutting is to help prevent the patch from falling out. Wetting down areas that will be in contact with new cement prevents old concrete from drawing moisture out of the patching before the patching has had time to cure properly.

Replacing a Brick, Block, or Stone

If a brick, block, or stone in a masonry wall is broken and loose, it should either be put back or replaced.

1. While wearing leather gloves and safety goggles, chisel away enough old mortar to remove the damaged unit (brick, block, or stone).
2. Either clean up the old unit by removing old mortar, or if the unit cannot be reused, find another that is as close a match as possible. If an exact match is not available, select one slightly lighter in shade for the most conservative look.
3. Soak the replacement unit in water for 5 minutes. Also wet the surrounding units or section of wall surrounding the vacancy.
4. Prepare enough premixed mortar to set the new masonry unit in place.
5. Trowel the mortar onto all sides of the hole. Set the unit in place. If too much mortar is present to accommodate the new unit, remove mortar a little at a time. Keep nudging the replacement brick, block, or stone with the trowel handle or a piece of wood. Avoid using a hammer or you will risk cracking the new unit.

MASONRY WALL MAINTENANCE

- Trim foliage that may be gradually overtaking a wall.
- Open up or establish "weep holes." Walls situated where the ground on one side is higher than the ground on the other side should contain "weep holes" to prevent water from building pressure against the wall. (See Figure 4-1.) Weep holes

should be located near the bottom of the wall. If they get sealed off or even temporarily plugged, water could build pressure against the wall and eventually cause structural cracks and other problems.

4-1. Weep holes.

- Clean out existing holes. If no holes exist and there obviously is a water problem, consider having a masonry contractor drill a series of weep holes for adequate drainage.
- Clean the whitish salt residues from efflorescence. It can usually be taken care of with the application of a trisodium phosphate solution, mixed and applied per the manufacturer's instructions. Some vigorous scrubbing with a wire brush is also in order. Again, while using the trisodium, as with any cleaning chemical, remember to wear rubber gloves, goggles, and a long-sleeved shirt.

  To retain the natural appearance of brick or stone, and to fight the effects of efflorescence, after all minor and major problems are corrected, a coat of clear silicone finish will work wonders.

MASONRY WALL SAFETY

- See the safety section on driveways.
- Resist the urge to walk along on top of the wall.
- Use the proper personal protective equipment, such as gloves, goggles, and hard-toed safety shoes because rocks, blocks, and bricks are heavy.
- Check for tripping hazards. Masonry walls are often constructed along uneven terrain. Be careful when transporting bricks, stones, or other heavy

supplies.

▪ Watch for lifting hazards. Again, masonry ingredients are heavy. Subscribe to proper lifting techniques. Get help when needed.

MASONRY WALL QUICK CHECKLIST

❏ Replace crumbling mortar.
❏ Repair, reset, or replace broken or loose bricks, blocks, or stones.
❏ Rebuild or replace buckled or caved-in sections of walls.
❏ Ivy and other ground cover can be trained to grow along a masonry wall, but should not be allowed to grow on the wall.
❏ Trim encroaching foliage.
❏ Clean the whitish salt deposits from efflorescence, if present.
❏ On walls separating different ground levels, open existing weep holes, or provide weep holes at the bottom of walls having none.
❏ Seal clean masonry walls with a clear silicone or similar finish.

Fences

Fences can be designed to keep things out or to keep things in. Fences delineate property lines, serve as barriers between feuding neighbors, reduce noise, increase privacy, or hide a particularly ugly view.

Remember the scene from *Tom Sawyer*, when Tom fools his friends into whitewashing a long wooden fence? It may be fiction, but the truth is that fences need maintenance. They are exposed to the elements, day in, day out. The sun, wind, temperature extremes, and moisture in its many forms all conspire against the typical fence. Paint peels. Wood rots. Metal fence posts and fabric oxidize and rust. Children climb fences because fences are there. Animals burrow from one side of a fence to the other. Weeds and trees snake their shoots and limbs between chain-links.

For all practical purposes, there are two main types of fences: wood fences and metal fences.

WOOD FENCE INSPECTIONS

- Dry rot at the base of posts, where the posts enter the ground. Rot usually originates at the soil line. Probe with a screwdriver to check for soft decay.
- Insect damage at the base of posts. Carpenter ants, termites, and other insects can make their homes in wooden fence posts. Again, check the posts at the soil line by probing with a screwdriver for decay. Look carefully for insect holes and trailings as well.
- Inspect the tops of wood posts for cracks. Cracks will allow water to enter and be retained by the posts. Water will cause rot. Furthermore, the tops of wood posts should either be cut at a 45-degree angle, pointed so they will shed water, or capped with a piece of copper or aluminum for the same reason.
- Pull against the posts to make sure they are secured into the ground, not wobbly.
- Examine the pickets, rails, or slats for deterioration. Look for loose, broken, cracked, or missing parts.
- Check wood railings for open splits which, if not

repaired, will crack the piece entirely or hasten the rotting process.
- See if the fence needs a new coat of paint, stain, or sealer.
- Check the operation of gates. Are they level? Do they line up properly for latching and locking?
- Is the fence free from encroaching weeds and other undesirable foliage?

METAL FENCE INSPECTIONS

- Check the posts at and a little below soil level for deterioration. Poke the metal slightly below the ground with a screwdriver. A metal post can look brand new above ground, but be practically rusted away below.
- Look for rusty sections of fabric or chain-link sections.
- Pull on the fabric to see how sturdy and taut the fence is. Make sure the posts are not wobbly.
- Check the operation of gates. Are they level? Do they line up properly for latching and locking?
- Is the fence free from encroaching weeds and other undesirable foliage? Chain-link fences have traditionally been deformed by trees, vines, and shrubs that actually envelop and grow completely around portions of chain-link fabric.

FENCE REPAIRS

One reason to keep fences in good repair is simply to maintain harmonious relationships with neighbors. A neat fence may or may not increase the value of a property, depending on potential buyers, but an unkept fence will invariably detract from the value of all surrounding properties, including that of the property on which it is erected.

Fence Post Replacements

If posts have deteriorated below ground they must be repaired or replaced. Replacing fence posts can be a rather tough task that you probably should not try to tackle alone. You may want to call a fencing contractor. But here is a general procedure just in case.

1. Obtain a clamshell post-hole digger or another hand tool with a long handle and spoon-shaped digging blade resembling large tongs. A gasoline-powered auger will also work. Both can be rented.
2. Remove the deteriorated post.
3. If possible, locate a new post hole alongside the old post's hole. If you need to use the exact same location, so be it. In either case, the hole you dig should be about 2½ feet deep and about 6 inches wider than the post's diameter.
4. Shovel about 4 inches of crushed stone into the bottom of the hole.
5. Compact the stone by striking or tamping it with the bottom end of the post or a piece of lumber. Put a flat stone (about the same diameter as the hole) on top of the crushed stone at the bottom of the hole, to help support the post and to prevent the post from settling. Try to arrange the thickness of the compacted stone and flat stone so the post is set at the correct height.
6. Set the post in the hole. While a helper holds it steady, place a carpenter's level against one side of the post. Adjust the post until the level indicates that it is vertical from both sides.
7. If the post is wood, shovel more crushed stone into the hole around the post and tamp the stone to within about 8 inches of the surface. Finish filling the hole with soil, tamping it firmly in place in successive 2-inch thick layers.
8. If the post is metal, prepare enough instant concrete mix to fill the hole. Brace the post so it will stay straight. Pour the concrete into the hole, around the post.

Supporting the Base of a Deteriorated Post
You might encounter a post that is decayed below ground but is fine above.

1. Dig another hole alongside it, touching the old post. Shape the new hole and add stones as mentioned in the previous post-hole replacement procedure. (See Figure 5-1.)
2. Install a short length of post, perhaps a third the standard length, beside the damaged or loose post. If wood, the new post should be treated with preservative and angled across the top, or capped with copper or aluminum.
3. Set the new partial post so its top is a foot above ground level, and the new post is touching the old.
4. Drill three or four holes from the new post all the way through the damaged post.
5. Fasten the two posts together with carriage bolts, flat washers, and nuts.
6. Level the combination post and fill the new post hole with stones, soil, or concrete.

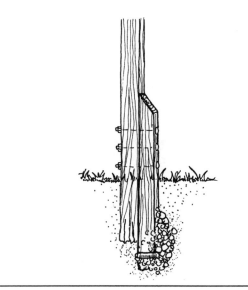

5-1. Reinforcing a deteriorated post.

FENCE MAINTENANCE

1. Treat small portions of dry rot on wood fencing with injections of dry-rot cures available in hardware and builder's supply stores.
2. Treat insect infestations with pesticides available from a local exterminator, or contract those services.
3. Cover the tops of wood posts with thin sheets of aluminum or copper, or seal cracks with wood putty or crack-repair material. Cover with a good paint or other sealer.
4. Strengthen healthy but wobbly posts. (a) Cut a 4-foot length of treated 2" x 4" lumber into four 2-foot-long wedges measuring 1½ inches square at the thick ends. (See Figure 5-2.) (b) Drive the wedges into the ground along each side of the affected post so only 5 or 6 inches of each wedge are above ground level. (c) Bind the driven wedges and post together by twisting wire tightly around them.
5. Refasten or replace loose, broken, cracked, or missing pickets, rails, or slats.
6. Fill cracks in rails with wood putty or filler. When dry, apply paint, stain, or a clear sealer.
7. On metal fences, remove rust with steel wool. Apply a primer coat and then paint with a rust-proofing paint. It is best to use a heavy nap roller when painting chain-link fabric. Posts and top rails can be painted with hand brushes.
8. Oil all hinges, latches, and moving hardware on gates. If the latches do not line up properly, the hinges should be tightened or otherwise adjusted.
9. Remove encroaching vegetation and all undesirable foliage growing along the fence.

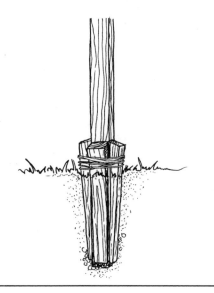

5-2. Reinforcing a wobbly post.

FENCE SAFETY

- Avoid working outdoors in hot temperatures. Prevent heat stress and heat illness by doing most work during early-morning hours.
- When handling wood posts, pickets and slats, rails, and chain-link fabric, wear gloves that will prevent slivers from entering your hands. Gloves will also prevent sharp edges of chain-link fabric from cutting your hands and wrists.
- Working with post-hole diggers. Use a helper who can relieve you if you get tired. Don't strain or push your luck. Stop to rest before you need it. An entire hole doesn't have to be dug at once.

FENCE QUICK CHECKLIST

❑ A fence should line up straight on both horizontal and vertical planes.
❑ The posts should be in sound condition and securely fastened into the ground.
❑ Treat dry rot or insect infestations in wood fencing.
❑ Fill and seal cracks in wood post tops and rails.
❑ Paint, stain with a stain/preservative, or seal wood fencing.
❑ Metal fencing should be kept free from rust and corrosion, and painted with a rust-proof paint when needed.
❑ Gates should be level and work smoothly, with latching and locking hardware correctly matched up.
❑ Weeds and other vegetation should be kept from overtaking fence lines.

Barbecues and Grills

Years ago, barbecues were often massive masonry productions that resembled free-standing fireplaces. Equipped with cast iron grates and oversized fireboxes for burning wood or coal, they frequently doubled as household incinerators when door-to-door trash pickup wasn't available.

Nowadays most barbecues and grills are purchased through a variety of retail stores and mail order catalogs. The units are a lot smaller and run the gamut from inexpensive to very costly. Practically all of them are portable, many with wheels so they can be moved from garage or patio corners to a backyard or driveway.

Three major types of barbecue grills are available: charcoal and wood burning, gas burning, and electric. Gas barbecue grills are by far the most commonly owned. They come in many sizes, designs, and colors, and offer a multitude of features in the top-end models.

BARBECUE GRILL INSPECTIONS

Barbecue grills are not complex appliances. They can be inspected quickly, and problems are usually readily detectable.

- Dirty, greasy surfaces.
- Cobwebs or other obstructions in gas supply tubes or lines.
- Loose or missing control knobs or fittings.
- Gas leaks.
- Rusty, corroded surfaces.
- Damaged electrical cords: frayed, cut, or cracked.
- Soiled, greasy lava rocks or charcoal briquettes.

BARBECUE GRILL MAINTENANCE

1. Keep the barbecue clean between uses. Grease buildups can cause fires that are not easily put out. Grills should be cleaned at least several times per season—more if used heavily. With a stiff, dry brush, scrub the grill free of ashes, drippings, and carbon "plaque." Wipe and remove loosened material with cloths or paper towels. Store the barbecue away from moisture.

2. Clean the burner system before using the barbecue if it hasn't been cleaned within one week. Pay special attention to the piping or tubes that supply gas. In some locations, spiders and small insects have been known to spin webs and make nests inside barbecue grill gas lines. Webs can block the flow of gas, which could result in a dangerous fire or "flashback." To clean the tubes: (a) Remove the burner assembly from the grill. (b) Bend a sturdy but flexible wire, such as a light coat hanger, so one end forms a small hook that will fit through the gas supply tubes. Run the hook up each tube past the bend and into the burner several times. (c) Use a small bottle brush with a flexible handle to clean the tubes in the same fashion.

    NOTE: It is a good idea to clean the gas supply tubes of new barbecue grills, in case some packing or other material might have lodged there during the manufacturing process.

3. Before each use, test the controls and major fittings to see that they are operating and not loose and ready to fall apart when the barbecue is burning. Adjust controls and attachments that are fastened incorrectly.

4. If you smell a gas leak on a barbecue grill while the grill is in operation, immediately shut the unit down by closing the gas supply at the propane tank. Is the line to the propane tank tightly affixed? If not, tighten the fitting. If the cause of a leak is not simple and readily apparent, a service person should inspect the unit and make necessary repairs.

5. Special heat-resistant enamel paint is available for use on stoves and barbecues. Before you can apply it, surface preparation requires cleaning and de-greasing. Grease can be removed with an ordinary oven cleaner or a less caustic degreasing spray made especially for outdoor barbecues. If a barbecue is stored outdoors, it will eventually fade from sunlight. The outside of the barbecue should also be painted with the same heat-resistant paint when needed.

6. Have damaged electrical cords and plugs replaced.

BARBECUE GRILL QUICK CHECKLIST

❑ Keep grills and cooking surfaces free of grease drippings and carbon residues.

❑ Make sure gas lines and fittings are securely attached and free from obstructions.

❑ Paint inside and outside surfaces, when needed, with barbecue heat-resistant enamel.

❑ Make sure control knobs are present and working, with legible markings.

❑ Keep electric units dry.

---

7. Clean dirty, greasy lava rocks by placing them in a large pot or other container with a few tablespoons of household cleanser, and then boiling them for about 15 minutes. Rinse the rocks several times with clean water to remove any cleanser residue, then lay rocks in the sun until dry.

BARBECUE GRILL SAFETY

Barbecue grill safety is no joke.

- If matches are needed, use long-handled ones.
- If gas burners won't light in five seconds, shut off the gas and wait five minutes before trying again. If an igniter fails to spark readily, use a match until the igniter can be replaced.
- If flashback occurs, immediately turn the control knobs to off and carefully turn the gas supply off at the propane tank. Consult the owner's manual to determine the cause and solution.
- Turn off or unplug the unit when it is not in use and before cleaning it. Allow the grill to cool before starting.
- Avoid using attachments not recommended by the manufacturer.
- Never move the unit while it is hot or in operation.
- Don't cook near or under combustible materials.
- Avoid wearing clothes with loose sleeves while cooking.
- If a flare-up occurs, reduce heat. If flare-ups persist, shut down the unit until flames cease.
- Never store a propane tank indoors. It vents gas if the pressure rises excessively, as it might on a hot day. The tank should be disconnected and kept outdoors in a well-ventilated area away from heat, direct sunlight, and children.
- Electric barbecue grills have these additional safety concerns: (1) To prevent electrical shock, never immerse cord, plugs, controls, or heating elements in water or other liquids. (2) Unplug the unit when not in use or before cleaning and servicing it. (3) Never, ever operate an electric barbecue with a damaged plug or cord or after the unit malfunctions or has been damaged in any manner. In other words, unless it is in perfect operating condition, don't use it. (4) Avoid exposing it to rain. (5) Keep the cord away from table and counter edges and hot surfaces. (6) To disconnect, turn off controls before unplugging the unit from the electrical outlet. (7) Use only properly grounded outlets. (8) If an extension cord is used, the connection must be kept dry and off the ground.

Wood Decks

Wood decks, while performing many of the same functions as concrete patios, are more versatile. Concrete patios, due to their weight and methods of construction, are most practical when located at or near ground level. Wood decks can be built at any height, from simple decks at ground level to complex, multi-leveled platforms that wrap around contemporary dwellings, blending a home's interior living spaces with the great outdoors.

However, wood—sturdy as it seems—can be affected by many kinds of destructive agents. The ones you should be most concerned with are water, sunlight, and biological organisms from fungi to termites.

WATER DAMAGE

All deck wood must be protected against water damage, even if the wood is pressure treated. During the manufacturing of pressure-treated lumber, a water-based chemical solution is forced into the wood. This solution includes chemicals that are hygroscopic, which means they readily absorb water. Within about thirty days the water evaporates, leaving the chemical protection behind, and leaving the wood protected against practically anything but water damage. Rain, melting snow, and other moisture can penetrate the wood fibers and cause the wood to expand. As the moisture evaporates, the wood dries out, contracts, and can develop long splits and cracks commonly seen on pressure-treated wood decks that haven't been waterproofed. This cycle will then repeat itself until the wood is extensively damaged. Waterproofing with a good sealant will prevent this from happening.

SUNLIGHT DAMAGE

All wood is subject to sunlight damage whether it is pressure-treated or not. Sunlight discolors or bleaches wood and dries out natural oils. Sunlight also speeds drying of wood, contributing to the splintering, cracking, and warping that untreated wood will develop.

BIOLOGICAL DAMAGE

One reason that pressure-treated wood is popular with deck builders is its fine resistance to biological agents. Once mold, mildew, or rot is present in untreated wood, it will literally eat the wood away, causing structural damage and discoloration. Attempts to cover untreated wood with even the finest of paints and sealers usually result in eventual deterioration. Moisture gets in somehow, through the ends, through scuffs in the paint, through nail holes, cracks, or knotholes. Termites and wood-boring insects can also cause severe damage to untreated wood. Termites are particularly dangerous, since they eat the wood from the inside out and can go unnoticed while the damage is occurring.

WOOD DECK INSPECTIONS

- Wood rot. (1) Look beneath deck crawlspaces—areas under the deck where rot and decay could go unnoticed, where there is not much ventilation or light. The most likely place for deterioration is where wood supports come in direct contact with the ground. (See Figure 7-1.) Also look for signs of insect infestations (see section on pests). Probe all suspected wood with a screwdriver. Mark areas on the wood and itemize on your worksheet where soft spots or related defects occur. (2) Check main deck supports. Again, carefully inspect the wood where it enters the ground. All structural members such as joists and girders should be checked. (3) Steps and flooring materials should be examined, from underneath if possible, for signs of fungus growth. This could be the beginning of wood rot. (4) Railings and safety guards should be inspected for wood rot.

- See that all deck components are securely fastened. Support posts should be stable and in solid footing. Check steps and railings for cracks or looseness. Do they bow under your weight? Walk along the decking and note any sagging, loose, or weak areas as you pass over them. All flooring and steps should be sturdy enough to support several pieces of heavy furniture without undergoing noticeable structural deflections. Railings should

7-1. In-ground deck support.

be strong enough to take a beating from children who like to climb onto or jump from the deck.

▪ Are all decking nails fastened so the nail heads are just below the surface of each board? Sometimes nails gradually "work up" from the flexing actions of the deck boards, and become a hazard to children and others in bare feet.

▪ Note any boards that have warped or bowed enough so they pose dangers to people using the deck.

▪ Note any spaces between decking boards that have become filled with leaves and other debris. This condition can keep the surrounding wood damp and cause decay.

▪ Dense shrubbery, vines, and other foliage can interfere with air movement and drainage near the deck, and might enable fungi to grow on deck supports or other structural members.

▪ Maintain proper drainage at the base of a deck. Downspouts should not discharge rain runoff onto ground on which a deck is constructed. Undrained soil around a deck can be a source of deterioration to deck supports that enter the ground. The ground that a deck is constructed on should slope away from both the house and the deck supports. Downspouts should discharge into drains, masonry gutters, or splash blocks that send the water outward at least several feet away from the deck.

▪ What is the condition of the deck's finish? Does it need restaining, resealing, or repainting? If a deck is stained, be aware that stain penetrates wood not only to color the wood but to lubricate and prevent cracking. If the stain has faded, or if you see hairline cracks in the wood, the oils have probably dried out and the stain is losing its protective abilities. This is natural. Sunlight will eventually dry out practically any wood that has been stained and then left alone.

Although most decks should automatically be resealed each year, you can determine what condition a deck surface is in by simply pouring water from a glass onto some deck planking. If the plank surfaces absorb water and turn noticeably darker, then the wood is vulnerable and needs the protection of waterproofing. If the water beads up and is not absorbed, the surface is already protected.

WOOD DECK REPAIRS

Replacing Damaged Planks

Replace all decayed, severely cracked, or warped wood members with pressure-treated lumber, preferably with lumber also treated with chemicals referred to as "CCA," which indicates the amounts of calcium chloride and arsenic forced into the wood fibers. If available, treated southern yellow pine and Ponderosa pine are excellent choices. Both have superior life expectancies against rot, fungi, and termites. Make sure all decking planks have the same thickness as the ones you are replacing, or you will end up with floors that are dangerously uneven to walk on.

Avoiding the Same Nail Holes

Whether replacing a board or merely turning it over, avoid using the same nail holes. If you must use the old ones, use screws that are somewhat larger than the existing holes, for secure holding power.

Replacing Deck Support Posts

Deck support posts can be replaced with procedures outlined in the section on fences. Their base holes should be filled with concrete.

Strengthening Weakened Joists

1. Obtain two pieces of new pressure-treated lumber the same width and thickness as the damaged joist but at least 4 to 6 feet longer than the damaged area.
2. Using galvanized or aluminum nails, nail the two new boards one on each side of the damaged joist.
3. Drill a zigzag pattern of holes at 10-inch intervals through the three boards. (See Figure 7-2.)

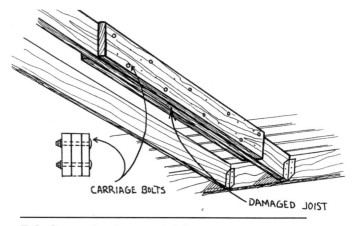

CARRIAGE BOLTS
DAMAGED JOIST

7-2. Strengthening weak joists.

4. Install carriage bolts with felt washers and metal nuts. Tighten the nuts until secure.

Replacing Damaged Sections of Decking

1. Saw the damaged section out with the inside joist edges on both sides of the repair. (See Figure 7-3.)

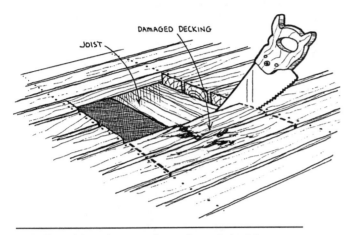

7-3. Repairing damaged section of decking.

2. Coat the remaining ends of the old decking planks with several coats of a good water sealer.
3. Cut two pieces of pressure-treated 2" x 4" lumber into lengths about a foot longer than the joist-end lengths of the repair. Nail one piece to the inside face of each exposed joist, to act as supports for the new flooring planks. (See Figure 7-4.) The supports should be even with the top of the existing joists.

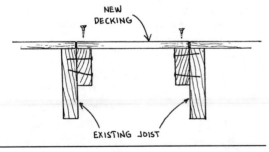

7-4. Installing new planking.

4. Cut new floor planks to the same size as those removed. Treat the ends with water sealer.
5. Fasten the new decking planks to the supports with brass wood screws to prevent rust.

NOTE: Always use non-rusting fasteners when working with wood decks. Galvanized or stainless steel, brass, or aluminum nails and screws will not rust away or leave ugly red and rust markings.

WOOD DECK MAINTENANCE

1. Tighten all loose wood members. Loose deck parts should be retightened as soon as they are noticed. By retightening, you will probably prevent wobbly parts that are more likely to break or cause injury to users. If nailed, renail with non-rusting deck nails. Avoid using old nail holes. If bolted, simply retighten the bolts and nuts. If certain parts continue to loosen, such as railings, consider converting them from nailed pieces to bolted pieces for greater stability.
2. Trim encroaching vegetation away from deck posts, supports, and decking. Some foliage may be desired, but don't let it interfere with the deck's air circulation or your ability to make visual inspections.
3. If ungalvanized steel nails are present and causing rust discoloration, scrub the rust marks with a deck cleaner. To prevent further staining, drive the nail heads at least $1/8$ inch below the wood's surface, swab the heads with water repellent sealer, and fill the nail-head depressions with stainable waterproof putty or with putty the same color as the wood.
4. If possible, avoid using paint on a wood deck. Often a coat of paint will actually trap water beneath its surface, which consequently causes decay. Outdoor wood steps and flooring especially do not hold paint well. A pigmented or clear stain that contains a preservative will protect the wood more consistently, and does not require extensive surface preparation when additional coats are needed. Stains can then be covered with a coat of water sealer.

   If a deck is not stained and you want to maintain the natural wood look, combination stain/wood protectors are available that contain waterproofing, preservatives, and ultraviolet light ray absorbers for protection against water, biological hazards, and sunlight. They can also contain non-drying oils which remain in the wood as a moisturizer to help prevent drying and cracking.

   Use the "water on the deck" test to see if a deck is ready for sealing each year; or, in harsh climate areas, you may opt to seal each year automatically.
5. To apply water sealer or wood preservative:
   - With a newly installed deck, wait at least 30 days before any treatment is applied to give moisture from the wood manufacturing process time to evaporate.
   - Clean the deck. Sweep away leaves, dust, and other debris. Remove materials that may have built up between the boards. Scrub the decking

with a household cleanser, warm water, and a stiff-bristled brush. For a more effective cleaning, purchase a bottle of deck cleaner and follow the package directions. Make sure you wear rubber gloves, sturdy shoes, goggles, long trousers, and a long-sleeved shirt. Mix the cleaner and apply it with a mop, paint roller, or sprayer. After it works for 15 to 20 minutes, scrub the deck with a brush. Then rinse the deck and surrounding area thoroughly with water from a garden hose.

▪ Allow at least two days following a washing or a rainstorm before you start to seal.

6. Get rid of any pitch that oozes to the surface. New lumber often develops this tacky residue on the wood's surface. Pitch forms when wood resin is activated by heat. Just scrape it off with a paint scraper. Don't try to remove it with solvents. That will only dilute the pitch and allow it to repenetrate the wood.

7. If any mold or mildew exists, scrub the infected areas with a solution of one cup trisodium phosphate, one cup household bleach, and one gallon warm water. Or use one of the special deck cleaners available at hardware and builder's supply stores. Select one that cleans and protects against mold and mildew.

8. When it is time to seal or stain, make sure the temperature conforms to the specifications of whatever material you are using. A safe range is at least 40 degrees F. for water sealer, and 50 degrees for wood protectors.

9. Wear goggles and rubber gloves when you work with stains and sealers. Take care not to breathe concentrated fumes.

10. If you've never used a particular product before, do a test patch first. Apply your treatment solution to an inconspicuous part of the deck to see exactly what will happen.

11. Apply the stain, sealer, or protectant easily with a brush, roller, or garden sprayer. Cover all exposed wood surfaces. Let dry for several days. Clean tools with turpentine or paint thinner.

NOTE: Avoid using steel wool on deck wood because steel wool might blacken the wood's finish.

WOOD DECK SAFETY

You may be working high off the ground. Use safe ladder practices. Don't lean outward against wobbly railings or safety guards.

Be careful no one stands, walks, or plays directly below a deck while you're working on it. Rope off an area wide enough on the ground so windblown dust, dirt, sawdust, cleansers, or sealing solutions will not be blown into anyone's eyes. Do this also so pieces of boards or tools that accidentally fall will not injure a child or bystander.

When working with pressure-treated wood, follow these precautions:

▪ Wear rubber gloves, goggles, and a dust mask when cutting, sanding, or drilling.

▪ If you accidentally get a splinter of pressure-treated wood in your finger or anywhere else, get the splinter out as soon as possible. While untreated wood may eventually soften and disintegrate within your finger, pressure-treated wood will not. It should be removed right away to prevent adverse reactions to its chemicals.

▪ Pressure-treated lumber should not be burned. If you have old or leftover scraps, or you have torn down a damaged deck, dispose of the material in the manner specified by your municipality or county.

▪ Pressure-treated wood shavings, chips, and sawdust should not be used for animal bedding. Dispose of such materials as mentioned above.

WOOD DECK QUICK CHECKLIST

❑ All deck components should be securely fastened and solid.

❑ Check that safety railings and attachments are present and in good condition.

❑ Support posts, structural members, and decking should be free from rot, fungi, and wood-damaging insects.

❑ Waterproof deck surfaces. Sealers and stains containing preservatives should be favored over paints.

❑ Opt for pressure-treated wood whenever possible.

❑ Use non-rusting fasteners: aluminum, brass, galvanized, or stainless steel nails and screws.

Landscaping

It is safe to say that a property's landscape is more often than not in a state of change. Things are sprouting, growing, going in or out of dormancy, or dying. If left to themselves, trees, shrubs, grass, weeds, and other plants inevitably engage in a survival-of-the-fittest free-for-all that will result in chaos. Chaos will yield a terrain that looks unkept, and unkept terrain will detract from both the value of a home and the occupants' enjoyment of the grounds.

Proper landscape planning, when combined with sound maintenance practices, can make a yard or grounds an asset to your property and lifestyle. There are many considerations to take into account.

Consider first the sun. The sun is one of the most important environmental factors that affect your home's heating and cooling requirements. Deciduous trees (ones that lose their leaves during fall) planted along the southwest side of a house will block hot summer sun rays. During winter, after the leaves have fallen, those same trees will allow winter sun rays to reach and warm the home. In such a way, landscape planning can help or hinder year-round comfort levels of a dwelling. Well-planned shade trees can reduce utility bills by as much as 10 to 40 percent per year.

Next, consider the wind. It too can be affected by plantings. Evergreen trees growing close together in a windbreak can form an effective wall against winter winds along the north side of a home. When tall enough, evergreens deflect the winds upward over a home's roof and minimize wind chill factors.

Plantings can also create privacy in a yard and block sound. Or they can provide small patches of wilderness for wildlife.

But no matter what the purpose, landscaping must be maintained. You have to keep after it or it will quickly overgrow and become unruly. It is much simpler to cut a lawn once a week, or just as it needs cutting, than it is to wait until the grass is so thick that hours are needed to rake, collect, and dispose of the clippings. That is how most landscaping maintenance works. By keeping things in check, trees, shrubs, hedges, and weeds won't grow out of control.

LAWNS

A lawn can be thought of as a landscaping backdrop against which the home and the rest of the property's trees, shrubs, and plants are placed. It is often the focal point and as such demands frequent attention during the growing season. Here are some lawn care points to consider.

Types of Grass to Plant

When faced with the question of what type of grass to plant, your best bet is to check with local garden stores and lawn care companies. The type of grass to plant is a variety specifically adapted to your area. To plant Oregon-developed grass seed on a front lawn in Florida may not result in a successful yard. Grasses not common to your location are more likely to fail. The most well-known grasses are rye grass, bluegrass, and fescue. But check with the experts in your location to see what has worked well for them.

Seed, Sod, or Plugs?

Spring is the best time to make most lawn repairs. There are three ways to replace or rejuvenate damaged or bare lawn sections: seed, sod, or sod plugs.

Grass seed is the least expensive way to make repairs. Just prepare the area by removing old thatch (dead grass lying on the sod) and roughing up the soil. Spread or broadcast grass seeds at a rate prescribed by the seed manufacturer. Cover with a light layer of straw to minimize erosion, to help hold moisture, and to prevent birds from eating the seeds. Keep the ground moist so the seeds will germinate.

The use of sod is popular with people who don't want to wait several weeks for seeds to grow. In a sense, sod provides an instant lawn. Early spring is the best time to install sod. The soil base must be carefully prepared, smoothed, and fertilized. The strips of sod should be firmly tamped into place and kept moist so the grass roots can reach the ground and become safely rooted by the time hot, dry weather comes along. Unless you are willing to baby-sit the sod for several months, never try to install it during summer.

In fact, it may not even be sold during the hottest months of the year. Sod becomes available once again in the fall; however, it then requires substantial watering and a richer mixture of topsoil than sod installed during spring.

Sod plugs are small rounds of grass sod a few inches in diameter. They can be planted to help thicken lawns with thin, spotty grass coverage. Simply plant the plugs in scattered fashion throughout the thin areas, then water them.

Fertilizers and Herbicides

During spring it is usually appropriate to put down an application of grass fertilizer to encourage lawn growth and greening. At the same time, a weed-control mixture can be applied to kill existing weeds and to inhibit new weed growth. There are a number of "weed and feed" fertilizers available that greatly simplify lawn care nutrient and weed-killing applications.

When deciding which one to use, make sure the weed and feed you select will destroy the following weeds:

> Dandelions
> Crabgrass
> Common chickweed
> Mouse-ear chickweed
> Ground ivy
> Wild garlic
> Goose grass
> Henbit
> Knotweed
> Nimblewill
> Plantain
> Quackgrass
> Sheep sorrel

These are problem plants. If you can, identify weeds in advance. Purchase or borrow a lawn care manual with color photos of the worst weed offenders. Ask your garden store clerk or lawn care representative what it will take to control your particular weeds.

The most popular method of spreading dry, granular weed and feed is with a drop spreader. (See Figure 8-1.) Here are some guidelines for using this simple piece of equipment:

1. Pick a calm day when the grass is damp but not soaked. Ideal conditions occur just after a light rain when no additional precipitation is forecast for 48 hours. Never spread on windy days, when the material can be blown off. Never spread when the grass is bone dry because the granules will not stick to the grass blades. And never spread when a rainstorm is about to drench the grass and

wash the granules into the base of the sod.

2. Wear work shoes and long pants. Handle the fertilizer or weed and feed with gloved hands. Avoid inhaling dust from lawn-spreading activities.

3. Set the spreader to the setting recommended by the fertilizer manufacturer, usually to a discharge number between 1 and 5. Make sure the discharge chute is closed until needed.

4. Fill the spreader bin with the material to be spread. Gently crush large lumps of material so they will drop into the spreader's moving machinery. It is a good idea to fill the spreader bin or hopper over a driveway, patio, or other place where spilled material can be harmlessly swept up. Spillages on grass or plantings will be in such high concentrations that severe burns and dead spots will result.

5. With the spreader's discharge chute still closed, push the spreader to the part of the lawn where you want to start.

6. Instructions on the package will show exactly how to spread the material. For the most part, first lay two strips of fertilizer at each end of the area. To do so, open the discharge chute and immediately start walking forward at an even gait. After the end strips are laid, complete the section by laying strips perpendicular to and between the initial four. (See Figure 8-1.)

The completed end strips let you shut off the spreader's discharge chute when you reach them. It is important to shut off the spreader as you reach the

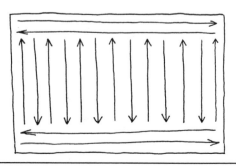

8-1. Drop spreader and spreading pattern.

end strips so those areas are not overlapped with a double dose of weed and feed. If you try to spread without the end strips, by turning at each strip end while spreading, the fertilizer will be applied extra heavy in the inside of each turn, and light on the outside. Grass won't grow properly in thin spots, and will turn yellow or brown along the inside of turns where the fertilizer was put on too heavily.

Try not to overlap or leave spaces between the fertilized rows. Use the spreader's wheel impressions in the grass to judge where the next row should be laid. A correct method is to keep the "inside" spreader wheel inside of the outer wheel mark of the previous track. (See Figure 8-2.)

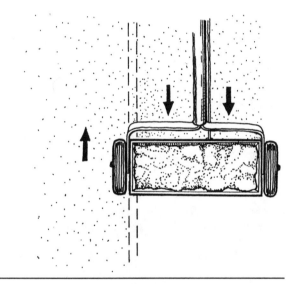

8-2. Drop spreader technique.

Drop spreader maintenance is extremely important. After each use, the spreader should be thoroughly washed with water from a garden hose. Wear goggles while doing so to protect against fertilizer residues splashing into your eyes. Even if the bin or hopper is plastic, the working parts are likely to be metal. They need to be cleaned and dried before the spreader is stored, to prevent rust from forming.

Fertilize at recommended rates and on a schedule that fits the growth cycle of your cool-season or warm-season grass. Again, local garden shops will know when you should fertilize. In general, it is advisable to apply a second treatment of weed and feed during the summer. During fall, an application of winter fertilizer will force grass roots to grow deeper for better survival during winter freezing temperatures.

When spreading liquid fertilizers with a pressurized spray unit, or through sprayers using pressure from a garden hose, wait for a calm day. To apply, simply walk slowly in a straight line and spray the liquid back and forth.

Pesticides

In addition to fertilizers and herbicides (chemicals for weed control), pesticides are available to rid a lawn of root- and leaf-eating insects, worms, grubs, and other lawn-damaging critters. With pesticides, safety is a major concern. Use only pesticides that specify use for lawns. Read and obey all warnings and instructions on the manufacturer's label.

Identify pests by inspecting sections of grass sod and looking for grubs, beetles, or other signs of infestation. Show them to your local agricultural extension representative or to experts at a lawn and garden store. If you can't find the pests, take a color photo of the lawn damage.

Try to purchase only the amount of pesticide you will need. This avoids problems with storage and disposal of excess material. If any chemicals are left over, package them and store them where children and pets cannot reach. Avoid keeping pesticides near food or food preparation equipment such as barbecue grills.

Apply pesticides on a calm day. Follow the same procedures used to apply fertilizers and herbicides. Don't permit lawn pesticides to contact fruit or vegetable crops unless the package label says otherwise.

Keep children and pets away when applying chemicals, and have them stay off the grass for the time specified by the pesticide manufacturer.

NOTE: Many large companies specialize in lawn care. These companies will apply liquid and granular fertilizers, herbicides, and pesticides at competitive rates. Check into their services and compare costs of contracting out this part of your landscape maintenance versus your cost of purchasing a spreader and materials.

Lawn Dethatching and Aerating

Springtime is also time to dethatch and aerate a lawn. Dead grass, or "thatch," that has built up in the lawn should be removed with either a rake or power landscaping equipment designed for that purpose. Excessive thatch can block moisture from getting to new grass roots. It can also promote insect infestations, and can encourage the development of a wide variety of lawn diseases. Small areas of heavy thatch can be cleared with garden rakes or stout grass rakes. Big lawns need power equipment. Dethatching machines can be rented, and they are fairly simple to run. Or consider contracting out the job — since it is not needed very often—to a local landscaper.

Kentucky bluegrass and Bermuda grass are notorious when it comes to heavy thatching. As a general guideline, if your lawn has ½ inch of dead material within the healthy, new blades, it is time to dethatch.

Aerating the lawn is accomplished by a machine that plucks small round plugs out of the sod. It opens up the soil and allows easier penetration by water, fertilizer, and air; it also increases the speed of grass clipping decomposition.

Lawn Mowing

Fertilizing, weed killing, and pesticide applications are important, but not as important as lawn mowing. Proper lawn mowing is the most time-consuming and critical lawn care activity required by a healthy landscape. It is an activity that will need to be done throughout the growing season. Mowing a lawn in a timely manner and to the right height will help grass resist weeds, insects, and disease.

When deciding on mowing height, keep in mind that if the grass in your lawn is a bluegrass, rye grass, or fescue, the recommended pre-mowing height should be no more than 4 inches, and the mowing height should be between 2 and 2½ inches. This will keep a lawn at its best without stunting the growth of the root system. If your grass is a different variety, check with local seed or sod suppliers to determine optimum mowing heights.

Remember that mowing the grass too short puts it under stress and tends to create a shallow root system. Shallow roots do not absorb moisture well, and have a hard time during hot, dry weather. During hot spells the mower should be adjusted to cut a little higher than normal, and the lawn should be mowed less frequently so grass roots will reach deeper into the soil.

In normal weather, mow to the proper height on a steady basis. If possible, don't let the lawn grow too long before cutting it to its regular 2 to 2½-inch height. If the rain pattern is such that the lawn grows to 6 or 7 inches before it can be mowed, when it dries enough to be cut, set the mower to 4 inches, cut the lawn, wait another day or so and cut it again, back to its normal cutting height of 2 to 2½ inches.

Change or alternate directions of mowing. This will keep the grass growing upright rather than leaning in the direction it is always mowed. Alternating mowing patterns will also prevent the soil from being compacted and forming wear patterns that could eventu-

ally show in the grass.

Never attempt to cut a wet lawn. The cut will not be even, and the clippings can mat and suffocate the grass. It is also tough to keep a solid footing on wet, slippery grass.

If you cut on a regular basis and never let the lawn get too high, grass clippings should be left on the lawn to help maintain sufficient nitrogen levels. It is easier, too.

Keep mower blades sharp. Dull blades will shred and pull grass tips and make a lawn weaker and more susceptible to disease and insects.

At the end of the cutting season, just before winter, mow the lawn extra short, to about 1½ inches. This will permit better air circulation that can prevent mold from developing and ruining the grass. Longer grass, when left for winter, will likely die and form a thick thatch that will make spring growth more difficult.

Lawn Watering

A lawn should be watered only when needed. Signs of a thirsty lawn include: wilting grass, a blue-green color under trees where grass competes with tree roots for water, or soil that has dried 2 to 6 inches deep.

Whenever natural rainfall is not enough and the grass needs watering, water it deeply to promote healthy, deep root growth. Lawns that are watered lightly and too frequently will develop shallow roots that cannot support healthy grass. Too-frequent waterings will also turn a lawn a pale yellowish-green. A proper watering will soak a lawn to a depth of 6 inches, which should take between 1 and 2 inches of water over the total lawn surface. Be careful, however, not to overwater. Grass, like other plants, can be harmed by too much water. Different soil types need different watering schedules. Clay soils tend to hold more water longer, while sandy soils are thirstier and tend to drain more quickly and need more frequent waterings.

It is best to water in the hours just before and after dawn. If that is not possible, the next best time is late evening. In any event, lawn watering may be a tug in the opposite direction of water conservation. You will have to decide for yourself which is more important. Keep in mind that grass can come through some very difficult dry times, and snap back as good as new with the onset of the next good rainstorm.

Lawn Edging

There is a world of difference between a properly edged lawn and a lawn with grass growing over and across sidewalks, driveways, curbs, and plantings. An edged lawn has that manicured look sought by architectural and home-design magazines. A straight, sharp edge is much more pleasing to the eye than a haphazard, uneven line. On a weekly basis — or whenever you mow your lawn—try to keep the grass trimmed where it borders driveways, sidewalks, trees, fences, and flower beds.

Raking Leaves

During fall, unless there are too few leaves to bother with, leaves should be raked and removed from the lawn. Otherwise, the grass may be smothered. You can use lawn rakes, leaf-sweeping machines, or yard vacuum units. You can even roll out sections of green nylon netting and weight them down on the grass with rocks. Every few days carry the net, with its catch of fallen leaves, to the compost pile.

TREES, SHRUBS, AND OTHER PLANTS

A landscape without trees and shrubs is like a still life painting of a bowl of fruit without the fruit. Trees and shrubs can add a lot to a yard, from both practical and aesthetic viewpoints. They can even provide the fruit.

But trees, shrubs, and other plants are living, evolving things that require maintenance if they are to thrive and nicely complement your surroundings.

New Plantings

Plantings—combinations of trees, shrubs, and other plants—are frequently installed to define borders: the head of a driveway or other outdoor feature, for instance, or boundary lines between one property and another. Shrubs or hedges can block wind, sun, noise, a distasteful view, or encroachment by neighbors and roaming pets. Shrubs or hedges can help screen a fence, patio, deck, or pool.

Whenever you plan to landscape a certain section of yard, design the entire job from the outset, even if you only intend to plant one or two items at a time. Landscapers suggest to mark spots you select with wooden stakes and string, and live with those staked-out areas for a while before you start digging.

Choose trees and shrubs that complement each other, and make sure their mature sizes will correspond to the size and style of your house. For example, avoid placing shrubbery that will eventually get 10 feet high below a window that is only 5 feet off the ground. Keep in mind how large the trees and shrubs will eventually be when mature. Keep a sense of propor-

tion to your selections. When in doubt, go smaller.

Before you allow a landscaper to deliver and install plantings, visit the nursery to look at samples of the items you will be getting. Do you like their shape, color, smell, and foliage? Before purchasing, investigate and consider how fast the trees or plants will grow and how big they will get. Will leaves be dropped every year? Is it a male or female tree? One may drop horrible black berries all over your white concrete patio. Will the tree or shrub need pruning every year? Is it susceptible to diseases or insects?

Planting Trees

If you plan to replace a tree or simply to add another to your property, make sure it is planted at least 10 feet away from the house, or its roots will compete with the home's foundation for space. Tree roots can also open seams in sewer lines and penetrate cracks in sidewalks, driveways, and patios.

Avoid areas around in-ground swimming pools as well, or you will have a maintenance nightmare keeping leaves out of the water and tree roots out of the pool.

When planting a new tree consider these points:

1. Plant trees as soon as you can after obtaining them. If weather and soil conditions prevent immediate planting, store the trees in a cool place with adequate moisture until conditions permit planting. Don't let trees or bushes in storage freeze.
2. When ready to plant, unpack the tree and soak the roots in water for 6 to 12 hours. Do not plant with packing material attached to the roots, and do not allow the roots to dry out at any time.
3. Dig a hole wider than seems necessary, so the roots can spread without crowding. Remove grass from within a 3-foot radius of the new tree's trunk.
4. Plant the tree at the same depth it stood in the nursery, without crowding its roots. Partially fill the hole with soil, moderately packing the soil around the lower roots. Avoid adding soil extenders such as peat or bark.
5. Shovel in the remaining soil. It should be firmly pressed but not tightly packed into a shallow "water holding" basin around the tree's trunk. (See Figure 8-3.)
6. Give the tree plenty of water.
7. Place a protective layer of mulch, such as wood chips, coarse bark, bark nuggets, or gravel, around the base of the tree after the water has soaked in. Tall, spindly trees that might be affected

by strong winds should be tied to stakes by running wires or ropes through pieces of rubber hose wrapped around the tree trunk.

8. Water the tree generously every week to 10 days the first year. Fertilize it after the branches have completely leafed out during the tree's first full spring. In the fall, completely soak the soil around the tree once a week until the ground freezes.

8-3. Planting a tree.

Tree Maintenance

Inspect trees at least once a year. Look for broken limbs, insect infestation, and signs of diseases. Are overhanging branches threatening to fall onto a house roof, a garage, or utility lines? Are tree roots encroaching on a house foundation, septic system, or swimming pool? They can also present serious problems to sidewalks, patios, and driveways.

Cracked and broken limbs should be trimmed back and removed before they fall. Overhanging branches that rub against roofs, gutters, siding, and windows should be trimmed before they cause serious damage. An occasional dead limb on a pine tree is to be expected; a giant tree with several dead limbs, one of which is about to flatten a house, means professional help is required.

Identify any dead or dying trees on your property. If a dead tree is left in place, a strong gust of wind could send a heavy branch or the entire tree crashing to the house or ground. If the tree is not completely dead and is an integral part of your landscaping, by all means get an expert's opinion as to whether the tree can be saved. If there is doubt in the expert's mind, it is usually best to remove the old tree and plant something else in its place.

Insects can be taken care of by pesticides applied by local landscapers or exterminators.

Tree roots starting to protrude above ground will pose tripping hazards to family, friends, and passersby. Offending tree roots can usually be cut off without damaging the tree as long as an equal proportion of branches and foliage is removed at the same time.

Tree Pruning

Sharp pruning shears and a pruning saw or bow saw are needed for pruning healthy tree limbs and removing dead and damaged branches. When using shears, place the blade next to the trunk and cut up. Remove any and all branches that are dead, broken, or diseased.

It is best to save branches that grow out at wider, more horizontal angles, and prune branches growing at narrow, more vertical angles. (See Figure 8-4.)

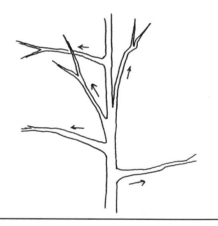

8-4. Pruning vertical shoots/branches.

When pruning diseased branches, dip the shears into or wipe the saw blade with household bleach afterwards to prevent spreading the disease to healthy limbs or trees. Most shade trees can be pruned during any season. But the removal of deadwood is best done during spring.

Avoid stubbing—cutting a large branch only partway to the trunk. Because of its weight, a large branch can tear loose during pruning, stripping bark from the trunk and creating edges that invite insects and disease. When pruning large limbs:

1. Cut partway through the branch from beneath at a point 1 or 2 feet from the trunk.
2. Make a second cut on top of the branch, several inches out from the first cut. This should allow the limb to fall by virtue of its own weight.
3. Complete the job by making a final cut next to the trunk, just outside the branch collar, with the

8-5. Cutting large branches.

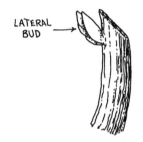

8-6. Pruning small branches.

lower edge farther away from the trunk than at the top. (See Figure 8-5.)

Small branches should be cut just beyond a lateral bud or small lateral limb. (See Figure 8-6.) The ideal cut will be sharp and clean and made on a slight angle.

Thinning works best by removing a branch at its point of origin, or shortening a branch by pruning from a lateral branch large enough to assume the main growth role.

Fertilizing Trees

Trees occasionally need extra nourishment to stay healthy. Solid tree fertilizer spikes are one way of adding nutrients to tree root systems. Landscapers have other methods, including liquid fertilizers that are injected directly into the tree.

Spraying Trees with Pesticides

Apple, cherry, peach, and other crop trees can be sprayed with pesticides to prevent insects from ruining the fruit. Other trees can be sprayed as protection against specific insect infestations, such as gypsy moths. It is best to seek advice from experts whenever pesticides are considered. A good source of information can likely be found at your local agricultural extension office.

One common pest is the black carpenter ant. Be on the lookout for black ants that swarm around the base of a large, old tree. It could be a sign of internal rotting from damages done by the insects themselves, or from a disease.

Hedge and Shrub Trimming

All shrubs and hedges can be trimmed monthly during the growing season so they will maintain their shapes. An acceptable substitute trimming schedule is to trim in late spring and early fall. Hedges and shrubs should be kept trimmed back so they grow slowly. The slower you allow them to grow, the more they will thicken and the better they will look.

Shrubs planted next to a house should not be allowed to become overgrown so they block sunlight from reaching the foundation or siding. Such overgrowth encourages decay-causing organisms to thrive and provides a refuge for insects and rodents. If shrubs have already grown too large for their spaces, it may be too late for neatly trimming them back. In that case, it is better to replace them with new plants that can be trained from the start.

Shrubs and plantings at the front of the home should highlight the main entrance. If the house is constructed low, a ranch dwelling, for instance, then the plantings should be trimmed low. The kinds of plants that are most suited to low height growth are shrubs that grow slowly in a horizontal rather than vertical fashion. However, if the house is several stories high and the entrance door is above grade, taller trees and shrubs can be kept and trimmed in a more vertical manner.

Mulch

Each spring, apply mulch where needed around trees, shrubs, and flower beds to help discourage weed growth and to retain moisture. Mulches include shredded hardwood and softwood bark, pine bark nuggets, peat, wood chips, and a wide variety of stone, depending on your location. Some people maintain a compost pile in such a manner that it provides all the mulch they can use. Compost has the feature of supplying nutrients in addition to holding in moisture.

Vines

Any form of vine that is found growing directly on a house, even if the vine is attractive and quaint, should be removed or relocated. Vines will hold moisture against a home's siding, be it brick, stone, wood, vinyl, or aluminum. Climbing ivy or wisteria can do a lot of damage; there is an incredibly destructive power in a vine's tendrils and shoots. They can rip siding loose and damage mortar between bricks and stones. They can literally destroy window frames and practically anything else that gets in their way. The moisture they hold will cause paint to blister and peel, and mold to form. They make a convenient path for termites and other wood-eaters to reach a dwelling's woodwork, plus mosquitoes, bees, spiders, and bats tend to nest in the foliage.

If you want creeping vines on your home, let them climb a trellis set at least 18 inches from the siding. Check the growth several times a year during the growing season to be sure that the plant's tiny tendrils have not reached for and attached themselves to anything they shouldn't.

While on the subject of ivy, be careful that ground cover with shiny leaves is not of the poison variety. Have someone identify plants growing in your yard if they are unfamiliar to you.

Before Winter Arrives
Plan ahead for winter. Protect plants from freezing temperatures and heavy snowfalls. Young evergreens are particularly susceptible to freezing winds. Partially screen or cover them to protect tender branches and needles from drying wind burns.

In cold-climate areas, shrubs should be watered thoroughly before the ground freezes. Give them a good soaking once a week from late fall until the ground freezes. If temperatures during winter rise above 40 degrees F. and stay there long enough for the ground to thaw, shrubs should be watered then, too, if the ground is dry.

A heavy drift of snow that falls from a roof can ruin shrubs. Protect shrubs and hedges by setting up a temporary shelter during winter. Although such a shelter arrangement may not win any beauty awards, at least the shrubs will be protected. (See Figure 8-7.)

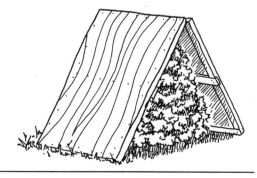

8-7. Shrub protection.

DRAINAGE

No one wants problems with water. Improper drainage is usually caused when some of the land surrounding a house slopes toward the house. If rainwater runs downhill to the home's foundation, it will seep through cracks, openings, and weak joints. Undulations and depressions near the house can also trap and hold water.

To protect the foundation and prevent leaky basements, refill areas that may have settled around foundation walls, make sure gutters and downspouts are operating correctly and are conveying water to a storm sewer or at least away from the house, and avoid sprinkling the lawn and plantings against the house to a point of saturation.

CONTRACTING HELP

If a yard has been neglected for a long time and resembles a jungle, there is no reason to tackle everything at once, or even to do everything by yourself. If you need a head start, call any of the following professionals. They have the tools, the knowledge, and the man- and womanpower to get you caught up in a hurry.

Landscape Architect
This may sound a bit too "high class" to suit some people's budgets, but landscape architects shouldn't be ruled out. Good ones can earn back what they cost by saving you all kinds of maintenance labor and expenses. They can design picture-perfect borders, flower beds, and other plantings. And they can design energy-efficient and reduced-maintenance landscapes with long-term comfort and savings in mind.

Landscapers
Landscapers can do it all: tree removing and planting, pruning and trimming, power raking, lawn aeration, seeding, mowing, edging, sodding, rock garden construction, garden preparations, and so on. They will diagnose your pest problems and tell you what disease has been leaving large, round bare spots in your backyard.

Weed-Control and Fertilizer Companies
Known for their colorful trucks run by uniformed attendants who spray and spread fertilizers, herbicides, and pesticides, these companies have what they do down to a science. They are cost efficient and eliminate the need to handle and store lawn chemicals in

the household. Some companies now offer organic services also.

When selecting landscape contractors, it is a good idea to ask friends, colleagues, your builder, or neighbors whose landscaping you admire for suggestions on whom to use. Be sure to ask the contractor for several names and addresses of his or her most recent clients. Then do some checking.

LANDSCAPING QUICK CHECKLIST

- ❑ Ideally, fertilize your lawn at least three times per year, during spring, summer, and early fall. But any fertilizing is better than none.
- ❑ If needed, apply weed control with the fertilizer, or resort to one of the "weed and feed" combination treatments.
- ❑ Make lawn repairs during spring.
- ❑ If needed, dethatch and aerate your lawn during spring.
- ❑ Mow a lawn when it reaches or exceeds about 4 inches in height. Cut it to between 2 and 2½ inches high.
- ❑ Keep lawn mower blades sharp.
- ❑ Mow a lawn often enough so you won't need to pick up clippings.
- ❑ Water a lawn only when it needs watering. Do it near dawn or late at night.
- ❑ Keep lawn edges trimmed.
- ❑ Select trees and shrubs that will complement, not clash with your house type.

- ❑ Arrange plantings so they will perform several functions: a row of pine trees situated along the north side of a home, for instance, can provide both privacy and protection from winter winds.
- ❑ Avoid planting trees closer than 10 feet to a home.
- ❑ Remove cracked, diseased, and dead tree limbs.
- ❑ Read a good book on tree pruning or watch an expert in action. Then apply what you learn to your trees, shrubs, and hedges. Remember that frequent prunings and trimmings are the key to developing healthy, attractive specimens.
- ❑ Fertilize trees when needed.
- ❑ Control insect infestations.
- ❑ Keep vines and other climbing vegetation off the dwelling.
- ❑ Winterize shrubs and young evergreens toward the end of fall. Protect shrubs and plantings from heavy snowfalls.
- ❑ Correct a neglected landscape a little bit at a time, not all at once.
- ❑ Don't be afraid to contract professionals, at least to get things started. Landscape architects, landscapers, and weed control companies can straighten out major problems in a hurry, and help you set up a program of regularly scheduled maintenance.

Landscaping Equipment

Equipment required to maintain a household's landscaping depends on several factors. Naturally, the more you do yourself, the more equipment it will take. Most people elect to do at least some of their own maintenance. From there, equipment selection depends on how large the yard is, what the yard contains or will contain, and how extensively you want to care for the grounds.

Typical equipment includes a lawn mower or garden tractor/mower combination, a weed or grass trimmer, a pair of trimmers for shaping shrubs and hedges, and a variety of hand tools from garden rakes, shovels, hand pruners, bow saws, wheelbarrows, fertilizer spreaders, and spray units to the less common power edgers and drip-irrigation systems.

LAWN MOWERS

There are several theories on lawn mower ownership. Some people will purchase the most expensive mower they can find—the one with the most horsepower, the sturdiest deck and wheels, and the longest warranty. Then they will baby it for years, changing the oil, cleaning the air filter, replacing the spark plug, sharpening the blade. At season's end they will follow to the letter the manufacturer's recommendations for winterizing the unit. A good mower, when kept that way, will last for years.

Other people will purchase the least expensive model they can find, and they will use it for one, two, perhaps three years without ever doing anything to it, except perhaps adding oil. When it wears out or will no longer start and run, they simply replace it with another cheap mower.

Still others go for middle-of-the-road mowers, and maintain them in a reasonable fashion.

Consider that lawn mowers are available with three power drives: manual, electric, and gasoline (or diesel). For someone with a small area of light, spindly grass, a rotary push mower may be all that is needed. It can even supply a limited but healthy amount of exercise to whoever pushes it. Its only maintenance is

occasional blade sharpening and lubricating. An electric mower can fill the same niche: light-duty cutting over small or medium-sized yards. Much of electric mower maintenance is in the handling and lubrication, as specified in the manufacturer's guides.

The most common lawn mowers by far are mowers powered by small gasoline engines. Gasoline mowers offer a greater selection, with more features, capabilities, and mobility than their manual and electric cousins.

No matter which type of lawn mower you prefer, to get the longest life out of the unit and the most for your dollar, consider the following maintenance points:

- The blades should be sharp. A dull blade won't cut cleanly. It will pull grass as it attempts to cut. It is a lot harder to pull grass than to cut it, so additional stress is placed on the mower engine and revolving parts. The grass, too, will suffer. The cut ends will be bruised and ragged, and will not have that healthy look given when cleanly cut. You can sharpen the blade yourself, but only if you know how. It can be tricky. If you are mechanically inclined and are used to sharpening things, fine. Otherwise, you might do better to have it done by a professional.
- Use correct amounts of motor oil in the mower or fuel. There are two kinds of mower gasoline engines. One takes oil in a separate reservoir and has a gauge from which you can check the level. The other kind requires the oil to be pre-mixed with the gasoline at an exact ratio. Probably the quickest way to ruin a lawn mower engine is either to let the oil level fall to nothing, or to forget to add the correct amount of oil to the fuel (depending, of course, on the type of engine).
- Keep the air filter clean. A dirty air filter can create a noticeable loss of power, and because it causes the engine to work harder to accomplish the same amount of cutting, it will definitely shorten the mower's useful life. The air filter should be cleaned or replaced after about every 10 hours of operation.

If the filter is made of paper, it should be replaced. Foam rubber filters can be washed with kerosene or with water and laundry detergent, then wrung out and treated with 10 to 15 drops of clean oil. Squeeze the filter several times to distribute the oil evenly. Replace the filter with the cleanest side facing the carburetor.

- Keep the mower clean and dry. Instead of just shoving the mower into the garage after every use, it should be brushed off and dried if wet. Disconnect the spark plug and use a flexible or medium-strength wire brush to clean the blades and interior housing beneath the deck. Remove accumulations of grass, leaves, and dirt that could otherwise hold moisture against the blades and deck. Clean the upper deck with a whisk broom or cloth. The point here is not to be obsessive, it is to prevent grass and debris from building up above and below the deck, so moisture will not rust the deck or other metal parts.
- Keep the spark plug reasonably clean. A dirty, oily, or carbonated spark plug will make the mower more difficult to start and can cause overall poor performance. It is best to begin each new cutting season with a new spark plug. Depending on how much you use the mower during the year, change the plug again about halfway through the season. Follow the manufacturer's recommendations for setting the point gap.

    At the same time you change the spark plug, inspect the wire that leads from the spark plug's metal socket to the terminal at the coil, where it reconnects to the engine. Feel the wire with your fingers and check for broken or cracked insulation. These cracks are sometimes difficult to detect, so look closely. Defects, including a broken spark plug wire, should be repaired or taken care of by a qualified service person.
- The blade must be straight and balanced. A bent or unbalanced cutting blade is usually caused by striking a solid object such as a stump, large rock, sidewalk, or patio edge. A damaged or unbalanced blade will cause a loss of power and vibrations that tend to loosen other mower components.

    To check for this condition, empty the fuel tank and disconnect the spark plug terminal for safety, then tilt the mower sideways so the blade is exposed. Place a yardstick across the bottom of the housing, front to back. Rotate the blade until one end is aligned with the straight edge. Measure the gap between the straight edge and the blade. (See Figure 9-1.) Again rotate the blade until the other end is aligned with a yardstick. Measure that gap. If the gaps are not within about

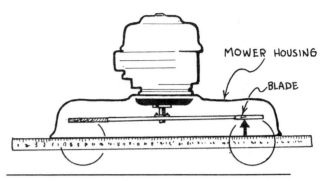

9-1. Lawn mower blade protection.

$^1/_8$ inch of each other, the blade will need tightening or replacement.

If the blade is loose, tighten the blade bolts with a wrench. If the bolts can't be tightened, a mower service person should make the necessary repairs. Never, under any circumstances, operate a mower until the blade is properly tightened and reasonably balanced.

- Lubricate all parts as recommended by the manufacturer. This could include oiling the throttle, a self-propelled cable, and the control cable during the start of the season or after every 50 hours of operation. Grease the front and rear wheels and adjustor brackets as well. At the same time, check for deterioration of or leakage from the fuel line.
- Winterize the mower at the end of the cutting season. Clean and dry the mower. Drain the fuel tank or mix additives with the remaining fuel, as recommended in the mower's operator manual.

WEED AND GRASS TRIMMERS

After lawn mowers, weed and grass trimmers are the second most frequently used power landscaping tools. They are used to control vegetation where lawn mowers can't cut: along sidewalks and curbs, driveways, fences, foundations, steps, patios, poles, trees, shrubs, and plantings.

As with lawn mowers, both electric and gas-powered models are available. Maintenance points include:

- Inspect a trimmer before each use. Make sure all components are in place and securely fastened. A power trimmer cuts by means of rapidly rotating plastic lines or plastic or steel blades. Trimmer head parts that are chipped, bent, cracked, or damaged in any way can fly apart and cause serious injury. Damaged parts must be replaced only with original manufacturer parts before the trimmer is used again. Follow the manufacturer's instructions to replace all parts. If the instructions recommend that a repair be made by an authorized dealer, make sure that is how it is done.

Use only string or blades specified by the manufacturer. It is extremely dangerous to try similar blades from another manufacturer, or substitute wire, rope, or string of a different size. On string trimming heads, use only flexible, non-metallic monofilament trimmer line of the correct diameter.

Make sure the shield guard is properly attached to the cutting end of the trimmer.

- Use the correct fuel/oil mixture or levels.
- On electric-powered units, follow the operator's manual lubrication instructions.

OTHER POWER LANDSCAPING EQUIPMENT

Other equipment can include rototillers for tilling gardens, chain saws for thinning and cutting wooded sections, hedge trimmers, post-hole diggers, backhoes, and to a certain extent, four-wheel drive carts or all-terrain vehicles. Most are gasoline powered, and must be maintained in a manner similar to that of gasoline mowers. In all cases, become familiar with the operator's manuals and follow safety procedures to the letter.

LANDSCAPING EQUIPMENT SAFETY

If you're wondering why this section seems unusually long, it is because landscaping with power tools is a rather dangerous activity. You are dealing with whirring, cutting machinery. With uneven terrain. With hot summer days. With things that fly into the air. With loud noises. With muscles you haven't used in months. Due to the nature of the landscaping tasks, the equipment can easily cut, crush, or otherwise damage fingers, hands, and feet or other body parts. Pets, too, are susceptible to injury.

While most safety procedures regarding equipment maintenance and use are covered in the manufacturer's operator's manuals, following are some general points to consider.

Electric Units
- Use only the voltage recommended by the manufacturer.
- Avoid using electric tools in the presence of flammable liquids or gases. Sparks from the electric motor could cause a fire or an explosion.
- Don't use in damp or wet locations or if exposed to snow, rain, or water to prevent the possibility of an electrical shock.
- Use extension cords specifically marked as suitable for outdoor service.

- Inspect the insulation, connectors, and extension cord before each use. Have damaged components repaired before putting them back in service.
- If a trigger mechanism or switch does not turn the tool off and on properly, have repairs made by an authorized dealer.
- Avoid any bodily contact with grounded conductors such as metal pipes or wire fences, to prevent the possibility of electrical shock.
- Avoid carrying a tool by its cord. An irritating and dangerous hazard faced by people using electric trimmers and clippers is the possibility of cutting the extension cord with the tool itself. Keep the cord out of the way while you cut, and that means away from heat, oil, and other sharp edges, too.

Maintenance Safety
- See that all internal services are performed by qualified service personnel to avoid creating a hazard and/or voiding a warranty.
- Unplug the power connection or pull the spark plug wire before a tool is serviced or worked on, to prevent accidental starting.
- Use only genuine manufacturer's replacement parts. The use of any other part or accessory not specifically designed for the tool could create a hazard.
- Watch how you lift or maneuver a tool, even when it is not running. On trimmers, avoid grasping the line limiter.
- Never douse the tool with water or other liquids. Clean with a damp sponge and household detergents.

Lawn Mower Operating Safety
At the risk of sounding like a doting mother, lawn mowers and other power landscaping equipment can be hazardous to your health and the health of bystanders.

- Wear sturdy, close-fitting non-slip shoes or work boots.
- Carefully inspect a lawn before cutting. Pick up stones, sticks, pine cones, apples, golf balls, tent stakes, wire, dog bones, and anything else the blade could strike and throw.
- Remember to avoid any hard, solid obstacles that exist in the yard, such as an old tree stump hidden in the grass.
- Always adjust the cutting height before starting the mower, not while the mower is running.
- Add fuel over a neutral surface other than your lawn, where accidental spills can be cleaned before starting the mower. Gasoline spilled on the

lawn will burn the grass.

▪ An electric mower should be plugged into a three-pronged grounded outlet.

▪ Always start a mower outdoors, near the lawn you're going to mow. Avoid starting it in the garage and then pushing it to the lawn while the motor is running.

▪ Mow forward as much as possible so you can see where you're going and so you can keep your eyes on the cutting end of the mower.

▪ Cut across slopes with walk-behind mowers; travel up and down slopes with riding mowers. Because the center of gravity on a riding mower is rather high — especially when an operator is present—to travel parallel to or to make a turn on a slope is extremely hazardous. People doing so have been critically injured and killed.

▪ Keep electric cords out of the cutting path.

▪ Stay clear of the blade housing edge and the discharge chute. Do not remove discharge guards.

▪ Point the discharge chute away from others. Be aware of bystanders, especially children and pets.

▪ Most lawn mowers will automatically stop if you leave them. Older models may not have "dead man" switches. If you have to leave such an older model—even for a minute—turn it off until you return.

▪ Remember to disconnect the spark plug wire when you have to work on the mower; for instance, when grass cuttings need to be cleaned from the discharge chute. With electric units, simply pull the plug to achieve the same "zero energy" result.

▪ With riding mowers, remember always to look before you back up. Keep children away from the mower at all times. A riding mower is not a pleasure vehicle. Small children should never be permitted to ride on or operate garden tractors or mowers. Never pull a cart or other vehicle carrying passengers behind a riding mower. Keep children away.

Power Trimmer and Clipper Operating Safety

A lawn mower operates with its blade near the ground, covered by the mower deck. With weed trimmers and hedge clippers, the cutting parts are right out in the open, sometimes at face level. For safe operation of trimmers and clippers, consider the following points.

Wear safety goggles. Wear gloves to minimize vibrations. Wear sturdy work shoes. Wear long-sleeved shirts and trousers. Avoid loose clothing, jewelry, and sandals. Wear long hair tied up or in a bun. Being fully covered will also help protect you from pieces of harmful plants such as poison ivy, which, when thrown from a trimmer or clipper could be more of a hazard than merely brushing up against the uncut plant.

Wear hearing protection if the unit is gas powered.

Refrain from operating landscaping power tools when you are tired, ill, or under the influence of alcohol or drugs.

Allow only individuals fully trained in the tool's operation and safety procedures to use power trimmers and clippers.

Inspect an area to be cut before starting the job. Remove all objects such as rocks, broken glass, nails, wire, string, toys, and other items that could be thrown or entangled by a trimmer or clipper.

Keep others, including children and pets, outside of a 60-foot hazard zone around your work area. Stop the motor immediately if you are approached.

Avoid accidental starting. Keep your hands and fingers off the trigger switch while handling the tool between cutting tasks. Even if the tool has a neutral gear, it is a good idea to turn off the engine for any reason other than a brief pause in the cutting. Unplug electric models when they are not in use.

Don't force a tool. It will do a better job with less risk of injury when used at the speed and manner for which it was designed.

Use the tool only for tasks as outlined in the operator's manual.

Try to keep the trimmer head or clipper blades below waist level if possible. In all cases, hold the tool firmly and maintain a steady balance. Take frequent breaks. Trimming and clipping can easily tire the strongest individual who is not used to holding his or her arms in the positions required for cutting.

Be wary of using power tools when a tree, bush, or shrub must be reached by ladder. It is often better to get what you can from the ground and then resort to hand clippers with an extension to complete uppermost work. Or simply hire a landscaper to do hard-to-reach trimming.

Store power trimmers and clippers high out of children's reach.

LANDSCAPING EQUIPMENT QUICK CHECKLIST

❑ Keep cutting blades sharp, straight, and balanced.

❑ Use correct kinds and amounts of motor oil.

❑ Keep air filters clean.

❑ Keep equipment clean and dry between uses.

❑ Keep spark plugs clean.

❑ Keep equipment lubricated.

❑ Store power equipment high out of children's reach.

❑ Inspect power equipment before each use.

❑ Use outdoor-rated extension cords.

❑ Avoid using electrical power tools in damp or wet conditions.

❑ Wear safety equipment when operating mowers, trimmers, clippers, and other power equipment.

❑ Pay close attention to recommended safety procedures for whatever power tool you use.

Gardens

Gardening is a huge industry. It is getting people back to the land. Gardening is catalogs of seeds, tools, and clothing to review in the dead of winter. It is churning up the earth, mixing and fertilizing. Gardening is watching green sprouts rise from your soil. It is matching wits with aphids, moles, rabbits, and your neighbor's baseball-playing kids. It is yanking weeds by hand and trying to prevent overloaded tomato plants from cracking to the ground. Gardening is begging people to take just one more zucchini, please! It is the satisfaction of growing prize-winning roses or pesticide-free produce. It can be good exercise, relaxation, and a stress reliever all at the same time.

Gardening is a lot of things. But mostly, once the planning and planting get done, gardening is preventive maintenance. Preventive maintenance will make or break the whole experience. In a nutshell, gardens need to be watered, fed, and groomed. Sometimes they need to be protected, too.

From year to year, gardens follow the same basic scenario, with the following steps:

1. Garden Planning
2. Obtaining Seeds and Plants
3. Soil Preparation
4. Planting
5. Watering
6. Weeding
7. Mulching and Composting
8. Thinning Excess Plants
9. Protection
10. Controlled Harvesting
11. Preparation for Winter

No matter what anyone says, most gardening is rather labor intensive. It won't get you up in the middle of the night, of course. But it will get you up early in the morning on a variety of weekday and weekend occasions. In short, gardens become ugly, overgrown, underproducing weed-infested plots if they don't receive their fair share of preventive maintenance during the spring, summer, and fall. But don't let that discourage you. Maintained in the proper way, gardens can certainly be worth the effort.

GARDEN PLANNING

It is better to start with a small, conservative garden plot, especially if you're a beginner. A 10 by 10 foot area is fine, particularly if you plan to dig by hand and the ground has never been worked. The reasons for a small plot will become apparent as the summer wears on. Expand, if desired, a little more every year until you reach what you feel is an ideal size.

Favor plants that are easy to grow, especially at first. Tomatoes, lettuce, radishes, beans, and green peppers are good to start with. Steer away from finicky plants such as cauliflower, eggplant, and celery until you have broadened your gardening experience. Beginners need confidence more than they need cauliflower. Crops that take lots of room, such as corn, are best left out of a small garden.

Favor plants and vegetables that you like to eat (or look at, in a flower garden). There is no sense in planting a half-dozen tomato plants if you don't like tomatoes.

Draw your plan on paper. If you want to do additional research, many excellent gardening books are available, with a wide variety of planting schemes and themes you can follow, for every gardening situation imaginable.

A few words on the number of seeds or plants with which you will populate your garden. Many conservative, sane, trusting individuals, when faced with instructions from books, articles, or seed manufacturers, will take a radical turn to the left and do all but call those professional gardener types liars. The feeling is if a single tomato plant is recommended to be planted per square foot of ground, then wouldn't *two* plants be better?

The answer is no. When plants are crowded, they won't develop fully. They will be stunted. And their ability to produce vegetables or flowers will be zilch, or greatly impaired. In all cases, resist the urge to overplant.

When putting a flower garden together, consider that perennials are plants that come up year after year. They require less work and expense than do annuals

—plants that flower and die after a single growing season.

Here are some tips to make the most of your space:

- With some plants, space can be better used by planting wide rows instead of the traditional single line of seeds. Radishes, carrots, and beans are good examples.
- Sprawling ground crops such as cucumbers, peas, and some beans can be encouraged to grow up on fences, trellises, or other supports instead of along the ground.
- If your garden slants downhill, place rows perpendicular to the slope to discourage rapid water runoff.
- By making raised beds, you can make up for soil problems or sloping ground problems and make harvesting easier.
- If your garden area is partially in the shade, you can consider growing shade-tolerant lettuces and herbs in that portion of the garden. They need only a few hours of sun daily. Spinach, Swiss chard, parsley, endive, tarragon, and mint are suitable choices.
- Use successive plantings. For instance, a week or ten days after planting a crop of peas, plant a second crop. Then, as one crop is harvested, another is on its way to maturity. Successive plantings will keep a garden producing the vegetables you enjoy throughout the season.
- When setting up a flower garden, plan for constant blooming by timing your plantings so some flowers are fading while others are starting to open. For example, tulips bloom early; irises mature later.

OBTAINING SEEDS AND PLANTS

You can purchase packages of seeds or bulk seeds in person at stores, or through the mail. It may be more fun to study major seed catalogs in the privacy of your home where there is more time to read about individual varieties, and there will probably be more kinds to select from. It is best not to rush past a seed-packet display in a supermarket at the beginning of April, grabbing some as you go by.

Don't assume that the most expensive or the most exotic seeds are best, or that the larger the package, the better. Seeds come in tiny quantities, which is good. Planting too many is easy to do. Typically, home gardeners resist thinning plants back—which is gardener's talk, meaning pulling them out or *killing them*. But it must be done, so try not to purchase more seeds than you will need. For the beginner, the

amount in a typical packet is usually more than enough.

One advantage (or disadvantage) to seeds is you can become involved earlier in the year. Many plants can be started indoors a number of weeks before their outdoor planting dates.

If you decide to start with plants instead of with seeds, don't wait until planting time to purchase them or you will probably only find sick, spindly specimens left. Instead, buy seedlings—also called transplants—early and keep them in a cool garage or shed, in filtered sunlight, until it is time to plant. Water them daily as they dry out quickly in flats or peat pots.

SOIL PREPARATION

Some professional gardeners claim that soil preparation can account for 90 percent of gardening success.

The soil should be turned over by hand, with a shovel, or with a gas-powered rototiller. Big clumps of soil should be broken. Dead roots and old plants should be discarded, and the soil should be worked with a hoe or garden rake. Loose, aerated soil will promote better root growth for vegetables and flowers.

It is prudent to have a sample of your garden's soil tested by the local cooperative extension service. After the results are known, the extension can tell you what, if anything, your soil is lacking. They can advise you on what organic fertilizers to use, such as blood meal and rock phosphate, as alternatives to granular chemical fertilizers. Organic additives may be more expensive, but they promote the growth of beneficial microorganisms in the soil. Chemical fertilizers do not. Remember that too much fertilizer is worse than too little. Excessive amounts of fertilizer can burn the roots of plants so they will never reach their full potential.

PLANTING

Plant at proper times. The soil warms less quickly than air. Many seeds will simply not germinate in cold ground. Seed packets usually show a calendar-map on the back which indicates when to plant, depending on what part of the country you live in. Local garden stores and greenhouses will also be able to give you the same information.

Plants that can grow vertically, such as peas, tomatoes, and some cucumbers and beans, should be kept tied to stakes or other supports with strips of cloth.

Be sure to water seeds and seedlings immediately after planting.

Inspect the area surrounding your garden. Have adjacent trees grown to block the sun's rays? If so, you might have to trim offending branches back.

WATERING

Watering depends on the weather. Plants should not be watered so often that they become waterlogged. Too much water can cause problems: uneven growth spurts, mold and fungus attacks, cracked fruits, and unhealthy, dying plants. Plants also need periods when their surrounding soil is *not* saturated with water.

The best rule is to water when needed—after the soil has dried and when the plants look as though they need water. They will start to droop a bit when they are thirsty. If you watch the garden, you will learn to recognize the signs.

When you water, apply a gentle spray or trickle to the base of the plants. Sprinkling cans are great. Avoid using a hard stream of water that could damage foliage or undermine root systems.

WEEDING

Before you begin weeding, learn to identify your vegetable or flower seedlings. It is usually fairly easy—they are the ones coming up at the same time, in the places they were planted.

Even if you have mulched the garden with materials meant to discourage weed growth, it is likely that some weeds will take root among your tomatoes or roses. It is up to you to pull them out. If you don't, weeds have a funny way of overtaking everything. Have you ever noticed how quickly weeds will sprout in abandoned asphalt or concrete parking lots? Weeds have had hundreds of thousands, even millions of years to develop. They are hardy. And they will get the better of you and your garden if they are not pulled at least once a week.

MULCHING AND COMPOSTING

Mulches are materials placed on the surface of a garden, around the cultivated plants, to prevent moisture from evaporating, weeds from sprouting, and roots from freezing. The most common organic mulches include straw, shredded leaves, bark, and newspaper. Various inorganic mulch materials are made of thin layers of black plastic and similar garden-type fabrics.

A garden should not be mulched too early. In most areas, mulching before June will keep the ground too cold, inhibit vegetable and flowering plant growth, and actually help pests and plant diseases gain a head start on your plants.

Compost is a decomposing mixture of vegetable and plant material that is used to fertilize soil. Composting will help practically any soil, and it is the environmentally correct thing to do. It prevents a substantial portion of kitchen and landscaping wastes from ending up in our landfills. Although elaborate composting equipment is available through garden supply catalogs and stores, a less expensive setup is simply a trash can with the bottom cut out and holes punched in the sides for aeration. A wire mesh enclosure pen will also work fine.

Set the trash can or wire enclosure on the ground in an out of the way place, preferably near the garden. Then:

1. Spread one to two days' worth of kitchen vegetable or fruit waste on the bottom, on the ground in the composter. Shred or break up large pieces such as watermelon rinds. Avoid large amounts of the same material. Acceptable raw materials include potato peels, apple cores, lettuce leaves, onion skins, pea pods, corn husks, coffee grounds, eggshells, and wastes from practically everything that grows from or in the ground. (See Figure 10-1.)
2. Cover with a layer of dry leaves, grass clippings, weeds, and soil. Keep the pile loosely packed and exposed to the air.

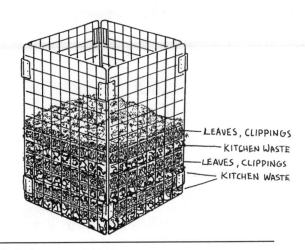

LEAVES, CLIPPINGS
KITCHEN WASTE
LEAVES, CLIPPINGS
KITCHEN WASTE

10-1. Compost bin.

3. Repeat layering daily. Keep the pile damp. An offensive odor means the pile is packed too tightly or the wrong materials have been used.
4. The materials will take about six to eight weeks to break down. Periodically, the bottom material—a black, loamy mixture—can be removed and mixed into garden soil or into soil of decorative plantings throughout the yard. Or the completed compost can be stored in a separate pile and worked into the garden and other soil after the growing season, to prepare for the following year.
5. Never place pet feces, grease, fat, charcoal, synthetics, floor sweepings, diseased plants, or large bulky materials in the compost pile.

THINNING EXCESS PLANTS

As mentioned before, new gardeners tend to sow seeds thickly and expect the plants to grow in clumps. Invariably such gardeners are disappointed with poor harvests from stunted plants. If you don't believe in the importance of proper thinning, run a test with radishes. Radishes can be planted early in the year, and they grow rapidly. In one square foot of ground, plant them thickly, and don't thin them out. In another equal-sized plot, plant them according to the instructions on the seed packet, and thin them by pulling out excess seedlings. Wait the prescribed number of days and harvest both plots. Can you guess which will yield plump radishes? And which will contain little but spindly tiny tap roots?

Sure, it is tough to snip off a perfectly good looking baby cucumber plant or a healthy zucchini vine. But in many cases it has got to be done to avoid crowding. Overplanting and crowding are probably the most frequent gardening problems. Better that plants have a little more room than not enough.

PROTECTION

Depending on where you live and where your garden is located, it may need protection from intruders: from insects, from small furry animals, from birds, from household pets, from large animals, and even from people.

Beat the bugs by enveloping plants with a feather-light polyester row cover. This thin, gauze-like fabric allows sunlight and moisture to reach the plants while protecting your tomatoes, peppers, and lettuce from pest, frost, and wind damage.

Some plants naturally fend off pests. Marigolds, when planted as a border around a garden, discourage insects and other intruders. Entire books have been written about "natural" pest controls.

Chicken wire or other wire screen materials can be used to keep rabbits, dogs, and some children from entering a garden.

A wide variety of insect-controlling chemicals is available for dusting or spraying on garden plants. Follow the manufacturer's instructions carefully and keep children away from all pesticides.

CONTROLLED HARVESTING

Don't be afraid to pick what grows! As soon as vegetables mature—perhaps even a little before—pick them and enjoy. If you don't keep picking cucumbers or peas or beans as they become ready, the plants won't bother to produce additional fruit. Instead, the cucumbers will overripen and rot. The peas will dry up, and the beans will turn as hard as stones. To keep many plants "active," you must keep picking their fruit.

GARDEN PREPARATION BEFORE WINTER

Vegetable gardens should be turned over, cleared of refuse, and planted with a cover crop such as winter grass or wheat to protect the ground from freezing temperatures. Tender plants such as roses should be protected by mulch placed around their bases, against their main stems. Spring bulbs should be planted. The trunks of young fruit trees should be surrounded by wire screening to prevent rabbits from chewing on the bark.

GARDENING SAFETY

- Prevent heat stress and heat illness by doing most work in the early morning hours. Get help for strenuous jobs such as turning over the soil for the first time. Drink plenty of fluids. Rest often.
- Use proper lifting techniques. This includes pushing rototillers around, lifting garden ties, using wheelbarrows, carrying bags of mulch, and many other related tasks. Get help when needed.
- Gardening involves a lot of bending. Use kneeling pads. Don't spend a lot of time bent toward the ground. Kneel when possible. Change positions often. Take frequent breaks.
- Watch out for insects. Mosquitoes, bees, hornets, and flies can be discouraged with bug bombs or balms available at any hardware or pharmacy.

▪ Use caution with pesticides and fertilizers. Pick calm days to spray or dust plants. Keep children away from sprayed plants. Make sure vegetables are washed before eaten.

GARDEN QUICK CHECKLIST

❑ Plan a garden on paper in advance.
❑ Prepare the soil before planting.
❑ Start small; plant only what you like to eat or look at.
❑ Avoid overcrowding. Plant fewer seeds or seedlings than you think you should.
❑ Try to include some plants that grow up a fence, trellis, or other support.
❑ Water only when necessary, with gentle sprays or trickles.
❑ Ruthlessly thin excess plants as needed.
❑ Weed a garden once per week.
❑ Mulch after the ground has warmed and the plants have gotten a good start.
❑ If possible, set up a compost pile to recycle vegetable, fruit, and plant wastes.
❑ Protect a garden from pests.
❑ Pick what grows, even if you have to give it away. Avoid letting vegetables, fruit, and flowers go to waste.
❑ Close out the garden toward the end of fall, and prepare it for winter.

Lawn Furniture

Lawn furniture is furniture used on patios and decks or anywhere else outdoors. It is often exposed to the weather, receives rather rough handling, and is frequently stored for long periods of time in cramped, out of the way locations.

Practically every material has, at one time or another, been used to manufacture lawn furniture. At the lowest end of the scale, chairs have been made from common PVC plastic pipe, from discarded milk crates, and from scrap wood ripped from used skids and pallets. Old wooden cable reels have been turned on their sides and used for tables. Available through retail stores and specialty catalogs are furniture groupings made of wood, wicker, plastic, aluminum, wrought iron, canvas, bamboo, and other materials. The most popular are wood, aluminum, wrought iron, plastic, and combinations of the same.

WOOD LAWN FURNITURE INSPECTIONS

- Dull, porous wood surfaces.
- Peeling paint or other surface coatings.
- Rot.
- Broken or loose joints, especially where chair or table legs are attached. Besides normal wear and tear, dry air can cause wooden furniture to shrink and come apart.
- Warped table tops.

WOOD LAWN FURNITURE REPAIRS

Lawn furniture made of wood, other than a naturally resistant variety such as redwood, will require a protective coating. Paint, however, is not the best option in every case. Paint can seal off much of the wood's outer surface, but it won't seal all of it. Moisture invariably enters through small cracks, nail holes, and joints. Once inside the wood, moisture will cause decay from within. It is better to coat wood furniture with an exterior wood stain that contains a preservative. Even redwood, which is a very durable material, greatly improves its appearance and life span when coated with a clear or pigmented sealer that prevents the wood from absorbing food and liquid stains, and

retards harmful effects of sunlight and moisture.

To Resurface Wood Finishes

1. If practical, take the piece apart. Strip or sand the components to bare wood. You can accomplish this by scraping and sanding, or by using chemical stripping compounds, which will work much faster. Chemical strippers, however, can soften more than paint or varnish. They can also damage the furniture's wood and the glue that holds the furniture together. It is recommended that a "neutralizer," another chemical compound that will stop the action of the stripper, be used as the last coat of paint or varnish is being softened. Then rinse and clean off the stripper, neutralizer, and old finish at the same time. After the stripping is completed, give the wood time to dry. Sand with medium to fine sandpaper to smooth the surface and to bring out the wood's natural grain.

2. If you want a clear wood look, treat the bare wood with a clear undercoating to bring out the wood's true color and grain and to help moisturize the wood so it won't dry out. Then apply a clear (or pigmented) all-weather seal.

3. If you decide to change the appearance of the furniture to match a different color scheme, prime and paint with several coats of all-weather paint.

To Repair Unglued Table/Chair Legs or Arms

1. If the pieces are loose, finish knocking them apart with a wood block and mallet.

2. Remove old glue with a dull knife or scraper and sandpaper. Scrape glue out of the holes, too. Remove only the old glue. If you sand any wood at the actual joints, the joints will become too loose when put back together.

3. Reassemble the pieces, using white vinyl glue in the joints. Follow the glue manufacturer's instructions.

4. Wipe glue spills or runs before they dry. With a rope or clamp, fasten the pieces together until the glue dries. (See Figure 11-1.)

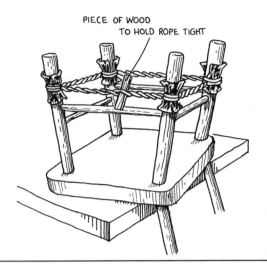

11-1. Gluing wood joints.

5. It is relatively common to have a chair or table break where the legs cross. Repairs can be made by joining the pieces with a splint that is glued and reinforced with several screws. (See Figure 11-2.) Chances are, a new joint made this way will be stronger than the original one.

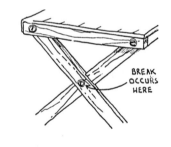

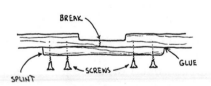

11-2. Repairing broken chair legs.

To Straighten a Warped Table Top
Warping is caused by uneven drying. After a top is straightened, it will have to be treated with a waterproof coating to keep it from warping again. Although the following procedure will greatly help straighten out most wooden tables, the top may never be exactly as straight as it once was.

1. Strip any table-top paint or varnish from both sides of the top.
2. Soak the wood top by piling wet newspaper, saw-

dust, or towels on it for five or six days. Keep the newspaper or other materials wet for the duration.
3. When the wood is soaked through, remove the wet materials.
4. Move the table to a warm, dry room.
5. Place weights on the warped boards, or clamp the warped boards against something that is sturdy enough to remain flat.
6. Let the table stand in the warm, dry room for several days, changing the positions of the weights or clamps every 24 hours to help the wood dry evenly and to prevent cracking.
7. When the boards have dried straight, refinish both sides of the table top to keep moisture from entering or leaving the wood.

Repairing Director's Chairs and Cord-and-Canvas Chairs
Director's chairs come apart easily. Disassemble a damaged chair. Refinish the wood. Use the old canvas back and seat as a pattern for new ones. Purchase ready-made replacements or sew your own. Consider obtaining two new sets for each chair and keep one set as a spare.

On cord-and-canvas chairs, remember to knot the ends of cords after you string them through. (See Figure 11-3.)

11-3. Cord-and-canvas chair repair.

WOOD LAWN FURNITURE MAINTENANCE
The combination of rain and sun can be harmful to clear finishes used on wood furniture. When small drops of water collect across the surface, they act like tiny magnifying glasses, concentrating rays of the sun into points of heat that can, over a period of time, ruin the finish. If you don't want to move furniture indoors each time it rains, an option is to cover the pieces with plastic dropcloths or set the furniture at an angle so water will drain from the flat surfaces. Another possibility is to construct a lattice-style roof — one that diffuses sun rays and reduces their intensity.

Over the years, wood furniture develops small scratches. One way to "erase" those scratches is with a touch-up stick that resembles a crayon. Touch-up sticks come in a wide variety of colors and shades to match most finishes. Another method is to use a similar color of shoe polish.

Larger cracks—cracks that cannot be filled with the soft touch-up stick—can be filled first with wood putty. When the wood putty dries, sand it smooth, then rub stick shellac over the repair. Stick shellac can also be applied with a heated knife blade. After applying the shellac, rub the repair with felt to help smooth it out. Then touch up the color with a touch-up stick or shoe polish.

Wood furniture not damaged enough to need stripping to bare wood can be washed with a wood cleaner available at hardware and builder's supply stores. A wood cleaner will get the dirt and grease off. Then apply a coat of clear lacquer, sealant, or varnish, depending on what was previously used.

NOTE: Be careful not to apply lacquer over varnish or solvent-based paints. It will remove that finish just as easily as a paint stripper would.

Wood furniture tends to last longer if it is stored between seasons in unheated areas such as garages or sheds. If it is stored in a place heated artificially, or worse yet, in a hot, musty part of an attic, the wood can dry out and crack, or seams and joints can shrink apart. It is particularly important to avoid storing wicker and rattan pieces in heated areas. The fibers will dry out and crack easily.

If you don't have a suitable garage or shed for wooden lawn furniture, rather than storing tables and chairs in an attic, protect them with covers and leave them outdoors. Just block them up off the ground with flat stones or bricks.

WROUGHT IRON LAWN FURNITURE

Wrought iron is durable. It is heavy and stable, yet susceptible to rust. It can be touched up with anti-rust metal paint. First remove rust with steel wool. Treat prepared areas with one or two coats of primer followed by several coats of rust-resistant paint.

Iron furniture should not be stored in damp locations. During off seasons, it should be kept indoors in a heated area.

ALUMINUM AND PLASTIC LAWN FURNITURE

Both of these types of lawn furniture are relatively maintenance free. If they are not abused, they will last a long time, even faced with weather and temperature extremes.

When plastic or cloth webbing, strips, or tubes wear out, they can be replaced. When re-webbing, as one chair or lounge is taken apart, save the old grommets and screws. Consider doing one piece of furniture at a time, so at least one is intact at all times, to be used as an example of how to arrange the new webbing or strips.

To replace the webbing or strips, twice fold the end of the webbing slat or strip, then puncture a hole in the correct place. Insert an old grommet to protect the strip. Attach the strip to the chair frame with a screw. (See Figure 11-4.) Weave the strip or slat through to the opposite side of the chair and attach it to the opposite end of the frame in the same manner.

11-4. Replacing chair strips.

LAWN FURNITURE QUICK CHECKLIST

- ❑ Seal dull, porous wood surfaces.
- ❑ Refinish peeling paint and other deteriorated surfaces.
- ❑ Repair broken or loose joints, especially where chair or table legs are attached.
- ❑ Straighten warped table tops.
- ❑ Protect wood furniture from sun rays by putting it away or covering it between uses.
- ❑ During the off season, store lawn furniture in unheated garages or sheds if possible.
- ❑ Replaced damaged webbing strips, cloth strips, and similar parts of aluminum, wood, and plastic lawn furniture.

Swimming Pools

Swimming pools can be a lot of fun—and a lot of work. In a way, they can be compared to aquariums. An aquarium provides a safe environment for fish and other aquatic life. A pump and filter take impurities out of the water, an aerator supplies fresh oxygen, and perhaps there is a heater to prevent the water from getting too cold. There is also a layer of gravel or sand in which tiny microorganisms break down and help condition the water. A swimming pool will rarely have a heater or an aerator or a layer of sand or gravel, but it will have a pump for recirculating and filtering the water.

For healthy aquarium fish, the condition of the water is all important. The same goes for a healthy pool. Keeping the water clean and properly conditioned is the main goal.

SWIMMING POOL WATER

Four main factors contribute to healthy pool water: free available chlorine, pH, total alkalinity, and calcium hardness.

Free Available Chlorine
Free available chlorine fights bacteria and algae in the pool. Inadequate levels of chlorine have a direct effect on pool cleanliness. Free available chlorine levels are expressed in parts per million. Ideal levels of free available chlorine are generally accepted as 1 to 3 parts per million (ppm). Simple test kits are available to check concentration levels on the spot.

PH
The measure of water acidity and basicity is called pH. A correct range for pH is between 7.2 and 7.6 on the pH scale. Again, simple test kits are available to check the pH. The proper pH is important toward maintaining healthy water. Levels of pH outside the desired parameters may cause eye and skin irritation, cloudy water, and chemical buildups on pool equipment.

Total Alkalinity
Total alkalinity is a measurement of the elements that help stabilize the water's pH. It is measured in parts per million, with between 60 and 100 ppm as a desired range. A hard-to-maintain pH balance, cloudy water, and scaling may indicate that the total alkalinity of pool water is not within acceptable limits.

Calcium Hardness
Calcium hardness measures the amount of dissolved calcium in water. Insufficient levels can corrode pool equipment; increased levels may cause cloudy water. A desirable range is between 200 and 1000 ppm.

ROUTINE WATER MAINTENANCE

Free available chlorine and pH should be checked daily, total alkalinity monthly, and calcium hardness two or three times per season.

Pool water is much easier to maintain if you keep on top of changing conditions. During the swimming season, the water can be significantly affected by a number of common occurrences. Unusually heavy rains, above average temperatures, and frequent pool use can all cause increases in chlorine demand. Peak demand conditions require special maintenance measures called superchlorination and shock treatment.

Both superchlorination and shock treatment involve the addition of chlorine in amounts required to elevate temporarily free available chlorine levels. Superchlorination is the addition of chlorine to achieve 5 ppm available chlorine to remove organic contaminants and prevent most common pool water problems. Shock treatment is the remedial addition of chlorine to achieve a 10 ppm available chlorine to kill visible algae. Pool experts recommend you superchlorinate or shock treat once every two weeks.

POOL WATER CLEANING

A clean pool is a healthy pool. To keep the water clean,

the pool itself must be attended to weekly. A number of components are required to keep the water clean. They include circulation systems, filters, skimmers, etc.

Circulation Systems

The typical circulation system includes skimmers, pump, pump strainer, main drain, and filter. The system must be maintained regularly for the chlorinator to work properly for effective water sanitization. It is important that the pump is run long enough each day to filter the water completely. All working parts must be kept clean and in proper running condition.

Some homeowners believe if they don't use a pool, they don't have to monitor its condition. Nothing could be further from the truth. Swimming pools can become maintenance nightmares if they are left alone for days and weeks at a time. Actually, they need daily attention to be kept clean and healthy.

Filters

Filters trap particles that don't dissolve in pool water, and prevent the particles from reentering the water. Common types of filters include sand, diatomaceous earth, and cartridges. Read the manufacturer's instructions carefully regarding the operation and maintenance of your particular filter arrangement.

Skimmers

Skimmers should be cleaned frequently, at least once a week. They operate at full efficiency only if free of leaves and other debris. To prevent buildup in skimmers, hose down the pool deck or pool area by washing objects away from the pool. This action will help prevent much dirt and accumulated debris from otherwise being tracked into the pool by swimmers.

To control the amount of leaves and airborne debris entering the water, it helps to cover the pool each night. Of course, it is hard to motivate pool owners to do so. A full day in the sun and water tends to tire out the swimmers, who may not have sufficient energy toward evening to worry about the cover. Consider installation of an automatic pool cover. A push of a button will send the cover on its merry way, similar to the operation of a car sun roof.

Surface Skimming

A long-handled leaf skimmer can be used to remove floating debris—leaves, insects, and wind-blown objects. (See Figure 12-1.) The purpose is to remove as many floating particles as possible. Once sunk to the

12-1. Hand skimmer.

bottom, the debris is much more difficult to collect and dispose of.

Brushing

Regular brushing of pool walls and bottoms prevents unsightly buildups of dirt, and will, in turn, help to prevent the discoloration of pool water. The type of brush you use depends on the construction of the pool. Concrete pools take a stiffer bristle than do vinyl-lined pools. Brush sediment toward the main drain if the pool is so equipped. There it can be caught by recirculating filter currents, or it can be easily vacuumed. In pools without main drains, follow the brushing with vacuuming.

Vacuuming

Weekly vacuuming is essential if a pool is to remain consistently clean and the water sparkling clear. Vacuuming will remove particles loosened by brushing and debris that has outmaneuvered the filter system. If the pool vacuum attaches to the skimmer, be sure to keep air out of the vacuum hose. To prevent this, submerge the vacuum head and hose before hooking the vacuum to the filter.

SOLVING POOL WATER PROBLEMS

Algae

Algae are tiny plants that grow in water. Three types of algae that occur most often in swimming pools are green, black, and yellow. Follow these steps to remove them from a pool: (1) Check the pH. It should be between 7.2 and 7.6. Once the pH is set correctly, shock treat to 5 ppm free available chlorine. (2) Scrub the pool bottom and sides with a commercially available algae treatment and a brush designed specifically for algae. (3) Treat the water with an algae preventive solution.

Cloudy Water

Cloudy water can be caused by a number of different factors: high pH and total alkalinity levels, intense algae growth, poor pool filtration, or a buildup of swimmer waste.

- Check the water balance. Adjust pH to between 7.2 and 7.6, and the total alkalinity to between 60 and 100 ppm, if necessary. Free available chlorine concentration should be between 1 and 3 ppm.
- If the cloudy water has a greenish cast, algae could be the cause. Treat accordingly.
- If the clouding problem persists, you might need to run the filter longer. Make sure the filter is operating correctly.

Scale

Scale consists of white, gray, or brown deposits commonly found on metal surfaces. Scale is the result of excessive alkalinity and a high pH. Keep the total alkalinity between 60 and 100 ppm, and the pH between 7.2 and 7.6. Scale removers and preventers are commercially available from pool supply stores.

Stains

Stains are usually caused by metals that leave deposits on pool walls. This happens when pool water pH, calcium hardness, or total alkalinity levels are consistently low.

Stains can be effectively removed if treated as soon as possible with stain controller solutions. Follow the instructions on the product label. If stains are left untreated, they can become permanent.

Eye Irritations

The two common causes of red and irritated eyes are improper pH and chloramine. Chloramine is a substance produced when chlorine in the water reacts with body wastes such as perspiration, saliva, and miscellaneous other compounds. When this happens, the free available chlorine concentrations are reduced to levels less than desirable. Check the pH level. If it is too high, add an adjuster chemical. Check the free available chlorine level. If it is below 1 ppm, shock treat.

Strong "Chlorine" Odors

Ironically, the cause of strong "chlorine" odors is usually from too *little* free available chlorine. It is the chloramine you actually smell, not the chlorine. First, adjust the pH. Next, shock treat the water.

Discolored Water

The most common discolorations are red, brown, and green. The solution is the same for all: (1) Adjust the pH. (2) Shock treat the water. (3) Inspect the filter for proper operation, and run it frequently until the discoloration disappears.

Too Much Chlorine

If you have dark brown hair when you jump in, and blonde hair when you get out, there is too much chlorine in the water. People have mistakenly added enough chlorine to bleach swimsuits and irritate eyes.

Simply stop adding chlorine until the free available chlorine concentration is between 1 and 3 ppm.

Commercial products are available that will immediately reduce chlorine levels, but they must be used exactly according to the manufacturer's instructions.

POOL EQUIPMENT CARE

In general, it is always a safe bet to follow manufacturer's guidelines for pool equipment care. Swimming pool contractors and sales agents are also good sources of information on this subject.

The Pump

In season, the pump should operate long enough each day to maintain clear, clean water. Clean the hair and lint basket weekly. Check to see if there are any leaks between the pump motor and the pump, or if water is dripping from any portion of the pump motor assembly. There shouldn't be any leaks. The pump should hum smoothly. Sharp gurgling or rattling sounds within the pump could signal cavitation—the pump is not getting enough water from the pool for its design. If this condition exists, have an expert evaluate the situation.

The Filter

Because the filter removes insoluble particles from the water, it acts like a strainer. It is important to backwash or change the filter regularly and with increasing frequency during periods of heavy use or during weather extremes. The system should run efficiently and should circulate the water at a brisk rate. Be sure you disconnect the power before cleaning or servicing the filter. Also, check the filter system's valves. Make sure they open and close easily and all the way.

The Main Drain

It is important that the main drain is cleaned regularly to prevent plugging. It is common to find chrome-plated grates that look fine, but hide totally plugged drains at pool bottom.

Heaters

Heaters are nothing to fool with by yourself. They should be checked by a pool service person once a year. Familiarize yourself with the manufacturer's operating manual.

Cleaning Equipment

To avoid mishaps, store skimming and vacuuming equipment when it is not in use.

Test Kits

Store test kits in a cool, dark place out of children's reach. Replace test kit chemicals every pool season. Rinse collection tubes several times before filling. Take water samples from at least 18 inches below the surface and away from walls and inlets. Wait 24 hours after superchlorinating or shock treatment before testing for free available chlorine or pH. Read and follow all label instructions.

Pool Decks and Liners

Check the decks and coping for breaches and cracks. (See Figure 12-2.) Cracked decks should be repaired quickly to prevent water from eroding the under-deck areas. Coping should be sound; its grout should be intact and form a good seal between the pool and deck edge.

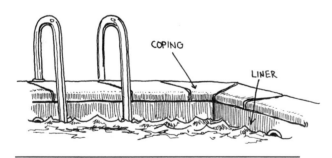

12-2. Swimming pool coping.

Pay attention to the condition of the pool liner. Look for any bulging or uneven walls that can indicate expensive troubles, and disaster if not repaired.

POOL START-UP

When warm weather arrives, here are steps for the quickest, easiest way to achieve the pleasure of sparkling clear pool water.

- Before you remove the pool cover, eliminate as much accumulated water and debris as possible.
- After removing the cover, clean it thoroughly and let it dry before storing it for the season. Otherwise, it may develop mildew and deteriorate prematurely.
- Hook up the pool pump and filter, reconnecting any hoses and electrical contacts that had been detached.
- Make sure the skimmer, filter, pump, and drains are clean and free from winter debris.
- Scoop all surface and submerged debris that you can safely reach with a long-handled leaf net.
- If the pool walls are dirty, clean them with a pool brush and cleanser.
- Bring the pool water up to the proper level.
- With all hoses and electrical hookups in order, and the pool filled to the proper level, turn on the filter pump. Check that skimmers, bottom drains, and filters are functioning.
- Vacuum any remaining debris.
- After the pool filter has been running for three to four hours, test the water for free available chlorine, pH, alkalinity, and calcium hardness. Make necessary adjustments.

CLOSING A POOL

By closing a pool correctly at the end of a swimming season, considerable labor and chemical supplies can be saved at the start of the following season.

In Cold Climate Areas

- Adjust the pH to between 7.2 and 7.6. Add a dose of commercially available winterizing treatment to the water.
- Run the filter for 24 to 48 hours. Do a thorough vacuuming, especially of the sides and bottom. Remove floating debris.
- To keep algae from forming before the water freezes, add an algae preventive.
- Follow the manufacturer's instructions and lower the water level, shut off the filter pump, then drain the pump, filter, heater, and all other applicable equipment.
- After the water level is below the water return fitting, remove the filter hoses from the return and skimmer.
- All equipment should be properly stored to prevent damage from freezing temperatures.
- Cover the pool. Position and anchor air pillows inside the pool. Tie down the cover securely. A properly fitted cover will save hours of cleanup time when the pool is reopened.

- If water bags are used to secure the cover, fill them only halfway to allow for expansion if they freeze.
- The cover edge should be sealed to prevent wind from getting beneath it.
- Drain water from lines and equipment, then add antifreeze at recommended strengths.

In Warm Climate Areas

In locations with mild climates, you might opt for a reduced maintenance program during the off season that does not involve covering the pool.

Begin shutting down by cutting the filter running time in half. Limit water tests to once per week—keeping the pH between 7.2 and 7.6, and the free available chlorine concentration to between 1 and 3 ppm. Follow the pool equipment manufacturer's instructions for proper care during this time.

Even though the pool will not be completely closed, you may want to cover it. A cover will reduce the labor needed for cleaning, and will also help conserve pool chemicals.

POOL SAFETY

Having a swimming pool is a big responsibility — to yourself, your family, friends and relatives, your neighbors, and even to total strangers. Not surprisingly, safety is a major concern around swimming pools.

- Locate and maintain lifesaving equipment at poolside. Never rely on inner tubes or water wings to keep children afloat. Such items can too easily slip off.
- Maintain a climb-proof fence to separate the pool from the rest of the yard. This is especially important for families (or neighbors) with children under twelve years old. The fence, however, should not block views of the pool from the house. Always use gates with self-closing, self-latching spring locks. Latches should be at least 54 inches above ground to prevent tampering by youngsters. The fence should keep unsupervised children from using the pool. It may, indeed, be a law or requirement in your community or by your homeowner's insurance policy. It will also prevent neighborhood pets from literally dropping in.
- Watch nearby children at all times. Never assume a child is water safe, even if he or she has had swimming lessons. If a lone adult must leave the pool area, he or she should take the children along. *Never* leave children unsupervised at pool side.

- It makes good sense to establish safety practices that anyone using your pool must follow. Stress the list to visitors, especially at the beginning of each swimming season. A sample list might include:
1. No running or horseplay around or in the pool.
2. No eating or carrying food into the pool.
3. No diving in the shallow end.
4. No pets in the pool.
5. No swimming alone.
6. Children must have at least one adult swimmer present to supervise them.
7. No swimming when it is thundering (lightning can strike several miles ahead of a storm).
- Make sure that all extension cords used near the pool are properly insulated and protected.
- Keep glass and other breakables away from poolside.
- Keep a well-stocked first-aid kit nearby, out of children's reach. Encourage all members of your family to become proficient at CPR and artificial respiration. Keep an artificial respiration guide with the first-aid kit. Contact the Red Cross for related lifesaving information.
- Pre-swim showers for pool users will reduce the amount of bacteria and other contaminants introduced to the pool.
- Establish a 10-minute rest period every hour or so for younger children using the pool.
- Mark the pool depths so visitors know what to expect. Most important, identify shallow areas where it is safe for small children to play.
- For lap swimming, serious swimmers need a depth of at least 3½ feet so they won't touch bottom while swimming. Monitor the water depth to make sure it hasn't gradually become too shallow.

Pool Chemical Safety

Keep all chemicals out of children's reach. Use the exact quantities specified; never overuse. Add chemicals to the pool water, not vice versa. Carefully seal containers after use. Be sure to store them in a cool, dry place.

If chemicals come in contact with your skin, brush them off and flush with cold water for at least 15 minutes. If irritation persists, get medical attention. Never smoke while handling pool chemicals. Keep pool chemicals away from lawns, shrubs, and trees. Carefully dispose of any spillages as directed on each label. Avoid using a vacuum cleaner to take care of spilled chemicals.

SWIMMING POOL QUICK CHECKLIST

❑ Keep levels of free available chlorine in the water between 1 and 3 ppm.

❑ Maintain pH level between 7.2 and 7.6.

❑ Keep a total alkalinity level of between 60 and 100 ppm.

❑ Maintain calcium levels between 200 and 1000 ppm.

❑ Check free available chlorine and pH levels daily.

❑ Check total alkalinity at least monthly, more frequently during periods of hot weather or heavy pool usage.

❑ Check calcium hardness at least two or three times per season.

❑ Superchlorinate when needed.

❑ Shock treat when needed.

❑ Maintain and operate water circulation systems on a regular basis, even if the pool is not used during times of inclement weather.

❑ Clean skimmers and filters regularly.

❑ Skim as much debris off the water's surface as you can with a manual long-handled leaf skimmer.

❑ Brush pool walls and bottoms to remove dirt build-ups.

❑ Vacuum the pool bottom at least once a week.

❑ Watch for and correct water problems, including the presence of:
algae
cloudy water
scale
stains
water that causes eye irritation
strong "chlorine" odors
discolored water
too much chlorine

❑ Operate the filter pump long enough each day to maintain clear, clean water, even if the pool isn't being used at the time.

❑ Backwash or change filters with increasing frequency during periods of heavy use or weather extremes.

❑ Keep the main drain clean and open.

❑ Pool water heaters should be inspected and serviced by a professional, usually at the beginning of each swimming season.

❑ Follow proper pool start-up procedures at the beginning of the swimming season.

❑ Follow proper pool shutdown procedures at the end of the swimming season.

PART 2

The Exterior Shell

The exterior shell of a dwelling is what people see from the outside. Some individuals in the real estate industry, when faced with marketing a particular home that has been "let go" on the outside, will often remark, "But you should see the *inside*." But a home that has not been carefully maintained on the outside is bound to start falling apart on the inside as well. Roofs deteriorate and leak. Caulking around windows and doors will shrink and crack. Corners of siding will fall off. Gutters and downspouts will become full of debris. Rust and rot will set in.

Little by little, if small problems are not taken care of, if preventive measures are not taken, the house will be opened up to the elements. Warm air will escape from living spaces during winter, and cool air during summer. Moisture will make a slow, relentless assault, harming wood, plaster, and any other material that can absorb moisture. Musty odors, mildew, and uncomfortable levels of humidity will take residence. Gradually, the malaise that invariably sets in over the exterior shell will work its way inward. That's why the appearance and integrity of a home's outer shell are so important, so tell-tale to can be expected on the inside.

The exterior shell is the only thing that separates living spaces of a home from a multitude of harmful conditions and hazards found outdoors. It is vitally important that proper inspections and preventive maintenance steps are taken to keep the exterior shell healthy and intact.

Roofs

A roof receives a lot of wear and tear from the elements. The sun bakes it, the wind drives rain and sleet at it, below-zero temperatures freeze it, and tree limbs fall on it. Shingles curl up, come loose, wear out, and get attacked by corrosion, mold, and mildew. Keeping a roof in top shape is necessary to avoid major headaches and repairs down the road.

ROOF INSPECTIONS

The best preventive maintenance for your roof is to inspect it twice a year, once during fall and once during spring. In between, also get into the habit of looking the roof over after major storms.

While inspecting roof conditions, you might as well also look at flashing and trim, gutters and downspouts, chimneys and skylights at the same time. They are all in the same area.

Realize that you don't have to go up on your roof if you don't want to. In fact, it is best to minimize the amount of walking done on a roof. The more walking you do on shingles, the greater the chance of damaging them. Inspect as much as possible from a ladder. If all or most of the roof can be seen from the ground, or from a neighbor's attic window, you can inspect from there. Use binoculars for close-up views if a certain section of the roof can only be seen from afar.

If the roof is extremely high and steep, or if it is constructed of slate or asbestos shingles, or if you simply feel uncomfortable about leaving the ground, then by all means hire a reputable roofer to do the inspections. He or she can, at the same time, make necessary repairs if needed.

If you prefer to go onto the roof yourself, here are some guidelines.

Go onto the roof only during good weather, when there is no rain and little or no wind. The roof must be dry, too. Never, ever go onto a wet or slippery roof. Snow and ice mean "keep off." Another roof to stay off is a roof covered with fungi-coated shingles. Such a roof is nearly impossible to walk on. That is a job for roofing professionals.

Wear soft shoes with good traction soles. They will help keep you from slipping and help prevent damaged shingles.

Walking on a roof is always dangerous, even if all precautions are taken. Often a roof is not as solid as it seems. Test the roof's integrity with a partial step before putting down all of your weight. Try to "feel" for where the supporting rafters are beneath the roofing, and step on them as you walk. You can also tie yourself to a safety line looped around a chimney or sturdy vent pipe, as long as the rope is not long enough to let you fall from any of the roof's edges. Another safety method is to hook a ladder to the ridge of the roof, so you can ascend the roof on the ladder's rungs or steps. (See Figure 13-1.)

13-1. Securing a ladder to a roof.

In any event, always be thinking of safety when on a roof. Use slow, calculated movements and don't let yourself get distracted.

The following are what you should look for when inspecting your roof.

Leaks

First look below the roof, from inside the house, for leaks. Do it during a rainstorm. The first sign of a leak is usually a wet spot or water dripping in the house somewhere. A leak can be difficult to find. If a wet spot were always kind enough to appear beneath the corresponding leak, the solution would be simple. But that is not always the case. When water comes through a roof, it often travels some distance before it becomes visible. That is why you look for leaks during a rainstorm. If that doesn't work, enter the attic or crawlspace beneath the roof on a sunny day. Turn off any lights and cover windows so the area is darkened. Then look for sunlight entering the attic or crawlspace through the roof. If you see daylight from inside, find the hole and push a wire or long finishing nail through it so you can see where the hole is from the outside, too.

While in the attic or crawlspace, check for obvious signs of wood rot or decay. With a screwdriver or an ice pick, probe into the wood beneath the roof for soft, rotten spots that may indicate the frequent presence of moisture from leaks.

Missing, Loose, or Damaged Shingles
Six types of roofing materials make up 99 percent of all residential roofs: asphalt shingles, fiberglass shingles, wood shingles and shakes, slate shingles, tile shingles, and metal roofing.

ASPHALT AND FIBERGLASS SHINGLES
Asphalt and fiberglass shingles are, by far, the most widely used. In those shingles, look for curling, cupping, blistering, and bald spots without protective granular coverings. Asphalt and fiberglass shingles can turn brittle from age and from weathering, and are also subject to ripping loose in strong winds.

WOOD SHINGLES AND SHAKES
Here the term "shingle" means that the wood has been sawn, and "shake" means that the wood has been split. A shake is usually thicker and has a more rustic appearance. Regardless of the type, shakes or shingles should not be cracked, warped, or worn away at their edges. A certain amount of mossy growth is not necessarily bad, but if the wood has been chemically treated for increased longevity and fire retardancy, mossy growth is an indication that the treatment is losing its potency.

SLATE SHINGLES
Slate is an excellent material for roofing. So excellent, in fact, that it tends to outlast the wood structures that support it. When roof framing members and underlayments sag or are pushed out of shape by the slate, individual slate shingles can crack or come loose. Other indications that slate shingles are wearing out include the presence of discoloring, pitting, cracking, or peeling across their surface. Also, the nails securing the slate may fail before the slate does.

Due to its smooth surface, slate roofing is difficult to walk on. It can also be difficult to match up exactly, and is not easy to repair. Slate, then, is a roofing material best taken care of by experts. Keep an eye out for leaks, for damaged and missing shingles, and for areas of the roof that appear to be sinking or bowing out of line.

TILE SHINGLES
Tile shingles are very weather resistant, especially to sunlight, high temperatures, and low, arid humidity. Because of their characteristics and because the raw materials needed for tile manufacturing are plentiful throughout southern areas, tile is a popular roofing in those locations. Still, it can be found on homes in northern areas, especially homes constructed with Spanish styles and influences.

Like slate, tile is a heavy material that needs to be well supported. Uniquely finished tiles can be impossible to match up. Due to the difficulty in handling and making repairs, tile is another roofing material best left to professional roofers.

METAL ROOFS
Metal roofs, especially those made of high-quality copper, terne (a tin/lead alloy), or aluminum are very durable. Look for holes, seams that have come apart, or roofing that has come loose from the underlayment.

Ridge Caps
Give special attention to the roof ridge caps—roofing shingles installed along the roof's ridges to seal the uppermost peaks. (See Figure 13-2.) From the ground, look for uneven sections where shingles might have lifted or even blown away.

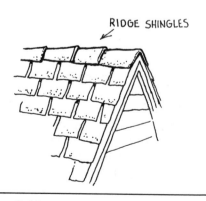

13-2. A roof ridge.

Mildew and Moss

Mildew and moss can grow on wood shingles and shakes, or even on flat tar roofs. Their tiny roots can penetrate roof materials and cause serious damages. If you need to determine whether a discolored area is mildew, dip a cloth in laundry bleach and apply it to a small suspected section of roof. If the spot you touch lightens or disappears altogether, you are dealing with mildew, not just dirt.

Roof Fixtures

Are television or other antennas standing straight? Are all support cables tight and secure? If an antenna is leaning to one side, it could mean that a support cable or bracket has pulled loose, leaving a hole in the roof.

Flat Roofs

On flat roofs, a low spot where water collects is a potential for leaks. Look for bubbles in a tar and gravel roof, which may mean that moisture has worked its way beneath the roofing felt. Luckily, flat roofs are most often found on garages, sheds, and other less conspicuous parts of a dwelling.

Roof Ventilation

Roof ventilation units should be checked for signs of water penetration. Look for corrosion or deterioration on the units themselves, as well as for signs of joint failures between the vent and the roof.

Gutters

Gutters should not be positioned to block the roof rainwater runoff. Their roof edges should not be raised above the shingles that abut the gutter. In fact, their roof edge should lie both below and behind the roof's edge, so ice cannot build up in a crack between the roof line and gutters. (See Figure 13-3.)

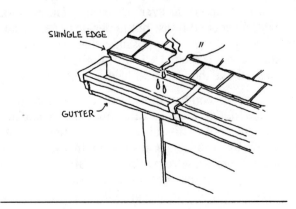

13-3. Roof edge and gutter.

Plumbing Stack Vents

Plumbing stack vents protrude through roofs to convey and disperse sewer gases. Roof connections should be carefully checked for cracks and holes that could allow water to enter the home. (See Figure 13-4.) Joints between the vent pipes and roof are vulnerable to shrinkage, peeling, and freezing/thawing temperatures.

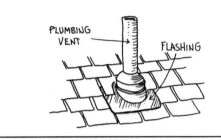

13-4. Plumbing stack vent.

Southern Exposures

Pay particular attention to roofs, or parts of roofs, facing south. They receive the most weathering from the sun, and often deteriorate faster than their counterparts facing other directions.

ROOF REPAIRS

Asphalt or Fiberglass Shingle Repairs

Missing, cracked, ripped, or otherwise damaged asphalt and fiberglass shingles can often be spotted from the ground, and should be repaired or replaced as soon as possible. Once a shingle is missing or "lifted up," the wind can begin to pull others away. Soon, instead of one or two minor repairs, a whole section of roof will have to be replaced. Since most leaks are caused by loose or torn shingles, shingles can be repaired or replaced, depending on their condition. Follow all safety procedures. Work only on dry, warm, windless days. Roofing cement will adhere better in warm temperatures, and you will work better when not bothered by the wind.

Repairs can be made with roofing cement and galvanized roofing nails. Apply the roofing cement beneath the shingle. Press the shingle down and nail tightly with broad-headed galvanized roofing nails. After the nails have been driven, apply roofing cement to the nail heads so water won't leak through.

If your inspection of shingles found only minor problems with the way the shingles are lying, apply roofing cement beneath the offending shingles, then press them flat by placing a heavy object on them, such as a thick catalog or a piece of 2" x 6" board. This will keep pressure applied until the cement has had a chance to fasten. If the problem cannot be resolved in this manner, use roofing nails in addition to the cement.

To patch a torn or badly damaged shingle, cut a thin piece of aluminum sheet metal, metal flashing, or aluminum siding to a rectangle large enough to cover the damaged shingle and to extend 3 inches beneath the adjacent shingles on each side. Spread roofing cement on the underside of the metal rectangle and slide the piece of metal into place beneath the raised shingle and beneath the edges of each adjoining shingle. (See Figure 13-5.) Then spread more cement on top of the metal piece. Apply roofing cement liberally underneath the shingle being repaired. Press down upon all affected shingles, including the damaged one. Place a weight on the repair until the cement has dried.

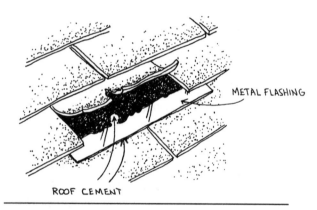

METAL FLASHING

ROOF CEMENT

13-5. Repairing a damaged shingle.

Replace shingles that are too damaged to be repaired. Lift the shingle and run a hacksaw blade beneath it to cut off the nails holding it in place. If needed, put down a tarpaper patch with roofing cement. Apply roofing cement to the underside of the new shingle, slide the shingle into place, and nail it down with galvanized or aluminum roofing nails. Apply roofing cement to the adjacent shingle edges that fit over the new shingle, especially to those from the row directly above the replacement.

Wood Shakes and Shingles
If a wood shingle or shake is damaged, a tarpaper or metal patch underneath the shingle or shake will often stop or prevent leaks.

Remember that wooden shingles and shakes swell as they age, so they must fit loosely between existing shingles when installed. Use only rust-resistant nails to fasten wood shingles and shakes to a roof. Replace wood shingles and shakes in a manner similar to re-

placing asphalt or fiberglass shingles.

Slate and Tile Shingles
Slate and tile shingles should be left to the experts to repair.

Metal Roofs
To repair metal roofing, you can solder patches onto copper or tin. But solder will not hold on aluminum. Aluminum repairs require patches of the same material using roofing cement and rust-resistant roofing nails. Cover each nail head with roofing cement to prevent leaks.

ROOF MAINTENANCE

Keep debris off a roof. This means tree limbs, leaves, tools, and other items that don't belong there. Dead leaves, pine tree needles, pine cones, and seeds of various kinds can collect in roof valleys or elsewhere. Eventually dirt will build up around the debris and before you know it, water will back up and seep uphill and under individual shingles. Keep children off roofs, too. Often a ball will get caught in a gutter— an invitation to children to climb onto and play on a rooftop. The less a roof is walked on, the better.

In cold northern climates, snow and ice can become a problem for roofs. Huge snowdrifts and heavy icicles at a roof's edge can pose hazards for both people and roof. Icicles can cause water to back up onto the roof and work its way beneath shingles. You can remove snow and icicles yourself, with a long-handled broom, but that can be difficult. Frequently the buildups are way out of reach, and it is a dangerous business as well—watching out for falling chunks of snow and heavy, pointed icicles.

One way to handle a snow and ice problem is to have a licensed electrician install electric heat wires or tape that zigzags along the roof's edges and valleys to prevent such buildups from ever occurring. These work well under most conditions, but in periods of extremely cold temperatures, it is possible that some of the snow and ice that is melted will form other, secondary "ice dams" above the electrical heat wires or tapes.

Another way to combat snow and ice buildup is to prevent the initial melting of snow that eventually freezes to the roof. This initial snow melting is usually caused by insufficient insulation in the attic or crawlspace beneath the roof. Enough warm air gets to the roof to prevent the roof's surface from achieving the freezing temperatures that will, in turn, allow snow to blow off its surface without sticking. By installing enough insulation, you can prevent household heat from escaping through the roof and melting snow and ice there.

Keep the shingles lying flat. Use a combination of roofing cement and nails if you must, but keep those shingles flat. It is the only way they will be able to protect the roofing underlayment from wind and moisture.

Periodically renew roofing cement and caulking around the various joints in a roof. At times, a leak will develop around a valley flashing where two roof surfaces meet. You won't be able to locate a hole because it is covered by the overlapping shingles and flashing. But water is getting under the flashing by running beneath the adjacent shingles, shingles that partially cover the flashing. On an asphalt or fiberglass roof, you can simply lift up the shingle ends and apply more roofing cement to bond the shingles to the flashing. If the roof is made of wood or other rigid material, the best approach is to apply the same roofing cement carefully along the shingle edges to create a tight seal with the flashing. (See the next section for more information on flashing and exterior trim.)

Keep the roof clean. This is typically no problem. The rain, wind, and sun do a number on dust and dirt that happens to land on wide-open spaces on a roof. Watch out, though, for rusting pipes, supports, vents, or other roof attachments. The rust will run down and streak practically any roofing material.

You can't just scrub off mildew, however. It should be sprayed with a solution of one part laundry bleach and three parts water. Let the bleach solution dry completely, then scrub it with a powdered detergent. Let the detergent solution dry without rinsing for added effect.

Keep the area beneath the roof ventilated. This is very important. Roofing materials—especially asphalt shingles—can be baked by the sun, but can also be baked from below. If the attic or crawlspace beneath a roof becomes oven-hot during the summer from lack of ventilation, its hot air will rise and curl or otherwise damage the roofing. (See Figure 13-6.) Make sure you have adequate ventilation to prevent this from happening.

ROOF SAFETY

Naturally, if you tread on a roof, tread lightly and slowly, with great caution. Falling from a rooftop—no matter what its height—can cause a multitude of serious injuries up to and including death. Think before you act. In addition to going up ladders, people have used all sorts of ways to get onto roofs, from crawling out of attic windows, to hoisting themselves through skylights, to dropping down out of trees. Whatever method you use to access a roof, there should be something to grab onto—something to steady yourself while stepping onto the shingles, and some way of catching yourself if you slip.

ROOF QUICK CHECKLIST

- ❑ Inspect as much of a roof as you can from the ground, from a neighbor's home, or from a ladder.
- ❑ If you have any reservations about going up on your roof, arrange for someone else to do it.
- ❑ Never venture onto a roof during windy, rainy, or wintry weather. Consider that the acts of getting onto and getting off of a roof can be the most dangerous parts of the inspection or work.
- ❑ Keep off slippery or very steep roofs.
- ❑ Wear soft shoes with good traction soles while walking on a roof.
- ❑ Trace and repair any leaks.
- ❑ Repair or replace missing, loose, or damaged shingles. Keep shingles lying flat.
- ❑ Re-caulk or reseal roof accessories such as antennas, guide wires, cable brackets, vents, and plumbing stacks.
- ❑ Keep debris off a roof.
- ❑ Prevent heavy snow and ice accumulations on your roof.
- ❑ Keep the area beneath a roof well ventilated year round.

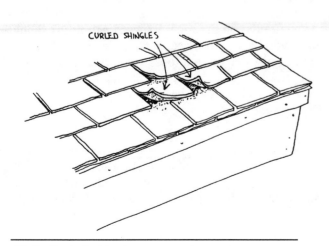

13-6. Curled shingles.

Flashing and Trim

Flashing is sheet metal or other building materials designed to prevent leakage, or "driving in" by rainwater. It is supposed to prevent moisture from infiltrating through joints around exterior house features such as windows, doors, dormers, chimneys, vents, roof valleys, and stacks. (See Figure 14-1.)

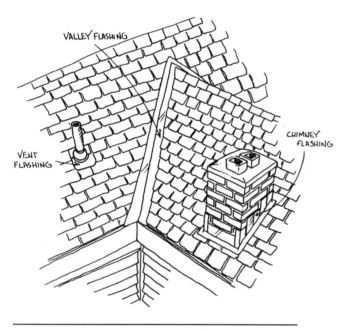

14-1. Roof flashings.

Trim refers to similar materials whose purposes can be both decorative and functional. It often consists of wood moldings that are stained or painted to match siding, windows, doors, or other exterior features. Both flashing and trim combine to give a house that "complete" look, so there are no large cracks or other openings at places where different materials meet.

Because flashing consists of materials that won't rust, such as aluminum, plastic, or copper, it is relatively maintenance free. Wood trim, on the other hand, needs occasional work. In recent years, more builders have been installing plastic and aluminum trim that provides years of service with hardly any required maintenance.

FLASHING AND TRIM INSPECTIONS

Because much of a home's flashing and trim is located on the roof, the same safety procedures that were discussed in the previous section on roofs apply here. In fact, it is best that this section's inspections be done at the same time.

Loose Flashing and Trim

Look for pieces of flashing and trim that have come loose or been damaged. This could happen if the pieces weren't correctly installed, or if a shingle gets caught by the wind, lifted up, and pulls up part of an adjacent strip of flashing. Sometimes a piece of flashing or trim will vibrate in response to the wind, and work its way over a nail head. A neighbor's child may strike some flashing with a baseball, knocking a piece loose or cracking it apart. Aluminum or other siding might fall or blow down, taking flashing or trim with it.

Roofing Paper

In some cases, builder's have simply used heavy roofing paper as valley flashing. Such flashing is almost always black, and is not as durable as aluminum, plastic, or other more substantial materials. Look for cracks, rips, and holes.

Exposed Nail Heads

This demands a close-up inspection that can be done with binoculars from the ground or a neighbor's second-story window, or from a ladder if you don't want to venture out on the roof. Exposed nail heads should be driven back into place, then sealed with a dab of caulk. Nails that are too loose when refastened should be removed, the hole filled with caulk, and replacement nails should then be driven in new locations an inch or so away.

Valley Flashing

Valley flashing on a roof seldom causes any problems if it has been properly installed and waterproofed. But if the valley has only a slight pitch (not steep), debris such as leaves and seeds can collect there and create a blockage that may back water up under adjacent shingles, where it could leak into the house.

Vent, Stack, and Chimney Flashing

Inspect flashing where vents and stacks protrude through a roof.

Inspect the chimney flashing that runs under the roof shingles and comes up the chimney sides. The lower part is called base flashing, and the upper vertical part is known as counter-flashing. (See Figure 14-2.) The ends of the counter-flashing are bent at right angles so they can be slipped into the chimney joints where they are held in place by mortar. Sometimes the flashing pulls out. Because the flashing around chimneys is generally installed in more than one piece, leaks can sometimes occur between sections of flashing.

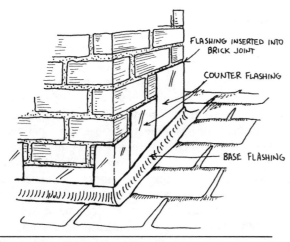

14-2. Chimney flashing.

Window and Door Trim Flashing

Inspect flashing on all places that stick out horizontally from the house, such as over window and door trim, or where the insulation and exterior wall start from the foundation. Flashing over exterior window and door trim is simply a piece of sheet metal or plastic bent or formed at right angles. (See Figure 14-3.) One flange of the piece is nailed beneath the siding. The other stands out from the house to deflect any water running down the siding away from the window or door. In this way, flashing helps prevent rot that could otherwise occur if moisture seeps into a window or door casing. As siding and window or door frames deteriorate, make sure the flashing isn't pulled out of line, leaving an opening for water to work its way into the house.

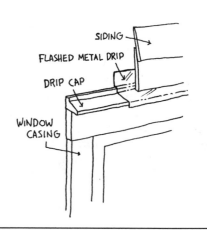

14-3. Window/door trim flashing.

Tight and Secure Trim

If the trim is made of wood, check to see if it is sound or in need of replacement. If sound, is the paint in need of attention?

FLASHING AND TRIM REPAIRS

Flashing and trim, if left completely alone over a long period of time, will eventually loosen. Once the flashing is no longer tight, water will quickly find its way through the small cracks between the flashing and the siding, window, chimney, or whatever is being protected. That is why flashing and trim should be inspected at least once a year. The best time to make repairs or to perform maintenance is when the roof is warm and completely dry, both from a safety viewpoint and because roofing cement or caulking is frequently used. You will get a better seal during warm weather.

Choosing New Flashing

If all of your flashing is in need of replacement, consider the following when choosing new material.

- Aluminum is the most common flashing and trim material. It is produced in long rolls of several widths and is inexpensive, lightweight, and resistant to corrosion except in industrial and seacoast locations. One drawback to aluminum is that it must be painted.
- Galvanized steel and terne are also used as flashing, but they must also be painted.
- Stainless steel and zinc alloy hold up well, but are more expensive.
- An excellent but expensive choice for flashing is copper. It weathers well — after turning a dull, antique-looking greenish bronze. It requires little if any maintenance, other than seeing that its joints with the house remain intact.

FLASHING AND TRIM QUICK CHECKLIST

❑ While inspecting or working on flashing and trim, follow the same kinds of safety precautions discussed in the previous section on roofs.

❑ Repair or replace damaged, loose, or missing flashing and trim. It should all be tight and secure.

❑ Keep roof valley flashing free from dirt and debris.

❑ Make sure the flashing and trim are kept painted if needed.

❑ Periodically apply roofing cement or caulk to all flashing joints around vertical protrusions such as chimneys, stacks, vents, antennas, and other attachments.

▪ Vinyl materials are available in many colors. They are inexpensive and durable, and a good all-round choice for many homes.

▪ Be aware that asphalt roofing material is sometimes used for valley flashing on roofs, and plumbing stacks are frequently flashed with special neoprene collars.

Replacing a Damaged Piece of Flashing

If any piece of flashing is rusted or damaged beyond repair, it should be replaced. Remove the old piece, trying to keep it intact. Take the piece to a hardware or builder's store so it can be used as a template for a replacement piece. When the new piece is installed, make sure its edges are tucked beneath the adjacent roofing shingles, window casing, or other material. Always seal the new piece with fresh roofing cement or caulking.

Patching Flashing

To patch holes larger than 1 inch square, cut a piece of patching from a similar material at least 1 inch larger on all sides than the damaged area. Attach the patch with roofing cement and place a heavy item on the repair until the cement dries.

Replacing Chimney Flashing

If chimney counter-flashing pieces are pulled out, clean loose mortar from the joint, push the flashing flange back into the chimney, and seal with new mortar.

FLASHING AND TRIM MAINTENANCE

▪ Refasten loose pieces. Aluminum nails can be used as fasteners. They won't rust and bleed rust colors down siding, roof, or other surfaces. When joints are involved, use roofing cement or caulk to weatherproof each piece that is refastened. Touch up nail heads with a paint that closely matches the color of whatever siding or material you are using.

▪ Reset nails that have loosened or worked partway out of place. Seal heads with a dab of roofing cement. If a nail goes in so loose that you can pull it back out with your fingers, then use a slightly thicker and longer nail. Seal with roofing cement.

▪ Clean debris from valley flashing so water runoff from the roof has a clear, unobstructed pathway.

▪ Apply a liberal coating of roofing cement or caulking to all flashing joints around vertical protrusions such as chimneys, stacks, antennas, and other attachments fastened to the roof or side walls.

▪ If you have flashing made of metal that has rusted, sand with steel wool or a light sandpaper. Wipe flashing with a clean wet towel and let dry. Once dry, the flashing can be painted with a rust-preventive paint suitable for outdoor metal service. Use a paint color that most closely matches the color and shade of the roof.

▪ If your trim is wood, touch up painted surfaces where needed, and reseal unpainted pieces of trim.

Gutters and Downspouts

Gutters and downspouts act in tandem. They work together to collect runoff from the roof and divert it away from a house so the side walls of the home are protected, so water won't erode soil around the foundation, and so the foundation and basement won't become saturated. Although they are vital accouterments in most cases, gutters and downspouts can be troublesome to maintain. Tree leaves, seeds, and twigs tend to collect in them and clog downspouts; squirrels and chipmunks use them as pantries for storing winter food; and ice hanging from their not-too-strong edges can cause damage.

GUTTER AND DOWNSPOUT INSPECTIONS

Pools of water that collect near the foundation, streaked house paint, damp or flooded basements, or ridges in the ground under the eaves are all signs that the gutters are not working properly. Gutters and downspouts should be thoroughly checked at least twice per year.

The best time to inspect gutters and downspouts is during a heavy rain. There is something wrong if:

- Water flows over the tops of gutters.
- Water leaks at seams or other places.
- Gutters are sagging.
- Downspouts leak or do not convey water at all.

Look for:
- Rot, rust, or corrosion.
- Loose spikes, hangers, or straps. Do the gutters completely span the roof edges? Are there any large sagging sections because supports have either rusted away or become unfastened? Are downspouts securely fastened to the sides of the house? Are the bottoms of downspouts angled away from the home onto splash blocks or into storm sewer pipes?
- Leaves or debris causing obstructions. Check gutter outlet openings. The gutter entrance to a downspout is often protected by a wire basket or strainer designed to prevent leaves and other debris from washing into a downspout. (See Figure 15-1.) Naturally, the leaves and debris will catch

on the basket or strainer. If not cleaned out regularly, the outlet openings will block the passage of water to the downspouts. Water will then build up and simply run over the sides of the gutters.

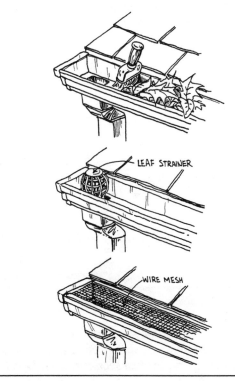

15-1. Leaf strainers.

Nearby trees, especially conifers like pine and fir, tend to deposit their needles in house gutter systems. Add leaves and twigs to the mixture and the end result is a mat of debris that will hold moisture for long periods. Moisture sitting in steel gutters will eventually work through paint coatings into the metal, causing severe rust damage.

- Cracks or splits.
- Loose joints.
- Make sure the entire system is connected. Lengths of gutters or downspouts may have become separated from each other.
- See that the water goes where it should once it exits the downspouts. Some downspouts discharge

their water onto splash blocks—concrete or plastic troughs about 2 feet long that are positioned below downspouts to channel water away from the home's foundation wall. (See Figure 15-2.) These inexpensive devices play an important role in keeping basement walls dry. Other downspouts send their water directly into pipes that tie into the home's storm sewer lines. The sewer lines can connect into the street storm sewer system, or the water may be conveyed into the street or some out-of-the-way location in the yard. Watch for water backing up out of downspout storm sewer pipes. It is a sure sign of trouble.

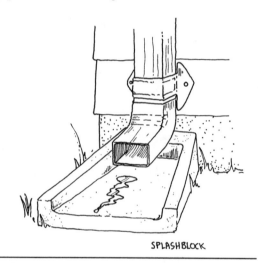

15-2. Splash block.

If the entire gutter and downspout system evolves to a point where major repairs are needed to correct splitting, rust, holes, and broken sections, your best bet is simply replacement.

The least expensive gutters to buy are galvanized steel models, but they have to be painted before they can be attached to a roof. Another inexpensive option is to use unpainted aluminum. It is durable enough unless exposed to salt air near seacoasts or air laden with chemical contaminants. Even when no pollutants are present, however, aluminum gutters should be painted for the sake of appearance.

Other choices of gutter materials are much better: aluminum with factory baked-on enamel, and aluminum covered with a thin layer of vinyl. Solid vinyl gutters are also manufactured. All three are, in the long run, durable and economical, and require little maintenance. Vinyl tends to be brittle in very cold weather, but it never requires refinishing because the color is integral to its form. Copper gutters are also available at substantially higher prices.

Metals used in gutters and downspouts vary in thick-

nesses; 26-gauge galvanized steel is quite strong, but 28-gauge (a thinner metal) is more commonly used because it costs less. Aluminum is measured in a fraction of inches. The most frequently used thicknesses of aluminum are .025 and .032 inches.

The gutters should be mounted on the roof fascia boards so the gutter backs are offset slightly, with an airspace between the fascia so the fascia surface will not deteriorate from lack of ventilation.

Large houses with great expanses of roof require that both gutters and downspouts have sufficient capacity to handle expected volumes of rainwater. Small houses up to 30 feet long are adequately serviced with standard 5-inch gutters and two downspouts. Standard building formulas state that a 4-inch gutter is the minimum size to be used for roofs that are no larger than 750 square feet. Roofs up to 1,400 square feet can be drained with 5-inch gutters, and larger roofs with 6-inch material. Downspouts 3 inches in diameter will do if the roof is under 1,000 square feet, and 4 inches in diameter if the roof area is greater. In either case, for locations that are subject to freezing winters, opt for corrugated downspouts instead of smooth ones. The corrugated material can expand to handle freezing/thawing water without damage.

GUTTER AND DOWNSPOUT REPAIRS

To make repairs and do routine maintenance on gutters and downspouts, you will need the following tools and supplies:

Hammer
Screwdrivers
Ladders
Metal gutter straps (made of the same type of metal as your existing gutters and straps)
Galvanized or aluminum spikes and ferrules (if your existing setup uses them)
Galvanized or aluminum screws and nails
Asphalt roofing cement
Plumber's snake or clean-out tool
Wire brush
Putty knife
Aluminum sheet patching material
Hacksaw blade

Installing Protective Gutter Screens

If you don't already have protective screens over your gutters, consider installing them. Lightweight plastic or metal screens can be positioned over gutters to keep out leaves and twigs. They are designed to snap into the rims of the gutters.

Repairing Pinhole Leaks, Small Leaks, Thin Spots

Pinhole leaks at connections can be sealed with silicone caulking compounds. To repair small leaks or thin spots, before beginning, check the weather report. You will need a dry, warm day, with no rain in the forecast.

1. Clean the area. Wire brush as much rust, debris, and loose material away as possible. If the gutter is made of wood, cut or sand away the rotted material.
2. Wipe the area clean of all dirt and dust with a damp cloth.
3. Cover the hole or thin spot with asphalt roofing cement. Apply it with a putty knife, feathering the edges of the putty into the surrounding sturdy gutter material around the spot being repaired.

Repairing Large Cracks or Holes

For cracks or holes that are more than ½ inch wide after the cleaning process is done, a layer of roofing cement should first be applied. Then it should be covered with an aluminum patch. After the aluminum patch and roofing cement have had a chance to set up, a second coat of roofing patch should be applied over the aluminum patch.

Adjusting the Gutter Pitch or Slope

If you are having trouble with gutters not draining properly, it could be because there is not enough pitch, slant, or slope toward a downspout. Gutters should slope about ⅛ inch per running foot toward their downspouts. If they need to be adjusted, they will have to be rehung.

There are two basic types of hangers that hold gutters into place: straps, and spikes and sleeves or ferrules. (See Figures 15-3 and 15-4.)

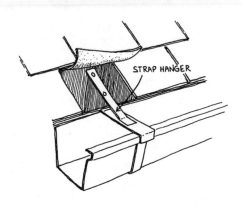

15-3. Gutter suspension—gutter strap.

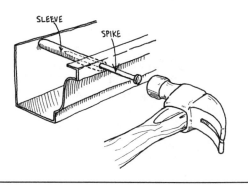

15-4. Gutter suspension—sleeve and spike.

WITH STRAP HANGERS

1. Lift the edge of the roof shingle or roofing material for access to a trap end so the strap can be removed. Remove this end of the strap.
2. Unscrew or unstrap the other end from the gutter.
3. Move the roof end of the strap to a higher (or lower) position on the roof. Renail with galvanized or aluminum nails. Any new nails should not be located within an inch of the old nail hole for best results.

WITH SLEEVE AND SPIKE HANGERS

1. Remove the spike that holds the gutter by cutting it with a hacksaw blade.
2. Move the sleeve into an adjacent location a minimum of 1 inch away from the old location.
3. Adjust the gutter level as desired, then fasten the gutter to the roof board by nailing a new galvanized spike through the gutter and sleeve into the board. (See Figure 15-4.)

GUTTER AND DOWNSPOUT MAINTENANCE

1. Clean leaves, seeds, and other debris from gutters, gutter screens, and downspouts. Pay special attention to clearing elbows and bends. A clogged downspout can be opened up with a plumber's snake.
2. Keep hangers securely fastened.
3. Plug holes, splits, and cracks.
4. Repaint rusting (but still intact) gutters and downspouts with rustproof paint, inside and out.
5. When worn out, certain heavily used parts such as the lower sections of downspouts should be replaced instead of repaired.
6. If snowdrifts and icicles or ice dams form along your roof slopes during winter, consider installing electrical snow melting wires. Heat wires or cables should then be inspected before each winter and repaired as needed.

GUTTER AND DOWNSPOUT QUICK CHECKLIST

❑ Inspect gutters and downspouts at least twice a year, during heavy rainstorms. This will reveal major leaks and obvious problems.

❑ Inspect also during dry days to look for minor defects.

❑ Gutters and downspouts must be kept free of leaves, seeds, twigs, and other debris that could impede the system's capacity for carrying away rainwater.

❑ Gutter and downspout hangers should securely fasten the entire system to the house.

❑ Leaks should be repaired.

❑ Rust and corrosion should be addressed and covered with rustproof enamel paint.

❑ Downspouts should discharge water onto splash blocks or into pipes that convey water away from the home's foundation walls.

❑ Prevent snowdrifts, icicles, and ice dams from forming and damaging gutters and downspouts during winter.

❑ If an entire gutter/downspout system has rusted and otherwise deteriorated to a point where extensive repairs are required, it is usually best to replace the system.

GUTTER AND DOWNSPOUT SAFETY

Follow all safety procedures as outlined in the section on roofs. Be careful with ladders. Wear heavy-duty gloves when cleaning out gutters. Get help when needed.

Exterior Wall Sidings

Exterior walls are generally covered with weather-resistant sidings. Their main purpose is to keep out rain, sleet, snow, and other moisture, to shield a dwelling's interior spaces from sun rays, winds, cold, heat, and other intrusions. Certainly, brick, stone, aluminum, and vinyl sidings offer years of almost trouble-free service. Some painted wood sidings, on the other hand, can be maintenance nightmares. In fact, no matter what paint companies call their paints, eventually painted wood siding will need to be scraped, sanded, or otherwise prepared for the application of additional coats.

EXTERIOR WALL SIDING INSPECTIONS

- Cosmetic damages. Stains and soils. Scratches, dings, and dents.
- Water damages. Peeling or blistered paint. Warped, split, or cracked wood shingles, mildew stains, rotting boards.
- Cracks and gaps. Open seams in siding and trim. Open gaps at outside corners. Missing or damaged caulking. Loose, missing, or rusty nails. Holes needing to be re-puttied. If repairs are not made, moisture will seep into a wall, eventually swell the wood and, in the case of stucco, push the outer material away. Fungi can establish itself in the cracks. Rot comes next and soon there is nothing for nails to hold onto, or stucco to adhere to.
- Insect damages. See the section on pests.
- Siding hardware and accessories should also be checked. Any iron or other metal items such as bolt heads and shutter hinges could be corroded and leaching rust stains down the siding's surface.

EXTERIOR WALL SIDING REPAIRS

Except for the simplest of repairs, such as renailing a piece of wood or aluminum siding here and there, most siding repairs are best left to professionals who know how to remove, replace, and blend various siding parts to match existing materials. A home's appearance is largely dependent on how its siding looks. Siding that doesn't match, or is crooked or otherwise ineptly installed, can make a big difference in how the entire property is viewed.

Masonry repairs are especially tricky. They often involve repointing brick, block, or stone walls, which is the process of replacing damaged and weak mortar joints with fresh mortar.

Repairing Masonry Cracks

A common repair to masonry exteriors is repointing: replacing damaged or weakened mortar joints with fresh mortar. Here's how it is done.

1. Clean out loose or deteriorated mortar with a chisel and hammer. (See Figure 16-1.)

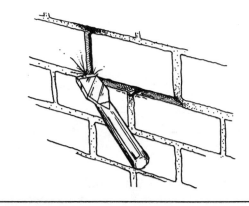

16-1. Repairing masonry cracks — cleaning out old mortar.

2. Remove the smaller particles by flushing with a strong stream of water from a garden hose (being careful to wear goggles in case of splashback), or by using a wire brush and water. (See Figure 16-2.)
3. Prepare enough premixed mortar, following the manufacturer's instructions. Try to match the new mortar mix with the old.
4. Wet the areas to be filled and then press the mortar into the open joints with a trowel. (See Figure 16-3.)
5. Use a joint tool to finish off the joints. After about 10 minutes, clean excess mortar from the surface of the brickwork with a brush, and make another pass with the joint tool so the joints will look the same.

16-2. Repairing masonry cracks—flushing joints.

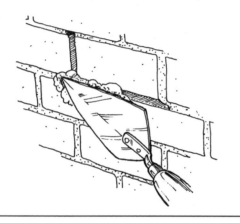

16-3. Repairing masonry cracks—troweling on new mortar.

Repairing Cracks in Stucco

Hairline cracks in stucco can easily be concealed by painting over them with latex paint. Larger stucco cracks must first be filled with latex caulking and then puttied over. Small holes can also be repaired in the following manner:

1. Remove all loose material and debris from the hole. Make sure that the bonding underlayment is intact.
2. Widen the crack with a stiff-bladed putty knife. Try to angle the side of the crack so the opening is wider inside than at the surface, to help the repair material to stay in place. (See Figure 16-4.)
3. If the wall lath or wire mesh is damaged, replace it with similar material.
4. Thoroughly wet the hole so the new patching material will adhere to the older and drier surrounding material.
5. Mix enough stucco patch compound, available at hardware and builder's supply stores, and use it to fill the hole. Follow the manufacturer's instructions.

Alternative stucco patching materials include silicone or latex caulking compounds that come ready mixed in cans. Tinted stucco repair compounds are available. If you use white patching material on a light green stucco, make sure you use the kind of patching material that can be painted.

Holes larger than 6 inches should be left to the professionals.

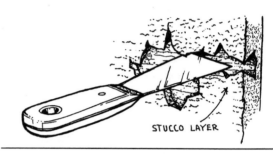

16-4. Widening a stucco crack.

Repairs to Metal Dents

Dents in metal siding can be pulled out by fastening a self-tapping sheet-metal screw to the dent, then pulling on the attached screw.

1. Drill a small hole into the center of the dented area.
2. So as not to split the siding metal, attach a piece of rubber ferrule or several small washers to the screw's head, as a spacer.
3. Drive in the screw, then grasp the end of it with a pair of pliers. Gently pull until the dent has flattened out.
4. When the dent is nearly gone, remove the screw and apply aluminum or steel filler to the screw hole. Work quickly before the material hardens.
5. Once the filler has hardened, sand it until the surface feels smooth. Touch it up with primer followed by several coats of exterior paint. Feather the new paint into the surrounding areas.

Wood Shingle Repairs

1. Begin by removing the damaged shingle. Split it into pieces by driving a chisel into the shingle's bottom edge or "butt."
2. Wiggle the pieces out from beneath the overlapping adjacent shingles.
3. The nails that had fastened the removed shingle will be hidden beneath the shingles in the overlapping row. Those hidden nails must be removed. Slide a hacksaw blade beneath the overlapping shingles. Saw the hidden nails off flush with the surface (see Figure 16-5), so replacement shingles can be slid or gently driven into place, using a 2" x 4" board as a buffer. (See Figure 16-6.) Use

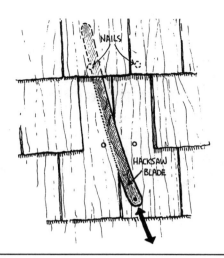

16-5. Cutting siding nails.

16-6. Installing a replacement shingle.

galvanized or aluminum ring nails to fasten the new shingles.

Siding Replacement

Major replacements are best done by professionals. If you want a low-maintenance siding, consider vinyl or vinyl-covered aluminum siding. Vinyl will not corrode, chip, peel, or blister. Another consideration is the replacement of wood overhangs or soffits with ones made of aluminum or vinyl, to eliminate the need for frequent painting. But if you have a small piece of siding to replace, here's how to do it.

1. Using a specially designed siding implement called a zip tool, which "unlocks" one piece of siding from another (see Figure 16-7), either remove the entire damaged strip or cut out the section that contains the damage by making a vertical cut about 12 inches from each side of the damaged material, as wide as the damage is. Remove the damaged piece by making horizontal cuts above and below the damaged section, between the vertical cuts, leaving the upper portion of the siding strip intact to provide a gluing surface for the replacement piece.

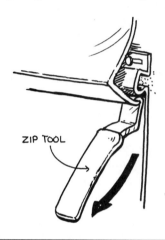

16-7. Using a ziptool to unlock pieces of siding.

2. Measure and cut out a replacement patch that is at least 3 inches longer and wider than the piece that was cut out. Be sure to trim off the upper edge with the fastening slots.
3. Spread roofing cement over the edge surfaces of the damaged siding that remains on the house.
4. Fit the new piece of siding into place. Press it tightly to spread the adhesive. (See Figure 16-8.) If needed, use several rustproof nails for additional support.

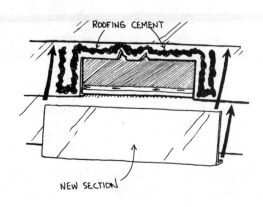

16-8. Cementing a piece of replacement siding.

EXTERIOR WALL SIDING MAINTENANCE

Keep the Siding Clean

Most sidings will come clean with soap and water and a little elbow grease. Some homeowners choose a nice warm summer day, get into their bathing suits, fire up their garden hoses, and grab a pail filled with a solution of household cleanser and warm water, and a scrub brush or sponge on an extension handle. Depending on the house type, a ladder may be needed as well. Before using any solutions on siding, though, test a small inconspicuous spot, to check for colorfastness.

Aluminum siding can be cleaned by washing it with a hard spray of water from a garden hose. If the siding is still soiled after washing, use a solution of strong non-abrasive household cleanser and water—usually one cup of cleanser can be combined with a gallon of water. Follow the cleanser manufacturer's instructions. Wash with a sturdy sponge.

Glazed tile or bricks can be cleaned with a soap and water solution. Stubborn discolorations and stains will often come out with gentle scrubbing with a brush and a non-abrasive household cleanser or a brick and tile cleanser.

Wood shingles can be brushed clean when dry. Use a stiff-bristled brush or a push broom. It is best to wait until after several days of warm, sunny weather so the dirt and dust will be dry and easy to remove. Stains can be removed from shingles by washing them with a solution of household cleanser and water. Use a scrub brush, then rinse the shingles well with a strong spray of water from a garden hose. Rust stains can be removed by treating them with oxalic acid solution available at paint supply stores. Wear gloves and goggles while working with oxalic and other cleaning solutions. Rusty nail heads should afterwards be covered with sealer to prevent further staining.

Mildew can be removed by spraying affected areas with a solution of one part household liquid bleach and three parts warm water. Let the bleach solution soak in for 15 minutes. Scrub the area with a stiff brush. Let the siding dry.

Stain or Paint Wood Siding as Needed

Stain lubricates or moisturizes wood and helps keep it from drying out and cracking. If a stain has faded or if you see hairline cracks, the stain should be replenished. Simply apply several more thin coats of stain or preservative.

Painted siding is a different story. Siding should not be overpainted. Overpainting builds up unnecessary

and harmful thicknesses of paint that may crack and peel under their own weight. Clean, sand, and prime all bare areas before painting. Select a quality paint. Two finish coats should be applied. Wait until the first coat dries before applying the second.

If wood siding is in such a condition that it requires the entire removal of old paint, compare the time, effort, and supply costs required to paint to those required by installations of aluminum or vinyl sidings. Figure that paint may have to be renewed every six years or so, while synthetic sidings can last 10, 20, or more years with barely any maintenance.

To paint or touch up steel or aluminum siding, wire-brush the damaged areas or sand them to remove rust or other corroded surfaces. Bare areas should then be primed with metal primer. Repaint with a matching color. Unpainted aluminum surfaces will accept paint better if they are first allowed to weather for a while and then given an undercoat of zinc-chromate metal primer.

Fill in Small Cracks

Joints between siding boards can be puttied over. Nail heads should be set below the wood surfaces and puttied over. Caulk and seal any open joints.

Remove Encroaching Vegetation

Vines are especially troublesome. They can work their way between joints or under a stucco finish and destroy a siding's integrity with their probing tendrils. Trees and shrubs planted too close to siding can hold moisture against the house and cause mildew and rot.

EXTERIOR WALL SIDING SAFETY

- Use caution with ladders.
- Wear gloves and goggles when working with cleansers, and sanders and other power tools.
- Never sand asbestos siding. If you have any doubts about whether your siding shingles have been made with asbestos, have the siding tested.

**EXTERIOR WALL SIDING
QUICK CHECKLIST**

- ❑ Keep siding clean.
- ❑ Maintain a weathertight exterior by filling cracks and gaps and making necessary repairs.
- ❑ Repaint or reseal wooden or metal sidings as needed.

Chimneys

There are two parts of chimneys to be concerned with: chimney components that are exposed to the elements, and those that are exposed to heat, smoke, and fumes from wood, gas, or oil combustion. In other words, the chimney's outside and inside. And don't think that because there isn't a fireplace in your home, you don't have to worry about a chimney. Not true. The typical home has an internal chimney that rises from the boiler or furnace up through the home and through the roof where boiler or furnace gases are vented into the outdoors. That means part of the outside of a chimney will run through the inside of a dwelling.

CHIMNEY EXTERIOR INSPECTIONS

According to most building codes, the portion of the chimney that runs through a house, as a fire-safety measure, should have a minimum of 2 inches clearance between the chimney and any wood framing or other combustibles.

That creates a special problem. Because the chimney perimeter space runs from the boiler or furnace room through the roof, in case of a fire it could draw flames throughout the center of the home, through the open air space. To eliminate such a hazard, the open area between the chimney and wood framing should be covered, or fire-stopped, with a non-combustible material such as sheet metal or fireproof insulation. This will block the movement of air around the chimney that would effectively turn the area into a fire-feeding flue in the event of a fire in the boiler or furnace room.

Inspect the part of a chimney that is exposed within an attic or crawlspace below the roof. After the furnace or fireplace has been operating for several hours, go to the attic or crawlspace and feel around the chimney for hot spots and cracks. Look for leaking smoke.

Look at the outside of the chimney that protrudes above the roof, as well as any part that is exposed along an exterior wall. Note eroding mortar, loose bricks or stones, and cracks. Note any deterioration on the chimney cap. (See Figure 17-1.) If the cap becomes cracked, water may get into mortar joints between chimney bricks. When water freezes, it will expand and cause larger cracks. Eventually the entire top section of chimney may have to be rebuilt. Look at the chimney flashing to make sure the seals have not shrunk loose or pulled away from the bricks or adjacent roofing.

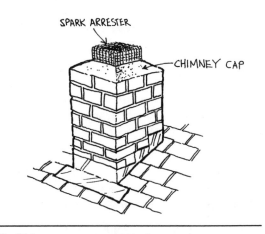

17-1. Chimney cap and spark guard.

Any small cracks should be highlighted for repair. If left alone, they will soon grow into larger cracks.

Note any evidence of efflorescence, which is caused by moisture in masonry that brings salts from the mortar to the outer surfaces of brick or stone. It appears as a whitish discoloration or scale. It is common in new brickwork and is usually washed off by rain. But if it appears in masonry that has already been standing for several years, it probably means that water is getting inside or between the inner and outer parts of the chimney. The source could either be from the chimney top—the cap may not be weathertight—or the quality of mortar is poor, allowing water to seep through the outer layer.

Check the condition of the chimney's spark guard. If there is no guard preventing sparks from emerging from the chimney onto the roof, one should be installed. (See Figure 17-1.) Most spark guards are made of 1/8-inch mesh hardware cloth. Smaller meshes will plug with soot. A spark arrestor screen or "weather cap" also keeps wildlife out of the chimney.

While looking at the top of the chimney, note branches that have grown too close to chimney flues. Such foliage could become a fire hazard, and it could also hinder the air flow needed to maintain proper chimney draft levels.

If there is a television antenna affixed to the chimney, consider having it removed. Strong winds can cause serious strain on chimney walls from flexing television or radio antennas or other fixtures. Cracks and eventual water damages may result.

With metal chimneys, look for signs of rust, corrosion, and holes in the metal. Check the condition of the rain cap—a cap on metal chimneys which prevents rainwater from running down inside the flues where it could cause internal corrosion.

Throughout living spaces that are adjacent to the chimney, do you notice any water stains on floors, ceilings, or walls? Is insulation around the chimney damp? Can you see daylight from the lower chimney connection up through the roof?

Where there are fireplace openings, no woodwork should be placed within 6 inches of those openings on the sides. Above the opening, a minimum of 12 inches should be kept open between wood components.

On the lower end of the outside part of the chimney, see if a clean-out door at the chimney's base closes tightly. Gaps through which smoke and sparks could emerge pose considerable safety hazards and unwanted drafts.

Check flue pipe connections from heating appliances to their own flues that run through the chimney. Are they tight? Any openings are a cause for concern because hazardous gases could escape into the basement. Special care should be taken when inspecting connections from wood-burning stoves. All pipes and mounting brackets must be secure, clean, and run into connections that are tightly fastened and sealed.

The foundation beneath a chimney is generally visible in a basement or crawlspace. If there is a tilt in the chimney, look for problems in the chimney's footer. Is there any evidence of uneven settling?

CHIMNEY INTERIOR INSPECTIONS

Chimneys where fireplaces or wood-burning stoves are involved demand considerably more attention than do chimneys in homes where fireplaces have not been included.

Have soot and ash accumulations been removed from ash pits or collection boxes? Most fireplaces in newer homes have an ash-pit beneath their firebox. There might be a little metal trap door in the hearth. When it is opened, ashes can simply be pushed into the pit below. The ashes can then be shoveled out of the pit through another metal door accessed in the basement or wherever the back of the chimney is situated—possibly inside of a garage or even from outdoors. Ashes can be mixed into soil; they make fine fertilizer.

Does the fireplace damper operate correctly? (See Figure 17-2.) Check how well it closes. If it is loose or partially open in the closed position, it should be tightened to prevent unnecessary heat loss.

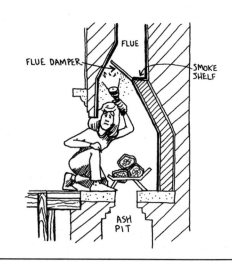

17-2. Inspecting a fireplace damper.

During the day, open the damper. Put goggles on and poke your head into the fireplace opening so you can look up the chimney. Can you see daylight through the top? If you don't see daylight, perhaps a bird has built a nest in the flue, or if you have a wire screen spark arrestor on the top of the chimney, it could have become coated with soot.

Is there a buildup of creosote around the firebox or inside the chimney flue? Creosote and soot can drastically decrease the air draw of a fireplace. Creosote is a shiny, black tar-like substance released from the wood by combustion. It can gradually build up in sticky, thick layers that can ignite and burn fiercely once caught. When a flue's insides are coated with uneven surfaces of this black, gummy-looking material, and you can't tell where inside tile and mortar joints are, it is way overdue for a cleaning.

If at any time creosote is noticed on the *outside* of a chimney, that is a cause for concern. It probably means there is a crack in the flue lining.

Using a screwdriver, poke around the firebricks that line the fireplace to see if any are loose, broken, or chipped. Test the grout between the bricks.

CHIMNEY REPAIRS

It is best to rely on a mason or qualified contractor to make most major chimney repairs.

CHIMNEY MAINTENANCE

1. Avoid large buildups of creosote and soot. Because it is such an infrequent and important task, and specialized tools, procedures, and skills are needed, it is recommended that you use a commercial chimney-sweeping company to rid chimneys of creosote and soot. Creosote is so hard and gummy that it can't simply be chipped away from masonry with a blade. Care must be taken not to ruin flue linings and create more problems than are being solved.

    Chimneys should be cleaned whenever needed, but the materials burned in a fireplace or stove will have a definite effect on the frequency. If soft pine woods are burned, generous amounts of their resins will be deposited along chimney flues. Cleanings should be scheduled at least twice per year. Chimneys over open fireplaces that burn hardwoods every so often can be cleaned as needed, or about every five years. Burning well-seasoned hardwoods such as oak and apple reduces the amounts of creosote and soot buildup. Chimneys used for oil-fired systems should be cleaned as needed or at least every other year. Chimneys serving gas-fired systems experience the fewest problems with chimneys, and rarely need the cleaning services of a chimney sweep. They will, however, need their insides inspected occasionally.

    In general, although guidelines are available, the condition of the inside of a chimney depends on how well it was constructed, how weatherproof it has been, and how often—and to what intensity—it has been used.

2. Keep moisture from entering a chimney. Chimney caps and rain caps should be kept in good condi-

tion. The cap and upper portion of a chimney that rise above the roof can be protected with several thin coats of liquid clear silicone. The silicone or a similar clear waterproofing will also help seal porous masonry surfaces that could otherwise be penetrated by water.

3. Oil the damper and make sure it doesn't stick in an open position.
4. Keep cracks and joints sealed.
5. Clean out fireplace ash pits whenever needed.
6. Refer to the section on masonry walls for additional maintenance items that apply to chimneys.

CHIMNEY SAFETY

1. The greatest danger is from chimney fires. Chimney fires are caused from buildups of creosote, from combustible materials located too close to hot flues, from cracks or breaks in a flue lining that sparks can get through, from wood components positioned too close to a firebox, and from sparks emitted through the unguarded top of a chimney where no spark arrestor has been installed.
2. Another serious hazard is noxious gases. These gases can enter a home if the damper is not working properly, if the chimney is plugged, or if other heating appliance pipes are not securely attached and vented through their own flues in the chimney.
3. A third hazard can come from the condition of the chimney itself—the part that protrudes from the roof. Chimneys have literally deteriorated over the years to a state where they can blow apart in strong windstorms and fall from a roof.
4. Use caution when inspecting chimneys on a roof. See the sections on roof safety and ladder safety in the sections on roofs and equipment.
5. If at any time smoke pours back into a room, it is a sign that the entire flue and damper system needs a close inspection.
6. A low chimney or a chimney that does not protrude much from the roof is a dangerous design feature. The chimney should extend at least 3 feet above flat roofs, and at least 2 feet above a roof ridge or raised part of a roof within 10 feet of the chimney.

CHIMNEY QUICK CHECKLIST

❏ There should be no combustibles located closer than 2 inches away from a chimney's outer sides, and 4 inches around fireplace fireboxes (where logs are burned).

❏ The envelope of space surrounding a chimney should be closed off or "fire stopped" with metal, fire-resistant insulation, or other non-combustible building materials.

❏ Creosote and soot levels should be cleaned from chimney insides as needed.

❏ Damper systems must operate correctly.

❏ A chimney's structure should be kept sound, with no cracked, tilted, or "rotten" sections. There should be no breaches, cracks, or deteriorated sections.

❏ Moisture must be kept out of chimneys. Rain caps or chimney caps should prevent water from getting through the top. Clear sealers should waterproof a chimney's masonry surfaces. Caulked flashing can take care of the cracks or joints between chimney materials and roofing.

❏ Structural repairs to chimney foundations or other major components should be done only by experienced masons or chimney repair and cleaning specialists. Chimney cleaning should be done by contractors having the correct equipment and knowledge.

❏ A spark guard should be installed at the top of every chimney to prevent sparks from discharging onto roofs.

❏ Television or radio antennas should not be affixed to a chimney.

Caulking

Have you ever watched old film clips of comedians W.C. Fields or Laurel and Hardy when they encountered some sticky material — like flypaper — they couldn't get rid of? In a sense, similar scenarios are still occurring year after year when thousands of homeowners arm themselves with caulking guns and head for the cracks in their houses, where they promptly apply caulking not only to crevices, but to their fingers, clothes, eyebrows and even, at times, to their children. Although caulking can be a sticky, nasty task, it doesn't have to be.

WHY CAULKING IS NECESSARY

If modern construction workmanship was as good as that practiced in ancient Egypt—where you couldn't slip the edges of a razor blade between the pyramid stones—we wouldn't have much need for caulking. Unfortunately, that is not the case. As a rule, wherever two different building materials meet, a sizable crack occurs. Through that crack any number of unwanted things can pass, including water, moisture, wind, cold air, hot air, gases, sounds, dust, dirt, insects, and even crumbs of food.

18-1. A home's many exterior surface joints.

In a nutshell, "to caulk" means to stop and make tight against leakage. One of the first uses of caulking was to fill seams in wooden boats so water wouldn't seep inside. Now we use it in houses also, to accomplish a variety of things.

To Reduce Energy Loss

Studies estimate that about one-third of average home heating and cooling energy costs are due to air leaks. Effective caulking of exterior and interior cracks and joints helps to keep cold air out during winter, and cool air inside during summer. (See Figure 18-1.)

To Guard Against Moisture Damage

Caulking provides an excellent weather seal around door frames, window frames, and any other components built into the home's outer shell. If the cracks surrounding them were left open, rain and snow could be driven in or could seep inside the walls. Moisture inside the walls will easily rot framing members, plaster, and other construction materials. Caulking also seals cracks in concrete and asphalt sidewalks, driveways, and patios to prevent destructive freezing-thawing cycles called "frost wedging."

To Seal Against Sound, Dust, Dirt, and Insects

Caulking helps soundproof a home's interior. It also keeps airborne dust and dirt from entering on windy days. Further, it denies access to all kinds of nest-building insects, including wood-loving termites and carpenter ants.

To Help Control Radon Gas Infiltration

Radon is a radioactive gas byproduct of decaying uranium and radium, small amounts of which are found naturally in most soils. It is considered a potential health risk to humans and has been known to collect in various concentrations in basements — especially basements with cracked or porous walls and floors. By sealing holes and cracks in slab openings, foundation walls, and basement floors, caulking can help reduce the flow of radon into a home.

To Improve Cleanliness and Housekeeping

Caulking around sink, tub, and shower drains and perimeters will prevent liquids, soaps, soils, and other residues from collecting out of sight and causing slime, mold, and unpleasant odors. Caulking around kitchen counters and built-in appliances will keep food particles from falling behind those components —where cleanup is difficult, if not impossible.

To Improve a Home's Appearance

Caulking helps prepare surfaces for painting and improves interior and exterior surface appearances by blending construction seams together for that "finished" look.

CAULKING INSPECTIONS

When you get to the item on your master PM Schedule that says to inspect the caulking, it means you will want to determine whether any existing caulking has deteriorated. You will want to know where it has "disappeared," leaving open cracks; and you will also want to determine where else caulking might be needed. The following list, though not all-inclusive, will give you a good idea of the kinds of things to check.

From the Outside

- Cracks in driveways, sidewalks, and patios.
- Small foundation cracks.
- If exposed, along the foundation sill—where the home's wood framing and siding rest on the foundation.
- Between driveways, sidewalks, patios, porches, decks, and the main house.
- Wherever masonry meets the siding (i.e., chimneys or siding that ends over the foundation walls).
- Along mortar joints.
- Places where pipes, cables, or wires enter the house.
- Around window frames.
- Around window air conditioners.
- Around door frames.
- Around pet door entrances.
- Underneath metal or wooden door thresholds.
- Around exhaust fan vents.
- Around clothes dryer vents.
- At corner joints formed by siding.
- On split or broken pieces of siding.
- Around electric receptacles.
- Around mail slots.
- Around post bottoms.

- Around the base of outdoor lights attached to the house.
- At joints, seams, cracks, or leaks in gutters and downspouts.
- At eaves/moldings and eaves/siding joints.
- Around all roof, dormer, and chimney flashing.
- Where skylights meet a roof or wall.
- Around vent stacks that go through the roof.
- Where an antenna connects to the house.
- Between any dissimilar materials such as wood and masonry, wood and metal, or masonry and metal.

From the Inside

- Cracks in foundations, slabs, basement floors, and walls.
- Along the foundation sill plate — where wood framing rests on the foundation.
- Around the access door to a crawlspace.
- Places where pipes, cables, or wires enter the house.
- Around window frames.
- Around exterior door frames.
- Around flues and chimneys, with heat-resistant caulk.
- At joints in fireplace masonry, with heat-resistant caulk.
- At joints in flooring/baseboards along exterior walls. If a lot of air comes in through the crack between baseboards and the floor, remove the baseboard and then caulk the seam where the wall meets the floor. Then replace the baseboard and caulk its seam.
- At gaps where a chimney passes through an attic. If the gap is too large, it should be filled with insulation instead.
- Around ceiling fan mounts.
- Around the perimeter of ceramic tile.
- Around bathtubs, showers, shower heads, and shower door tracks.
- Around toilets, sinks, faucets, and soap dishes.
- Around pipes beneath sinks.
- Around splash boards in bathrooms and kitchens.
- In seams and cracks along kitchen counters, in tandem with inserts that cover cracks between appliances to keep particles of food from falling between counters and appliances.

TYPES OF CAULKING: STRENGTHS AND WEAKNESSES

Practically all caulking comes in tubes or cartridges about 11 inches long by 2 inches in diameter. These tubes will all fit a standard caulking gun—essentially an inexpensive lightweight tube holder with a handle and trigger mechanism that operates a plunger. The plunger, in response to your finger pulling the trigger, pushes the round bottom of the caulking cartridge up toward the applicator tip (much like squeezing a tube of toothpaste from the bottom).

Before purchasing caulking, consider what you are going to use it on. The following chart notes strengths, weaknesses, and suggested uses of the four main types of caulking.

CAULKING TYPE	Oil Base	Butyl	Acrylic Latex	Silicone
Weather Resistance	Poor	Good	Good	Excellent
Effective Life (yrs.)	3	10-20	10	20-50
Tack-Free Time	1 day	12 hrs.	30 min.	45 min.
Paintable	Yes	Yes	Yes	Some
Wood Use	Good	Good	Good	Excellent
Metal Use	Good	Good	Good	Excellent
Masonry Use	Good	Good	Good	Excellent
Adherence to Water-Based Paint	Good	Good	Can't Use	Excellent
Adherence to Oil-Based Paint	Good	Good	Can't Use	Excellent
Suggested Use	General Purpose	General Purpose	Roof Gutters Lap Joints Wood Metal Masonry	General Purpose

You can see from the chart that silicone is often the best option, although it doesn't take paint finishes very well. On the other hand, silicone caulking comes in different colors. It is usually wise to steer away from bargain caulking. It is more difficult to apply, takes longer to dry or set up, and has a much shorter life span. Oil-base caulking, especially, tends to shrink and dry out in cracks as its oil gradually disappears. A few extra dollars for a better grade of caulking are almost always worth the labor you will save, the aggravation you will save, and the increased protection you will realize.

HOW TO CAULK

When caulking outside, you will need a warm, dry day. Moderate temperatures are best. Extremely cold weather will form frost or condensation on the joints, which will prevent the caulking from adhering. In very hot weather, the joints may be unnaturally closed through expansion, so not enough caulking can be applied. Rain will prevent the caulking from adhering and hinder it from curing properly.

Caulking is also sensitive to heat while in its tube or cartridge. Store it in a cool, dry place.

The tools you will need for caulking include:

Caulking gun
Tubes or cartridges of caulk
Common nail a few inches long
Ladder
Utility knife
Putty knife
Bristle brush
Wire brush
Paint scraper
Backup filler
Cleansers
Sandpaper
Isopropyl alcohol
Clean dry cloth

First, remove all or as much old caulking as possible from the area being prepared. Use the putty knife to scrape away old caulking that can't be easily peeled from the surface. Caulking that isn't "gummy" anymore, or that cracks and falls out of a crack or joint when you probe it with a knife, needs to be removed and replaced.

On concrete, masonry, and stone, use the wire brush to remove old caulking and any dust, dirt, or other loose particles. All impurities such as water repellents or other surface treatments should be removed as well.

On porous surfaces softer than masonry, clean lightly with sandpaper.

Metal, glass, and plastic surfaces should be cleaned with a solvent such as isopropyl alcohol. Make sure you read the safety instructions that come with the solvent before starting, and don't let the solvent air dry without wiping it clean.

With the utility knife, cut off the tip of the cartridge at about a 45-degree angle at a width of about ¼ inch or less. It is better to start out with a narrow bead. You can always enlarge it later.

Puncture the interior membrane of the tube with a common nail (a few inches long, 16d or 20d size), so the caulking will be able to come out when you operate the gun.

Load the caulking tube or cartridge into the caulking gun. Turn the plunger in back of the gun to engage the trigger mechanism.

Place the tip of the caulking tube on the crack to be filled. Hold the gun at about a 45-degree angle—the same angle as the cut on the tip of the cartridge. Then pull the gun trigger while you move the caulking gun along the crack, squeezing caulking into the crack while holding the angled opening fairly flat along the crevice being filled. Press the tip firmly over joints and push the caulking ahead of the tip to force it deeply into the crack.

You will have to judge the best speed to work with. Go too fast and the caulking will look stringy, with depressions and gaps. Go too slowly and the caulking will overfill the crack and look sloppy. If caulking looks too rough and uneven, simply wet your finger or the round end of a small spoon and run it down the filled crack, smoothing the caulking into a uniform line. Dip your finger or spoon in water often, or the caulking will stick and pull out of the crack.

On vertical cracks, start at the bottom and pull upwards while filling. (See Figure 18-2.)

18-2. Caulking.

For good control, don't let the bead of caulking get any bigger than the open tip.

Excess caulking can be removed with a rag dampened with water or a mild cleaning agent.

For cracks and gaps over ¼ inch wide, first use a backup filler such as oakum, caulking cotton, sponge rubber, wood strips, or fiberglass insulation. Pack the backup material in and then caulk over that.

If the caulking sinks in at any spot, allow it to dry and apply more. Wipe away any excess.

To stop the flow of caulking, twist the gun slightly as you disengage.

As soon as you finish with a caulking job, turn the plunger at the back of the gun to take the pressure off.

When finished, always reseal the tube by inserting a wide nail or screw into the tip opening and twisting it tightly.

Latex caulking can be painted shortly after being applied, in about half an hour. Let the other kinds set about a day before painting over them. Most silicones will not take a paint finish well, but some are currently being developed that are paintable. Read the instructions carefully when shopping for them.

Latex cleanup can be done with warm water. Silicones and oil-based or butyl caulking must be cleaned with isopropyl alcohol, mineral spirits, or something similar.

CAULKING: DO IT YOURSELF, OR CONTRACT IT?

While caulking is a relatively easy technique to learn, until you learn how to do it, your results are likely to be a bit sloppy. Unless you practice, it is difficult to do a smooth, even job.

It all depends on you. Do you want to learn the skill? Or is your main goal to have the best possible caulking job available? If excellence is desired, you may be better off going with a painter or siding contractor who has developed his caulking skills to an art. It depends on your goals and your budget at the time.

CAULKING SAFETY

There is nothing elaborate here. Follow procedures for high work, paying particular attention to ladder and roof safety if you go up high with the caulking gun.

CAULKING QUICK CHECKLIST

❑ Learn how to caulk, and practice your techniques before you attempt to caulk high-profile areas such as the window frames at the front of your home.

❑ Buy premium caulking even though it costs a few dollars more. Bargain caulking is difficult to apply, wears out quickly, does not look as nice, and will not provide good protection.

❑ Store caulk in a cool, dry place.

❑ Select a warm, dry day to apply caulking.

❑ Prepare the areas you will be caulking. They must be clean and dry for caulking to adhere properly.

❑ If possible, don't cover old caulking. Remove as much of the old material as you can for a better end result.

❑ Insert a nail or screw into the applicator tip to keep caulking in the tip from drying out and plugging the applicator nozzle while the caulk is being stored.

Windows

Windows come in all shapes and sizes. They come in single-panes, double-panes, and triple-panes. They come in different types of glass and Plexiglas. They come with special coatings, and they come plain. They come in wood frames, metal frames, plastic frames, and combination frames. Some can be opened. Others can't. Most are see-through clear. Some are partially transparent, or translucent, like "frosted" glass.

WINDOW INSPECTIONS

- Cracked or broken panes. Broken windows should be repaired as quickly as possible to prevent energy losses.
- Chipped, cracked, or missing putty.
- Condensation.
- Incoming drafts.
- Rotten wood frames and sashes.
- Loose or missing fasteners or locks.
- Dirty or sticking frames.
- Corrosion on metal frames and sashes.
- Loose joints.
- Peeling paint on frames and sashes.
- Broken window sash cords.
- Damaged screens.
- Twisted frames.

WINDOW REPAIRS AND MAINTENANCE

Glass can be very sharp. Even when it is not broken, edges can slice tender skin. Always wear cut-resistant gloves when handling glass. Many individuals will simply prefer to take windows and screens in need of repairs to local hardware or glass-repair shops. That is probably the best idea for most homeowners. To repair a broken pane, you will need the following tools and supplies:

> Pliers
> Hammer
> Narrow chisel
> Putty knife
> Regular large screwdriver
> Window glass cut to fit
> Putty

> Glazier points (small wedge-like inserts for holding the glass in place)
> Gloves, tight-fitting and reasonably cut-proof
> Ladder
> Waste container to hold scrap glass

Here are some window glass replacement guidelines.

1. Windows are typically removed from the outside of their frames. Put your gloves on and place all the tools and materials outside near the window that is being repaired. Wear your gloves during the entire repair.
2. Set up the ladder, if needed. Have a helper hold it as you perform the repairs. While you're removing broken glass from the window, the helper should be wearing goggles and a hat, and standing as far out of the way as possible, while still holding the ladder.
3. Remove all broken glass with the pliers.
4. Use the putty knife to remove the old putty.
5. Use the pliers to pull out all the old glazier's points.
6. Clean out the recess in the sash where the glass fits, using a narrow chisel. (See Figure 19-1.)

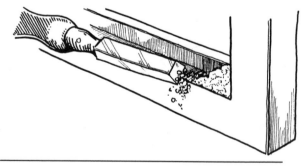

19-1. Cleaning a window sash.

7. Place a new layer of putty in the frame. Fresh putty can be rolled between your hands to stretch it out into a string of putty $1/8$ to $1/4$ inch thick (before you climb the ladder).
8. Insert the pane of glass against the putty.
9. Insert the new glazier points by tapping them in carefully with the head of a screwdriver. Start at a corner and work out every 4 to 6 inches.

10. Finally, fill the groove with putty. Press it against the glass with a putty knife or your fingers. Use the putty knife to smooth out the surface to complete the installation.

Painting Wood Frames and Sashes

Wood frames should be painted whenever the house or trim is painted, about every four to six years. Aluminum, vinyl, and vinyl-clad wood do not need painting. Aluminum can be left to age to a uniform gray color.

All wood window parts that do not have a vinyl covering and are exposed to the weather should be coated with paint or a wood preservative. Pay particular attention to the joints where the sides of the window frame meet the window sill. Fine cracks can be sealed with paint. Large ones will need a wood filler first, before painting.

Avoid painting windows shut. Windows that have already been painted shut will need to be freed by cutting through the paint with a putty knife. Never pry a window — you will damage the sash or sill. Some windows may have to be removed from their frames to get unstuck. The sliding part of the window, called the sash, is usually held in place by two strips of wood called stops. Carefully pry up the stops so you can use them again. Once the sash can be removed, sand or scrape the old paint from its surfaces.

Paint or preservative protects the wood frames from swelling. If moisture gets into the wood, expansion occurs. Never sand or plane or otherwise try to correct a wet window frame or sash. Wait until the parts dry out. Then after repairs are made, rub paraffin wax or soap along the parts of the sash that slide up and down, to make their movements easier.

Regluing Loose Corners and Joints

Reglue loose corners and joints. Reinforce them by installing corner plates available at hardware and builder's supply stores. (See Figure 19-2.)

Repairing Window Sashes

Older style single- and double-hung windows sometimes operate with pulleys, ropes, and weights that are hidden to a side of the window, within the wall, to help slide the window up and down. If a sash cord breaks, or a weight comes loose, the window may hang crooked or not stay up.

To fix the cord, first pry off the stops. Find the sash weight door and remove it (it is usually held in place by two screws). Reach inside and take out the weight. If the sash cord is still good, the weight probably just came untied. Retie it and put everything back together. If you need a new sash cord, here's what to do.

1. Make sure the new cord is the same thickness and length as the old one. Consider that the cord could stretch. If you think that is the case, make it a little shorter than the cord you are replacing, so the weight won't hit bottom later and keep the window from opening all the way.
2. Feed the new cord through the pulley, tying one end to the sash and the other end to the weight.
3. Move the window up and down to see if it works.
4. If it works, put everything back the way it was. But when you put the stops back, use new nail holes. Tap the stops into a slightly different spot. To avoid hammer dents, stop hammering before you hit the frame. Finish driving the nails with a nail set. Cover up the nail holes with putty. When the putty is dry, touch up the repair with paint.

Weatherstrip to Prevent Drafts

On a cold, windy day, if you can feel cold air coming in around a window, it needs to be sealed. Weatherstripping is usually installed on windows where the sash and frame meet. The most durable weatherstrips are made of bronze, aluminum, steel, and rubber or plastic strips. The less durable ones include adhesive-backed foam rubber, felt strips, and foam rubber with

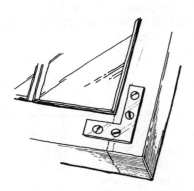

19-2. A window corner plate.

19-3. Installing weatherstripping.

wood backing. Some of the less durable weatherstripping may have to be replaced almost every year, depending on how often windows are opened. Simply cut the weatherstripping to fit, and follow the manufacturer's instructions. Usually, it is installed against the inner edge of the sash. (See Figure 19-3.)

Repairing Window Hardware

The cranks that operate casement and awning windows sometimes need to be replaced. Their gears or sprocket teeth can break and strip, or the set screws that fasten the crank to its sprocket will wear out their threads. Replacement parts are readily available at hardware or builder's supply stores. Loose window latches should be screwed down tightly, with larger and longer screws if necessary.

Storm Window Installations

Storm windows should be installed or put in place every fall as protection against cold temperatures and wind. "Sticking" can be corrected by cleaning the tracks and applying some graphite or silicone lubricant. Make sure that the weep holes — small holes at the bottom of the storm windows—are not blocked. If they are, unplug them. If they don't exist, drill two small $1/8$-inch holes in the storm window frame that will allow rainwater or moisture to drain out or evaporate.

If you have aluminum windows and aluminum storm windows, you may have moisture forming on the frame of the inside windows during cold weather. This is caused by condensation. Prevent this by installing a strip of insulation or weatherstripping between the storm window frame and the regular window frame. The same procedure can be used to take care of any other window condensation problems as well.

Treat wood storm windows the same way you would care for regular wood windows. Make sure loose joints are repaired, putty is in good condition, and all wood parts are sealed with paint or a preservative. Consider putting adhesive-backed foam weatherstripping on the inner edge of a storm window sash to make the fit more airtight.

Screen Repairs

A hole in a screen should be repaired as soon as possible, to keep the hole from spreading and to keep insects from entering the house. Screening is relatively inexpensive to purchase, so if the hole is large, or if it is in a noticeable place, consider replacing the entire screen instead of making a repair.

To repair a hole in a screen, you will need a piece of

19-4. Trimming screen hole into a rectangle.

new screening, a small block of wood with a straight edge, and a pair of heavy-duty scissors or shears.

1. Trim the hole to a rectangular shape. (See Figure 19-4.)
2. Cut a rectangular patch of screening an inch larger than the hole.
3. Remove the three outside wires on all four sides of rectangular piece of patching. (See Figure 19-5.)

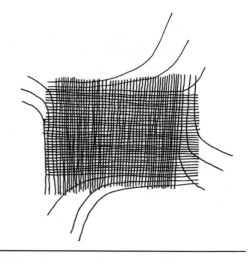

19-5. Removing outside wires of screen patch.

4. Place the patching over the block of wood and bend the loose ends of the patching all down in the same direction.
5. Set the piece of patching over the hole from the outside. Hold it tight against the screen so the small bent wires go through the screen, toward the inside of the house.
6. The loose wires sticking through the screen should then be bent toward the center of the hole. Someone should be outside to press against the patching piece while you push the wires in. The pushed wires will hold the screen patch tight. (See Figure 19-6.)

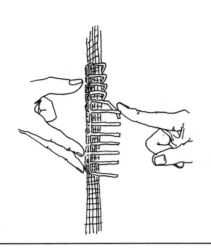

19-6. Installing screen patch.

To repair a small cut in a screen, use a needle and a fine piece of wire or nylon thread to stitch the cut back together.

Screen Maintenance

Screen frames can be maintained in the same manner as storm-window frames. Screening should be cleaned at least once a year. Use a soft-bristle brush with a sudsy cleanser and warm water. Rinse with a garden hose spray of water. Let the screens dry. Corrosion on aluminum screening can be cleaned with a light rubbing action of steel wool. A coating of household wax on the frames will help keep them clean and shiny.

Screening that encloses outdoor porches can be hosed from inside, so dirt, cobwebs, insects, and other tiny debris are all forced outside the screening.

NOTE: When taking down screens and installing storm windows, remember to write an identifying mark or number on each window frame and sash, so you will know where they go next season. Put any hardware—screws, wing nuts, or latches—in separate bags taped to the corresponding windows or screens.

Repairing Twisted Frames

Structural changes in a house can cause settling that may twist an entire window frame and cause the window to become jammed. In that case, the entire frame must be removed and reset in the wall. A project of this nature is best left for a carpenter or contractor.

Cleaning Windows

If the outside of the glass is extremely dirty, wash it with a solution of 1 tablespoon household ammonia to a quart of warm water. Or use a commercial glass cleaner containing ammonia. Lightly soiled glass can be cleaned with a solution of one cup vinegar to a gallon of water. A rubber squeegee is ideal to dry a window without leaving streaks. If you don't have a squeegee, paper towels are the next best thing. Most cloths will leave tiny pieces of lint on the glass.

WINDOW SAFETY

It is important that windows can be opened and closed easily, especially windows located in bedrooms, in case they are needed during a fire or other emergency. If a wood window does not slide as easily as it should, rubbing the channel with a piece of paraffin or an old wax candle should help. Another method is to spray the tracks with a silicone lubricant.

Windows should also be able to be securely locked, so a burglar cannot simply slide open a window to gain entrance. There are locking mechanisms available for every window. A trip to your local locksmith is worth the effort. Take along a list of the different types of windows you have and where they are located. Ask the locksmith for suggestions. Don't forget to add any basement windows to the list.

Always wear cut-resistant gloves when handling glass.

WINDOW QUICK CHECKLIST

- ❑ Replace cracked or broken windows.
- ❑ Eliminate window condensation.
- ❑ Windows should be practically airtight; they should allow no drafts.
- ❑ Repair or replace rotten wood window frames and sashes.
- ❑ Make sure all window hardware is present, securely fastened, and in working order.
- ❑ Seal window frame and sash surfaces against moisture and the weather.
- ❑ Keep window tracks clean and lubricated with wax or silicone.
- ❑ Windows should operate smoothly.
- ❑ Windows should be equipped with locking mechanisms.
- ❑ If repairs to old windows are too overwhelming, consider replacing those windows (all at once or several at a time) with new energy-efficient models. The payback in energy savings can be surprisingly quick.
- ❑ Install and use storm windows and screens.
- ❑ Keep windows clean.

Exterior Doors

Exterior doors receive far rougher handling than do doors hung within a home's interior spaces. Exterior doors must keep the weather out, and must be sturdy enough to keep unlawful intruders out as well. A typical exterior door is about 1³/₄ inches thick, 36 inches wide, and at least 81 inches high, so large appliances and pieces of furniture can be moved through its opening. There should be a burglar-resistant deadbolt lock and hardware, plus a peephole—a safety feature that lets the homeowner see who is calling before the door is unlocked.

All exterior doors should have a step down to the outside, a sill forming the bottom part of the door frame and entrance to prevent water from entering the house during heavy rains or snowstorms.

From all perspectives, steel doors make more sense than doors made entirely of wood, except, perhaps, when varying levels of artistic beauty are argued about (where the wood door continues to come out ahead). The better-grade steel doors have steel sheets fabricated over a wooden frame in which urethane foam or other insulation is sandwiched to protect effectively against cold and heat.

STEEL DOOR INSPECTIONS AND MAINTENANCE

Steel doors are designed to prevent the chief cause of wooden door failures—warpage that results in improper closing and gaps that allow air infiltration. By sandwiching insulation between their inner and outer surfaces, steel doors eliminate condensation problems that used to (and still do) plague wooden doors.

Steel doors are remarkably durable, requiring little maintenance. Their finishes are often baked on, and resist weathering for years. Keep them clean. Make sure their weatherstripping is intact. To prolong the life of vinyl/rubber weatherstripping, apply a bit of petroleum jelly to it occasionally. Also, see that door locking mechanisms are in order.

Fiberglass doors can be handled the same way. They need little other than an occasional cleaning.

WOODEN DOOR INSPECTIONS AND MAINTENANCE

Here's where the maintenance problems come into play. On doors that do not close correctly, needing minor adjustments, those adjustments can be easily made. But a wooden door with major defects, especially warpage, and especially when used as the front door to a home, should probably be replaced by a modern steel or fiberglass model.

The main concern about wooden doors is to prevent them from absorbing moisture. Moisture will cause them to swell, to warp. Warpage will affect their fit. Air gaps will result, and the door's operation may become difficult to handle. Wood exterior doors should be painted, varnished, or resealed every four to six years. That includes their bottoms, tops, and edges—places where moisture is most likely to enter.

For hints about maintaining wooden doors, see the section on interior doors. The same procedures are used.

STORM AND SCREEN DOOR INSPECTIONS AND MAINTENANCE

Screen or storm doors that don't work properly can be a real problem. Screen doors are supposed to let in ventilation and keep out insects and other creatures. They are simple to maintain. Just see that their screens have no holes or rips, and their closing mechanisms work as they should. Storm doors are supposed to keep out the weather. Their glass or aluminum panels should be intact, and their closers should operate correctly. Pneumatic closers can usually be adjusted by turning a slotted screw in the center of the end cap. Turning the screw counterclockwise generally makes a door close faster. Turn it the other way to make the door close more slowly.

SLIDING GLASS DOOR INSPECTIONS AND MAINTENANCE

Sliding glass doors are fairly maintenance free. Occasionally clean or vacuum debris from the bottom track so the doors can slide more easily or screen doors can roll more easily. The wheels, whether used in the glass door or a screen, will turn more freely over the aluminum track when the surface of the track rib they slide on is clean and lightly oiled.

EXTERIOR DOOR SAFETY

Steel doors with deadbolt locks provide the greatest measure of safety from fire, burglary, and inclement weather.

- Door hinge pins should be located on the *inside* of all doors that lead outside a home. Otherwise, an enterprising intruder could gain entrance simply by popping out the hinge pins with a screwdriver.
- Quality glass peepholes should be installed in all exterior doors that afford no other view of callers. Plastic lenses will fog, scratch, and deteriorate quickly.
- Sliding glass doors are usually situated in the back of a home, facing the rear of the property. That gives burglars plenty of confidence. Although most sliding doors consist of two glass panels, usually only one of them is permanently mounted. To safe-proof sliders, you must prevent an intruder from sliding the movable door open by force, and prevent him from prying the movable door up and out of its track. A common way to prevent someone from opening the movable panel by force is to place a long wooden dowel or piece of broomstick in the bottom track. This is not foolproof, however, because it won't prevent someone from simply prying the door away from and out of its track. A special steel or wood bar that locks into the sliding track, often called a "Charley bar," will prevent potential housebreakers from prying the panels off the door tracks. Charley bars can be purchased at hardware, locksmith, or builder's supply stores.
- Door locks are important. Forget about skeleton keys. And forget about key-in-the-knob locks. A key-in-the-knob lock is the easiest (and most common) lock to defeat. It can be thwarted by force: by placing a piece of wide-mouth pipe over the outside handle, the knob can be snapped off. Because the locking bolt is usually rather short and beveled, a crowbar or similar tool can be used to pry the door open. A key-in-the-knob lock can also be "loided." That means opening a lock by inserting a thin plastic strip, such as a celluloid credit card, between the bolt and jamb so the plastic strip releases a spring-operated catch.

The safest lock is a single-cylinder deadbolt, operated by a key from outside, and a thumb-latch inside. It throws a minimum 1-inch rectangular (not beveled) bolt into its receptacle, and if installed properly, cannot be pried or loided. One problem with the single-cylinder deadbolt is if there are panes of glass next to the door, an intruder could break the glass, reach inside, and turn the thumb-latch from the inside. In that case there are two options: (1) Replace the glass. (2) Replace the single-cylinder lock with a double-cylinder lock—a lock operated by key from inside and out.

The first option is the safest. That is what most locksmiths and law enforcement agencies recommend, because a lock that requires a key on the inside could be hazardous in case of a fire or other emergency.

EXTERIOR DOOR GENERAL MAINTENANCE

- Adjust the door so it closes completely, without sticking or rubbing. Tighten hinges and other hardware. Plane or sand sticking parts.
- Replace deteriorated weatherstripping. A good way is to use foam-edge strips that attach to the trim around the doorway. The strips come in long lengths that must be cut to fit. Follow the manufacturer's instructions. (See Figure 20-1.)

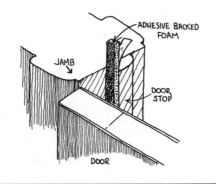

20-1. Doorway weatherstripping.

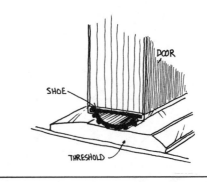

20-2. Door bottom seal, shoe, or "sweep."

▪ Replace the bottom seal if it has deteriorated. Constant opening and closing of an exterior door will eventually wear down or loosen a plastic or rubber "sweep." (See Figure 20-2.)
▪ Repair cracked glass, missing putty, broken peepholes, and malfunctioning hardware.
▪ Refinish door surfaces that are peeling, scratched, stained, or otherwise damaged.

EXTERIOR DOOR QUICK CHECKLIST

❑ Weatherproof exterior doors, with no gaps to let moisture or cold or hot air through.
❑ Equip doors with single-cylinder dead-bolt locks.
❑ If there is no other means to observe callers, install glass peepholes in exterior doors.
❑ Refinish peeling, scratched, or deteriorated surfaces. All surfaces of exterior doors must be able to repel moisture.
❑ Repair or replace warped doors.
❑ Keep exterior doors clean.
❑ Make sure latches, locks, closers, and other hardware operate smoothly.
❑ Keep sliding glass door tracks clean, and sliding track ribs lightly oiled.
❑ Equip sliding glass doors with "Charley bar" locking mechanisms.
❑ Make sure exterior door hinge pins are located on the inside of an outside door.

Foundations

Foundation problems typically occur shortly after a house is completed, while things are settling. A foundation should provide a solid base for the home's upper works and living spaces. It should also keep out moisture and creatures while being in constant contact with the surrounding earth. Foundations more often than not are constructed of masonry—concrete blocks or poured concrete. Occasionally you will find one made of stone, or brick, or even wood. But those instances are fairly unusual.

FOUNDATION INSPECTIONS

Water and Dampness
You will need to check for water streaming in through porous walls, through cracked walls, or up through holes or cracks in the floor. Water can come in through and around window wells, or places that pipes or other utility lines come through foundation walls. It can be caused by a variety of conditions: by gutters and downspouts not working correctly, by surrounding ground that slopes toward the foundation, from too many hedges and plants holding moisture next to the foundation walls, from inoperable French drainage systems, from plumbing leaks, from snow melt, from condensation, from driveways or walkways sloped toward the house, from underground springs that become active after winter, and from a host of other conditions.

Malfunctioning Sump Pump Systems
Sometimes, due to the ground and water table conditions surrounding a home, sump pump systems are the only way a basement can stay dry. See that the pump works properly and, when it does pump water out and away from the foundation, be sure that the water is sent away from the house and not merely to a place where it runs right back in again.

Foundation Cracks, Small and Large
Small cracks can be expected. Cracks that are wider than 1/16 inch warrant further investigation best accomplished by a professional. Severe cracks in a founda-

tion are generally caused by heaving or settli soil, or by the exertion of lateral pressure a foundation.

Pests
Foundation pests are mainly termites and oth destroying insects. See the section on pests.

FOUNDATION REPAIRS

Major foundation repairs, ones involving modifications or improvements, should on tempted by a qualified contractor. There is at stake for something to go wrong. If you wall starting to bow inward, or large cracks up, call in a contractor as soon as possible.

FOUNDATION MAINTENANCE

1. Do what you can to keep water and away from foundation walls.
- Grade the surrounding ground so it slo from the foundation. (See Figure 21-1.) have to add soil. If so, make sure you us

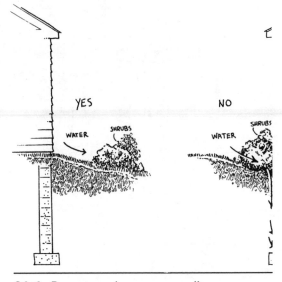

21-1. Proper vs. improper grading.

or loam with some clay content. Clay will help shed rainwater and snow melt. Avoid using sand, gravel, or coarse soil that will act like a sieve and let the water through. Try to establish a slope of 1 or 2 inches per horizontal foot, and continue the slope as far as possible away from the foundation.

- Keep gutters and downspouts repaired, with downspout angled bottoms or "shoes" and splash blocks in place. (See Figure 21-2.)
- Insulate basements to reduce condensation.
- Repair leaky pipes and fixtures.
- Make sure basement floor drains work correctly.
- Caulk and seal around basement windows.
- Keep window wells free of leaves and debris.
- Install clean plastic covers to window wells.
- Keep sump pump systems in operation.
- Paint the insides of foundation/basement walls with waterproof paint or concrete sealers.

2. Fix hairline cracks or cracks up to $^1/_{16}$ inch wide. Hairline cracks can be repaired in the following manner: (1) Prepare enough of a heavy paste made by mixing dry cement base paint with a little water. (2) Force the paste into the crack with a putty knife. (3) Let the paste dry; paint to match the rest of the wall.

3. Have large cracks looked at and repaired by a contractor. Horizontal cracks that travel from concrete block level to level can be very serious. They may have occurred in response to considerable lateral pressures being applied to the side of the foundation.

FOUNDATION QUICK CHECKLIST

- ❑ Keep foundations dry.
- ❑ Keep sump pump systems in working order.
- ❑ Watch for and repair small foundation cracks.
- ❑ Watch for and have a professional contractor evaluate and repair large cracks and structural defects.
- ❑ Look out for termite and other wood-destroying insect activity.
- ❑ Review the sections on basement floors, basements, and environmental/radon.

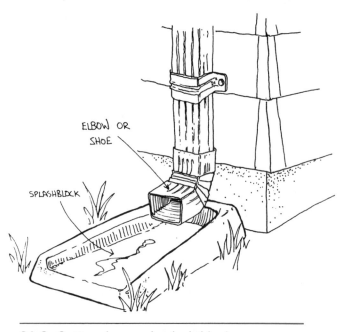

21-2. Gutter shoe and splash block.

Pests

Pests. These uninvited guests can make trouble in a number of ways. They include a huge number of individual species of creatures, from tiny insects to huge, furry mammals. To someone in the backwoods of Quebec, a moose can be an enormous pest, while someone in southern Florida might rattle off the names of eight or ten pinching, biting, and stabbing bugs. Skunks can be a problem. Mice, moles, and rats are unappreciated at times. Raccoons can drive homeowners crazy. So can chipmunks and squirrels and even woodchucks. Bats can be a problem. Bees and hornets can build nests in barbecue grills and attic eaves. Snakes can thrive beneath wood decks. Fleas will literally invade a family room.

There is no doubt that we share the planet with numerous creatures that often find their way into our yards and homes. Usually the instances are isolated and not threatening. Sometimes, though, we must take action.

Unless you are thoroughly familiar with a pest, or a colony of pests that has invaded your terrain, we advise you to seek help from a qualified exterminator or an agency (such as a wildlife department or game commission) to either exterminate or trap and remove whatever has encroached upon your living space.

Certainly, most pests will make their presence known without you having to inspect for them. But not all. One notable exception is that class of insects known for its wood-loving tendencies. Included in this insect group are termites and carpenter ants.

TERMITES

You have probably seen cartoons in which Bugs Bunny or some other character was up against a swarm of unruly termites or carpenter ants. Inevitably the insects would destroy wood items one at a time on a rampage that seemed entirely unstoppable. It's funny on television, but in real life, when termites devouring a main house beam do damages that cost upwards of $20,000 to repair, it turns serious.

Most termite infestations in homes occur in areas where the presence of termites has already been documented. The individual homes are often infested when termites gain access to wood that contacts or is too close to the ground. Porches, steps, and terraces are frequent stepping stones for termites to enter a dwelling. Once on board, termites will find their way into the home's main framing members such as the sill plate — heavy wood planks that rest upon the foundation walls to which the upper part of the home is attached. From the sill plate, termites can reach other parts of the home's frame and structure, including the main support beam that runs across the basement, beneath the first floor.

Look for earthen tunnels that termites will build as pathways from the ground onto parts of a dwelling, particularly along masonry foundations and basement walls, around openings where pipes enter walls, along the surfaces of metal pipes, and at expansion joints. These tunnels are also called shelter tubes. They are ¼ inch to 1 inch wide, and used by termites as passageways from the ground to the wood on which they are feasting.

Inspect all wood and wood structures that are near the ground. Pay special attention to any that touch the house. Look at the undersides of porches, outdoor stairs, and crawlspaces. Termites tend to be drawn toward wood where moisture is present. If you see insects swarming near your home, watch out! They could be termites.

Termite Prevention
If you live in a known termite zone, your best bet is to hire exterminators to treat the perimeter of your home every spring. Keeping them out of a home in the first place is a lot less expensive than getting rid of them once they have moved in. Other precautions include:

- Keep basement windows and crawlspace foundation vents closed during hot humid weather. Uncontrolled condensation may cause wood joists and sub-flooring to rot. Rotting wood tends to attract wood-destroying insects.
- Use a dehumidifier in the basement during the summer.

- To prevent an unfavorable moisture buildup in the soil around a house, the ground should be sloped away from the foundation, so water drains away from the home on each side.
- All wooden parts to a home, including steps, decks, and porches, should be at least 4 to 8 inches above the soil level.
- Dead trees and stumps near the home's foundation should be pulled out and removed so they won't attract wood-destroying termites and carpenter ants.
- Homes with stucco exterior walls need to be carefully inspected. Stucco sometimes does not stick close to concrete. So termites can crawl up into the home beneath the stucco and foundation walls.
- In places where termites are common, metal shields are installed between the foundation and the sill plate. The shields extend about 2 inches from the concrete at a 45-degree angle to block the ability of termites to build tube passages directly from the ground to the wood sill plate. (See Figure 22-1.)
- If wood in a home already appears to be infested — if there are clusters of small holes, insect wings lying about, small piles of sawdust here and there, and a pen knife sinks into solid oak as it would into balsa—the wood should be treated by a professional exterminator. This goes for infestations of big black carpenter ants as well.

When looking for a competent exterminator, it's important to find one who will not overtreat the problem. Be aware that the chemicals needed to control termites and other insects or pests are toxic to animals and plant life. That is why only licensed exterminators should be used.

PEST SAFETY

When in doubt, call professionals: exterminators, game commission personnel, veterinarians. Don't try to bag that rabid skunk yourself. Refrain from letting your kids try to spray that huge hornet nest with a garden hose. Get some qualified help instead.

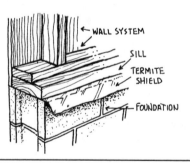

22-1. Termite shield.

PEST QUICK CHECKLIST
❑ Find out if you are in a wood-destroying insect zone.
❑ Look closely for signs of wood-destroying insects.
❑ If you are likely to encounter termites or carpenter ants, take preventive measures.
❑ Unless you are familiar with the pests and their solutions, call professionals in to take care of the situation.

PART 3

The Interior Shell

A home's interior shell directly reflects the kinds of wear and care that are given to it. A single elderly woman or man can live in a house for years and years and have little effect on the condition of the furnishings. Carpets will stay clean, walls will be kept free of smudges, paneling and trim will receive no dings and scratches, and doors will work properly. The same dwelling, when populated by a married couple with three children, a Labrador Retriever, seven goldfish, and a cat, can, without generous ongoing doses of maintenance, be trashed in a month.

A dwelling's interior shell is what the inhabitants see and live with on a daily basis. Unfortunately, because it is often considered a "private" part of the home, the outside of the dwelling is given more attention.

That should not be the case, because inside is where the action is. Life unfolds more within a home's walls than it does without. Enjoyment of the home is appreciably stronger when the inside of the home is kept in good condition—clean, orderly, with all components working as they should.

Some people have been known to fix up the insides of their homes only when preparing to put the home up for sale. What a misguided effort that is. Why not fix things up while they can enjoy them, and keep things that way until time to move? For certain unexplained reasons, replacing that threadbare carpet, refinishing deteriorated woodwork, or resealing the open cracks along the base of an upstairs shower just never work their way into many homeowners' plans until time comes to sell. The repairs will have to be done eventually. Why shouldn't they be completed and enjoyed well in advance of time to move?

Once completed, interior shell repairs need only be kept after to stay in tip-top condition. All it takes is a little common sense, some routine inspections, and a bit of preventive maintenance here and there to keep the interior shell of your home as it should be kept.

Interior Walls

While there are many ways to finish off interior walls, three make up about 95 percent of what you will find: drywall, plaster, and paneling.

The main ways to prevent wall problems are to keep water leaks and humidity levels under control, keep furniture from banging into walls, and keep children from using walls as part of their daily play activities.

GENERAL WALL INSPECTIONS

- Look for water stains around damaged floors near doors and windows. Cracked caulking, damaged weatherstripping, or a poor seal may be responsible for water intrusion here. Or the stains could be the result of leaving a window partly open during a storm, or from condensation dripping from glass or metal trim.
- Look for damaged or missing caulking between bathroom walls and tubs, sinks, and toilets.
- If mildew and musty odors are a problem, consider that closets may become musty because of poor air circulation. Often the best solution is to install a ventilating fan or louvered doors.
- When trying to prevent damages from furniture, a simple option is to install chair-rail molding about 2½ feet above the floor around the perimeter of a room. Doorstops installed at the floor line will also protect walls from being struck by door handles and knobs.

DRYWALL INSPECTIONS, REPAIRS, AND MAINTENANCE

Drywall consists of large (usually 4 by 8 foot) panels of prefabricated gypsum plaster sheathed on both sides in paper. The panels are measured to fit, cut to fit, and nailed to the rough walls. The nails are driven to countersink slightly into the drywall. A smooth continuity between panels is obtained by troweling over the joints with a plaster-like joint compound after a thin water-saturated paper tape has been applied to each crack or joint line. The nail depressions are then filled in with the same joint compound and troweled smooth. Light, sturdy metal angles are installed wherever two pieces

of drywall form right angles, to give the corners strength. The "plastered" edges are then troweled smooth with a thin layer of joint compound. Once the joint compound dries, it is smoothed out with sandpaper.

Final finishing is accomplished with more sanding and last-minute "point-up" work—taking care of any minor irregularities and making edges sharper. When everything is dry and sanded smooth, the entire surface can be painted, usually white. Once painted, there should be no evidence of panel joints or nail indentations. The surface is then ready for special finishes which add "skim" coatings of topping compounds similar to plaster. They can be finished off to look like any number of textured surfaces. Another possibility is wallpaper.

When compared to plaster wall finishes, drywall is easier to install and repair. It is also less expensive. It can be installed quickly, without the long drying times needed by plaster work. Here are some points to consider about drywall.

- Look for water damage from leaks or general dampness, for bowed-out or buckled sections caused by poor installation methods (usually insufficient backing support and poor nailing), and for nails that have not been properly set and covered.
- If tiny cracks develop where two pieces of drywall abut, fill them in with ready-mix drywall patch. (See Figure 23-1.) Let the filler material dry, then sand until smooth. Handle other imperfections the same way. If any of the cracks return, try filling them again, this time with flexible caulking. Then touch up the repair with paint.
- Minor hairline cracks occurring parallel to and about 1½ inches away from an outside corner are usually caused by poorly installed corner reinforcements. Correct the situation by securing the metal corner with more nails, then apply joint compound over the area. Let the joint compound dry. Sand it smooth, then repaint.
- Nail popping. When a dwelling's framing expands or shrinks in response to humidity changes, nails can "pop" out and become visible beneath

drywall or paint or wallpaper. If the nails are tight, simply drive them back into the wall with a claw hammer. If the nails are loose, pull them and drive new drywall nails nearby. Cover the nail heads with joint cement.

▪ Split tape. Split drywall tape is caused by house settling. The tape will bubble or crack. Cut and pull off the loose tape. Sand the area and spread a thin coat of joint compound over it. With a wide putty knife, work new tape into the compound, until the tape is smoothly fastened in place. Let the tape and compound partially dry, then apply another thin layer of compound over the tape. Let dry. Sand the repair smooth.

23-1. Crack where two pieces of drywall meet.

PLASTER WALL INSPECTIONS, REPAIRS, AND MAINTENANCE

Until drywall was invented, plaster was the overwhelming choice of contractors and homeowners for finishing walls. Plaster is a mud-like material that is troweled over plasterboard lathing — an understructure that gives the plaster a secure base to adhere to. It is applied in either a single coat about ½ inch thick, or two ³/₈ inch thick coats one on top of the other. Plaster can be finished in smooth or textured surfaces to complement any decor style.

Plaster's advantages over drywall include better fire resistance, more rigidity in construction, better soundproofing, better insulation, and a greater variety of artistic and creative finished effects are possible.

On the other hand, plaster cracks more easily than drywall does, and is more difficult to repair. Plaster costs more, takes longer to install, and is far more difficult to work with. Here are some points to consider about plaster walls.

▪ When inspecting plastered walls, look for signs of

moisture and cracks. Water leaks or general dampness can have disastrous effects on plastered walls. The leaks must be stopped, and the humidity taken care of before repairs are made.

▪ Minor defects can be touched up with premixed plaster putty available at hardware, builder's supply, and paint stores.

To repair plaster cracks:

1. Moisten the crack by misting it with water from a spray bottle, or rubbing it with a wet sponge.
2. Allow the moisture to soak into the plaster for a few minutes. This will prevent the plaster from absorbing water from the filler material during repairs. If that happens, the filler will not adhere properly within the crack.
3. Spread joint compound into and over the crack with a putty knife. Force the material into the crack, smoothing the surface and eliminating air pockets.
4. Let the filler dry, according to the manufacturer's instructions.
5. Apply a second layer if cracking or a depression forms.
6. If necessary, sand the repair smooth and level. Use a fine-grit sandpaper (about 100 grit) wrapped around a wooden block or a rubber sanding block.
7. Before covering filled areas with paint or wallpaper, apply a sealer (such as shellac) according to the filler manufacturer's instructions.

Major problems should be referred to professional plasterers. Some plaster cracks may be caused by structural problems such as a settling foundation. Be wary if cracks appear over a short period of time. A shifting of the foundation could be the cause.

Sometimes plaster will pull away from its lathing. If you notice a bowed-out section of plaster wall, and it sounds hollow when you tap it lightly, that is probably what has happened. If the location is in the middle of your living room, and a large section of wall needs to be repaired, you should probably call a professional. If the problem is in an out of the way location and you want to attempt repairs yourself, here is how to re-anchor plaster that has pulled away from its lathing:

1. Plaster buttons, or dished-in metal washers, and screws are available from builder's supply and paint stores. Purchase enough screws and buttons (one each per 1-foot interval will be enough) to make the repairs.
2. Install the buttons so their convex sides face out. Drive the screws through the buttons into the plaster and into the lath boards until the buttons flatten. Use an electric drill or a drywall screw

gun. Fasten the screws enough to countersink their heads, so the heads will not protrude above the wall's surface. Attempting to use nails will not work. The threads on the screws are what draws the lath and plaster together. The buttons help fasten the plaster so it will not work loose over the screw heads.

3. Cover the buttons and screw heads with joint compound or plaster to conceal them.

PANELING INSPECTIONS, REPAIRS, AND MAINTENANCE

Prefabricated panels or individual boards and planks of wood and other materials are used to cover walls because of the material's beauty, variety, low-maintenance qualities, and simple installation methods. Wood planks and paneling are the most popular, but panels are available that resemble a wide selection of building materials, including marble, stone, brick, and stucco. There are even panels that simulate a wallpapered surface. Such prefabricated sheets are becoming increasingly popular in kitchens, bathrooms, foyers, and even in main living areas.

Plywood makes a very good wall paneling. It is durable and can add a rich look to a family room, recreation room, study, den, or dining area. Wood species such as elm, pecan, birch, and certain kinds of walnut lend themselves nicely to use as plywood veneers.

Paneling should be installed against walls that have already been roughly finished in drywall or plaster, so the paneling will have sufficient backing to prevent waviness or buckling. Care must be taken, in both installation and when repairs are needed, that all sections of paneling are plumb and fitted nicely together, with adequate nailing along their edges.

Paneling will not show cracks in the walls, is easy to install, and can create many different moods for a room or an area. On the other hand, matching certain types of paneling and making repairs can be very difficult. Often entire panels will have to be replaced. In the case of wood panels, an exact match may not be available because old sections frequently become duller over time, through bleaching by sun and other light rays.

OTHER WALL COVERINGS

Wallpaper can be difficult to repair. To replace a small greasy or torn spot, carefully tear (don't cut) a piece of matching wallpaper from the front of the new paper, so backing will be torn away from the edges. Remove the old piece that needs repaired. Match the pattern, tear the new piece to match, then paste down

the new patch. The seams will always be slightly visible, but the ragged edges will make them less obvious. Some wallpapers are easier to repair than others. Styles with "natural" dividing lines, in which seams can be hidden, are the easiest to repair. Plain wallpapers and styles with odd patterns can be more difficult to match.

Wallpaper can develop bubbles. When this happens, try cutting a slit in the bubble and forcing a bit of paste behind the bubbled material. Roll or press the wallpaper flat. The cut will be less visible if made along a straight line in the wallpaper's pattern.

WALL COVERING SAFETY

- When painting, plan to do as much as possible in early summer, when windows and doors can be left open while the paint is drying.
- Many acoustical ceiling materials and wall coverings installed before 1976 may contain asbestos. Never cut or sand materials containing asbestos, since airborne particles are created by doing so. Before working with a material you think may be asbestos, have it tested. Refer to the section on asbestos.
- Always wear dust masks when sanding plaster or drywall patching.
- Handle razor-sharp butt knives and putty knives with caution.

INTERIOR WALL QUICK CHECKLIST

- ❑ Keep water and moisture away from wall surfaces. In places that are likely to encounter water or grease spattering, such as kitchen and bathroom areas, use easy-to-clean wall coverings such as vinyl-coated wallpaper.
- ❑ Inspect for and repair potential house problems that could result in leaks.
- ❑ Repair cracks and minor imperfections.
- ❑ Resurface deteriorated wall coverings.
- ❑ Hire professional plasterers to make major plaster repairs.
- ❑ Make minor repairs easily with plaster putty or drywall patching.
- ❑ Install chair-rail molding where furniture is likely to come in contact with walls (dining rooms, eat-in kitchen areas).
- ❑ Prevent children from using walls as part of their play schemes.

Ceilings

Ceilings are simple to inspect and a pain in the neck to work on. They are taken for granted unless they leak, sag, fall down, or are constructed of unusual materials.

CEILING INSPECTIONS

Stains

Ceiling stains near or beneath a bathroom can be caused by a variety of circumstances. They could simply be a plugged toilet or from someone letting a sink or bathtub run over. They could be from a deteriorated toilet floor gasket, or the behind-the-wall plumbing that services any of the bathroom's fixtures. If pipes are boxed inside the wall and can't be accessed, a contractor may have to cut a hole in the wall so the leak can be found and repaired. If that is the case, the hole should be covered by a panel that can be removed again in the future without cutting or damaging the wall.

On ceiling stains that develop below an attic, check for leaks in the attic plumbing. If an air conditioner has been installed in the attic, look for leaks around the condensation pan and drain line. On the other hand, perhaps someone just failed to close an attic window during a rainstorm.

Cobwebs

Cobwebs sound harmless, but they are not. They tend to collect airborne oil and other particles. Oily particles will then attract other airborne soils. Soon there is a considerable amount of dirt on the ceiling.

Other Items

Other items to look for include acoustical ceiling tiles made of asbestos (see the section on environmental factors), leaks, mildew, sagging, and cracks.

CEILING REPAIRS

Ceilings are difficult to work on because they are out of the typical person's reach.

Sagging

A sagging ceiling may signify loose wallboard or plaster and should be inspected more closely from above, or from an attic if possible. Sagging could be caused by a water leak above or behind the area in question. Water can travel along the house framework to areas surprisingly far away from the point of entry. Sometimes you have to observe what happens during an actual rain. Another common cause of sagging is loose, cracked, or missing caulking around bathtubs and showers.

Just because a portion of ceiling is sagging or bowed a little doesn't mean it *must* be repaired. But if it deteriorates to the point of falling down, and the material is plaster that has pulled away from a lath backing, you are usually better off having a contractor make the repairs. If the problem is with plasterboard or drywall, you can make the repairs by cutting out the damaged section and patching with new, then filling in the cracks with drywall tape and patching material. A coat of paint will further blend the repairs into the rest of the ceiling. Naturally, the leak or whatever else caused the cracks should be repaired.

Cracks

Cracks parallel to drywall joints are common and easy to repair. Just fill in and feather out the cracks with paintable flexible caulking or a drywall patching material. Touch up with paint.

Cracks perpendicular to each other, or at odd angles, can be more serious. If the cracks develop over a short period of time, try to find the reason for their appearance. Has the building shifted? Inspect the foundation. Have you had recent problems with drainage? Maybe you will find something obvious, something that can be fixed. On the other hand, maybe you will find no other problems. In that case, just fix the cracks, as described above.

Asbestos Tiles

Some acoustical ceiling tiles installed before 1976 contain asbestos. Asbestos fibers can harm your health if inhaled or ingested. Never sand, rip apart, or do anything else to cause dust from asbestos tiles to become airborne. Asbestos requires special handling and equipment to be contained or removed safely. Don't fool with it yourself. If you are unsure about tiles or similar materials, contact your local health regulatory agency. Again, see the section on asbestos.

CEILING MAINTENANCE

Wood ceilings and exposed beams need little maintenance other than occasional cobweb removal. Remember that cobwebs should be removed as soon as they are seen: they attract airborne dirt, tars from cigarette smoke, cooking greases and oils, and other cobwebs. Cover a long-handled broom head with a damp cloth or towel, and swish away. The webs will stick to the towel instead of just falling from the ceiling to the furnishings.

With wood ceilings, pay special attention to waterproofing whatever is above the ceiling, because even the slightest leak may cause permanent discoloration. Look at living spaces above your ceilings. Joints between bathroom walls and sinks, bathtubs, shower stalls, or other water appliances require caulking. Caulking is a simple, inexpensive method of moisture proofing that can save you hundreds or thousands of dollars in ceiling repairs.

If mildew and musty odors are a problem, spray with a solution of half bleach, half water. Be sure to wear safety goggles. Add a fungicide to a good quality ceiling paint. Check with your paint store for exact recommendations. Repaint the ceiling, then look at

increasing ventilation to affected rooms. In kitchens and bathrooms, install exhaust fans that vent moist air to the outdoors, not into the attic. In closets, elevate closet doors about an inch off the floor to allow additional air circulation.

CEILING SAFETY

Be careful with ladders. Whenever possible, work from the ground. Use implements with long handles. Wear safety goggles when cleaning or repairing ceilings, because whatever you dislodge from ceiling surfaces will likely fall straight down into your face. It is a good idea to use dropcloths to cover exposed carpeting and furnishings when you are working on a ceiling.

CEILING QUICK CHECKLIST

❑ Repair leaking roofs and fixtures.
❑ Block out and cover stains, including mildew.
❑ Remove cobwebs.
❑ If possible, correct sagging ceilings.
❑ Repair ceiling cracks, gouges, and missing sections of plaster.
❑ Replace asbestos acoustical tile and related materials in a manner that doesn't expose anyone to asbestos fibers and dust.

Lighting

Lighting is a feature proven to be extremely reliable and trouble-free. As long as you use correct wattages of bulbs or lamps in your fixtures, practically all that is ever needed is to change the bulbs when they fail.

But even though lighting is expected to be trouble free, it still makes sense to inspect it every so often, because electricity goes hand in hand with lighting, and that deserves attention.

LIGHTING INSPECTIONS

- Switches that sound, strange, won't stay in one position, work only when pushed to the end of their throw, double click, or feel warm or hot to the touch.
- Pull-chains that are frozen and won't work.
- Old-fashioned push-button and toggle switches. These should be replaced with modern types.
- Decorative globes or other units that enclose light bulbs must be removed to be cleaned. Inspect the globes for "overstamping" and cracks, which could lead to the globe falling from the ceiling someday. (See Figure 25-1.) Check the permissible wattage on each fixture—it is usually stamped somewhere on the fixture's body. Remove any bulbs of greater wattage than the fixture was designed for. The use of higher wattage bulbs may cause heat to build up in the fixture, which could result in a fire. Note any melted shades, scorching, or heat discoloration. If evidence of past or present overheating is found, do not use the fixture until an electrician checks it out.

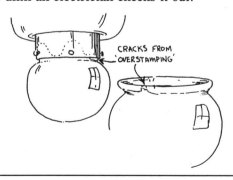

CRACKS FROM OVERSTAMPING

25-1. Cracked globes.

- Recessed lighting fixtures set into ceilings may also overheat if they protrude into an attic or a second floor where insulation has been packed around them. If you haven't already done an attic inspection, go to the attic and take a look. Fixtures set into ceilings below other living levels can only be inspected from below, by opening up the fixture. A properly installed recessed lighting fixture is surrounded by a sheet metal or wire cylinder vented so heat can escape, but nothing flammable should touch the fixture inside the sheet-metal or wire cylinder.
- If you notice that a light bulb flickers when turned on, it could be caused by a switch that is on its last legs. It may also be a problem with the light socket or the wiring between the switch and fixture. A constantly flickering light bulb needs investigating.

Of course, just because a light bulb flickers doesn't means there is something wrong with your system. It is more likely the bulb is wearing out, getting ready to fail. Maybe the bulb has gradually come loose from the socket. Tighten it, and if that doesn't work, try a new bulb.

If all the lights in a home flicker at the same time, it could be a sign of a brownout, or power problems at the utility company. In that case, other homes nearby will be affected. If your home is the only one with problems, there may be a defect or excessive wear in your main switch, in the main breakers, or in the incoming power link. Problems of this nature should be referred to the local utility company for inspection and recommendations for repairs.

If you notice your lights dimming when the clothes washer, dishwasher, garbage disposal, refrigerator, or other appliance is turned on, question the house power first. The temporarily lowered light level is usually a sign of an overloaded circuit.

LIGHTING REPAIRS AND MAINTENANCE

Unless you are formally trained or very experienced with electrical equipment, you are better off letting a licensed electrician make most lighting repairs, replacements, and new installations. These have to be done right.

The most important thing you can do is to be observant. Watch for trouble signs, flickering lights, fixtures or switches that get hot, increasingly loud humming sounds, circuits that blow out or don't act as they should.

LIGHTING SAFETY

Again, most of the dangers have to do with working with electrical circuits. See the section on electrical safety.

▪ The most important rule to live by is, before working on a lighting fixture of any kind, make sure the electrical supply is shut off to that fixture.

▪ Lighting is, in the first place, installed for our safety—so we can see when no natural light is available. Make sure everything that should be illuminated is. Stairways, hallways, entrances, basements, laundry rooms, garages, and workshops all need enough lighting for activities that go on in those locations.

▪ There is another option when it comes to lighting outdoor areas near gas grills, decks, patios, swimming pools, and hot tubs. Gas-powered lamps are both efficient and safe. They offer no shock hazards. Their non-glaring soft illumination is considered elegant and nostalgic by some, plus their yellow-spectrum light does not attract insects. A gas light will also provide security in the event of a power outage.

LIGHTING QUICK CHECKLIST

❑ Electrical switches and outlets should function exactly as they were designed to do.

❑ Recognize the bulb wattages at which individual fixtures are rated, and avoid overloading them with bulbs that are too powerful.

❑ Make sure recessed lighting fixtures are positioned within vented metal cylinders, cages, or protectors to shield surrounding insulation and construction materials from the fixture's heat.

❑ Before working on any lighting fixture, make sure the electrical supply to that fixture has been shut off.

❑ Consider gas-powered lamps for outdoor use, especially in areas where water is often present, such as near swimming pools and hot tubs.

Interior Doors

Interior doors operate in the same way as their exterior cousins, but they aren't exposed to the outdoors. So they needn't be *as* concerned with locking mechanisms, insulation qualities, and weatherproofing. However, interior doors are concerned with two major factors: privacy and noise reduction. To be effective, they must be well fitted.

If the house heating system depends on a free flow of air from room to room, interior doors should be undercut at least ½ inch above the finished floors to permit air passage. (See Figure 26-1.) This does not apply to doors bordering areas having their own air supply and return outlets or doors leading to any unheated areas such as garages, basements, and attics. The gaps around those doors should be weatherstripped.

26-1. An undercut door.

On the other hand, doors should not fit too tightly. You don't want door bottom edges to have to be forced open and closed over carpeting, or scratching vinyl flooring because the fit is so tight.

If you ever have to replace an interior door due to wear or remodeling, consider a solid-core flush door made of wood blocks or composition material formed into a solid piece. It provides greater security, better insulation of heat and sound, and more fire resistance and rigidity than hollow-core flush doors, which are constructed of veneered plywood with cores of wood cross braces or cardboard strips.

INTERIOR DOOR INSPECTIONS

- Loose hinges.
- Loose handles.
- Edge surfaces that stick between the door and jamb.
- Surfaces that are peeling, scratched, gouged, or otherwise damaged.
- Squeaky hinges.
- Doors that are not aligned properly.
- Locks that are tight or won't turn.
- Gaps around doors that lead to unheated areas such as garages, basements, and attics.
- Excessive humidity.

INTERIOR DOOR REPAIRS

Have the following tools and supplies ready when interior doors need repair or maintenance work:

Screwdrivers
Hammer
Pliers
Sandpaper
Wood glue
Light lubricating oil
Graphite

Tightening Loose Hinges

If door hinge screws are not holding, replace them one at a time with longer screws. Or insert a glue-covered sliver of wood about the size of a matchstick into the hole before putting the old screw back in. To work on the hinges, the door should be removed. Remove the bottom pivot pin first. If you take out the top pin first, the weight of the door may tear the bottom hinge loose.

Tightening a Rattling Door Knob

Loosen the door knob set screws. Remove the knob. Place a small piece of modeling clay in the knob. Push the door knob back on and tighten with the set screw. (See Figures 26-2a and 26-2b.)

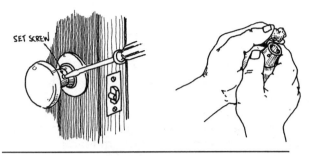

26-2a. Removing a door knob.
26-2b. Pressing clay into door knob.

Sticking Doors

Look for a shiny spot on the edge of the door that has been rubbed smooth from sticking. Open the door slowly to find the spot. Sand down the shiny spot a little at a time until the door opens and closes freely.

If the door or frame is badly out of shape, you might have to remove the door and cut or plane down the part that is fitting too tightly. Close the door and see if the top edge and the lock edge are even in the frame. If the crack in either area is uneven, or if it reveals a wedge of air, the fit is wrong. The door opening is probably not square.

Always paint or varnish parts of wood doors that have been sanded or planed. Paint and varnish or wood sealers protect wood from moisture and help to prevent additional problems. Sand the edges of the door before painting to prevent a paint buildup that can cause the door to stick. Moisture is most likely to enter a door through the door edges because the edges are most often not painted, varnished, or sealed at the time of installation.

To fix doors that have absorbed enough moisture to swell or warp, you will either have to wait until the weather gets less humid (so the door will dry out and revert to its previous dimensions), or the door will have to be removed and placed in a dry place until the swelling goes down. Never sand or plane a swollen door. A door that has warped too much to revert back to normal may have to be straightened by applying weights on the bulging parts while the door dries out.

Strike Plate Repairs

Strike plates are the metal inserts affixed to door frames to receive latching mechanisms from door knobs. When a door frame or door sags or warps, the latch in the door may travel across the strike plate without meeting the strike plate's hole. The door then cannot be closed all the way and will not latch securely. The strike plate should be removed and placed in a vise. With a file, enlarge the hole enough to ac-

commodate the latch. (See Figure 26-3.) If a bolt hole is also present in the strike plate, enlarge that as well. Before replacing the strike plate, chisel out the wood behind the enlarged holes to accept the latch and bolt.

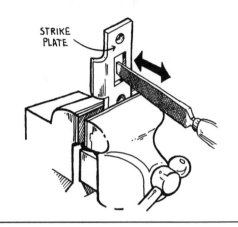

26-3. Enlarging a strike plate.

Repairing Scratches and Gouges

To repair scratches and gouges, fill them in with a crayon of stick shellac. Just rub the stick along the crack or gouge. Wipe off excess shellac. Blend into door by re-treating the surface with furniture polish or similar surface conditioners.

INTERIOR DOOR MAINTENANCE

- Paint or varnish wood sections that have been sanded or planed. This will seal the door and keep moisture from being absorbed by the wood. Make sure top and bottom edges are sealed.
- Keep interior humidity levels under control. Humidity can eventually cause doors to warp.
- On doors requiring a close fit to restrict the passage of air, especially on doors leading to unheated areas, install adhesive-backed foam insulation strips along the sides and top of the door frame. This will enable the door to work properly while fitting tightly. First, clean the door stop section of the frame. Remove any grease or dirt, then press the weatherstripping into place.
- Stop or prevent doors from squeaking by putting a few drops of lubricating oil at the top of each hinge. Open and close the door several times to work the oil into the hinge. If the squeaking persists, raise the hinge pins and add more oil. If the hinges still squeak, remove the hinge pivot pins. Dry them and sand off any rust. Coat the pins with paraffin wax, silicone spray, or graphite lubricant. Replace the pins.

- A lock that is too tight should be lubricated with graphite. All door locks should be lightly lubricated with graphite at least twice a year.
- Polish door knobs and other hardware at least once a year to help protect their finishes from tarnishing.

INTERIOR DOOR QUICK CHECKLIST

❑ Make sure hinges and other door hardware are firmly attached and work smoothly.

❑ Align doors correctly. Latches should engage their strike plate receptacles.

❑ Weatherstrip interior doors leading to unheated areas to prevent heat or cool air losses.

❑ Seal wood doors to prevent moisture absorption. Sand or plane and reseal sticking spots.

❑ Refinish or repair surface peeling, scratches, and gouges.

❑ Lubricate squeaky hinges.

❑ Lubricate locks twice a year.

❑ Keep doors clean.

❑ Keep the home's humidity level under control.

Wood Paneling and Trim

Prefabricated panels of wood and products that simulate wood are frequently used to cover walls because of the material's beauty, variety, ease of installation, and low-maintenance qualities.

A home without interior wood trim is like a shirt or blouse without a collar or sleeves. Trim gives the home's interior those finishing touches. It can be installed wherever different construction materials intersect: along joints, corners, door frames, windows, and other built-in house features.

Trim also has functional applications. It can tightly hold down edges of paneling, carpeting, and linoleum, and when placed in dining areas at chair-back height from the floor, it will prevent chairs from scraping the walls. (See Figure 27-1.)

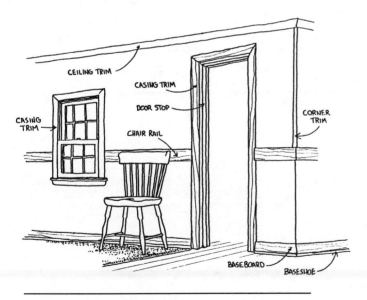

CEILING TRIM
CASING TRIM
DOOR STOP
CASING TRIM
CHAIR RAIL
CORNER TRIM
BASEBOARD
BASESHOE

27-1. Types of trim.

Wood paneling and trim are relatively maintenance free. Unless you have a home full of very active dart-throwing, finger painting, carving-their-initials-in-the-walls children, about the worst you can expect are a few scratches, dust and dirt, drying out of the wood, and gradual fading.

WOOD PANELING AND TRIM INSPECTIONS

- Scratches and gouges.
- Dust and dirt.
- A dull surface.
- Peeling paint.
- Loose pieces.

WOOD PANELING AND TRIM MAINTENANCE

- Scratches and gouges can be filled in with a crayon of stick shellac purchased in a color that closely matches your paneling or trim. Fill nail holes, scratches, gouges, and miter joints by rubbing the crayon back and forth over these imperfections. Wipe surplus shellac away with a clean cloth. Buff lightly and apply the same moisturizing wood polish that you use on the rest of the paneling or trim.

- Dust, dirt, fingerprints, and splashed materials can be removed with an all-purpose household cleaner or a commercial wood cleaner. Always test an inconspicuous spot first, to see if the cleaner has an undesirable effect on the wood. Wait until it dries before making the final judgment. Some paneling is treated at the factory to be stain resistant, but few people realize that. If you know who the supplier was, it would be helpful to find out the manufacturer's recommendations for care. Avoid using harsh abrasive cleansers. Overall, it is best to clean paneling and trim just as you would fine wood furniture.

- To prevent wood paneling and trim from drying out and discoloring, it should be treated with a moisturizing polish. Such a treatment will remove dust buildups and will protect the wood against drying, humidity, and other moisture damage. A good wood treatment will restore the appearance of the wood by helping bring out the natural color and grain, which may be several shades darker than the pre-application wood. There is a world of difference between paneling and trim that is allowed to dry out and collect dust, and paneling and trim that is regularly cared for.

▪ Trim that has been painted will need additional maintenance if the paint starts to flake or peel. It is usually much easier to remove trim before refinishing it. Be sure you keep track of which pieces go where. Once it is removed, fill cracks and gouges with wood putty before painting.

▪ Loose pieces of trim and paneling should be renailed or reglued, depending on whether the loose part is over a wall stud or joist. Use finishing nails closest in color to the woodwork. If a loose section of paneling is not over a stud or joist, panel cement or glue can be forced behind the loose piece. Hold a padded block against the repair—perhaps a piece of 2" x 6" board wrapped in a bath towel—and pound the block with a mallet while the glue is drying, to push the paneling tight against the wall.

ADDING PANELING TO A ROOM

If you are thinking about adding paneling to a room, consider the following points:

▪ The size of the room will shrink by the thickness of the furring and paneling used. Furring is strips of wood fastened to the walls to act as a support and nailing medium for the paneling's installation.

▪ Paneling that is dark-colored will make a room look smaller.

▪ Electrical outlets and wall switches often have to be moved forward to be level with the paneling's surface. Extended collars for electrical wall boxes are available for this purpose.

▪ Heating and air conditioning registers will also need to be moved or extended. Electric baseboard heaters will have to be removed and reinstalled.

▪ Door and window frames, baseboards, and ceiling moldings can be removed and trimmed to fit the new paneling, or new paneling can be cut to fit around the present trim.

WOOD PANELING AND TRIM QUICK CHECKLIST

❑ Keep paneling and trim clean.
❑ Limit the amount of direct sunlight that falls upon paneling, to reduce fading.
❑ Refasten loose and bowed pieces.
❑ Touch up scratches and gouges with stick shellac.
❑ Periodically treat paneling and natural wood trim with a moisturizing polish.
❑ Remove peeling or flaking trim. Repaint if desired, refinish to natural wood, or replace with stained natural wood trim.

Wood Flooring

Wood flooring has been around for centuries. It is available in hardwood and softwood varieties that can be used in almost every part of a house. Hardwoods have excellent wearing qualities. The most popular species are white and red oaks. Softwood floors are made from pine wood planks. Pine is a lot less expensive than oak, but does not wear as well. On the other hand, pine has a very attractive grain and will accept staining and sundry wood finishes for a variety of looks from rustic to modern.

Wood flooring is extremely durable when properly installed and maintained. The important thing to remember is that its surface pores remain sealed to keep out moisture and other foreign agents. A wood floor that has been sanded, sealed, and periodically resealed with protective layers of wax, shellac, varnish, lacquer, or hard polyurethane is a floor that will give many years of service. However, no finish is permanent—all of them must eventually be renewed. In between finishings, wood flooring needs little other special treatment. Minimal dusting and cleaning will keep it fresh looking.

WOOD FLOORING INSPECTIONS

- Shrinking appears as gaps between floorboards, which is more likely to happen with pine planks. It is caused by the wood drying out from lack of moisture in the air.
- Swelling is another humidity-related condition. But it can also be caused by direct water damage from leaking rainwater or a leaky plumbing fixture. It appears as warped, swollen, or buckling floorboards.
- Squeaking does not sound like a serious problem, but it can be very annoying to a home's occupants. It is usually caused by loose floorboards.
- Sagging is caused by too little support beneath the wood flooring, or by the floor being overloaded beyond its carrying capacity.
- Worn, peeling, stained, or otherwise damaged finishes can usually be made to look new again. Unlike badly damaged or worn carpeting or vinyl flooring, wood flooring can be refinished: the old

finish taken away and a new one put down.

WOOD FLOORING REPAIRS

Filling Gaps

Gaps of up to ½ inch or more between boards can be filled in with wedge-shaped fillets or pieces of any available wood, preferably of the same type and color. Make sure the thick edge of the wedge is slightly larger than the gap it will fill. Pound in the fillet, using a block of scrap wood. Once all of the large cracks have been filled, the floor should be sanded or planed smooth and refinished. Plank shrinking can be kept to a minimum through the use of a penetrating finish absorbed by the wood. It usually takes several coats to seal off the wood's surface and protect it from moisture.

Warped or Swollen Flooring

To repair warped or swollen flooring, you may be able to level the floor by drying the wood as much as possible with a dehumidifier. Then nail the boards through and all the way into the floor joists, or fasten them from below, with wood screws, to the subfloor they are laid upon.

For swelling that cannot be reduced enough with drying, the affected planks will have to be removed and replaced. This problem is more likely to occur with narrow tongue-and-groove boards than with wide planks. A long-term solution includes better ventilation in the area, both below and above the wood floor.

Squeaky Flooring Repairs

To repair squeaky flooring, if the boards have been surface nailed, make sure all the nails are hammered at least flush with the surface of the floor. Many carpenters say it is better to set the nail heads a little below the surface, using a nail set or punch to avoid making hammer marks or "moons" in the flooring.

If the floor is not surface nailed, you can still try nailing at the squeaking point anyway. Drive two nails at opposing angles and make sure they reach well into the joist below. Set the nails and fill the holes with plastic wood to match the floor.

Another potential cure is to wedge the floor from underneath if you can get to it. Drive wedges between the squeaking boards and the joists on which they rest. (See Figure 28-1.) Other things to try include squirting powdered graphite or talcum powder between the offending floorboards, or, with first-floor squeaking, by screwing into the squeaking boards from below, and drawing them tightly to the subfloor.

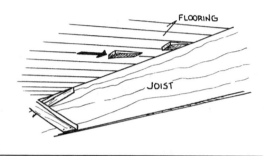

28-1. Wedging a squeaky floorboard.

Sagging

Sagging can be repaired more easily when it occurs on a first floor. The entire set of joists can be jacked up slowly, no more than ½ inch per week, to allow everything to rise gradually without exerting sudden, potentially damaging strain on the rest of the structure. It is probably best to get help from a builder who has had previous experience with adjusting the structural members of a floor.

When sagging occurs to an upper floor and it is not possible to erect an adjusting post beneath it, the only possibility is to install new or additional support joists. That means ripping out ceilings and doing major restoration work. If that sounds like more effort than it is worth to you, try rearranging the furniture in affected rooms so there is as little weight as possible over the sagging areas.

Refinishing Floors

Floors with bare, damaged, or worn surfaces should be refinished. Unless you are familiar with wood floor finishing and all of the sanding, scraping, and other tasks involved, you are better off to have it done by someone who makes a living working with floors.

Sanding floors is something that has to be done so infrequently, it is worth doing right. If a floor needs very little preparation, and you opt to do it yourself, fine. But just as a precaution, have someone with professional knowledge go over your plans—what finish

you plan on using, and what equipment you plan to use to complete the job. Should the bare wood be stained first? Is polyurethane the right choice? Make certain you also understand how to maintain the floor afterwards; for instance, that polyurethane requires no waxing.

Also consider that you don't have to remove an entire finish before you recoat a floor. If the finish hasn't been worn down to bare wood and is free of wax and grease buildup, you may be able to get away just sanding with 100-grit or finer sandpaper, vacuuming, wiping, and recoating with whatever type of finish was previously used. In fact, most floors can stand to be recoated up to six times before complete removal is needed.

Be careful not to overlook boards that have cupped or buckled slightly above the floor's surface. Such protruding edges could trip a visitor. Boards with unevenly worn edges can give slivers to bare feet. Such offending planks should be sanded and refinished, or replaced.

WOOD FLOORING MAINTENANCE

Vacuum and damp mop or dust mop weekly or whenever needed. Vacuuming is preferred because it will pick up dirt and grit not only from the surface of the boards, but from the crevices and seams as well. Damp mops should be damp only, not wet, and they can only be used on finished floors. Avoid damp mopping of an unfinished floor because moisture will be drawn into unsealed wood. If there is only dust on the floor, a dry dust mop will work well. It should be treated with dust mop spray to better attract and hold the dust. Varnished, shellacked, waxed, and oiled wood flooring should never be washed. In fact, no wood flooring benefits from sloshing a lot of water and soapsuds on its surface. Water can cause the wood grain to rise and, through frequent soakings, may cause cracks from expansion and contraction cycles.

Wax or surface-treat wood flooring before it really needs it. That is the key to a beautiful wood floor. Never let it get out of shape. A floor that receives moderate wear needs waxing only two or three times a year. The best wax is a "spirit" wax, either liquid or paste. Avoid "self-polishing" water-based waxes. Wax can be buffed or polished most easily with an electric floor polisher that can be rented at a neighborhood hardware store or supermarket. It is worth the effort. When applying the wax, go lightly near the wall baseboards. Little traffic occurs there and you will minimize wax buildup and extend periods between removal.

If you want to be sure that a floor has been waxed, scrape near the walls for evidence of wax buildup. Or apply a few drops of ammonia and let it stand; if it turns white, wax is present.

Occasionally, old floor wax will have to be removed so a fresh, thin coat can be applied. Wood floor cleaners are available at hardware stores, paint stores, and builder's supply stores. Follow their directions to remove the old wax and dirt.

The most critical wear areas on a wood floor are the home's traffic lanes, near doors for example. Those are the places that wear first. The traffic lanes will need more attention than the rest of the flooring. On moderately soiled floors where traffic is not heavy, cleaning and polishing can be done in the same operation with new clean-and-wax products.

If the wood floors are near entrances, make sure you position entry mats at each entrance. Entry mats will help remove soil tracked into a home on people's shoes.

Remove spots and stains as soon as possible. White rings can be removed by dampening a soft cotton cloth with equal parts of ammonia or turpentine and linseed oil. You can also use camphor spirits. Rub the spot lightly. To remove black heel marks or marks left by furniture casters, rub with No. 00 steel wool dampened with mineral spirits (squeezed nearly dry). Then apply fresh wax, blending the area into the surrounding floor. Buff the area by hand, with a clean cotton cloth. To remove oil and grease stains, saturate a gauze pad with hydrogen peroxide and place it over the stain. Saturate a second pad with ammonia and place it over the first. Wait about fifteen minutes, then inspect the results. Repeat if necessary. Apply fresh wax to the affected area after you wipe it clean and let air-dry.

To remove persistent stains, cross-sand the stained area, then sand with the grain. Heavy stains may need to be bleached. Deep discolorations caused by water damage or pet urine may require board replacement or coverage with a dark wood stain.

Touch up scratches and gouges with a crayon of stick shellac. Just pencil it in across the imperfection. Wipe away excess material, polish with a clean rag, apply wax, and blend the repair into the surrounding floor, buffing by hand or with a machine.

Watch what you allow on your floor. If you have a household full of young children, perhaps it would be best to put large area rugs or carpets down on fine hardwood floors, or to restrict their milk and juice drinking to the kitchen and dining room.

WOOD FLOOR SAFETY

On the negative side, wood floors are hard and noisy, and they can get very slippery when wet. Babies, young children, and elderly people should be steered to carpeted areas if possible.

Any way you look at it, stripping old finishes from wood floors is a messy business. It takes either the application of horrible-smelling chemical strippers, or enough power sanding to create a dust storm. In either case, you will need to protect your lungs and eyes from fumes, splashes, and dust. With liquid strippers, the floor will get extremely slippery, so keeping your balance, especially while operating a power buffer, can be quite a challenge. The safest way to proceed is to do it in an orderly manner, attacking small portions at a time, finishing one section before going to the next. Wear rubber gloves when handling the strippers, and see that there is enough ventilation in the area so fumes don't become concentrated. Wear shoes with sure-grip soles.

WOOD FLOORING QUICK CHECKLIST

- ☐ Keep wood floors sealed to protect them from moisture.
- ☐ Vacuum and clean frequently with a dry dust mop treated with dust mop oil. Damp mopping (damp, not wet) should be done only on well-sealed floors.
- ☐ Avoid using wet mops or sudsy water. The less moisture a wood floor sees, the better.
- ☐ Try to maintain consistent levels of humidity in rooms with wood floors.
- ☐ Correct ailments such as wide gaps between planks, warped or swollen flooring, sagging, and squeaking.
- ☐ Refinish worn, peeling, stained, or otherwise damaged surfaces.
- ☐ Wax or surface-treat wood flooring *before* it really needs it.
- ☐ Place entry mats at entrances to rooms having wood floors.
- ☐ Remove spot- and stain-causing materials from wood flooring as soon as possible. Treat spots and stains right away.
- ☐ Touch up scratches and gouges with stick shellac.
- ☐ Use sound safety practices when refinishing wood floors.

Tile and Vinyl/Linoleum Flooring

Tile flooring is exceptionally durable when correctly installed. It withstands wear and tear well, comes in a huge variety of shapes, colors, and composition, and works wonders in areas of a home likely to encounter water or other liquids, such as bathrooms and kitchens. The tile itself is practically maintenance free. The main drawback from a maintenance point of view is that grouted joints are susceptible to cracking, crumbling, staining, and mildew.

Vinyl/linoleum floorings are easy to maintain, and should have very few seams. They are used in the same kinds of places you will find tile, and then some. If not abused, vinyl/linoleum flooring will give years and years of trouble-free service.

TILE FLOOR INSPECTIONS

- Cracked, loose, or missing tiles. (See Figure 29-1.) In addition to being unsightly, damaged tile flooring—in areas where water and other liquids are splashed on the floor—can lead to moisture seepage and decay of wood structural members located beneath the floor. If loose tiles are allowed to stay that way, they can cause adjoining tiles to follow suit.

29-1. Damaged tiles.

- Soiled or stained tiles are usually simple to clean, but like any stains, the earlier you get to them, the better.
- Missing grout is a serious problem. It will allow water and other liquids to get behind the tiles, where it can seep through and undermine the integrity of adjacent tiles and flooring beneath.
- Stained grout is more an annoyance than a serious problem, but stained grout can turn a beautiful glazed floor covering into an ugly mess.
- Mildew traditionally occurs in bath areas, especially showers. It thrives on spatters of body oils and soils, shampoos, and hair conditioners in the warm, moist, dark confines of poorly ventilated showers.

TILE FLOOR REPAIRS

As mentioned above, the actual tiles are likely to last many years without problems. You are more likely to have difficulties with the grout or cement holding the tiles in place. On the other hand, it is not a bad idea to have a handful of spare tiles available, just in case. Some tiles are "one set of a kind," from a place such as Spain or Italy or Greece. You may lose touch of where they were purchased, or they may just be unavailable. If you can find duplicate tiles, try to obtain a few to have on hand for future repairs. Tools needed for tile repairs include:

> Tile adhesive for the kind of tile you have
> Old paintbrush or putty knife
> Utility knife or small saw
> Grout for ceramic or plastic tile
> New tiles, if required

To Replace Ceramic or Plastic Tiles
1. Scrape off the old adhesive from the floor or wall and from the old tiles, if you plan to reuse them.
2. If you have to cut pieces of tile to fit, mark them carefully to the right size and shape. Cut plastic tiles with a thin-toothed saw. Make straight cuts on ceramic tile by scoring them first with the saw, then snapping pieces off by pressing the scored lines against the edge of a hard surface.

Practice both methods on pieces of scrap tile before attempting to cut tile you plan to install.

3. Spread adhesive on the wall or floor and on the back of the tile. Follow the adhesive manufacturer's directions exactly.

4. Press the tile firmly in place.

5. Joints on ceramic tile should be filled with grout after the adhesive has set. Mix grout powder with water to form a stiff paste. Follow the manufacturer's instructions. Press the grout mixture into the joints with an applicator or with your fingers. Smooth the surface and carefully remove excess grout from the tile surface before the grout dries.

   If you need to buy additional grout for replacement, consider the following improvements in grout formulation that are available in today's modern formulas:

   ▪ Grout comes in many colors to coordinate or contrast with any tile scheme.

   ▪ Latex additives make grout more flexible, more stain-resistant, and more moisture-resistant than ever.

   ▪ Epoxy grouts are more expensive than others, but are practically maintenance free; they are well worth the investment for use in a busy food preparation area.

6. Let grout dry overnight before it gets wet again.

TILE FLOOR MAINTENANCE

Keep the tile clean. Glazed or ceramic tile normally needs only a wipe with a damp cloth or mop, or an occasional wet mopping to stay clean and new-looking. A solution of white vinegar and water in equal amounts will remove most soil deposits, but test the mixture first on some inconspicuous part of the tile to make sure the vinegar does not etch the tile or erode the grout. Vinegar can damage some fine crystalline tile glazes. If necessary, a more thorough cleaning with a ceramic tile cleaner will remove most stains and grime. To remove particularly heavy accumulations of soil, you may need a stiff brush and a mild scouring powder cleanser.

Tile in bath areas is subject to frequent use. The simplest long-term maintenance tip is not to let surface soil build up. Regular care does the trick. The easiest way to keep a tiled shower wall clean is simply to wipe it down with a towel after each use. That way, soap scum, hard water film, and mildew won't develop. Once it gets dirty, though, use an all-purpose cleaner where deposits of soap scum, body oils, and hard water stains have accumulated. The cleaner should be applied and allowed to stand for about five minutes

before you scrub the area with a sponge. Use the same procedure for tile floors, except try a brush instead of the sponge. Nylon scrubbing pads may also be helpful. Avoid steel wool as part of a general cleanup if possible, to prevent discoloring the tile and grout with rust stains. Small spots can be removed with fine *stainless* steel wool, a material that won't leave ugly stains.

Routine wiping with a clean, damp sponge or towel will also maintain the brightness of tile vanity tops, walls, and floors.

Staining agents should be mopped up promptly, even though they rarely affect glazed tile. Grape juice or ink or some other notorious liquid could eventually work its way into tiny cracks in the grout, where it can cause difficulties in removal.

Keep the grout clean. Grout is more susceptible to soil and staining than tile is. Grout joints are more porous and absorb dirt more readily. Grout will even absorb dirt from soiled cleaning solutions as the surrounding tile is washed. Grout can be cleaned by scrubbing the joints with an abrasive scouring cleanser and rinsing thoroughly. Heavy stains can be removed by leaving a paste of the cleanser on the soiled area overnight before regular cleaning methods are used. There are also commercial grout cleaners available. Mildew can be removed with an application of half bleach, half water. Scrub with a fiber brush and let dry without rinsing.

After the grout has been cleaned and dried, grout joints should be treated with grout sealer to help them fight soil and stains. Acrylic joint sealers for this purpose are available at hardware or builder's supply stores. Apply three coats of sealer to the grout, allowing each coat to dry for one hour before applying the next. Use a small paint brush to avoid getting grout sealer on the tiles. Clean excess sealer from tiles with denatured alcohol. Once grout has been coated with an acrylic sealer, avoid using cleaners with ammonia for your general tile cleaning, because the ammonia may have an adverse effect on the acrylic coatings.

VINYL/LINOLEUM FLOORING REPAIRS

Some vinyl/linoleum flooring comes in flexible tile form. To replace flexible tiles:

1. Apply a warm iron over a towel to the face of tiles to be replaced. The warmth will help soften the adhesive and make the tiles easier to remove.

2. Scrape the old adhesive off the floor or wall, and also from the tiles, if you are reusing them.

3. Fit tiles carefully. Most can be cut with a utility knife. Some more rigid tiles, made out of asphalt, will have to be cut with a saw. The rigid tiles will be less likely to break when warmed.

4. Apply adhesive on the floor or wall with a paint brush or putty knife. Wait until adhesive begins to set before placing the tiles.

5. Butt one side of the new tile against the edge of an adjacent tile, gently curving the tile as it is lowered into place. Press the tile firmly, using a rolling pin if necessary. Place weights on the tiles overnight to hold them flat while the adhesive sets up.

If water seeps under vinyl/linoleum, the edges will come loose and begin to curl. (See Figure 29-2.) Dry out the area and work adhesive under the loose edges. Pile on weights. (See Figure 29-3.) Clean excess adhesive. Let set overnight.

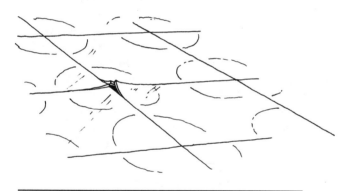

29-2. Curled vinyl/linoleum.

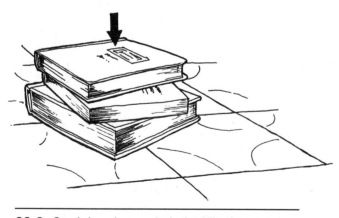

29-3. Straightening curled vinyl/linoleum.

To repair a blister in vinyl flooring, slit the blister lengthwise with a utility knife or single-edge razor blade. Try to follow a line in the flooring pattern to make the slit less conspicuous. Extend the cut about half an inch beyond each end of the blister. Place a

clean, dry cloth or some aluminum foil over the spot and heat the flooring with a warm iron to soften it. Force a liberal amount of adhesive under both sides of the slit blister with a putty knife. Press or flatten with a rolling pin. Place an old book or other weight on the repair and let it set overnight.

Small tears and holes in vinyl/linoleum flooring can be repaired with a homemade color-matching compound. Use a utility knife to scrape the surface of a spare piece of the same flooring if you have some. If not, scrape the surface of material from an inconspicuous location, such as the back corner of a closet. Build up the small hole or tear by adding the floor shavings to a drop or two of clear nail polish. Mix on the hole or tear with a toothpick. Let dry.

Large tears and holes must be patched. A damaged tile can be replaced with either a spare tile or one removed from an inconspicuous location. If you remove an undamaged tile to use as a replacement in a highly used area, buy a new tile to fill the space, even if it doesn't match exactly. It won't matter much when at the back of a closet.

VINYL/LINOLEUM FLOORING MAINTENANCE

1. Keep it clean. Use water sparingly with mild cleansers. When the floor is dry, apply wax in a thin, even coating. Never use harsh abrasives, except very fine stainless steel wool for the removal of stubborn spots. Even if the flooring says it is "no-wax," the finish will probably eventually wear to a point where a coating of wax will help.

2. Try to keep sharp objects away from the flooring. Never walk on it with your golf spikes. Keep children with ballpoint pens from poking the floor's surface.

3. Be careful when you move appliances on the flooring. When moving a heavy oven or refrigerator, consider placing a thick bath towel beneath the appliance, and sliding it away or toward the wall. It only takes one wrong furniture or equipment move to catch and destroy a vinyl floor.

TILE AND VINYL/LINOLEUM FLOORING SAFETY

▪ Both tile and vinyl/linoleum flooring can be very slippery when wet. Watch your footing.
▪ Putty knives, scrapers, utility knives, and other scraping and cutting instruments will cut flesh and bone in addition to tile.
▪ Chemical adhesive removers can produce strong

fumes. If you use them to remove tile cement residues, make sure you provide adequate ventilation. Open windows and doors. Run the air conditioning.

▪ Wear gloves and safety glasses with side shields, or goggles, while sawing and breaking tiles to custom-fit your application.

TILE AND VINYL/LINOLEUM FLOORING QUICK CHECKLIST

❑ Repair or replace cracked, loose, or missing tiles.
❑ Repair blistered, ripped, gouged or loose vinyl/linoleum flooring.
❑ Keep tiles, grout, and vinyl/linoleum flooring clean. Don't let soil build up.
❑ Treat grout joints with grout sealer.
❑ Remove stains and mildew as soon as possible.

Carpeting

Carpeting is a great idea. It is relatively inexpensive and easy to install. It can give a room a rich, modern look, or the appearance of something cool, clean, and clinical. It can create moods, deaden sounds, provide warmth, and offer padding for small children who can tumble and fall on it without scraping their knees.

On the other hand, carpeting can also show various stains and soils. Chewing gum, grease, ink, and numerous foods and beverages can become embedded and absorbed in carpeting yarn tufts. Static electricity can build up in its fibers, and so, unfortunately, can pet odors.

CARPETING INSPECTIONS

To inspect carpeting, just use your senses. Touch, smell, and look.

- Spots and stains. Entire books have been written on the hundreds of different common spots and stains a carpet can receive, and how to take them out. Spots are concentrated substances that have recently spilled onto a carpet. They haven't had time to soak in and set for a long time, and can be cleaned with general-purpose spot removers or shampoos. Stains have had a long time to soak in, saturate, and dry on the carpet fibers. They are a lot tougher to remove.
- Rips and holes. Picture a brand new wall-to-wall carpet in a large living room. A brand new puppy gets loose. The puppy chews up a good square foot of carpeting and is sitting there, wagging his tail, tufts of yarn still in his mouth, when his owner enters the room. Indeed, sometimes a new carpet will receive damage that just can't be overlooked.
- Unravelings. Sharp things have a way of catching in carpets and pulling fibers loose and out.
- Damage from furniture. Carpet pile that is beneath heavy furniture legs for 365 days a year will eventually get crushed past the point of repair.
- Loose carpeting. Is the carpeting taut or loose? Carpet that is loosely installed is nothing but

trouble. It poses a safety hazard and will not wear or clean as it should.
- Soil. If soil is allowed in the house, it will get on the carpets. Much of it comes in on the bottom of people and pet feet. Some soiling, however, comes from airborne cooking oil and grease particles, cigarette smoke, and other hard-to-prevent materials.
- Odors. Enter the puppy again. Cats and dogs are the biggest violators. Urine is especially troublesome.
- Wet spots. Carpeting installed in basements or other low-lying areas can be subject to moisture which can, in turn, cause rust stains and fungal growth.
- Are entrance floor mats present? Entry mats will remove a substantial portion of tracked-in soil before it reaches the home's carpeting. Naturally, the mats must be cleaned periodically, or they themselves will become a source of dirt. Entry mats should be large enough to allow both shoes to come into contact with the mat. You might want to consider two types of mats: plastic mats for winter and wet weather, and tufted nylon or olefin mats with rubber or vinyl backing for the rest of the year.

CARPETING REPAIRS

Carpeting repairs depend on what's wrong and where the damage is. If it is that square foot of brand new carpeting in the middle of your living room, your best bet is to have whoever did the installation make the repairs. If there is a section of indoor-outdoor carpeting that needs to be reglued in the laundry room, go ahead and do it yourself.

Most of the attention needed by carpets falls into the category of maintenance.

CARPETING MAINTENANCE

1. Vacuum carpeting at least once a week. Use a regular upright vacuum with a beater bar for best results. You don't need an elaborate one that will

play gin rummy with you when the cleaning is done, just a standard upright vacuum with at least a 6 amp motor. It is nice to have an extra-long cord, too. Never allow the vacuum cleaner bag to become more than two-thirds full, or you will lose considerable picking-up ability. Replace vacuum beater-bar brushes before they wear out completely. Vary your pattern of sweeping from time to time. Occasionally vacuum against the grain of the pile to remove the greatest amount of dirt and to help raise the carpet's nap and restore its springiness.

There are generally two kinds of soils in a carpet: dry soils and oily soils. Vacuuming removes most of the dry soils, but does not work well on the oily soils — soils from cooking vapors, air pollution, cigarette smoke, and greasy dirt that is tracked into the home by people and pets. The dry soil, if left in the carpet, acts as tiny pieces of grit that grind and cut against the fibers. The oily soils, if left in the carpet, attract more soil to themselves, and cause the color of the carpet to become gradually duller and darker.

2. Clean spots as quickly as possible. Carpet-cleaning companies say there are four basic categories of spots:

▪ Water-soluble. Luckily, these are the most common. They include substances such as ketchup, ice cream, mud, and maple syrup.

▪ Oil-based. Motor oil, oil paints, grease, cooking oils, nail polish, household cement, and various glues.

▪ Non-soluble. These are from soils that cannot be dissolved with any medium. Sand, grit, plastic particles, dust, and similar materials must be vacuumed from carpet fibers.

▪ Problem spots. These are the nasty, tricky ones — urine, vomit, blood, eggs, gravy, milk. Many have various animal proteins in them, which, if not immediately cleaned, will have to be treated with a chemical "digester" for complete removal.

In the typical household, a good carpet spot cleaner should be kept on hand. Obtain one recommended by a local janitorial supply company, and follow the product recommendations carefully. Here are some helpful spot removal hints:

▪ Always test cleaning solutions and powders on small, inconspicuous carpet areas for possible fiber damage or dye color changes, especially when using a solvent-based cleaner.

▪ Avoid over-wetting. If too much cleaning solution or water is added to a carpet, a larger stain may result than the one you are trying to remove.

▪ Never rub a spot or stain. Always blot. Work from the outside edges of the spot toward the center so you won't spread the spot. Blot with clean, white absorbent materials such as paper towels, napkins, or tissues. You can press down hard, just don't rub the surface vigorously.

▪ For stains that have set and dried already, treat and let the cleaner stand longer for better removal.

▪ A wet/dry carpet vacuum cleaner, while not necessary, can be a great help in removing many spots. Put on the attachment that gives the greatest suction and vacuum as much of the staining material as possible. Add a little water to the spot as you continue to vacuum. If detergent is required, use it sparingly. After removing the spot, rinse by slowly pouring water into the carpet pile as you work the vacuum wand to remove all detergent.

▪ Always dry an area affected by spot removal as soon as possible. A wet carpet will attract soil. Place towels or tissues over a wet or damp area and weight them down with canned goods or other heavy items. Once most of the moisture is absorbed, point a small electric fan toward the affected area to complete the drying.

▪ Certain spots might return after you thought they were gone. This happens when the spot-producing substance is dissolved by the cleaner or water and consequently sinks to the base of the carpet, out of sight. The blotting removed most of the material, but traces still left can migrate to the top of the carpet pile as the fibers dry. Just repeat the same spot-cleaning process, with more emphasis on blotting.

▪ If what you try doesn't work, call a janitorial supply company and ask for advice over the phone.

3. Keep entry mats at every entrance. Again, this point cannot be stressed enough. According to carpet-cleaning companies, about 70 percent of soil on carpeting is tracked into the house from foot traffic. This can be greatly reduced by placing entry mats — commercial quality mats made of nylon or olefin fibers on rubber backing — at each entrance.

Remember that the mats must be kept clean or you will defeat their purpose. But it is better to clean soil from a built-to-last mat than from your living room wall-to-wall carpet.

4. Do periodic maintenance cleaning. This is a step beyond vacuuming. It means either bonnet cleaning, surface extraction, or dry/absorbent powder cleaning.

▪ Bonnet cleaning uses a floor machine resembling a buffer that spins a revolving bonnet pad. It "polishes" the carpet clean by agitating medium-levels of soil and drawing them out of the carpet with the pad and various shampoos and chemical sprays. This is best done by someone who performs such work routinely, such as a janitorial contractor.

▪ Surface extraction uses equipment that will at the same time shoot a hot-water soap solution into the carpet, agitate the fibers, and vacuum the dirty solution back out. Many of the carpet cleaning machines for rent at supermarkets, carpet stores, and rental companies are surface-extraction machines. They are fairly easy to use but not foolproof. There is always the possibility of overwetting a carpet, which can, in some cases, ruin it. There are also safety concerns with lifting and using equipment you are not familiar with.

▪ Dry/absorbent powder cleaning uses a machine that brushes and beats the carpet so an absorbent powder can work its way into the fibers. To a certain extent, dry carpet cleaning can be accomplished with your regular upright vacuum. It may require more expensive cleaners (the dry/absorbent powder) and more time than the two previous methods, but there is less chance of making a mistake.

NOTE: Ultrasonic cleaning is another method that is gaining support. It is a wet shampoo or extraction method where a carpet-cleaning head vibrates at ultrasonic speeds for efficient mechanical agitation. Because no brushes beat against the fibers, it is easier on the carpet.

In addition to vacuuming all household carpeting at least once a week, you should perform or arrange one of the above maintenance cleaning methods at least twice per year on the rooms that receive the most traffic and soil. Perhaps upstairs bedrooms will need it only once every five years. You will have to judge based on your situation.

5. Deep extraction or restorative cleanings are recommended only if a carpet is very soiled. These cleanings should be done by professionals familiar with carpet conditions and the cleaning chemicals, equipment, and methods required for attempts at restoring a carpet to its original condition.

6. Keep up with minor carpet maintenance tasks:
▪ Clip snagged fibers off with scissors, don't pull.
▪ Minor burns can be clipped with curved fingernail scissors.
▪ Move furniture an inch or two every week so it doesn't always push down on the same fibers.
▪ Moldings and thresholds that hold carpeting down

must be kept firmly in place.
▪ Loose carpeting should be restretched and fastened down so it is tight. Consider having this done by professionals. At the same time, they might be able to reverse or rotate the carpet to put less-worn carpeting where travel patterns are heavier.
▪ Odors that do not come out with spot removal and maintenance cleaning should be referred to a janitorial contractor. You can also try carpet deodorizers. Odors in a carpet usually come from spilled materials or from bacteria within the material. Some deodorizers are little more than perfumes. Look for deodorizers that contain germicides or mildew attackers that will kill the bacteria that causes the odors.
▪ Moisture problems must be taken care of at their source. Carpeting exposed to continuous moisture will not be comfortable or practical in those conditions.
▪ Keep pets under control. If you won't banish them to the backyard, at least keep them clean and brushed.
▪ Change filters in your heating and air conditioning systems frequently. That is a cheap way of achieving an environment that is cleaner and easier on both you and the carpeting.

Remember, it is a lot easier to perform preventive maintenance on carpeting than it is to clean spots, stains, and ground-in soil.

CARPETING SAFETY

One of the main drawbacks to carpeting is its tendency to permit static electricity to build up within its fibers during the winter months when humidity levels in a home are much lower than normal. Most people have had the feeling of reaching to turn on a brass lamp and ZZZAPPP! a painful shock to the fingers. It may sound funny, but it could cause a serious problem to children or seniors, and especially seniors with heart ailments. The shock is caused by completing a circuit between the static electricity in the carpet and the conductive material of the lamp.

Preventive measures include the use of anti-static agents that can be applied to carpeting every other month or so. The trouble with this measure is that the same application will render the carpeting less resistant to soil. Treated carpeting will, in fact, tend to attract more soil. Another partial solution is to place light circuits and the controls of other electronic appliances on remote control devices.

If static electricity is a major consideration, be aware that most carpet manufacturers are now producing "no-shock" carpeting that has woven through its yarn tufts enough metal fibers to dissipate static electricity. You can't tell the difference by look or by feel.

Conflicting studies and reports have recently been issued on the possible emissions of hazardous substances from carpeting, especially new carpeting. To reduce those possibilities, make sure that there is adequate ventilation in your home through your heating and cooling systems, windows, and screens.

CARPETING QUICK CHECKLIST

❑ Remove spots and stains as quickly as possible.
❑ Repair rips, holes, and unravelings.
❑ Periodically move heavy furniture a few inches to give carpet indentations from furniture legs a chance to snap back.
❑ Re-lay loose carpeting. Tighten it down.
❑ Use entry mats at each entrance of a home to reduce tracked-in soil.
❑ Avoid getting carpeting soaking wet. Dry carpeting that has been accidentally soaked by vacuuming with a wet/dry vacuum or by setting up portable fans that will circulate air over wet areas.
❑ Vacuum carpeting at least once per week; more if necessary.
❑ Shampoo, surface extract, ultrasonic clean, or dry vacuum frequently used carpeting at least twice per year.
❑ Restorative cleaning is required only when a carpet is very soiled.
❑ Keep up with minor carpet maintenance tasks: trim snagged fibers, refasten loose moldings and trim, pick large items out of the carpet by hand.
❑ Use a deodorizer if needed.
❑ Try to keep pets out of carpeted rooms. At the very least, restrict the living and dining rooms from their use.

Basement Floors

The times of dirt floors in basements are long gone. Today any basement worth its salt is made of concrete. It is either a simple floor poured within the foundation and basement walls, or it is part of a solid slab that a house without a basement is constructed upon—in actuality, then, the first floor.

BASEMENT FLOOR INSPECTIONS

If the basement has been finished off, if it has carpeting or other floor coverings, the inspection is more difficult to complete. Generally, if there is no evidence of moisture or heaving, you needn't take up the carpet or flooring. If you are going to have carpeting, a thin carpet—of the indoor/outdoor type rather than a thick shag or velour plush — is better because thicker carpet can hide floor deficiencies. Bare floors are easily inspected. Check for:

- Plugged drains. Drainage is the most important feature of a basement floor. Floor drains should be able to prevent water from a burst pipe, a blown water heater, a malfunctioning sump pump, or other source from collecting in a basement. Run water from a garden hose down floor drains to test drain-carrying capacities.
- A wet basement. Keep an eye out for any metal equipment in the basement that develops heavy rust: a furnace, washing machine, dryer, or humidifier, for example. Rust is a sign of excessive humidity.
- A dull, porous surface.
- Cracks. With houses built on a one-piece slab, heaving may cause the slab to crack on a vertical or horizontal plane. Affected sections can tilt or lift out of line.

Although hairline cracks are common in any concrete structure, cracks wider than $1/8$ inch or cracks that are out of vertical or horizontal alignment by more than the same amount should be analyzed further by a building inspector or engineer. Trace cracks to see if they enter the foundation or basement walls, and look outside as well.

Be aware that radon can enter a house through holes and cracks in the foundation and floor. It collects in the highest concentrations toward the lowest places in the home, usually the basement. Radon levels can be minimized by sealing lower cracks and openings including where pipes and conduit come through the floor.

- Spalled or flaked concrete.
- Heaved or sunken sections.

BASEMENT FLOOR REPAIRS

See the section on concrete driveway repairs.

BASEMENT FLOOR MAINTENANCE

See also the section on concrete driveway maintenance.

- Neatly store belongings off the basement floor on shelves or in cabinets. This will allow quick, efficient cleaning of the floor.
- Use drain cleaners if the floor drains are sluggish or plugged. Or use your garden hose with a nozzle on high pressure to blast through debris. If all else fails, contract a drain cleaning company to get the job done.
- If you have a sump pump that keeps water from rising to floor level, service the unit according to the manufacturer's operating manual.
- If you have a wet or damp basement, you can patch cracks with hydraulic cement, a quick-setting compound sold at paint and hardware stores. Hydraulic cement expands when it contacts water. It can even be used to plug a hole while water is seeping through. Just follow the manufacturer's directions. Use a dehumidifier to help dry the basement air, walls, and floor.
- It is best to keep metal equipment off the basement floor. The ideal arrangement is to pour a concrete base about 4 inches thick on which to set the furnace, water heater, or other units. (See Figure 31-1.) Another solution is to put the equipment on bricks.

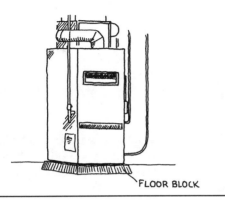

31-1. An elevated furnace.

- Basement floors should be sealed to resist dirt and stains. Remember that unpainted or untreated concrete floors should not be washed with soap before being treated. Instead, use a solution of 4 to 6 tablespoons baking soda to one gallon of hot water. Or purchase a concrete cleaner from your hardware or builder's supply store. Painted basement floors can be cleaned with plain water and a mild soap or detergent solution. Paint, however, will eventually wear out or will peel when subject to damp conditions. It is better to leave a concrete floor bare, treated with several coats of clear sealer.

BASEMENT FLOOR SAFETY

See the section on concrete driveway safety. When working in basements, make sure there is adequate ventilation when you use cleaning and sealing compounds. Wet basement floors can be slippery. Watch your footing.

BASEMENT FLOOR QUICK CHECKLIST

❑ If possible, avoid painting a basement floor. Apply several coats of a clear concrete sealer instead.
❑ Make sure the floor drains remain open and unobstructed.
❑ Repair cracks.
❑ Repair flaking and crumbling sections.
❑ Repair heaved or sunken sections.
❑ Keep humidity under control. Run a dehumidifier during periods of warm, wet weather.
❑ Keep sump pumps serviced and ready for action.
❑ Keep items stored in the basement off the floor for easier cleaning.

Garage Floors

Most of what was said in the previous section about basement floors also applies here. If anything, garage floors receive tougher use.

GARAGE FLOOR INSPECTIONS

Stains
To individuals who actually use their garages to park cars, the floor can become stained with oil, antifreeze, brake and transmission fluids, and grease. Such drippings should be cleaned up as quickly as possible both for appearance and for safety. See the section on driveway maintenance for clean-up methods. And for new driveways, the same section explains how to seal concrete so it is more resistant to car fluid drippings.

If such petroleum-based drippings are not cleaned, they will stain the concrete, they will pose a slipping hazard, and they can get tracked through the house to further damage carpeting and other floor coverings.

Plain Concrete Surfaces
Garage floors should not have any coverings such as carpet or vinyl flooring laid on their surface. Additional coverings could absorb gasoline and oil, which would create continuous fumes and a greater risk of fire.

Good Housekeeping
Housekeeping is important to garage floors. Many individuals, although their homes are kept clean and uncluttered, consider their garages to be a catch-all for everything. They soon fill the garage so full that their cars no longer fit. It becomes difficult to walk inside. Once this happens, it gets harder and harder to clean the floor, or to access what's there. The garage thus becomes a "no man's or no woman's" land—and a complete waste of good space.

As with basement floors, it is important to keep items off garage floors as much as possible. Only then can you periodically clean the floor and keep things under control.

GARAGE FLOOR REPAIRS

See the section on concrete (or asphalt) driveway repairs.

GARAGE FLOOR MAINTENANCE

See the section on concrete (or asphalt) driveway maintenance. Keep any floor drains open and unobstructed.

GARAGE FLOOR SAFETY

Again, refer to the section on driveways. Also be careful not to become preoccupied with some activity while a vehicle is running in the garage. Carbon monoxide is a lethal gas.

GARAGE FLOOR QUICK CHECKLIST

- ❑ Avoid painting a garage floor. Apply several coats of sealer instead.
- ❑ Clean automobile fluid stains as soon as possible.
- ❑ Make sure floor drains remain open.
- ❑ Repair cracks.
- ❑ Repair flaking or crumbling surfaces.
- ❑ Repair heaved or sunken sections.
- ❑ Keep most items stored in the garage off the floor, for easier cleaning and additional walking space around your vehicles.

PART 4

Utility Space

Mention "laundry room" as a topic of conversation to anyone and you will probably receive a polite nod and a yawn. Same with utility rooms. In fact, most homeowners don't even think about utility spaces until such areas are needed for a specific purpose. Basements, hallways, stairways, and attics fall into the same category. Even garages can be downplayed by the typical homeowner.

All of these utility areas supply something that no dwelling should be without—adequate working and storage space. A sufficient amount of both will make a home a much more pleasant place to live. Due to the nature of utility spaces, they receive considerable hard use, and need routine inspections, repairs, and maintenance just as the rest of the house does.

Attics

Here is a home feature that appears to be nearing extinction. Years ago, when two- and three-story houses were crammed together along city streets like Monopoly houses, attics were included with every dwelling. They held (as they still do) old cardboard boxes and wooden chests loaded with toys, clothes, school papers, Christmas decorations, antiques, photographs, and other mementos. Attics have always been cluttered, dusty hideaways for family memorabilia, largely because there was little other space built elsewhere within the homes for storage. At that time, garages were usually cramped, flimsy structures erected toward the back yard—if they were built at all—and basements were typically damp, dark, low-ceilinged affairs with barely enough room for a fat, squat gas gravity furnace.

The predominant reasons for the decline of attics have been modern methods and designs of today's home construction. Roof trusses—prefabricated triangular roof supports that rest upon and are fastened to opposite exterior walls — are reinforced with diagonal boards that greatly restrict usable attic space beneath the roof. Trusses allow improved design versatility because they are engineered to span entire distances between opposite exterior walls without relying on intermediate support or additional bearing walls.

Even with the space-restricting roof trusses, though, some usable attic space is usually available, over the main part of the home, and over the garage as well.

ATTIC INSPECTIONS

- Entrances. Some attics have little more than a thin piece of plywood covering a small rectangular access located in a bedroom or hall closet. In fact, it is possible to find a home that has many inches of insulation in the attic floor, but nothing over the entrance hatch cover. That means the heat will pass through the thin wood cover and be lost into the attic. The same goes for a pull-down stairway. If it is not insulated in some fashion, hot or cold air will be lost through the wood. (See Figure 33-1.)

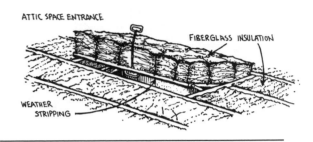

33-1. An insulated stairway hatch.

- Dry rot or fungi in rafters or trusses. Does a screwdriver sink into the wood? A lack of ventilation could cause damaging heat buildup during the summer, which could accelerate wood deterioration.
- Water leaks and stains.
- Chimney deterioration. Are bricks crumbling? Is stucco falling off? Look for water stains on the wood floor around the base of the chimney.
- Holes, gaps, or missing boards in the attic floor. There shouldn't be any openings you can look through to the living level below. Direct openings will undermine efficient insulation and fire-stopping properties.
- Note the condition of exposed utilities, ducts, and piping. All pipes, vents, and ducts should be properly supported. Wiring should be neatly installed and not allowed to wander haphazardly beneath and between stored items. Electrical fixtures should be rated "insulation safe." All heating, cooling, and plumbing lines should be separately insulated. The use of a lamp cord or flimsy extension cord to run lighting or attic fans is clearly a fire hazard. Such cords should be replaced by permanent wiring and fixtures.
- There should be plenty of ventilation, especially in a well-insulated attic. If the attic has windows, they should operate correctly and have screens. No open spaces should be permitted: vents should be screened to prevent birds, small mammals, and insects from entering. Do attic fans and ventilators work properly? Does the attic seem excessively humid? Check the attic for vent openings in the walls, roof, or eaves. A combination of

ridge vents, soffit vents, and gable vents works most effectively. An attic is rarely over-ventilated, especially one that is heavily insulated. Inspect the vent openings for signs of water penetration or general decay. Sometimes screens will warp and fall out. Make sure they are replaced to keep out insects, bats, and other wildlife. (See Figure 33-2.)

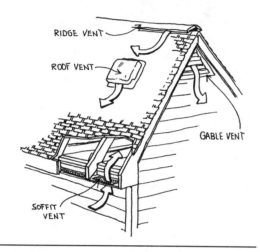

33-2. Vent openings.

As a rule, there should be equal amounts of ventilation in the inlet vents beneath the eaves (in the soffit) and in the outlet vents close to the roof's peak. (See Figure 33-3.)

▪ Make sure insulation does not cover exposed electrical components such as old knob-and-tube wiring, transformers, and junction boxes.

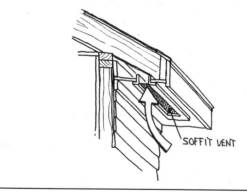

33-3. Soffit vent.

▪ No stack vents or ducts should end in the attic. They should all be carrying exhaust and other fumes up through the roof or at the very least, out the sides of a house.
▪ There should be a vapor barrier between the floor joists of the attic to stop the movement of moisture from heated rooms below to the unheated attic area. The vapor barrier should always be on the inside face of the insulation, between the insulation and the heated rooms of the dwelling.
▪ There should be a lighting fixture in the attic, operated either by a pull chain or a wall switch mounted in the room below.
▪ The attic's main runways, walkways, or crawlways should be kept uncluttered. If you can't move around in an attic, you won't be able to inspect it.

ATTIC MAINTENANCE

▪ Insulate and weatherstrip hatch covers or pull-down attic stairs.
▪ Keep the attic clean and uncluttered.
▪ Follow maintenance procedures for windows, fans, screens, ventilators, and all attic components.
▪ Caulk junctions of vent pipes, ventilators, fan units, and other components that pass through the attic roof or sides.
▪ Add more ventilation if necessary. A whole-house fan is one option. Individual power roof vents are others.

ATTIC SAFETY

▪ Be careful when you go into an attic, especially if you need to use a ladder.
▪ Remember not to blunder around in the dark. Use a light. Don't strike your head on a rafter or truss. It is not only the bump to watch out for—it is exposed nails, brackets, and other components as well.
▪ If the attic floor doesn't have a full covering (and parts of many attic floors do not), be careful where you step. Walk only on the tops of joists in that case. Avoid stepping between the joists because the plaster or plasterboard is not likely to be able to support your weight.

ATTIC QUICK CHECKLIST

❑ Attics should have safe, approachable, insulated entrances. Pull-down stair-cases are ideal.

❑ There should be no leaks in an attic's roof or side walls.

❑ There should be enough ventilation to minimize moisture accumulation and heat accumulation.

❑ Vent openings should be screened to prevent access by insects, birds, mammals, and other creatures.

❑ Old, outdated wiring and electric fixtures should be replaced.

❑ Attics should be illuminated with at least one lighting fixture near the attic's entrance.

❑ Chimneys, vent stacks, ventilators, and other components that pass through an attic to the roof or side walls should be properly caulked, flashed, or otherwise sealed.

❑ There should be at least a partial floor covering in an attic.

❑ There should be a vapor barrier between the attic joists and the attic insulation.

❑ An attic's access area and main crawl or walkways should be kept open, free from stored items and clutter.

Stairways

"Stairs. You go up 'em, and down 'em," said a grizzled old builder, "and that is all they are good for."

That may be the opinion of a majority of homeowners, but to others, stairways can be architectural focal points, showcases for special artwork, or opportunities for bathing a home in natural light through skylights and massive casement windows.

Still, their main function is so you can go up and down them and do so safely. As simple as stairways are, they must be sturdy and sound, and constructed to correct, expected dimensions.

STAIRWAY INSPECTIONS

- Loose, damaged, or squeaky steps. Identify any cracked, rotted, wobbly, or worn-out steps: treads or risers. Squeaks can be an annoying factor here.
- Steps without a good tractive surface. There is nothing like a set of slippery steps to give a person a good rush of adrenalin. Falls on stairways are notorious for producing crippling injuries and deaths. Painted wood steps can be very slippery. Consider installing individual rubber treads with anti-slip surfaces.
- Loose, wobbly railings. Check for firmness. Make sure handrails extend fully from the bottom to the top of each stairway. Handrails should be easily grasped by a hand of average size; flat and wide designs do not permit a firm grip. There should be at least a 1½-inch gap between the handrail and the wall. If a handrail vibrates when touched, it should be tightened.
- Broken or missing railing parts. Some people have removed safety railings so they can carry items up and down more easily. That is fine to do when some one-time lift must be made, such as wheeling down a clothes washer, but afterward the railing should be reinstalled. Look especially hard at staircases in old homes. They have traditionally been narrow and steep and full of hairpin turns that make carrying items on them very hazardous.

To put it simply, handrails, banisters, spin-

dles, balusters, and other railing or safety components should contain no damaged, loose, or missing parts. (See Figure 34-1.) If they do, get them repaired before someone gets hurt.

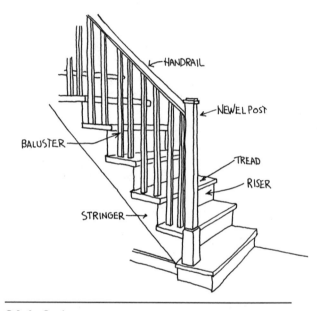

34-1. Stairway components.

Balusters, or posts supporting the handrail, should be spaced so a 6-inch sphere cannot pass through any portion, to prevent young children from sticking their heads through.

- Loose, torn, or frayed carpeting. Carpeting on any set of stairs must be kept tight, without wrinkles or other defects that could catch a heel and cause a tumble.
- Loose staircases. Sometimes an entire staircase, though sturdily fixed at both ends, will wobble or vibrate when someone is traveling on the middle stairs. It should be fully supported, so users do not feel swaying on the way up or down.
- Stairways constructed with odd dimensions. Most regular, straight stairways follow the same basic guidelines for stairway angles, stairway step dimensions, and stairway widths. For instance, on a good-quality interior stairway, the vertical risers from step to step should be 6½ inches. The

horizontal run should be from about 10 to 14 inches. The tread width should be 3 to 4 feet. The railing should be firmly installed. Baluster spacing should be 6 inches or less. (See Figure 34-2.)

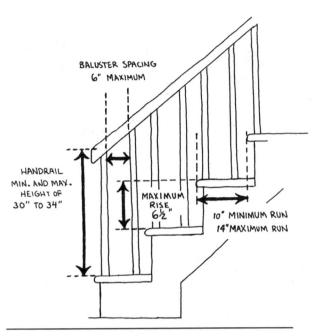

34-2. Stairway dimensions.

People expect stairways to consist of step sizes they are used to making day in, day out. Odd sizes, or steps that vary in dimension from one to another within the same staircase, are a definite hazard to anyone's health. Such a stairway should be remodeled into an arrangement featuring correct dimensions.

- A lack of illumination. Stairways should be well lit by a light that can be turned on from both the top and bottom of the stairs.
- Items stored on the stairs. Absolutely nothing should be kept on the stairs. Not shoes, boots, brooms, cleaning products, dog biscuits. Nothing.
- Concrete steps should be inspected for cracks, spalling or chipped surfaces, heaving, or tilting.

STAIRWAY REPAIRS

Repairing Loose Steps and Squeaks

Loose steps and squeaks can be fixed in several ways, depending on how loose a step is. If there is just a squeak, with very little movement, it can sometimes be taken care of with a simple application of powdered graphite or even talcum powder to the offending joint. For a more serious movement, assuming you have access to the stairway's underside, tighten the step's wedges that are often found beneath each

tread and riser. Drive the wedges in further to tighten an individual step. If there are no wedges, use short blocks of 2" x 2" wood screwed to the two adjacent parts, where the tread meets the riser. If you can't get to the underside of the stairway, try nailing or screwing through the surface on either the riser or the tread, whichever part displays the most movement. (See Figure 34-3.) Usually the tread is the culprit.

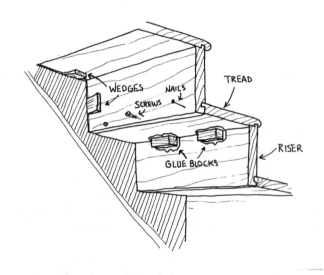

34-3. Stairway repairs.

The method of repairs can depend on how you want the finished product to look. If the staircase is constructed of hardwood finished to go with a room's decor, then you will want to take care that the repairs blend into the woodwork. If it is an old, open wooden stairway to a basement, appearance isn't so important.

If you decide to use screws, pre-drill the holes using a profile bit that matches the size of the screws. Profile bits widen the entrance to the screw hole so the head of the screw can be installed below the wood's surface and the hole can be filled and hidden with putty or a wooden plug. Profile bits, wood putty, and plugs are available at hardware or builder's supply stores.

Nails can be used if you have enough room to swing a hammer. Although they don't bind parts together as strongly as screws will, nails are easier to hide. Spiral-shank or ring-shank nails at least 1½ inches long have the greatest holding strength. You need to drive a pair of these nails angled toward each other into the squeaky spot. But first drill holes using an ordinary straight drill bit that is slightly smaller than the diameter of the nails. Sink the nail heads below the surface, using a nail set or punch. Fill the tiny depressions with wood putty. (See Figure 34-4.)

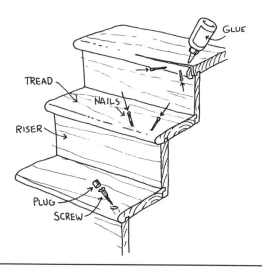

34-4. Step repairs.

Repairing a Cracked Nosing
To repair a cracked nosing (the edge of a step tread that sticks out slightly over the riser), work wood glue into the crack using a playing card or other thin item as an applicator. Wiggle the cracked portion gently as you apply the glue, and squeeze the crack together until an even line of excess glue is produced along the seam. Then drill pilot holes and drive nails as described in the previous paragraph, at angles into the edges of the nosing to help hold the split together. Wipe away excess glue with a damp cloth.

Tightening a Stairway Post
To tighten a solid newel post situated on your main living floor, you must first look to the basement. These newel posts are usually bolted to a joist beneath the floor. You should see the base of the post protruding vertically through the subfloor and extending past the joist, forming a right angle with it. To tighten the post, use a large adjustable wrench or an automotive socket wrench to snug the bolts that fasten the bottom of the post to the joist. (See Figure 34-5.)

Tightening Loose Spindles
Spindles that are loose or damaged are often more difficult to fix than wobbly newel posts and handrails. To tighten loose spindles, drive thin, glue-coated wooden wedges into the seam where the spindle meets the underside of the handrail, where they won't be noticed. After the glue dries, trim the wedges carefully

with a sharp utility knife to hide them further.

Repairing Cracked Spindles
Cracked spindles can be repaired with wood glue. Apply the glue, wipe away excess, then wrap the glued area tightly with adhesive tape. After the glue dries, remove the tape. Wipe the repaired spindle with mineral spirits or penetrating oil such as WD-40, which will remove sticky tape residue without damaging clear finish or paint.

Concrete Step Repairs
For concrete step repairs, see the section on concrete walkway repairs.

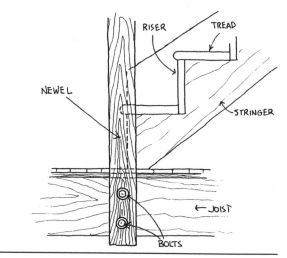

34-5. Post repair.

STAIRWAY MAINTENANCE

- Keep stairways solid. A squeak here and there is nothing to worry about, but parts that wobble or vibrate should be tightened. They could cause someone to lose his balance and fall.
- Keep stairways free from clutter. Avoid storing anything on stairways. If you see something on a set of stairs, remove it.
- Maintain slip-resistant treads. Don't paint wooden or concrete steps with slippery paints or other coverings. Avoid using wood polishes on stairways. Give bare wood stairs a light application of wood protective treatment that will not leave a slippery coating of polish or oils on the surface.

When possible, use individual rubber treads. Carpeting should always be kept tightly fastened to the stairs, and should be in good condition.

▪ Maintain good lighting over stairways. Replace bulbs as soon as they burn out.

▪ Make sure that handrails are in place in every stairway. Don't take a chance by leaving them off.

▪ The same concepts hold true for all types of stairways: spiral staircases, attic pull-down staircases, L-shaped and U-shaped staircases. All of the parts should be firmly attached, to give the users a feeling of security as they travel up and down.

STAIRWAY SAFETY

The main concern is the topic of slips and falls. Remember where you are while working on stairways. It only takes one misstep to ruin a person's spine for life.

STAIRWAY QUICK CHECKLIST

❑ Repair loose, damaged, or squeaky steps.

❑ Steps must not be slippery. Install individual rubber treads on slippery stairs. Make sure that carpeting on stairways is securely fastened from bottom to top.

❑ Railings and their components should be present and sturdily installed, with no missing parts.

❑ Stairways made with unusual step dimensions should be repaired or replaced with steps that adhere to standard, recognized sizes.

❑ Stairways must be well illuminated.

❑ Stairways must be kept clean and uncluttered. Nothing should be stored on steps.

Basements

Basements can take several forms. There is the old, low, dark, and dirty basement that is damp and full of rusting tools, cobwebs, and dryer lint. There is the modern, plain basement: neat, clean, and bright, with a clothes washer and dryer, a small workbench, and a few cabinets and shelves for storage. Then there is the modern fixed-up basement—a basement that is been remodeled into living space.

The first two types of basement are fairly straightforward and simple to inspect. The important structure and surfaces of a basement that is remodeled into living space, however, can be difficult (if not impossible) to view.

BASEMENT INSPECTIONS

Moisture

Wet basements can be a nightmare. Damp basements are bad enough. Basement floors and walls should look and feel dry. But a basement that appears dry during August may be 2 inches underwater in April. Stains on walls and floors are typical signs of wetness, as is mildew. Wooden beams that are moist, slippery, and mottled with mildew or fungi are also good indicators of continual or frequent dampness.

Any dampness problem that develops within a basement should be corrected. Moisture can lead to sticking windows and doors throughout the entire home. It can cause mold and mildew to form. It can bring condensation into the home, and will cause surface coatings to fail long before their expected life spans are reached. It will warp paneling and other wood furnishings, and it can help attract termites to the home.

Moisture can come from several sources. Inspect your basement after a heavy rain to see if there are spots where water is coming through the walls or floor, especially at corners and, of course, at cracks. Sometimes it can come straight through porous masonry walls. If that is the case, it needs immediate attention. Check first if something can be done on the outside of the foundation. Is a defective gutter splashing water along a foundation wall? Should a splash block be positioned below a downspout? Are there cracks in the wall? Does the surrounding ground hold water against the house, or is it graded properly, sloped downwards away from the foundation? Could dense shrubbery be holding moisture against the foundation walls?

Window wells (also called areaways) can be a source of unwanted seepage. These are excavations in the earth made outside basement windows which are set below ground level. They have walls of masonry or metal. The bottoms of window wells are usually lined with gravel, so water that finds its way into the well can be absorbed into the ground through the gravel. (See Figure 35-1.) Look into the window wells during a hard rainstorm to make sure water is not rising to a depth where it will pour into the basement through cracks around the window. A thick coating of leaves on the bottom of the window well will also cause water to build up there. Window wells can sometimes be accidental collection points for garden debris, grass clippings, and other materials. Such debris can reduce the ability of water to be absorbed into the wells.

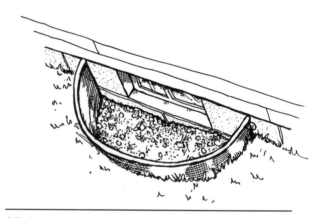

35-1. A window well.

Another source of moisture is condensation. During hot, humid weather, condensation can appear on the floor joists and subfloors and walls exposed in crawlspaces and basements as warm moist air penetrates and comes in contact with cooler surfaces. Cold water pipes and storage tanks are notorious for water from condensation building up to a point where entire lengths of pipe are dripping condensate onto the floor, equipment, or materials being stored in the basement. Although condensation rarely causes major damage to masonry surfaces, it will cause wood joists and flooring to rot, and will help attract wood-destroying insects.

Earthen-floor crawlspaces can have additional moisture problems. Soil can draw water up like a blotter, through a phenomenon called capillary action, which can make water travel considerable distances. Even though the soil in a crawlspace appears to be dry when you look at it, you can't be sure it is without touching it, and you can't infer that it is always dry, either.

Sump Pumps

Make sure that a basement sump pump operates correctly. A sump pump's job is to collect water that has accumulated below the basement slab or floor and pump it out and away from the foundation.

Termites

See the section on pests.

Structural Problems

These can be bowed-in walls, cracked walls, or problems with beams, joists, or support posts.

Look at the base of wood posts for signs of decay. Probe the wood, especially at the bottom of each wooden post, with a screwdriver. Is each post straight and level? Look for obvious defects in exposed I-beams.

Defects

Look for defects in basement components such as oil-storage tanks, heating systems, water tanks, electrical systems, plumbing, and other items, even though you will be inspecting those parts and systems on their own later.

Deteriorated Windows and Doors

Check the condition of windows located in basement window wells. Some are constructed with wood frames and are susceptible to termites or wood rot. Others are made of metal that may be in need of painting. Basement outside access doors should be sound, with steps that are solid and safe.

Insulation Problems

Some homes benefit from a layer of insulation placed

below their first floor, or just against the basement ceiling. Crawlspaces should almost always be insulated. If so, does the insulation have a vapor barrier installed between the insulation and basement ceiling? It should. (See Figures 35-2 and 35-3.)

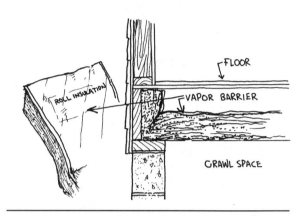

35-2. Basement ceiling insulation.

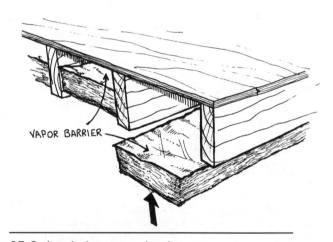

35-3. Insulation vapor barrier.

All bare soil in a crawlspace should be covered with a layer of plastic about 6 millimeters thick that is fitted against the foundation walls and weighted down with stones, bricks, or other heavy non-organic material. It is also a good idea for the plastic to be carried up the walls to a point above the outside ground level or grade, where it can be fastened to the walls with duct tape. When seams are unavoidable, the plastic sheets can be overlapped by at least one foot, then fastened together with duct tape.

Walls around a crawlspace should contain at least four screened openings about the size of small windows to provide adequate ventilation. (See Figure 35-4.)

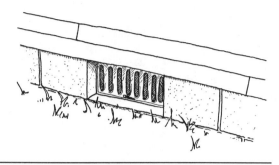

35-4. Basement window vent.

BASEMENT REPAIRS

Correcting Wet Basements

If you cannot stop water from entering a basement from the outside, and waterproofing the walls also fails, the last resort is to have a sump pump system installed. This should be done by a qualified contractor. Before that step is taken, however, make sure you can't correct the problem by repairing a gutter or downspout, by adding a splash block, or by re-grading some ground adjacent to a foundation wall.

Correcting Structural Problems

Bowed-in walls or major foundation cracks should be repaired by a contractor familiar with making structural repairs.

BASEMENT MAINTENANCE

1. To prevent moisture from seeping through concrete foundation or basement walls, apply a waterproofing paint to the inside surfaces.
2. If condensation forming on basement walls is a persistent problem, consider lining the walls with a layer of rigid-board insulation. Insulate plumbing pipes to prevent moisture from condensing and dripping from those surfaces.
3. Install a dehumidifier to draw excess moisture from a damp basement.
4. When the outside air is relatively dry, open basement windows to provide a source of ventilation.

5. Keep the bottom gravel surfaces of window wells free from debris that could trap water against the windows.
6. Remove dense shrubbery that abuts a foundation wall. The soil beneath the shrubbery will not dry out if sunlight can't reach it.
7. Keep gutters and downspouts clean and in good repair.
8. Seal openings around pipes, vents, electrical wires, and all fixtures installed in the basement walls.
9. Clean debris that may be plugging screen openings that provide ventilation to crawlspaces.
10. If a sump pump hasn't run in several months, prime it with water from a garden hose to activate and exercise the motor and pump.
11. At least twice a year, wipe cobwebs and dust from basement walls and ceilings. Keep heating and cooling appliances clean as well.

BASEMENT SAFETY

The basement is frequently the location of many of the home's major component centers. Understand what's down there, where it is, and how it works.

- The heating system. Know how to turn it on and off; how to reset the furnace or relight a pilot flame. Where is a spare filter? How often should filters be changed?
- The water system. Where is the main shutoff valve?
- A natural gas system. Where is the main shutoff valve?
- The electrical system. How do you replace fuses or reset circuit breakers? Is there a flashlight handy in case the lights go out? Are all the circuits clearly identified as to what parts of the house they service?
- Basement steps are notorious for causing slips and trips. Install rubber or other non-slip treads. Never store shoes, boots, boxes, or other items on the steps. Also avoid hanging so many jackets or coats at the head of the basement stairway that you can barely see down the staircase.

BASEMENT QUICK CHECKLIST

- ❑ Keep basement moisture levels under control.
- ❑ Have structural defects repaired by professionals.
- ❑ Maintain working windows for ventilation.
- ❑ Maintain a sump pump system on a regular basis. Test-operate the system during extended dry weather conditions to keep the sump motor and pump exercised.
- ❑ Watch out for termites and carpenter ants.
- ❑ Insulation against a basement ceiling should have a vapor barrier at the top or upper surface of the insulation, so moisture won't get trapped inside the insulation between the vapor barrier and basement ceiling.
- ❑ Cover crawlspaces with soil floors with a thick (6 millimeter) layer of waterproof plastic. Insulate ceilings.
- ❑ Understand the basics of all the important utility systems (electric, water, gas, sewer, heating and cooling) and know how to turn them on, reset them, and turn them off in case of an emergency.
- ❑ Keep basements clean, free from clutter, cobwebs, and dust.

Laundry Rooms

Laundry rooms are convenient. They are often located on the first floor of a household, near the kitchen, so a family member can do the laundry while concentrating on other things such as cooking or watching children in an adjacent family room. A typical laundry room should contain a clothes washer and dryer, a cabinet for storing soaps, bleach, softeners, and related supplies, a portable or built-in clothes rack, shelves to hold folded clothes, a hamper for soiled clothes storage, an ironing board, and a place to store the iron when not in use. There must also be a laundry tub or sink with hot and cold water for various cleaning duties. (See Figure 36-1.)

36-1. Laundry room.

LAUNDRY ROOM INSPECTIONS

- Soiled, corroded clothes washer and dryer. These major appliances are discussed further in the section on appliances. But for now, just make sure they operate correctly and are kept clean.
- Leaky pipes and dripping faucets. You want to keep the laundry room clean and dry. Moisture will be hard on your washer and dryer, and no one should ever handle an iron while standing on a wet floor.
- Outside dryer vent hookup problems. Some people will go for months before they figure out that their dryer vent — that accordion-like hose that

vents through the rear wall—has come detached at the base of the dryer. All the while it has been spewing moisture from the clothes drying process into the laundry room. Is the hose secure at both ends?
- If there is a drain on the floor near the washer, does it work? Check it by running water down it from a garden hose.
- Is there an open table or counter for sorting and folding clothes?
- If you have small children, is there a cabinet for soap, bleach, and other potentially hazardous cleaning supplies that can be locked for safekeeping?

LAUNDRY ROOM MAINTENANCE

1. Keep the area clean, dry, and uncluttered. Avoid storing non-laundry-related items here. If you fill the floor space with bicycles, canoe paddles, and boxes of off-season clothing, there won't be enough room to work. The cleaner and neater you keep the room, the smaller the chore of clothes washing and handling becomes.
2. Maintain bright lighting. Keep the maximum wattages of bulbs for which the fixtures are rated.
3. Maintain a good supply of fresh air. Make sure windows have screens that operate easily. Cross ventilation is the best. The windows should be able to be opened during a rainstorm if necessary. For winter use, consider installation of a fan.
4. Get in the habit of putting the iron away after each use. This applies even if children do not live in the household. On the same subject, never let children play at your feet while you are ironing clothes. It is just too dangerous.

LAUNDRY ROOM SAFETY

Laundry rooms are not known to be dangerous places, but there are a number of precautions you should take.

- Clothes irons get very hot. They need to be kept in high, stable places so children will not be able to reach them or knock them down. Get into the habit of plugging the iron in when it is needed, and unplugging it when you are through. Even if the iron has an automatic shutoff, keep it unplugged between uses.

- Laundry products can be deadly to children. Bleach, bluing, spray starches, detergents, softeners, stain removers, and related items such as measuring cups with chemical residues could all cause injuries to children. Even if you don't have children at home, you never know when unforeseen circumstances will bring youngsters into your house.

- One little-known hazard originates in the dryer's lint trap. Lint from drying clothes collects in a strainer in the dryer, and becomes a fire hazard when too much of it accumulates. Clean the lint trap after each dryer load run.

- Watch for sink drains that are plugged by a washcloth or sock or other item. Water from the clothes washer can overflow onto the floor if the drain isn't open for the washer's spin and rinse cycles.

LAUNDRY ROOM QUICK CHECKLIST

- ❑ Keep outside surfaces of the washer and dryer clean.
- ❑ Repair leaky water pipes, hose lines, and faucets.
- ❑ Keep the dryer vent attached and free from lint blockages.
- ❑ Avoid clutter. A laundry room is no place to store unrelated items.
- ❑ Keep soaps, bleach, starches, and other chemical products high out of children's reach.
- ❑ Keep the iron in a secure place, unplugged, between uses.
- ❑ Make sure the room is well illuminated.
- ❑ Check the sink drain for blockages before each load of wash.

Kitchen Utility Space

Kitchen utility space is probably the most abused utility space in the entire house. It is where food is stored, prepared, cooked, and sometimes eaten. It is counter space, cabinet space, sinks, and related nooks and crannies.

KITCHEN UTILITY SPACE INSPECTIONS

- Poor lighting. There is a lot of fine manipulation involved with food preparation: reading directions and ingredient labels; cutting, slicing, peeling, scraping, chopping, and measuring. Sharp blades are whirring about. Good lighting is needed to prevent eye strain and to provide a margin of safety. Bright lights should be located over the sink and countertop areas. A window over the sink is ideal for letting natural light in during the day. But if a homemaker must resort to preparing recipes on counter spaces darkened by overhanging cabinets, fluorescent lights should be installed along the bottoms of the offending units.

- Lack of ventilation. Window and door screens are great for ventilation during mild temperatures. But they are not much good when it is cold out. Every kitchen should have at least one exhaust fan. Many such fans are located in lighted hoods built into counter range tops. These units are okay, but not as effective as exhaust fans located at or near the room's ceiling, where cooking smoke and vapors tend to collect. The job of an exhaust fan is to remove airborne vapors, grease, oil, and smoke from the kitchen, and vent them outdoors. Check the unit's filter, fan blade, and light bulb for accumulated grease buildup.

- Leaking or worn-out faucets and other plumbing. Inspect the faucet's aerator, the water-saving insert that is screwed into the faucet's outlet. The aerator softens the faucet's stream of water. It should be replaced if plugged or deteriorated. Use a flashlight to look for leaking pipes, wet spots and damage from moisture, especially beneath sinks and behind disposals and dishwashers.

- A working telephone. More than ever, a telephone is needed in the typical kitchen. People have busy schedules, coming and going at irregular hours. Much of what little time is spent at home is now passed in the kitchen. A phone there makes sense. It should have an extra-long cord if it is not a cordless model.

- Cleanliness and organization. Are cabinets and drawers all working? Are they clean and organized? Or do they contain items (that hard-boiled egg slicer) that you haven't used in twenty years? Are counter tops clean and uncluttered?

- Is there a working garbage disposal? Some people love them. Others feel that disposals are yet another appliance to fail and need repairs. From every respect, disposals are "people interactive." Many a love/hate relationship has arisen between stuck or plugged-up disposals and heads of households.

- Does the kitchen sink drain? Some homeowners—bright, perceptive individuals—when faced with the question of what should go down the kitchen sink, have poured such incompatible materials as hot bacon grease, melted lard, butter, and even smoking-hot paraffin wax right down the drain. Naturally such materials solidify once cooled within household piping. Kitchen sink drains must be kept open. Check for a sluggish flow. The next step could be complete stoppage.

KITCHEN UTILITY SPACE MAINTENANCE

1. Replace burned out light bulbs as needed.
2. The kitchen range exhaust fan and hood should be cleaned as needed. Grease buildups on the filter, fan, light bulb, and metal surfaces should be removed. The filter can be washed in your dishwasher. A recent development by oven manufacturers has been to offer fans that vent fumes back into the kitchen after passing them through undersized charcoal and grease filters. Due to the ineffectiveness of this system, a separate kitchen exhaust fan must be used to vent fumes to the outdoors as well.
3. Plumbing work is best left to plumbers. Unless you have worked with plumbing before, you are probably better off to let licensed plumbers replace piping, stop leaks, and install additional

plumbing fixtures.

4. Wood cabinets should be cleaned and treated in the same manner as wood paneling or fine furniture. Counter tops are generally heat-resistant under proper care, but protect them from hot pots, pans, and baking dishes taken right from an oven, a broiler, or a burner. Never cut anything directly on a counter top. Keep all cabinets, drawers, and counter tops clean and organized. Remove appliances that you rarely use — keep them in the garage or other storage and bring them out when needed. Free up as much space as you can.

5. Learn to use the disposal correctly. Many people conclude that because their disposal is capable of grinding up most of their garbage, it can also handle grease and substances that would otherwise not go down a drain. False and untrue! Grease should not be put through a disposal.

   Most disposals have a reset button that works in much the same way as a circuit breaker. If the disposal becomes overloaded with something it is incapable of grinding, the disposal will turn itself off. If that happens, the power switch should be turned off right away. The problem is likely to be a bone, a bottle cap, silverware, or some other hard object that has jammed between the grinding wheel and the housing.

   Look down into the hopper of the disposal and see if you can spot the offending object. If you see it, turn off the electrical power to the disposal at the main electric box or panel. Check to make sure the power is off by pushing the reset button several times while operating the disposal start switch or control. You will hear a humming sound from the motor if the power is not off. Once you are certain that the power is off, use kitchen tongs or a similar implement to dislodge the stuck item. Never put your hands down into a disposal, even when the power is off.

   After the stuck item has been removed, try to get the flywheel to turn one way, then the other, with a short length of broom handle or something similar. If you can move it a little, take the broom handle back out and turn on the power. Run plenty of cold water and flick the disposal switch

on and off several times in quick sequence. The grinding action should return to normal.

6. Take care of the kitchen sink drain. Excess grease should be poured into a can and thrown out with the garbage.

KITCHEN UTILITY SPACE SAFETY

A kitchen is often full of danger.

▪ Improper food storage and handling can cause food poisoning.

▪ Sharp knives stored haphazardly in drawers can cut unsuspecting or forgetful fingers.

▪ Hot liquids, spattering grease, electric burners, hot pans in the sink, and even steam coming from a just-opened dish from the microwave—all can cause serious burns.

▪ Grease fires can start in a kitchen. Curtains can catch quickly.

▪ Tile and linoleum flooring can get very slippery when wet.

▪ Garbage disposals can wreak havoc with fingers, spit pieces of glass and metal back at you, and plug up at the most inopportune moments.

KITCHEN UTILITY SPACE QUICK CHECKLIST

❏ Keep kitchen work areas well illuminated.

❏ There should be plenty of year-round ventilation to rid the kitchen of cooking fumes and airborne waste particles.

❏ Make sure faucets, pipes, and drains are all working, with no leaks.

❏ Arrange to have a phone in the kitchen, preferably a cordless model.

❏ Keep cabinets, drawers, and counter tops clean and organized, with most of the equipment, cooking supplies, ingredients, and related items put away out of sight.

❏ Use the garbage disposal correctly.

Garages

At one time, having a garage was a luxury not many people could afford. In fact, years ago there weren't many cars on the road to use those few-and-far-between garages or "car barns." Nowadays, look at the number of automobiles, vans, and pickup trucks in service. They have practically become members of our families. And as such, they need shelter.

GARAGE INSPECTIONS

Structural Defects
Do the walls bow or sag? Does your garage remind you of the Leaning Tower of Pisa? Are the windows and doors difficult to operate because the garage has settled or heaved? In other words, is your garage dramatically out of kilter?

Condition of the Exterior Siding
Does it need to be painted or stained? Are there missing or decayed sections? Are the windows sound, with intact caulking?

Roof, Gutter, and Downspout Problems
See their respective sections. Just because a garage does not hold actual living space, it doesn't mean the construction can be any less weather resistant. A sound roof and a working drainage system are just as important on a garage as they are for the rest of the home.

Overhead Doors
There are a number of important things to look for on the large, overhead car bay doors, including:

- Examine cables for fraying or kinks.
- Inspect the condition of rollers. Metal rollers will rarely fail, but nylon ones can be easily damaged.
- See if the hinges are fastened securely to the door panels. The same hinges will also be attached to the door's rollers. (See Figure 38-1.)

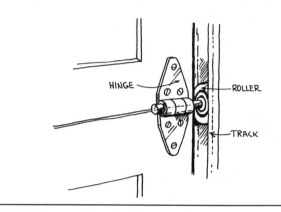

38-1. Garage door roller assembly.

- If a garage roll-up door binds, inspect the tracks for misalignment. Where the tracks are vertical, measure them with a builder's level. Overhead, measure the distances between them at several places; these distances should be the same.
- The lock bars—the metal rods extending from the door's handle lock to the tracks—can cause door locks and handles to work stiffly. The ends of these bars should slide in and out of their slots in the tracks when the door lock is opened or closed.
- Check the torsion springs and cables that provide the mechanical power assistance when the door is opened or closed. Do not attempt repairs or adjustments on torsion springs because a considerable amount of stored or coiled energy could be accidentally released at an inopportune time.
- Open and close the door several times. If the door mechanism is motorized, make sure it works properly without grinding noises or erratic, jerky movements.
- Does the door close tightly? Is there a gap at the foot that could allow wind, rain, snow, or animals to enter? Check the bottom of the door. Look at the piece of heavy rubber or plastic weatherstripping that fits along the bottom edge of the door. Inspect also the weatherstripping fitted along the sides of the door. (See Figure 38-2.)
- Does the door lock? It should.

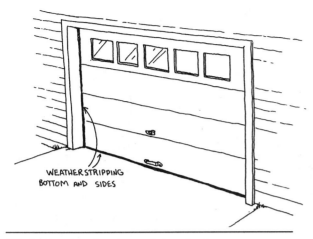

38-2. Garage door weatherstripping.

Automatic Openers

Do you have the model, make, and frequency of your automatic opener written down in case you eventually need to order another unit?

Place an object in the descending path of the overhead door. Activate the door. If it doesn't automatically reverse within two seconds of hitting the object, the opener should either be adjusted so it will reverse itself, or if that is not possible, it should be replaced with another unit that will.

Garage Entry Doors

Does the entrance from the garage to the house have a tight seal to prevent garage fumes from entering the house? Are all entry door locks deadbolts?

Lighting

Is the lighting adequate? Is it accessible to a driver who returns at night? Or must an obstacle course be run to reach the nearest switch? The best option is to have an automatic light included with the garage opener. (The light should stay illuminated for the average time it takes to get from the car into the house.)

Electrical Outlets

Are there at least two electrical outlets for the power tools you need to clean your car or garage?

Housekeeping

See the section on housekeeping. The main point is to keep as much as possible off the garage floor, so the floor can be kept clean and so you can walk around your cars without stepping across buckets and tools and supplies. Is the garage neat and orderly, or cluttered?

GARAGE REPAIRS

See the individual sections on roofs, gutters and downspouts, windows, doors, and other respective topics. It is usually best to have an automatic door repaired by a professional.

GARAGE MAINTENANCE

Again, see the individual sections for specific component maintenance. The most critical item is the automatic garage door opener. Have it serviced at least once a year by a qualified technician.

One special note on housekeeping. Be careful when it comes to storing firewood in a garage. It may be a lot simpler to have wood in the garage on those cold, wintry nights, but remember that you could be carrying wood-destroying insects into the house. A better option is to erect a wood storage rack along the outside of the garage, not directly touching the garage but not far away either. If you decide to store wood in a garage anyway, at least inspect each piece before you bring it inside.

GARAGE SAFETY

Home heating furnaces or boilers located in a garage should be partitioned off from the rest of the garage area to prevent accidental ignition of gasoline fumes from a leaky automobile tank or line.

If a water heater must be positioned in a garage, and cannot be placed in a separate enclosure of the garage, it should be mounted on a concrete or other sturdy platform at least 18 inches high. Gasoline vapors are heavier than air. If a car has a leaking gas tank, line, or gas tank cap, it will take many hours for the gasoline fumes to rise over 18 inches to the level of an open flame pilot light in a water heater.

Adequate ventilation should be present.

Again, make sure an automatic garage door opener has an auto-reverse feature. Keep automatic door opener wall switches and portable units out of children's reach.

See the section on garage floors for further safety points.

GARAGE QUICK CHECKLIST

❑ A garage should be structurally sound and weatherproof.

❑ Overhead doors should work easily.

❑ Automatic door openers should be serviced at least once a year by a certified technician.

❑ Only use automatic doors with an auto-reverse feature.

❑ Keep garages neat, clean, and uncluttered, with as much open floor space as possible.

❑ Arrange for easy access lighting and several electrical outlets.

❑ Keep major appliances such as water heaters, furnaces, and boilers in separate enclosures, or high off the garage floor so open-flame pilot lights cannot ignite low lying gasoline fumes.

❑ Maintain adequate ventilation.

❑ Keep up with repairs and maintenance on individual garage components such as the roof, gutters and downspouts, exterior walls, man doors, and windows.

Workshops

In some homes, a workshop could mean just a wooden workbench built into the corner of a basement, with a few pegboards affixed to the walls for tools, and an overhead fluorescent lamp. In other homes, this could mean elaborate woodworking shops, machine shops, or similar setups for hobbyists or for people who work out of their homes.

There are five basic factors to consider when looking at workshops: storage of tools and supplies, general housekeeping, lighting, ventilation, and safety procedures.

STORAGE OF TOOLS, EQUIPMENT, AND SUPPLIES

Proper storage of tools, equipment, and supplies will make any workshop a neater and safer place to work. When reorganizing workshop storage, consider the following points:

- If you have young children, store all tools in locked cabinets or drawers. As the children grow, introduce them gradually to locked up tools. But continue to lock up power tools until the children are old enough and mature enough to be trained correctly in tool use and safety.
- To make handy tool racks, drill a series of holes, ½ to 2 inches in diameter, through 1" x 3" boards. Mount the boards on the wall with angle brackets so tools can be suspended through the holes within easy reach of the workbench.
- Need a storage receptacle for pointed or sharp tools? Cut a block of plastic foam from the lining material in an appliance carton.
- Do your tool drawers pull out and spill their contents? Screw a small rectangular piece of wood to the inside of the drawer's back panel to act as a stop. Turning the stop to a vertical position will keep the drawer in place. To remove the drawer, turn the stop to a horizontal position. (See Figure 39-1.)

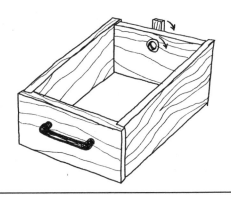

39-1. Drawer stop latch.

- To protect the teeth of a hacksaw blade, cut a length of old garden hose as long as the blade and slit lengthwise to fit over the teeth.
- To prevent metal tools from rusting, store them in sealed wooden bins with camphor and sawdust. Or after each use, wipe a light film of lubricating oil on the tools with an oiled cloth.
- Paint your initials or engrave your name on tools you loan to neighbors and friends.
- In your garage or basement, you can store lumber and pipe between exposed ceiling joists. Screw wooden cross members across the bottom of the joists to support materials you wish to tuck up and out of the way. (See Figure 39-2.)

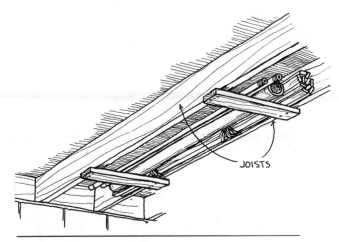

39-2. Basement ceiling storage.

- For convenient storage shelves, use unfinished spaces between wall studs on workshop walls. To make the shelves, nail pieces of 2" x 4" boards horizontally between the studs.
- Jars with screw-top lids, especially plastic peanut butter containers, are ideal for storing small items such as nails, screws, nuts, and bolts. You can double your shelf capacity by screwing the lids to the undersides of shelves. Place a lock washer under the head of the screw so the lid won't turn when you unscrew the jar.

GENERAL HOUSEKEEPING

Part 7 will discuss housekeeping and its importance at greater length, but for now, be aware that good house-keeping will go a long way toward the enjoyment, efficiency, and safety of any activity, and especially so with a workshop. Even the messiest person, when forced to earn a living from his or her shop, ultimately comes to the conclusion that proper house-keeping has a direct effect on the efficiency and productivity of the business. Those who never learn, never prosper as much as they otherwise could. Why spend hour after hour wondering where you put that tool, or sifting through sawdust on the floor for your car keys? Most workshops need all the available space they can get. A shop littered with raw materials, piles of waste, and equipment strewn about haphazardly will be neither a safe nor an enjoyable place to work. A few pointers are in order here:

- Clean and store tools when you are through with them. Resist the urge to lay tools down where you last used them. Always put them in the same place when you are through. Otherwise, it will be as frustrating as looking for your car keys if they aren't put in a specific place whenever you go home.
- Repair broken tools or get rid of them.
- Keep maintenance and operating manuals for all power tools and equipment. Follow their preventive maintenance recommendations.
- Avoid overfilling racks, bins, and other storage containers.
- Keep bench tops neat and free from clutter. This is one of the most important things you can do. Cluttered workbenches invite injuries, spillages, and other accidents. Give yourself some elbow room on your benches.
- Keep all drawers closed. Don't overfill them so they can't be closed all the way.
- Keep aisles clear of boxes, extension cords, and other tripping hazards.
- Stack and store materials and other items neatly,

keeping heavy items on bottom shelves.
- Put away sharp tools and items as soon as you are finished with them.

PROPER LIGHTING

Maintain proper lighting in your work and storage areas. If there is not enough lighting, install overhead fluorescent fixtures. Lack of lighting will tire your eyes and cause you to misjudge cutting, drilling, or other power-tool operations.

ADEQUATE VENTILATION

If you produce fumes in your workshop, make sure there is sufficient ventilation. If need be, install a fan unit that is vented to the outdoors. Paint and solvent fumes, welding and burning fumes, various wood, metal, and other dusts all can be harmful to your health. Vacuum units are available for attachment to sanders, saws, and other tools. Keep circulating fresh air for a healthy work atmosphere.

WORKSHOP SAFETY PROCEDURES

When operating power tools and equipment in a workshop, there is usually no one standing over your shoulder telling you what to do and what not to do. You are on your own. Understanding and following recommended power-tool and material-handling procedures is a must if you want to retain your eyesight, your hearing, and all your fingers. This is a serious matter.

1. Wear safety glasses or goggles whenever your work may endanger your eyes. That means when cutting, sawing, sanding, drilling, planing, routing, chiseling, hammering—in fact, you might as well get into the habit of putting on safety glasses with side shields, or safety goggles, the minute you enter your workshop, and keeping them on until you leave. Naturally, the heavier the hazard, the sturdier the eyewear protection should be. Different safety lenses are needed for welding or cutting and burning. But always go for a little more protection than you think you will need. Consider how important your eyesight is.

2. Wear hearing protection—ear plugs or muffs, the kind that muffle sound but do not block it out completely. Wear protection when operating loud power tools to protect your hearing against gradual damages that can occur from repeated exposures.

3. Even though you may have a good ventilation or

vacuum system, wear an appropriately rated dust mask or respirator whenever particles are airborne or chemical fumes are present.

4. Don't forget helpers and visitors. Keep extra safety eyewear, hearing protection, and dust masks on hand in case you have company.

5. Clothing should suit prevailing circumstances but should always be close-fitting so it won't catch on protruding items or worse yet, on moving equipment.

6. Wear sturdy work shoes or boots with thick non-slip soles.

7. If you have long hair, tie it back, wrap it into a bun, or stuff it under a hat. This goes for men and women alike.

8. Before operating power equipment, remove jewelry, especially rings, necklaces, bracelets, and wristwatches. Never, not even for a minute, wear a scarf, bandanna, or tie around your neck while operating or standing near moving equipment.

9. Get into the habit of wearing gloves whenever you can. Have several kinds: lightweight cotton, heavyweight cotton, leather, and rubber. You may not be able to wear them for tasks requiring fine manipulation skills, and you should not wear them if there is a chance they could get caught in moving machinery.

10. Avoid distractions. Refrain from speaking to someone while operating power equipment. Postpone activities if you are tired or ill or otherwise unable to concentrate.

11. Keep a first-aid kit nearby, including eyewash solution.

12. Have a phone handy, with telephone numbers of the fire department, ambulance, and poison control center.

WORKSHOP QUICK CHECKLIST

❑ Keep tools, equipment, and supplies neatly stored away between uses.

❑ Keep items off the floor. Workbench surfaces should be uncluttered. Practice sound housekeeping procedures. Put tools back after each use.

❑ Repair broken tools or get rid of them.

❑ Regularly refer to power tool and equipment maintenance and operating manuals.

❑ Maintain proper lighting levels.

❑ Maintain sufficient levels of ventilation.

❑ Wear personal protection when necessary, including goggles, dust masks, respirators, hearing protection, and gloves.

❑ Avoid interruptions and distractions while working.

❑ Maintain a well-stocked first-aid kit.

❑ Make sure a phone is nearby, in case of an emergency.

PART 5

Major Operating Systems

A home's major operating systems can be considered the actual lifelines of a house. Without them, practically all modern conveniences would be impossible. Due to this importance, many of their components and installations are regulated by strict local and national codes. Certainly, the systems in this section should be included as the most important items in your inspection program. The sections discussed here are Electrical, Cooling, Heating, Plumbing, Water Wells, Septic, Gas Wells and Fuel Tanks, and Security. Select the systems that apply to your situation, and note them for inclusion in your custom preventive maintenance checklist.

Electrical Systems

Electrical systems are not very dynamic in the usual sense of the word. Although electricity does indeed "run" through the system, there are not that many moving parts other than components that either make the current available (outlets) or start the current flowing and turn it off again, when desired (switches). In fact, practically the entire system consists of insulated wires strung throughout the house, hidden within walls and making themselves known through, in addition to outlets and switches, fixtures such as ceiling lamps and direct-wired appliances. Other than the main electrical box with old-fashioned fuses or more modern circuit breakers, the rest of the system, though hidden, is quite simple.

It is simple, but if not carefully maintained, it is dangerous. The electrical system is a system that you should consider as the household's number one concern, especially when something within it appears to be amiss.

Although entire books have been written on installing and caring for electrical systems, this section will highlight the main points. Some simple repairs can be undertaken by homeowners who follow detailed instructions complete with illustrations. The safest tack, of course, is simply to have a qualified electrician perform inspections, maintenance, and repairs. On the other hand, knowing how to change a light switch or repair a damaged electrical cord plug (see Figure 40-1) requires a basic understanding of electricity that every homeowner should possess.

40-1. A damaged plug.

ELECTRICAL DROPS

An overhead electrical drop is an energized overhead wire by which the main electrical supply enters a house. This main wire should clear by at least 12 feet any ground where vehicles may pass underneath, and where pedestrians may walk, by 10 feet. It must also be at least 3 feet above any relatively flat roof (where people could walk), and it cannot pass close to windows or balconies or anywhere else that someone could conceivably reach. Other hazards to electrical drops include vines, tree limbs, and other wires or cables that could rub against it, such as telephone or cable television lines.

If you notice any of these problems developing, or if the insulation from an overhead drop is starting to rot off, notify the electric company at once.

Another place that a main electric supply line can enter a house is beneath the ground. Many modern subdivisions boast of underground utilities. Here the electricity is brought through underground wires in conduits or piping made of plastic or metal, often about 2 inches in diameter. These conduits are fairly durable, and will last for years and years as long as construction excavations do not damage them.

In both cases, the main electrical service should be well supported where it reaches the house. Typically, the utility company is responsible for installing, repairing, and maintaining electrical supply lines to customers' homes. That is nice to know, but it won't do you much good if your power gets knocked out by a falling limb or tree. It is a good idea to report potential trouble to the electric company so they can have overhanging branches removed as a preventive measure. Whatever you do, never attempt to prune tree limbs that are over or even near electrical lines. That is a job best left to professionals.

ELECTRIC METERS

These mysterious-looking meters are, to say the least, quite confusing to individuals not trained in electric meter operation. (See Figure 40-2.) They are especially difficult to inspect for accuracy. About the only way is to shut off all electricity to the house, then peer at the spinning wheel to see if it has stopped. Usually, though, homeowners just take the electric company's word that the meter is accurate. Perhaps the best way to tell if your meter is working correctly is to obtain estimates of cost for various appliance operations. Then estimate what you use for a particular period, and match your estimates with an actual bill.

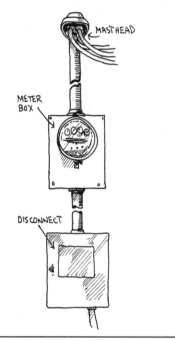

40-2. Electric meter.

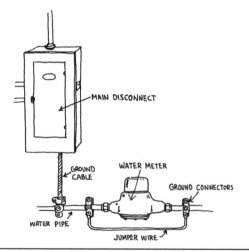

40-3. Grounded wire.

MAIN POWER GROUNDING

Your main electrical panel box should be grounded to a rod driven into the earth or attached to a metal cold water supply line. (See Figure 40-3.) Grounding reduces the chance of shock, fire, and damage to appliance electrical motors. It also helps protect a home from lightning. Sometimes it is difficult to tell if a

ground wire exists, because it may be hidden by a finished room or wall. If that is the case, an electrician should be asked to verify that a ground connection exists.

THE MAIN CONTROL PANEL

This is where electricity from the main power line is split into a number of separate circuits distributed throughout the house. It contains a number of circuits protected by fuses or circuit breakers, and a main disconnect switch. (See Figures 40-4 and 40-5.) Test the main disconnect switch by first turning lights on in every room. When the main disconnect switch is pulled, all the lights in the house should go out. If they don't, there is a serious and dangerous problem with the system. Call an electrician at once to track it down.

Ideally, everything on the panel should be clearly labeled. You should be able to open the door and see where each circuit runs. For example:

#1 Electric range, kitchen
#2 Dishwasher and disposal, kitchen
#3 Rest of kitchen
#4 Dining and living rooms
#5 Family room and outside patio
#6 Basement furnace
#7 Basement hot water heater
#8 Basement washer and dryer

The purpose of this customized list of circuits is so you can isolate a circuit that you may want to disconnect temporarily because it needs to be worked on or some problem has come up. You can then shut off a single circuit without disabling the rest of the home's electrical supply.

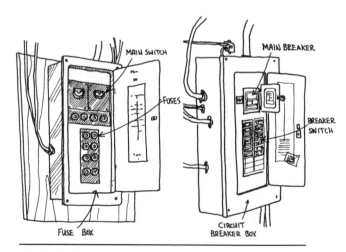

40-4. Fuse box panel.
40-5. Circuit breaker panel.

If circuit breaker switches or fuses are not clearly marked on your main panel, you can either call an electrician to trace the circuits and see where they go, or you can perform that task yourself, through a series of trial and error experiments. Turn on every electrical item — lamp, television, radio, clothes washer, etc., throughout the house. Then mark down what gets shut off as you turn off each circuit switch or fuse in sequence. Enlist the help of a friend or family member to simplify the procedure.

Safety Notes
- Never stand on a wet or damp floor (especially in your bare feet) while working with the main panel. Wear rubber-soled shoes and stand on dry boards rather than in a puddle of water.
- If you find fuses or circuit breakers that are very warm or hot to the touch, there is a serious defect present. Call an electrician right away. The same goes for any signs of melted insulation in the wires leading from the box. That means the fuses or circuit breakers might be too large for the wire that was used.
- The panel itself should be free from rust and in a location protected from dripping water or large amounts of condensation.

FUSES

An electrical fuse is a device designed to act as the weakest link in an electrical circuit. When too much electricity is drawn through the system the fuse is connected to, a small strip of metal visible through the glass window of the fuse "burns through" or "blows." Afterwards, the fuse may look burned or discolored. A burned fuse cannot be reset. Instead, it is replaced in almost the same manner as an electric light bulb. After shutting the main power switch off, simply unscrew the burned fuse and replace it with one of the recommended amperage—usually the same amperage as that of the fuse being replaced. The "bottom" rim of a fuse is insulated and is the only part of the fuse or fuse box you should touch when replacing a damaged fuse. (See Figure 40-6.) Using a fuse with a higher amperage could cause enough heat buildup to start a fire. Some electricians can "read" broken fuses. For example, when the fuse window surface is discolored, a short circuit is the likely cause. If the fuse window is clear and the broken fuse wire inside can be seen, an overloaded circuit is often the case. After unplugging some of the appliances that were on the circuit when the circuit failed and replacing the fuse, if it blows again with fewer items drawing power, there may be an appliance with de-

fective wiring that is causing the problem. Check each appliance on the circuit for visibly defective wiring or plugs.

BLOWN FUSE

40-6. Replacing a damaged or blown fuse.

The greatest danger with ordinary fuses is that they can be replaced with fuses of heavier capacities. That, of course, defeats the purpose of a correctly rated fuse which is supposed to blow before an overloaded circuit starts a wiring fire. It is recommended that only fuses of the correct size be kept on hand to prevent the temptation to put a larger fuse in place "just to get by" until one of the correct capacity can be obtained.

The clothes washer, dryer, refrigerator, dishwasher, water pump, and other major appliances that are heavy users of electricity should have circuits to themselves, usually 20 amps or more each.

CIRCUIT BREAKERS

Circuit breakers can be considered improved versions of fuses. If a circuit breaker turns off (or "trips") because too much demand or draw is placed on the part of the wiring the individual circuit breaker represents, simply follow the resetting instructions on the electrical panel box where the breakers are located. Usually this means flipping the thrown circuit breaker switch back on. The nice thing about circuit breakers is they can't be defeated or altered as easily as fuses. Even so, a tripped circuit breaker means that something has overloaded that part of the electrical system. The cause of the overload should be identified and corrected or prevented from happening again. Most often the overload results from too many appliances being operated at the same time, or from running defective electrical equipment. A malfunctioning switch, a worn appliance cord, or a broken plug connection can all cause circuit breakers to trip.

Sometimes a household can go for years without having a circuit breaker trip. Because of that likelihood, it is a good idea to trip breakers manually a few times per year to make sure the contacts are in working order. To see if they work, simply check the appliances on the circuit while the breaker is tripped. If the appliances still operate while the breaker is tripped, there is something wrong—the breakers aren't providing the safety measure for which they are intended. Circuit breakers can be reset by first switching the breaker all the way off, and then back to all the way on.

WIRING

If a circuit becomes overloaded because it is trying to draw more electricity than it was designed to provide, this is a major wiring concern. Overloads frequently occur when something that requires a lot of energy—a toaster or clothes iron, for example—is plugged in and operated while a number of other appliances are being run from the same circuit. Sometimes an overloaded circuit may not trip a switch or blow a fuse. It could manifest itself in other ways—light bulbs may dim, toasters and irons may heat slowly or never reach their potential. If the fuses or circuit breaker switches don't function properly, the appliances being run on an overloaded circuit may be damaged beyond repair.

In many older homes, the electrical systems are hopelessly outdated and should be replaced entirely. Knob-and-tube wiring and limited fuse-box services should be pulled out in favor of more modern, heavy-duty wiring. If you have doubts about any wiring system, warning signs include warm cover plates on switches and outlets, dead outlets, flickering lights, or smoke coming from outlets or appliances. Also watch out for live wires hanging from the ceiling, or switches, outlets, and junction boxes without covers—revealing the bare wires within. (See Figures 40-7 and 40-8.)

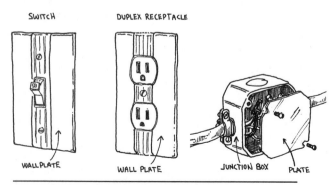

40-7. Wall switch and receptacle.
40-8. Junction box.

POWER OUTAGES

It happens. Entire cities have been without power for hours or days at a time, due to an overloaded transformer, a major accident, or a natural disaster.

Some individuals believe that when power is lost to the entire house, the home's appliances and miscellaneous electric components are at risk. That is true, but the problem exists when the electric service is first restored after the power failure is over. Most damage is done when the initial surge of power comes bursting through the lines. To prevent this surge from damaging equipment, especially equipment such as computers, stereo systems, televisions, refrigerators, electric water heaters, and others, simply unplug them. Keep the equipment unplugged and wait until your lights come back on and are not flickering before you start plugging in appliances.

Whenever you experience a total power failure, make sure you do leave at least one light in the on position, so you will know when the power is restored. And always check with your neighbors to see if they are in a similar situation. If they have power and you don't, you will know that the problem is probably not with the electric company. If that happens, and it is not something simple, such as your ten-year-old son just pulled the main disconnect switch to see what would happen, call an electrician immediately.

ELECTRIC MOTORS

All electric motors should be inspected, cleaned, and oiled (if needed) at least twice a year. If an electric motor is correctly matched for its job, beyond routine wear, the main thing to watch out for is dust and dirt. Electric motors are air cooled. If dust, dirt, or lint accumulate in the vents of a motor or motor housing, excessive heat can build up. Heat buildup will shorten a motor's life and cause fires by igniting dust or lint. After making sure that a motor has been unplugged or otherwise shut off from the electric supply, vacuum the motor's exterior with a brush or crevice tool, or use a small soft-bristle brush on smaller units. If any lubricating oil or grease has built up on an electric motor's housing, wipe it off. Oil and grease attract dust and lint and can ignite if the motor overheats. Oil and grease can also rot rubber insulation on wires.

Some electric motors need to be oiled. Others, with sealed bearings, don't require additional lubrication. On older motors or on motors you don't have instructions for, if they have small "oil cups" on the ends, that means the motor should be lubricated occasionally with a few drops of electric motor oil. Naturally, for motors you have instructions for, follow the recommended maintenance to the letter.

Here is a list of common pieces of equipment that come with electric motors:

Vacuum cleaner
Floor polisher and waxer
Fan
Air conditioner
Automatic garage door opener
Sump pump
Swimming pool filter
Water pump
Oil hot water heater
Oil burner
Circulating hot water boiler
Furnace
Exhaust fan
Clothes dryer
Washing machine
Trash compactor
Garbage disposal
Dishwasher
Freezer
Refrigerator
Compact disc player
Record player
Food mixer
Electric clock
Electric toothbrushes
Power tools

ELECTRIC LAMP SOCKETS

The average life span of a lamp socket with a pull chain is between two and four years if heavily used. The most common failure is when something inside the socket breaks so the pull chain "sticks" and the light cannot be turned either off or on. Lamp sockets, because they are relatively inexpensive to purchase and difficult to repair, should generally be replaced when they fail. In fact, you will save both money and inconvenience if you learn how to replace sockets and keep several on hand. Many hardware and builder's supply stores offer free pamphlets on replacing electrical wall sockets, switches, and lamp sockets. After making sure the item you are working on has been shut off from the electrical supply, it is really just a matter of correctly connecting a few wires.

Lighting fixtures should also be inspected. Are the mounting bases fastened tightly to ceilings and walls? Are the fixtures themselves well made? If they hang from swag or other chains, can you see any bare wires

within the chain? Replace fixtures that don't measure up.

While on the subject of lights, also consider that outside lighting fixtures should be watertight.

ELECTRICAL OUTLETS

Modern outlets have three holes. The third or odd hole is for the ground wire. Older two-hole outlets may be grounded inside, but you need to use an adapter to insert a modern, three-prong plug. The adapter, however, will not supply any grounding protection unless its pigtail is fastened to the center screw of the outlet cover.

Grounded three-prong outlets should be installed throughout a house. Outlets in areas where water plays an important part should have ground fault interrupters, especially in bathrooms and outdoor locations. A ground fault interrupter (GFI) shuts off the electrical current when it senses the presence of water. It has a test button that should be pressed and reset at least once a month. If the test button will not reset, the outlet should be replaced. Since replacing a GFI receptacle is more difficult than replacing an ordinary one, it is best handled by an electrician.

ELECTRICAL SAFETY

See the specific section on electrical safety. The main thing to remember is, until you are certain that an electrical circuit has been disconnected, assume that it is active and "hot." Never work on an electrical appliance unless it has been disconnected.

Heat-producing wires can be affixed to the edges of roofs in cold-climate locations to prevent snow and ice from building up, blocking gutters, and forming dangerous icicles. (See Figure 40-9.)

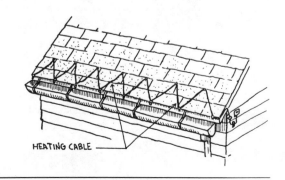

HEATING CABLE

40-9. Heat or snow melt wires.

ELECTRICAL SYSTEM QUICK CHECKLIST

❑ Make sure the main electrical supply wire is sturdily attached to the house, and free from encroaching tree limbs or other wires and cables.

❑ Make sure your main electrical panel box is properly grounded.

❑ See that the main panel's circuits are clearly labeled.

❑ Never replace a burned-out fuse with a higher-rated model.

❑ Major appliances that are heavy users of electricity should have individual circuits to themselves.

❑ Inspect, clean, and lubricate (if necessary) electric motors at least twice per year.

❑ Make sure bathroom and outdoor electrical outlets are protected by ground fault interrupters.

Cooling Systems

Years ago, enjoying cold air during summer meant a trip to an ice house to select frozen fish. Nowadays, anyone who can afford it can have cool, crisp air during the hottest summer weather. In warm climate locations, air conditioning has become a must in homes, public buildings, and automobiles.

There are two ways of looking at air conditioning: for individual rooms or parts of a house, or for the entire living area. That translates to window air conditioners or units, and central air conditioning. Whether you have one or the other, avoid waiting for the hottest part of a day to turn on the air conditioning. Instead, begin to cool your room, area, or home a short time before it starts to get hot. It is better to achieve a cool atmosphere gradually. If you try to turn up the air conditioning full blast to cool down a hot house, it will require a considerable effort that will strain the system and use more energy than necessary.

Another important operating tip is to shield the inside of your home from direct and indirect sunlight during the times you are air conditioning. Close drapes, blinds, and shutters. If that is not practical for you, consider installing special coatings or films to your windows. A quality window film will block much of the heat from direct sunlight and will also cut down on radiant heat produced by reflected sunlight.

Because cool air falls, it is best introduced to a room toward the ceiling, or aimed upwards through movable vents from a window unit so it can roll its way through the room or area, cooling additional air on its way.

WINDOW UNIT INSPECTIONS

Window units require the least amount of installation expenses.

- Is the unit firmly attached to a window opening? Are the support brackets in good condition? The installation should be secure and airtight. Wall-mounted units are generally set into sleeves that are built into an exterior wall. The sleeve should be caulked where it passes through the wall. After that, the unit itself should be weatherstripped so that it fits nicely, and without any open seams, into the sleeve. (See Figure 41-1.)

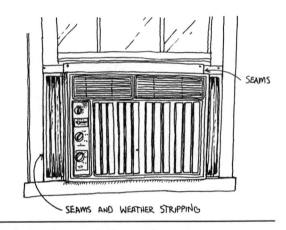

41-1. Sealing a window unit.

- Are weatherstripping and gaskets tight? Do they seal out unwanted warm air?
- Are shrubs, hedges, and trees trimmed so none block or interfere with the condenser? There has to be a free flow of fresh air for an air conditioner to work efficiently.
- Are drapes, curtains, or furniture items blocking the front of the unit?
- Are drain pans and outlets clean and unobstructed?

Summer is the best time to inspect an air conditioner. Unplug or disconnect the unit's power. Remove the outer cover so you can see the inside. Inspect the filter. Does it need to be cleaned or replaced? Air conditioners draw air from a room into and through the machine, so the front of the unit often collects large amounts of lint and dust that can cover and clog vital parts. Check the mounting screws, nuts, and bolts for snugness. Some could have vibrated loose during the last cooling season. Coils that are packed with dust and dirt will be inefficient. Inspect all motor and fan belts. A belt should not deflect (or "wiggle") more than between ½ to ³/₄ inch.

WINDOW UNIT REPAIRS AND MAINTENANCE

Air conditioners are similar in nature to refrigerators and freezers, in that most major repairs should probably be made by a qualified technician. And just as refrigerators and freezers need little maintenance attention, so do air conditioners.

1. Outside, keep nearby foliage trimmed so it won't encroach on the compressor. On the other hand, it makes good sense to keep direct sunlight from burning down on the unit during the afternoon, so usually a few well-positioned bushes or trees can help provide a certain amount of shade during the summer.
2. If the exterior fins on the compressor are dirty, shut off the electricity to the unit, open it up, and wash soiled sections from the inside out with water from a garden hose. (See Figure 41-3.)
3. Tighten bolts, nuts, screws, and any other fasteners which may have vibrated loose. One way to tell quickly if fasteners need tightening is if a window unit is making a lot of noise. Especially check for loose screws on exterior panels.
4. Recaulk brittle, cracked window seals.
5. Oil when necessary, according to the manufacturer's instructions.
6. Vacuum and wipe lint, dust, and dirt from the grillwork (see Figure 41-2), the condenser coils, and the insides, being careful not to damage the inner workings with vacuum crevice tools. Replace stretched or deteriorated belts. Carefully brush or vacuum dust and lint from the fan blades occasionally. This will help ensure a maximum air flow and will keep the unit operating near its original efficiency rating.

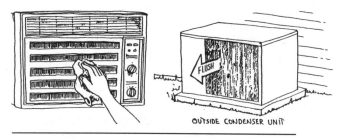

41-2. Wiping a window unit grill.
41-3. Flushing out condenser fins.

7. Keep drain pans and outlets free from rust. When rust starts to form, clean it with steel wool, then touch up the spot with rustproof paint.
8. After fall weather is officially over, remove air conditioners from windows. Clean them and replace their filters. Vacuum the insides again, win-terize according to the manufacturer's instructions, cover, and store in a safe, dry place. If the unit cannot be removed from the window, clean and cover it in place. But take greater pains to cover the unit's exterior portion so it won't be affected by winter weather.

CENTRAL AIR CONDITIONING INSPECTIONS

There is considerably more involved with central air than with window units.

- The main operating unit is usually located outside, on a slab of poured concrete, on concrete blocks, or even on formed plastic platforms. Is the unit level, or has it tilted? Look for cracks or settling of the concrete or other platform, which could cause the unit to make loud rattling noises while running. Settling could also fracture the refrigeration lines.
- Inspect the main unit's exterior. Listen for strange noises. Look for leaks and corrosion.
- Make sure that vegetation is not allowed to encroach on the main refrigeration unit. Every other week or so check the condenser's housing to make sure that vents are not being blocked by leaves, grass clippings, or other yard debris. On the other hand, shade from a nearby tree will help protect the same unit from working overtime under the heat of direct sunlight.
- Are the cooling ducts insulated? If they are not, the overall effectiveness of the system will be greatly reduced. If uninsulated ducts pass through a hot attic or crawlspace, conditioned air will be warmed up while it is being delivered. Look for cracks and open seams, too, from which cool air can escape.
- Have the entire system checked and serviced at least once a year by a qualified technician. The technician should check the condition of the refrigerant and look for possible leaks.
- Are filters plugged with dust and dirt? Are the outside finned surfaces of the condenser covered with leaves, mud, spiderwebs, or miscellaneous debris? Is the coil dirty?
- Check interior belts, blower motors, and condenser fan motors.

CENTRAL AIR CONDITIONING REPAIRS AND MAINTENANCE

Most of the repairs, and much of the maintenance, are nearly the same as for window units. Keep everything clean, make sure belts are kept in good condition, and see that blower motors receive proper lubrication, as recommended by the manufacturer. When the cooling season ends, cover the outside compressor to keep it out of the weather.

NOTE: When installing a new central air conditioner, locate outdoor compressors away from decks, patios, bedroom windows, and dryer vents. Also avoid interior corners that tend to accentuate the compressor noise and restrict proper air flow. Instead, look for a shaded area that is out of the way.

COOLING SYSTEM QUICK CHECKLIST

❑ Keep air conditioners and condensers from being blocked by encroaching vegetation, furniture, and other objects.

❑ Shelter outside parts of air conditioners and condensers from direct sunlight.

❑ Keep grills, coils, and all exterior and interior parts clean.

❑ Keep drain pans and lines clean and unobstructed. Change or clean filters when needed.

❑ Check and tighten all fastening hardware if necessary.

❑ Recaulk brittle, cracked, or missing window seals around window air-conditioning units.

❑ Winterize air-conditioning units and systems at the end of each cooling season.

❑ Make sure that cooling ducts are insulated if they pass through hot attics or crawlspaces.

❑ Have a central air-conditioning system inspected and serviced at least once a year by a qualified technician.

❑ Follow servicing recommendations for belts, blower motors, and condenser fan motors.

Heating Systems

Heating and cooling systems are probably the hardest working components of any home, especially in homes located in climates having temperature extremes. There are six primary types of fuel available for home heating use: electricity, fuel oil, gas, coal, wood, and solar energy. Electricity is a clean fuel that leaves no residues to contaminate or soil the house or atmosphere. Its maintenance chores are few. Fuel oil, if the burner is kept tuned, can be a relatively clean-burning fuel. But if the burner is out of tune—watch out. It will soil drapes and other furnishings throughout the house. It also needs to be stored on site in a large fuel tank. Natural gas and liquid propane are clean fuels burned by forced-air furnaces that require routine maintenance. Coal is an old-fashioned fuel rarely used anymore to heat homes. It is too dirty, even before it is burned, and it leaves large amounts of ash after combustion occurs. Wood heat may sound nice—and it can be a nice supplemental source of warmth—but it takes a considerable amount of manual effort to keep it on line.

Here is a rundown on the types of heat production and delivery systems, and how to keep them running through cold times.

FORCED-AIR HEATING UNITS

These systems burn fuel to create a supply of warm air that is blown (or forced) by a fan through a duct system to various parts of the house. During its operation, this type of furnace heats air that is drawn from the rooms and then sends it back through ducts and registers out again into the rooms. The sheet-metal enclosures that route the air back to the furnace are known as the return ducts, and those supplying the air are supply ducts. Before the air comes back into the furnace from the return ducts, it goes through an air filter where most of the airborne dirt and dust are filtered out to protect the furnace from fouling its working parts.

Forced-air units can operate with a pilotless ignition that uses an electrical spark generated only at the moment the fuel flow begins. Forced-air furnaces require fairly simple, low frequency maintenance. The filters need occasional cleaning or changing; the electric motors and a few moving parts need a few drops of lubricating oil from time to time; and the blower belts need to be checked at the beginning of the heating season. Typical natural gas-fired units need to be tuned by a professional every other year or so, but forced-air furnaces fired with other fuels such as oil will benefit from more frequent tune-ups that will pay for themselves by saving more energy than the tune-ups themselves cost.

Here are some points to consider about forced-air furnaces (see Figure 42-1):

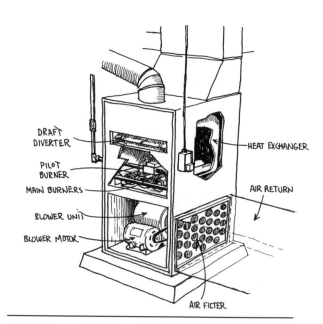

42-1. Forced-air furnace.

- On gas-fired systems, check the gas lines for rusty pipes and fittings. Run your hand along suspect areas. Do you smell gas? Is there an easy-to-use gas shut-off valve? There should be. If not, have one installed. Know how to light the pilot light in case it extinguishes unexpectedly.
- Usually the local gas company service person will adjust the pilot light level and the igniter controls.

To maintain everything functioning smoothly, keep the furnace clean. Periodically remove the grills and covers and vacuum all dirt, dust, and lint. Use a soft brush when cleaning around difficult areas such as the controls. Cleaning the furnace is important for a number of additional reasons. A dirty forced-air furnace will inevitably carry small amounts of airborne soot through the supply ducts and onto your walls, floors, and furnishings. This process is likely to be so gradual that the graying of white walls can occur without your realizing it.

▪ When the heating season ends and it comes time to shut down the furnace, extinguish the pilot light, but don't just blow it out. Instead, shut off the furnace's gas supply valve.

▪ Watch the gas flame as it flares up into the heat exchange chamber. If it angles off to the side, there may be a hole in the exchanger that is pulling it off course. If the flame is standing up straight and steady, the heat exchanger is probably in good working order. If the flames are flickering, the burners could need adjusting. Healthy flames burn blue. If the flames are orange or red, you are not getting the correct fuel-to-air combustion ratio. In that case, call a qualified service technician for help. Also look for corrosion on the burners. Buildups of rust can clog the burner jets. A simple cleaning can correct this problem.

▪ Listen to the furnace run. If you hear unusual clunking or growling noises while the blower is on, there could be worn fan bearings or a defective fan belt. Some units have permanently lubricated bearings, while other furnace bearings should be oiled at the beginning of the heating season and perhaps one more time as the season reaches its midpoint. Motor, fan, and oil cups can be reached when the front or side panels are removed. Fan belts, or V-belts that run from the electric motor on the furnace to the blower fan unit that forces the air through the ductwork, will fray and wear at their edges. They will also stretch. Fan belts should be adjusted, tightened, or replaced if they have more than ½ inch of play in them. Belt stretching can be corrected up to a point by taking up the slack. Loosen the bolts on the blower motor mount and move the motor slightly farther away from the blower. Naturally, before you attempt to adjust any of a furnace's moving parts, always turn off the unit's electric power.

▪ When a furnace is in active use, clean or change the air filters about once a month. Disposable filters are inexpensive. A clogged filter can reduce the efficiency of heat output by as much as 70 per-

cent, which will cause the entire system to strain unnecessarily to reach its thermostat setting. The air is drawn from the inside of the house. After being drawn through the filter, it gets warmed by the burning fuel then blown back into the house through a system of ducts and registers. If you live in a dusty environment, or if you own a pet that sheds a lot of long hair, you will have to change or clean the air filter more frequently.

HOT-WATER HEATING UNITS

With this kind of system, water is heated in a boiler by a gas, oil, or other burner and then pumped throughout the house through a piping network equipped with radiators. The hot water heats the radiators, and the heat is radiated into the rooms. A similar system can be operated with steam. Here are some guidelines for maintaining hot-water systems (see Figure 42-2):

▪ When you turn on your system at the beginning of the heating season, bleed or let out trapped air in each of the radiators. The trapped air is from gradual accumulations that build up in heating pipes, baseboards, and radiators. Early signs of this are gurgling noises or the sounds of running water every time the heat goes on. Air pockets will hinder the water flow, and the radiators or baseboard units won't heat properly. For radiators, just open the unit's bleeder valve at one end to allow the excess air to escape. When a stream of water squirts out (catch it with a rag or sponge), enough air has been released. Close the valve immediately. Many baseboard units have vent screws through which air can be released. Otherwise, look at the boiler operating manual to see if there is a purge mechanism near the boiler that allows air to be released from the system. Some baseboard systems run continuously around the house instead of dead-ending from room to room.

▪ Make sure that radiator shut-off valves do not leak. Even a few drops of water seeping out around a valve stem can leave stains on wood flooring or soften and stain the ceilings of a room below.

▪ Quite a few things can go wrong with a hot-water boiler heating unit. As a group, boiler systems are somewhat temperamental. Read your unit's operating instructions carefully, and have your boiler inspected by a professional at least once before each heating season. Watch what he or she does, ask questions, and take notes, because you should be repeating the inspection yourself at least once a month during the rest of the heating season.

▪ There should be a low-water emergency cutoff that

will prevent the boiler from running if not enough water is in the tank for it to run safely. The low-water cutoff should be purged about once a month to expel any rust or corrosion that might settle there and plug the line, and to see if the cutoff actually works. The level of the water in the boiler should also be checked through the unit's sight glass.

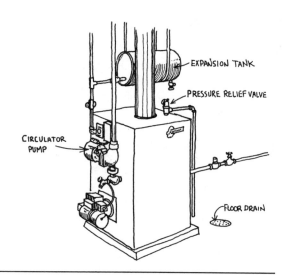

42-2. Hot water heating system.

- The temperature of the water inside some boilers is controlled by an aquastat (instead of a thermostat). The temperature setting should be carefully adjusted to meet but not exceed heating water requirements. Consider that lowering an aquastat can save fuel much in the same manner as lowering a thermostat can.
- The boiler's expansion tank—for the expansion of water within the tank—should have a pressure relief valve that will prevent excessive pressure buildups. Consult the owner's manual to see how to confirm that the pressure relief valve is in good working order.
- Make sure the water circulator pump and motor are serviced and lubricated, if necessary, every heating season.
- If your system is oil-fired, make sure you have your oil burner inspected and tuned up by a qualified service technician. The combustion chamber should be cleaned, the heat exchanger should be cleaned, the oil pump pressure should be checked and regulated if necessary, and the oil filter should be replaced. Final combustion ratios should also be tested and adjusted if required.
- Dust or vacuum radiators frequently. Avoid covering or blocking them with boxes, books, furniture,

or anything else that could hinder their heating performance.

ELECTRIC HEATING UNITS

Straight electric heating systems use electricity directly as a heat source. Simply put, electricity is converted to heat when it moves through conductors that resist the flow of current. The conductors or heating elements become hot and give off heat. The heat is then distributed via baseboard heaters that can be located anywhere. The system is simple to maintain because there is practically nothing to do. Electric heat uses no boiler, no furnace, no ductwork, no chimney, and few moving parts to wear out.

Then why isn't electric heat taking over the industry? Well, electric heat is a rather dry heat; humidification is usually necessary during times of low humidity. And sometimes the actual heating surfaces get hot enough to pose a danger to young children. But those aren't the reasons. The determining factor has been that electric heat has historically been more expensive to provide than that of other systems.

Practically the only maintenance chore required by electrical heating systems is periodically to clean off and vacuum dust and dirt from the baseboard heating components.

HEAT PUMPS

This system can make sense in locations having mild weather year round. It employs available cool outdoor air to chill refrigeration coils. The liquid in the coils compresses, and in the process heat is created and given off into the house. In summer, the entire process can be reversed and used to cool the home. Electricity is the fuel used to create the mechanical energy, which then converts unusable heat to usable heat. In simple terms, a heat pump can be described as an air conditioner that runs two ways. During warm weather, it removes heat from the inside air and pumps it outside. In cold weather, the unit takes heat from outside air and brings it inside, even during winter. The efficiency of a heat pump falls off as the outside temperature drops, so many of these units include conventional electrical heating elements to supplement their "heat pump" heat.

Maintenance of heat pumps is similar to that of cooling systems. Make sure the indoor coil on the heat pump is clean and free of dust and debris. Dirty coils reduce the unit's efficiency and lessen the system's operating life span.

SOLAR AND OTHER ALTERNATIVE HEATING SYSTEMS

These "maverick" heating units should generally be inspected and maintained as recommended by the manufacturers. Make sure you know where the emergency shutoff valves and switches are, and how to restart the system once it is off. Ask the service technician what you should be doing between his or her service calls. Know how to confirm that everything in the system is working safely and efficiently.

THERMOSTATS

All central heating systems have at least one thermostat that should be mounted on an inside wall, about 4 feet above the floor. No cold drafts should affect it, and neither should warm air from the heating system itself. A thermostat in direct line with an outside entrance will receive blasts of cold air whenever the door is opened, which will, in turn, kick on the heating system. On the other hand, a thermostat directly above a hot-air register will be bathed in warm air—a similar false alarm that tells the furnace to stop producing heat.

Check and clean a thermostat by removing its cover and carefully vacuuming the insides about once a month to prevent dust buildup. If problems develop, call a professional to inspect and calibrate the thermostat.

CHIMNEYS AND FLUES

When fuels are burned in a heating system, gases are produced. Those gases must be vented, usually through the home's chimney. They are most often vented through flue pipes that run to the home's main chimney. Flue pipes should be tightly connected to the chimney to prevent gases from poisoning the home's air. Within the chimney, a liner provides a measure of safety for transporting unburned fuel and exhaust fumes up and out of the home. If, during your inspection, you determine that flue pipes are heavily laden with soot and carbon deposits, have them cleaned before the heating season begins.

The topmost section of the chimney should also be inspected at the beginning of the season, to make sure that no birds, squirrels, or other creatures have built nests that will block the free flow and discharge of heating gases. To function safely, a chimney's insides must be clear. Some older chimneys require cleaning when bricks, stones, or mortar work loose and fall within the chimney. In any case, improper venting can cause a buildup of carbon monoxide—a gas that can kill practically without notice.

DUCTWORK

Heating (and cooling) ducts deliver warmed or cooled air throughout a house. When checking ducts, look at their joints. Are there any open gaps? If there are, seal them off with duct tape.

Make sure that all ducts and pipes running through unheated or uncooled areas are insulated. Places such as garages, basements, attics, and crawlspaces are notorious for losing heat or conducting cold air into the house when you don't want it there.

Many ducts end in heat registers and grills. See that those registers and grills are kept clean. Once in a while, remove their covers and vacuum as far down into them as the vacuum tool will reach.

INSULATION

Because a home's heating system is likely to be a major cost component in the household utility budget, it makes sense to try to reduce the amount of fuel needed to heat or cool a home's living areas throughout the year. Beyond purchasing a modern energy-efficient heating or cooling system, the second most important factor is providing as much properly installed insulation as is practical in your situation.

There are certain restrictions, of course. You can fit only so much insulation in old, thinly constructed walls. But generally, here's where you should consider adding more insulation, if possible (see Figure 42-3):

- Roofs.
- Ceilings with cold spaces above them.
- Exterior walls or walls between heated and unheated spaces.

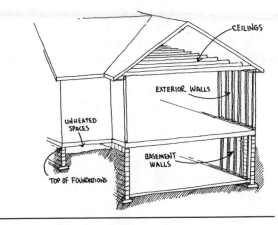

42-3. Where to insulate.

- Floors over unheated or outside spaces.
- Walls of finished or heated basements.
- Tops of foundation or basement walls.

Those are the big places. Small places include:

- Behind exterior wall light switches and outlets.
- Attic stairs or hatches.
- Around ducts and plumbing pipes.
- Around a water heater.

Insulating Finished Walls

This is probably the hardest insulating task. The only real choice here is blown insulation. Small holes are drilled into the side of the house between every pair of vertical studs or framing members. Insulation is then blown in under pressure through a hose. Care must be taken, however, when the passage of insulation is blocked by a horizontal framing member that spans and seals off a void insulation cannot reach. In that case, additional holes must be drilled to access those areas. There are two main types of blown insulation: foam and loose cellulose or mineral wool. Although the latter materials are less expensive, they may settle over the years, leaving uninsulated gaps. Another disadvantage of cellulose is that small rodents love to tunnel and make nests in it. The foam works by expanding to fill every available crevice, and then dries in place.

Insulating Attic Floors and Unfinished Walls

Attic floors are simple to insulate. Loose fill insulation comes in large, lightweight bags and can simply be poured between open attic joists that support the ceiling below—as long as there is no attic floor covering the joists. The loose fill material is made from a wide variety of materials, including fiberglass wool, cellulose, vermiculite, and perlite. Blankets and batts of insulation are even easier to handle. Both are made in various widths to fit between studs or joists spaced differently and in different thicknesses. Batts are manufactured in relatively short lengths. Blankets come in long rolls. Both kinds are available backed with foil or impregnated paper, which provides an effective vapor barrier wherever they are installed. They are also available without backing for use when adding to existing insulation where a vapor barrier already exists.

To be effective, the vapor barrier (which prevents trapping moisture within the house) must be positioned with the barrier side facing the heated area. And it must also be completely intact, without breaks or openings of any kind.

Seal all attic air leaks from the living spaces below. Weatherstrip around the edges of the attic access

hatch or door to prevent heated air from leaking into the cold attic atmosphere. This action will increase the effectiveness of the insulation, at very little cost. Remember to insulate the back of the hatch as well. (See Figure 42-4.)

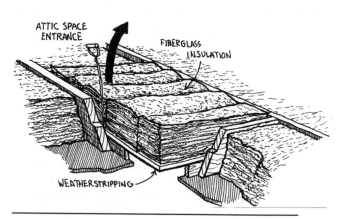

42-4. Attic hatch insulation.

Many homes have gable, soffit, or eave vents in their attics or roof crawlspaces. These vents allow air to flow up behind the insulation into the roof and out through attic vents, or, in some contemporary houses, through a continuous ridge vent at the roof peak. Eave vents tend to get painted over, and become blocked by wasp nests, dirt, or other debris. Some have screens on them to keep out insects. Make sure that such vents are still in place and in good condition. And see that your insulation isn't blocking them. If you have loose fill insulation, use cardboard baffles to keep the material off the soffit vents. (See Figure 42-5.) If the loose fill insulation is bunched up, use a rake to spread it evenly. Batts can be stapled back up or held in place with string or wire. Make sure that flammable insulation does not come into contact with any light fixtures or electrical boxes.

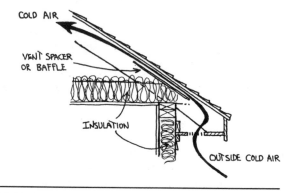

42-5. Attic baffles.

Insulating a Water Heater

Water heater insulation kits are available. Try to cut the insulation so it will fit around or encircle the tank in a single piece. Do not, however, cover the drain valve, pressure-relief valve, burner inlet, pilot access plate, or the draft hood at the top which might prevent toxic fumes from properly venting to the outdoors. Leave all the controls uncovered. (See Figure 42-6.) You don't have to cover every square inch of the water heater for the insulation to be effective.

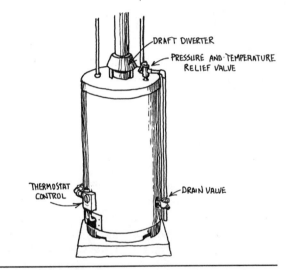

42-6. Hot water tank.

On oil heaters, it is important to keep insulation off the peep sight, oil burner mechanism, temperature controls, drain valve, pressure relief valve, and flue pipe.

Insulating Hot Water Pipes

Apply tubular or wrap-type insulation from the point where the pipe leaves the water heater tank to 2 or 3 feet up the vertical run. If the pipe makes a bend before that, just insulate to the bend. Tubular insulation must be cut the long way and "clamped" around the piping. The vertical seam can be sealed with duct tape. If desired, insulate additional lengths of hot water pipe in the same fashion, especially lengths that pass through cold or unheated areas. Wrap-type insulation can be trimmed with scissors.

Insulating Ducts

You will need a utility knife or heavy-duty scissors, pliers, duct tape, and foil-backed R-7 or R-11 insulation. All furnace and air conditioner ducts that run through unheated areas should be insulated. So should the plenum box or distribution duct located next to the furnace.

Cut the insulation 6 inches longer than is required to fit around the duct. Scrape the glass fiber or other insulation material off the foil backing from 6 inches at one end of the insulation piece. That will give you a 6-inch overlap that helps to hold the insulation in place. Apply the insulation, foil side out. Use duct tape to connect the overlap to the intact foil backing. Tape each joint between the separate pieces of insulation.

HUMIDIFIERS

In some locations and at some times of the year, dry air will occur naturally, or heat from the heating system can dry out the air inside a house and make it uncomfortable. This is particularly true of forced-air systems. If mechanical means for supplying moisture to the air are not available, the humidity inside a home can drop to levels approaching that of a desert environment. Such a condition can cause shrinking of wood and other materials, which might open gaps in the house structure itself. Dry air also damages furnishings. It can put a piano out of tune, cause fabrics to wear because they become more brittle, ruin plants, and cause cracks in ceilings and walls. On the human side, excessively dry air can cause nose, throat, and skin problems in household members.

Humidifiers are rather fragile mechanisms that put moisture back into the air within a home. In addition to correcting the ill effects mentioned above, more moisture will let you feel warmer at lower temperatures, so you can turn down the thermostat without sacrificing comfort.

Humidifiers are often installed as an add-on to the heating system, frequently in tandem with a forced-air furnace. Carefully review the owner's manual and follow the instructions to the letter. It is also advisable to have the unit serviced at least once a year by a professional heating and cooling technician. By far, most humidifiers eventually become either clogged with mineral deposits or become "dried up" and corroded beyond repair. But that is because they are neither understood nor cared for by their owners.

DEHUMIDIFIERS

A few paragraphs ago we were adding moisture to the air. Now we're taking it away. Dehumidifiers are for removing moisture from the home's air when there is too much moisture. That happens during periods of hot, moist weather when outdoor levels of humidity become oppressive.

Dehumidifiers are compact, heavy-duty appliances

that often run for years and years in harsh environments, needing little else but emptying. Some of them don't even need that if they can be attached by an outlet hose to the nearest floor drain. The main component is the automatic shutoff, with its signal that the water container is full and ready to be emptied. It is usually a small orange or red light on the front of the unit. Also, every so often clean and vacuum the compressor and coils.

The advantages of dehumidifiers are:

- They can economically convert damp rooms into livable space.
- They prevent warping of doors and furniture.
- They prevent drawers from sticking.
- They prevent costly moisture damages to windows, paneling, carpeting, paint, plaster, wall coverings, clothes, metal objects, and many other items.
- They help keep pipes from sweating and dripping.
- They are especially helpful in laundry rooms, recreation rooms, storage areas, basements, and workshops.

HUMIDITY FANS

These are small fan units that remove dampness and odors from bathrooms or other small enclosed places. Mount fans in the ceiling or wall, ideally near the bathtub or shower. Have a separate switch installed, or wire the fan to the light switch so that both go on simultaneously. Some city building codes require the simultaneous wiring for windowless bathrooms. For such a fan to work properly, there must be a passage for air to enter the bathroom from an outside source. Louvered panels in the bathroom door, or a door that is cut off slightly at the bottom, will be sufficient.

AIR CLEANERS

Forced air heating and air conditioning systems are ideal for the application of electrostatic air cleaners. They not only clean the air, but tend to make it smell fresher, which is a feature becoming more important with today's tightly-built homes. Other types of heating systems aren't as accommodating to the air cleaners, and separate units must be installed in individual rooms.

What will air cleaners clean? Pollen, spores, dust, and other microscopic irritants will be removed from household air. Ordinary fiberglass furnace filters screen out about 15 percent of airborne particles; high-efficiency air cleaners can remove up to 95 percent of the tiniest microscopic particles.

HEATING SYSTEM QUICK CHECKLIST

- ❑ Make sure pilot lights and burner flames are adjusted to burn efficiently: blue instead of orange or yellow.
- ❑ React immediately to the smell of natural gas and other fuels. Find the cause and have it corrected.
- ❑ Keep all furnace, boiler, and other heating components clean.
- ❑ Oil motors when needed.
- ❑ Replace or clean filters as scheduled.
- ❑ Tighten fan and blower belts.
- ❑ Have forced-air units professionally tuned up at least every other year. Tune oil-fired units and boilers at least once per heating season, and possibly twice, depending on the conditions.
- ❑ Bleed built-up air out of hot-water heating lines and radiators.
- ❑ Make sure that thermostats are positioned away from entrances and interior heat sources.
- ❑ Inspect and test all safety devices— boiler shutoffs, pressure- and temperature-relief valves, and related devices— several times during the heating season.
- ❑ Know where all fuel line shutoffs are. Operate them at least twice a year to keep them from "freezing" open or closed.
- ❑ Make sure unburned heating fuel and exhaust fumes are vented through flues and chimneys or other acceptable means.
- ❑ Insulate heating (and cooling) ductwork that passes through unheated areas.
- ❑ Find cold, drafty, and "bare" areas and insulate them.
- ❑ Insulate your water heater.
- ❑ Humidify dry air.
- ❑ Dehumidify overly moist air.

Plumbing Systems

There is a lot to plumbing, and a lot that can go wrong. Naturally, the most obvious conditions to inspect for are leaky pipes and fixtures. Those can generally be seen quickly enough; water dripping from a ceiling, a standing puddle of water in the basement, or ugly stained walls will all get noticed in a hurry. Look for dripping faucets, continuously running toilets, sluggish appliances and drains, and places that need to be sealed or caulked.

EMERGENCY SUPPLIES

There aren't many items you will need to make temporary repairs to plumbing. An immediate problem may be as simple as shutting off the valve to a sink or toilet or unplugging a drain. A few tools are in order, including:

- Screwdrivers, regular and phillips head models of varying sizes to fit faucet hardware, valves, and other key components.
- Adjustable pliers.
- At least two pipe wrenches.
- A rubber plunger or force cup.
- A clean-out auger or "snake."
- Pipe joint compound, used when connecting threaded pipes.
- Plumber's putty, used for a wide variety of tasks, including reseating the drain in sinks when leaks develop or when a new drain is installed.
- Assorted sizes of sheet rubber, up to 8 inches square.
- Several feet of old garden hose.
- A handful of wide and regular round hose clamps.
- And perhaps the most important item of all: two emergency phone numbers for plumbers who are on call or available 24 hours per day, seven days a week.

PLUMBING SAFETY

A number of important safety steps should be taken before working on plumbing.

- In most cases, turn off the water pressure.
- Disconnect electrical connections, if any.
- Drain hot water pipes.
- Make sure all electrical tools are grounded. Avoid using electrical equipment in wet areas. Dry everything first, or provide something else to stand or kneel on.
- Use the right tool for the job, and use it carefully. When wrenches slip off a pipe joint or handle, knuckles and fingers get bruised and cut.
- Handle pipes carefully. New pipes and pipes that have rusted through are very sharp. A good pair of gloves is a must when working with metal piping.
- Wear eye protection.
- Make sure the plumbing system is closed before turning the water on again.
- Natural gas supply lines can be considered part of a home's plumbing. If you ever smell gas, check the pilot lights to each gas appliance in the home. Stove burners may have been turned on without being lit. If you can't quickly locate the source of leaking gas, call the gas company immediately. While you are waiting, don't light any matches, and don't turn on or off electric switches or appliances. Open all windows. Turn off the main gas shutoff valve—the one located closest to the meter. Most gas valves require only a quarter turn, clockwise, with a wrench. When the emergency is over and the gas is turned back on, relight all the pilot lights. But make sure the gas to the pilot lights has been off long enough for ventilation to have carried away all gas that escaped from the earlier leak.

TRAPS

Plumbing traps are elongated, usually "U"-shaped sections of drainpipe (you will sometimes see "P" and "S" traps also, see Figure 43-1), constructed and installed between a drain or fixture and the rest of the plumbing or drainage system. Traps are constructed so that enough water remains at the bottom of the "U" to prevent sewer gas and odors from the home's plumbing system from backing up into the house. All fixtures that drain to the home's main sanitary sewer or line are trapped, except toilets. Toilets have similar mechanisms built into their bowl construction. If any fixture is used infrequently, such as a basement shower, it should be turned on at regular intervals to replace evaporating water so the barrier remains in place.

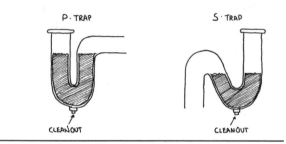

43-1. Traps.

Unfortunately, beyond trapping enough water to seal out gases created by waste matter, traps also do a fine job of occasionally trapping enough waste material and foreign objects to clog the pipe on which they are installed. On the other hand, this can be an advantage if your wedding ring slips down the kitchen sink drain while you are washing dishes. A threaded clean-out at the bottom of the trap can usually be unscrewed so the object, if small enough, can be recovered without disassembling the trap and pipes. Traps that have no clean-out plugs must, of course, be taken apart to be cleaned or otherwise accessed. Accumulations of hair, kitchen grease, and various other materials may find their way into the typical sink trap. That is why kitchen sinks, showers, bathtubs, and laundry tubs have strainers that fit over their drains. It is more practical simply to stop the material from going down the drain in the first place.

Cleaning a Sink Drain and Trap

To clean a sink drain and trap, there are a number of options. One of the simplest ways is using a plunger. Fill the sink basin with about 2 inches of water — enough for the rim of the plunger to be underwater. Plug the overflow opening (the hole toward the top of the sink) with a wet cloth or have someone hold a hand tightly over it while you are plunging. Double sinks or laundry tubs must have covered the part of the sink you are not plunging. That enables the force from the plunger to be applied to the pipe's obstruction instead of being wasted, blowing out of the overflow outlet or an adjacent sink drain. For a tighter plunger seal, wipe a little petroleum jelly along the plunger cup edge. Just place the suction part over the drain and pump up and down with the plunger handle. The goal with the alternating pressure and suc-

tion is to loosen the plug and push it to a larger size pipe. When you feel it loosen, send plenty of water down the drain behind it to push the obstruction out of your plumbing.

Another method for cleaning plugged drains and traps is with a drain cleaner. Liquid drain cleaners are the simplest to handle. The solid cleaners, if not used correctly, can solidify in a pipe or trap. And not all chemical drain cleaners can be used with plastic piping. Make sure you follow the manufacturer's instructions exactly. Don't improvise. Avoid putting larger quantities into your plumbing, or running hot water when the instructions say to use cold, or plunging a drain that is half full of backed up water and drain cleaner. (Keep in mind that if you use a chemical drain cleaner and end up calling a plumber anyway, he or she may charge extra to deal with the hazardous material.)

Consider periodic treatments with drain cleaners on traps that clog frequently or that can't be dismantled for cleaning.

A third to clear a drain is the trap clean-out. Place a pan beneath the clean-out plug to catch dripping water and debris. Unscrew the clean-out plug. If the blockage does not immediately gush out, bend the end of a wire coat hanger into a small hook. Gently poke the wire up the clean-out hole and run it up both sides of the trap. If that doesn't work, undo the slip nuts that hold the U-section to the sink and the rest of the plumbing. Or simply pull apart the friction connectors that hold newer traps. Remove the trap and clean it out with a bottle brush and running water from a different sink faucet. If the old trap is corroded, or if it falls apart when removed, replace the piece — and possibly adjacent components — with a plastic trap and connectors. The plastic won't corrode.

Another method is with a plumber's snake or an auger — a long coil of flexible steel with a point or hook at the end. By twisting or rotating the snake into a drain pipe, the snake will usually cut its way through the obstruction and will either push it into the main sewer line or enable you to pull it out. Depending on where the obstruction is, heavy-duty snakes up to 100 feet long can be rented.

Sometimes the obstruction might be closer to the home's sewer lines. If that is the case, sewer lines usually have one or more clean-out plugs that can be removed. (See Figure 43-2.) If the obstruction is near the clean-out, you may be able to remove the clog with a wire or short plumber's snake. A garden hose is another alternative, with or without water pressure. Where possible, the water should be turned on full force.

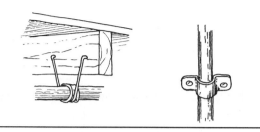

43-2. Pipe hangers.

If your washing machine, dishwasher, or other water-using appliance begins to leak, first check that the plumbing trap the machine drains through is completely open. Sometimes a partially clogged drain can cause an overflow within an appliance.

PIPING

Four different types of plumbing pipes can be found in homes today. Cast iron pipe is strong and durable. It is been in general use for drain, sewer, and vent lines for years. Galvanized steel pipe was used for transporting water before copper lines gained widespread acceptance. Copper pipe is the number one choice to supply hot and cold water throughout today's modern houses. Copper pipe can be bent or curved rather easily, an advantage not available with cast iron, galvanized steel, or most plastics. Plastic pipe is considerably less expensive than copper, galvanized steel, or cast iron. It is also simple to install, repair, and maintain. There is no need for torches and solder, or measuring and threading the ends. Instead, there are convenient plastic fittings, easy-to-cut plastic pipe, a can of plastic cement, and a brush. Almost anyone can work with it. There are other advantages to plastic pipe. It is extremely lightweight and easy to support. Plastic is chemically inert and unaffected by corrosive materials. The smooth inside surface of plastic pipe aids the movement of materials through the lines. On the other hand, it is not as strong as the other types, and it doesn't have the bending capability of copper.

Whatever the piping material, your first concern is leakage. Inspect all of the pipes you can see, and also the joists or beams to which they are attached. Be on the lookout for wet, moldy sections of wood or concrete and recent water stains. To repair leaking pipes temporarily, first shut off the water supply ahead of the leak. Next, wrap a single layer of sheet rubber around the leak. Place a wide clamp over the rubber and tighten the clamp screws so the rubber beneath the clamp is pressed against the leak. Another method is to use a section of garden hose held in place with two small clamps.

Although copper pipes should last the lifetime of a house, if a joint loosens, it will have to be re-soldered. Soldering copper piping is a tricky procedure that may not be worth gearing up for and learning. Most people are better off letting a plumber do it. Loose plastic piping joints are easier to tackle, but, depending on where they are, you may want to consider a plumber for those, too.

Copper piping should be suspended or fastened to joists or beams with copper, rubber, or nylon straps, never galvanized metal. Copper should not come in contact with steel beams, heating ducts, nails, or other dissimilar materials. If this is the case in your plumbing, and you notice corrosion or mineral deposits on the outside of any metal pipe or joint, there is probably a leak in the making.

If you hear a banging or vibrating sound when you turn faucets off and on quickly, this is a condition known as water hammer. It sounds a lot worse than it really is. It can often be stopped through installation of some additional hangers and supports so the pipes are affixed more firmly. It is usually the horizontal runs in the basement or in a crawlspace that are affected. Add enough hangers and supports so the pipe can't be moved by hand. (See Figure 43-2.) Another way to stop hammering is to install short lengths of capped vertical piping on the supply line to provide a cushioning air chamber. In certain cases, special coiled pipes and more expensive pneumatic cushioning devices will do the trick.

Although water hammer seems more of an irritation than a serious problem, in worst cases fittings can be loosened over time.

In cold climate locations, inspect all pipes that run through unheated areas. House trailers are notorious for frozen piping. Protecting water pipes from freezing can prevent the disastrous situation of a burst pipe during winter, with its accompanying damage and inconvenience. Insulate pipes with cellular foam tape or an asphalt-based tape with an aluminum covering. Lengths of round fiberglass pipe insulation are also available. Just cut them to length and snap them onto the pipes in question. Extreme conditions can be overcome with electrically heated wire or cable.

If a pipe does freeze, proper defrosting can prevent damages from occurring. The pipe must be thawed slowly to prevent steam formation that could burst the pipe. The first step is to restore heat to the part of the house affected. The pipe will most likely be on an outside wall or exposed to winter winds. Open all faucets connected to the line so that steam can escape if any forms during the thawing process. Begin the thawing at the frozen point nearest the faucet. Hold a thermometer against the exposed pipe to help locate the frozen section. A small butane or propane torch can be used to do the thawing slowly.

Outside faucets are entirely exposed to the weather. Simply closing the spigot outside the house may not keep the unit from freezing. The nearest inside shut-off valve should be closed, then the spigot handle should be turned slightly open to release standing water in the end of the line that might otherwise freeze. The best locations for shutoff valves are close to where the pipe in question goes through the outside wall. Two specially made water spigot valves are available for this situation: one has a drainage valve included with a threaded plug at its base, which can be removed for complete drainage, and the other is an anti-freeze valve where exterior spigots need to be used year round. The anti-freeze valve contains a plunger inside, which controls a supply valve located well inside the house, away from the possibility of freezing winter air.

When you are winterizing your outside spigots, remember to remove garden hoses, drain them, coil them neatly, and store them indoors.

No matter what your water supply source is—a private water well or a public water system—you should know how to shut it off. If you have a well with a pressure tank, you can shut off the water where it goes into the tank or where it comes out of the tank. If you need to drain the entire system for some reason —say you are closing up a dwelling for winter—then turn off the supply before it goes into the tank, and drain everything, including the tank. But if it is a question of just working on one section of house plumbing, you can turn off the valve controlling the water coming out of the pressure tank. Or, along that same line, you could instead turn off the water closer to the involved section, since many plumbing fixtures have their own shut-off valves. (See Figure 43-3.)

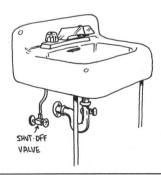

43-3. Sink shutoff valve.

In basements and along the rest of water supply systems, it is a good idea to operate individual shutoff valves at least once a year to keep the valve packing flexible and to prevent a buildup of corrosion. Leave valves one-quarter turn less than fully open to extend their useful life.

For safety's sake, know where all your fixtures' shut-off valves are located (this includes gas line shutoff valves). Also let other family members know where they can shut off lines in the event of an emergency. Consider marking the valves with color-coded tags.

Start with the main water line shutoff valve, which controls the flow of water into your home. It is usually in the basement. Where public water systems are used, it often comes through the lower basement wall on the street side of the house. Find the valve, make sure it operates freely, then tag it. If it is especially hard to find, place a second tag in a more visible spot.

Move to the kitchen next. Find the valves below the sink and see if they open and close easily. This is an important test because the valves can "freeze" and become inoperable if they aren't used for years at a time. Usually a wrench applied to the handle will free up the valve. If that doesn't work, call a plumber to remedy the situation. After freeing up and moving the valve, check for possible leaks around the stem. Minor leakage can often be stopped by tightening the valve's cap or packing nut. Apply tags that say "Hot water, kitchen," and "Cold water, kitchen," to their respective control valves.

Continue the process, visiting, testing, and tagging shutoff valves to bathrooms, wet bars, utility rooms, and various appliances that work with water, such as water heaters, dishwashers, clothes washers, water softeners, and every other place in the house where water is used.

Floor drains in the basement and garage should be tested at least twice a year to make sure they will work during an emergency. Just lift their covers and stick a running garden hose down them. If mud or debris has accumulated beneath the grate cover, shovel it out first.

WATER METERS

Many public and private water supply systems charge their customers by the amount of water used. Naturally, if you are on such a system, you want to make sure the meter hooked up to your water line is accurate and also that you are not losing water to leaks throughout the system. During your plumbing inspection, turn off all faucets and appliances that may be using water. Use a felt-tipped pen to mark the location of the needles on all scales or parts of the water meter. Then avoid operating water fixtures or appliances for several hours. If any of the needles move, there is likely a leak somewhere in the system that you will need to investigate.

A vent stack is a pipe that runs from the main drain of a house through all of the living area floors and out the roof. It provides an escape route for air and sewer gases emitted through various plumbing fixtures. Look at the top once in a while to make sure birds or chipmunks have not constructed nests there, and that it has not been plugged by leaves or other debris. Some home plumbing systems lack vents. One way to tell if a vent pipe is missing is the sound of gurgling and sucking noises after a plumbing fixture is drained. Foul odors, most likely from sewer gas, will also be evident.

FAUCETS

Leaking faucets should be repaired at the first sign of a drip. With compression-type faucets, if water drips from the spout after the faucet is turned off, the problem is usually from a worn-out stem washer inside. If water leaks from around the faucet handle, the problem is usually deteriorated packing or a worn O-ring.

To repair such a faucet, first shut off the valve that leads to the faucet and let standing water run out. Pipes will drain faster if you can open another faucet on a higher level to let air into the lines. Next, remove the screw that fastens the handle to the central shaft, called the stem. If the screw is not visible on the top of the handle, you will likely find it by removing a decorative cap that has the screw covered. Knurled caps (their edges resemble the rim of a coin) can generally be unscrewed with pliers. Wrap the jaws of the pliers with adhesive tape first, to prevent scratching any of the faucet's finished surfaces. If the edge of the cap is smooth, it can usually be gently pried up with a thin-bladed screwdriver. Once the cap is removed, remove the screw, then lift the handle off the stem.

Some faucet handles are tied into a metal or plastic sleeve along with the faucet's spout. Slide any such sleeve components off the stem as well.

On faucets without sleeves, next remove the packing nut. The packing nut holds the faucet assembly in place while allowing the stem to turn. It is usually a large cone-shaped nut with a hexagonal base designed to be turned with a wrench or pliers. Some packing nuts are hidden beneath decorative metal housings called bonnets. A bonnet can usually be slid off the stem easily.

After the packing nut is removed, you should be able to take out the stem assembly by turning the faucet counterclockwise, as if you were turning on the faucet. If it won't turn in response to considerable pressure, reinstall the handle on the stem for more leverage.

Faucets with sleeves usually have a thin lock nut instead of a packing nut. To remove the lock nut, turn the stem as if opening the faucet a half turn, then unscrew the nut.

Finally, at the base of the stem, you should find the stem washer, held in place by a screw. If, to your horror, no washer is present there, the faucet is not a compression type but a washerless faucet, it still can be repaired. You will have to take it in to a plumbing supply store for the necessary replacement parts. To free a stem washer, remove the washer's screw. If the screw is too corroded, cut off the washer with a sharp knife. Apply penetrating oil or "lock free" to the corroded screw, then remove the screw with a pair of pliers. Obtain a replacement washer and screw. Reassemble the faucet.

If the faucet has been leaking around a handle, pry out the packing washer and the packing. Either wind additional packing material around the shaft above the old packing, then push up the material and replace the old packing washer, or replace whatever packing material has failed.

While most faucets operate in a similar fashion, there are many, many designs, makes, models, and exceptions to a wide number of maintenance and repair rules. There are so many differences out there that individual units will have to be disassembled and repaired "as you go," in most cases.

Although many of the less expensive faucets manufactured today still rely on "washer construction," most quality faucets today are being designed and manufactured using washerless valving. Valve cartridges that contain ceramic discs and similar control mechanisms are making the old standard types of repairs obsolete. When replacing faucets, insist on washerless valving for reduced maintenance and longer life. Modern faucets are at the same time being designed to restrict water flows for maximum water and energy savings. Manufacturers are continually looking for better designs, so expect faucets to keep changing and improving in the near future.

TOILETS

Everyone, at one time or another, will probably have to match wits with a toilet. To most people, a toilet's insides remain shrouded in mystery—flushing mechanisms that gurgle and whine and send wastes heading somewhere into that equally mysterious network of sewer or septic lines that run below and away from the house.

There is probably no other fixture as annoying as a toilet when something goes wrong with it, especially when it is plugged and water runs over and out of the bowl. Toilets, however, seldom run over unless an item that doesn't belong in them gets dropped in. Often a plunger or a wire clothes hanger with the end bent into a hook can remove the offending object. Another way is through the use of a plumber's snake or an auger—a short snake with a crank at one end and a hook on the other. Start the snake into the bowl and slowly crank the coil of steel into the bowl until it reaches its entire length into the plumbing below. Then remove it by cranking the opposite way. Be careful when using the snake, however, since most toilets are made of vitreous china and can crack or scratch if an auger is roughly applied to their surfaces. If these methods fail to clear the obstruction, you may have to shut off the water, drain the tank, and take up the bowl to reach the object from below. When replacing the toilet, make sure you install a new preformed wax gasket between the toilet and soil pipe. (See Figure 43-4.) Signs of water and damp flooring around the base of a toilet often mean that the wax gasket is broken or deteriorated and needs to be replaced. Use caution when tightening the bolts so the toilet bowl doesn't crack.

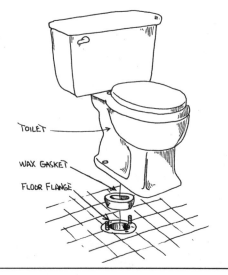

43-4. Toilet seal.

Beyond the immediate toilet plumbing, blockages also occur closer to the home's sanitary sewer line. Cleanouts are often positioned near the main sewer line access. (See Figure 43-5.)

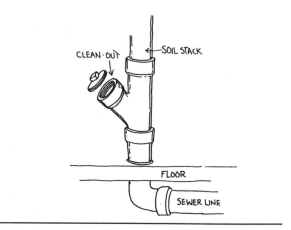

43-5. Cleanout.

Another annoying plumbing condition is when a toilet continuously runs or whines. Here are the causes and solutions to whining toilets:

- If water runs steadily into the tank, the problem can be stopped, but never prevented, by simply jiggling the toilet handle. Remove the tank top and watch the flushing mechanism in action. (See Figure 43-6.) On many toilets, the water level is controlled by a float arm and ball. The ball is hollow and floats on the water in the tank. When it rises high enough, the float arm closes the inlet valve. That stops water from entering the tank. At the bottom end of the tank, if a flush ball or plunger is not dropping squarely into the water outlet seat (the hole where the water runs out), maybe the metal connecting rods are not correctly aligned. Or perhaps they are not sliding through the guide attached to the overflow pipe. Try bending them back in place or adjusting the slide guide. If the ball looks as if it is dropping correctly into place, there may be a buildup of dirt, rust, or other deposits on the outlet seat that could be preventing a tight fit. Clean off impurities with steel wool. If the flush ball has deteriorated, or has become hard and worn, unscrew it from the rod and replace it with a new, supple ball.

When the flush valve does not leak but the tank keeps running down the overflow tube, the problem could again be the float valve. Shut off the water by closing the valve below the tank. Take apart the flush valve carefully, keeping the parts in order. Purchase individual replacement parts as needed, or obtain a repair

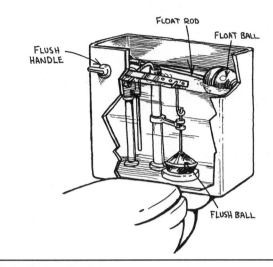

43-6. Toilet flush system.

kit with plastic fittings, as recommended by your plumbing supplier. Most kits come with illustrated directions.

- If water runs steadily into the bowl, this indicates that the water supply to the tank isn't being shut off when it should be. Lift the float by hand. If that stops the water running, try adjusting the screw at the end of the float arm (if present) or try bending the float rod down slightly, so the float will require less water to push it up. If that doesn't solve the problem, it could be an inlet valve washer that needs replacing. At this point, either consider calling a plumber or attempting to make the repairs yourself after a trip to a plumbing supply store.
- If a tank won't flush or the handle must be constantly held down while flushing, the flush handle may be loose. If so, tighten it. Is the bowl refill tube bent properly to allow water to go into the overflow pipe? If not, correct the refill tube alignment.

Condensation from a toilet tank can drip water onto a floor with such regularity that tile can be discolored, wood flooring can be stained, and baseboards can develop rot. Cold water piping can be wrapped with foam adhesive tape. Toilet tanks can be insulated as well. After draining their water and drying their insides, line their inner surfaces with a blanket of ½-inch thick foam rubber applied with a waterproof glue. This will reduce condensation by insulating the cold water in the tank from hot, humid air in the room.

When replacing toilets, consider today's many water-efficient one- and two-piece models. Standard toilets use about 3½ gallons per flush. Water conservation efforts by toilet manufacturers have reduced the number of gallons of water needed per flush to as few as 1½.

WATER HEATERS

Water heaters are heavily used home appliances that can greatly benefit from proper maintenance care. Here's how to get the most out of them.

Every few months, remove about a gallon of water from the drain valve at the bottom of the tank. (See Figure 43-7.) The drain valve is usually threaded so you can attach a hose, which can then be positioned to flow into a nearby drain. Simply open the drain valve and let the water run until it turns clear. Along with the expelled water will be any rust, sediments, and mineral deposits that have settled on the tank bottom and are hindering the efficiency of the unit's heat transfer process by which the water is heated. If you have an old tank that has not been "drained off" in quite a while, be careful when you try to open the valve. If it is "frozen" closed through disuse, opening it may make closing or resealing it impossible. You could end up with a leak that requires professional repairs. If you ever notice stains on the floor around a hot water tank, particularly stains in a circle, it could be a sign of a tank that is about to rupture, or one that has already developed a crack or a slow leak.

43-7. Water heater—drain.

Check the thermostat setting. The lower the temperature of the heated water inside the tank, the cheaper it will be to run the heater. If the water is so hot that you are constantly mixing cold water with it when the hot water is being used, it is being heated too hot by the water heater. That is a waste of energy and money. Gas water heaters have a single thermostat to adjust, but electric models frequently have two: an upper and a lower unit. The maximum benefit from a hot water heater comes when the temperature of hot water in the tank is kept between 140 and 150 degrees Fahrenheit. Higher temperatures are not necessary. Scalding water is dangerous to people and will deteriorate packing materials in certain faucets.

Most water heaters have an automatic temperature and

pressure relief valve at the top of the tank. (See Figure 43-8.) It is designed to leak if pressure builds up within the tank, so the tank will not explode. In some models, a probe inside the tank is connected to the pressure relief valve. If the heating control—the thermostat—malfunctions and the water is heated to a potentially dangerous temperature, the valve will automatically open to let off steam. Once a year, after placing an empty bucket beneath the end of the overflow pipe, lift the relief valve handle briefly to see if it is in operating condition. A spurt of hot water should be released. If nothing happens, the valve should be inspected by a plumber and either repaired or replaced.

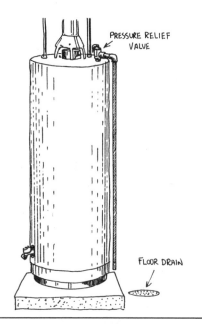

43-8. Water heater—pressure relief valve.

Increase the useful life of a water heater by making sure it is level. Most units have legs that can be adjusted to compensate for an uneven basement or garage floor.

The less a water heater has to run, the longer it will last. That means any fixture that leaks hot water, or piping that hot water loses heat through, will make a water heater work harder than it should. Fix any faucets leaking hot water. Insulate any exposed hot water lines, especially those running in or near cold locations such as unheated crawlspaces and basements. Insulate the water heating tank with a blanket insulation kit. Keep the water temperature between 140 and 150 degrees Fahrenheit.

To light a gas pilot light, follow the instructions on the tank carefully. The usual procedure is to hold the dial or lighting button down and light the pilot with a long-handled match. Keep holding the dial or button down

until the pilot stays lit. Then turn the dial to "ON" and set the thermostat between 140 and 150 degrees Fahrenheit.

On gas water heaters, have the pilot light opening and burner area cleaned out periodically. Also check where the vent to the chimney may pass through any walls, ceilings, or roof; those areas should not be hot to the touch. If they are, contact a plumber or heating specialist to reroute the vent line or have it insulated.

To drain a hot water tank properly, shut off the water entering the tank. Open any hot water faucet in the house to let air into the system so the tank will drain freely. Attach a garden hose to the drain spout or valve near the bottom of the tank. Drain the water into a floor drain that is lower than the drain spout. Wear gloves while handling the hose and to guard against any hot water that may splash. When the heater is almost empty, run more water into the tank, letting it drain until the water coming out the drain valve runs clear.

SUMP PUMPS

Sump pumps are pumps which, when rain or other water reaches a certain level after collecting in a sump hole in a basement or other low spot on the property, automatically activate and pump water from the sump, preventing the water level from getting high enough to overflow and do damage. Sump pumps should be serviced as recommended by their operator's manuals. If they are rarely used, put them into service manually several times per year to make sure they will operate when needed. Every three months, pour several five-gallon buckets of water into the sump so the float will be raised high enough to activate the motor and pump. If the motor runs and the pump removes the water from the sump, everything is working as it should.

Active pumps—pumps that are worked frequently—need more maintenance. Most pump systems have strainer screens that prevent sediments and debris from clogging the pump. If wash water is discharged into them, clean their strainers at least once a month. This will prevent large accumulations of lint on the strainer screens. Also make sure that the float-operated switches are working, and that the guides keep the float in place so it is free to move up and down in response to the sump water level.

One major drawback to sump pumps is that most of them are electrically operated. If you have a power failure along with some other emergency that causes water to flood a basement, you will need to call the fire department or a plumber who can set up a portable gasoline-powered pump.

SEDIMENT SCREENS AND FILTERS

First of all, your water should be tested occasionally by a local health department or private testing lab, even if it comes from a city water supply. If there is evidence of sediment or foreign matter, consider installing a purifying filter where the water enters your home. A variety of filters can be found. The two most common types are activated carbon filters and reverse osmosis purifiers. The carbon filter is used to remove such materials as rust, sulphur, chlorine, and organic matter. It can be installed on the main water supply inlet or just ahead of a major plumbing fixture. Filters on the main line will probably need to be changed about once every six months, while filters to major fixtures (such as the kitchen sink) can last up to a year between changes. Reverse osmosis units screen impurities through a cellulose acetate or similar membrane that can last up to two years. Other water treatment devices include softeners that will soften hard water supplies.

Many fixtures and appliances that use water have some form of built-in sediment screen to filter out impurities that could otherwise clog inner workings. On a clothes washer, for instance, a sluggish filling cycle could result from a switch malfunction. But it could also be from sediments trapped at the screens positioned at the ends of the water inlet hoses. These sediment screens should be cleaned periodically, depending on your water supply quality. "Hard" water can contain a considerable amount of sediment, causing screens to plug up more quickly than those using softer water. Most screens can be removed when the threaded hose fitting is unscrewed. Clean screens (or aerators) from faucet heads (see Figure 43-9), shower heads, sink spray heads, and washing machine inlets. Silt or sand particles stuck in the filter holes can be pushed out with a pin or needle.

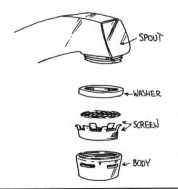

43-9. Faucet head aerator.

PLUMBING FIXTURE AND APPLIANCE MAINTENANCE

To prolong the life of plumbing fixtures and appliances, here are a number of points to consider.

- Don't let wastes stand in a sink. If you have a disposal, process food waste as it accumulates. Avoid grinding fibrous, stringy materials such as asparagus or celery. They can be ground into an unruly, tangled mass that may have to be removed by a commercial drain-cleaning company. Every month, flush your disposal with one pot of hot water mixed with a half cup of baking soda. During daily use, grind small amounts of food at a time while running cold water through the drain. Grind ice cubes to clean the disposal, and orange or lemon peels to freshen it.
- Pour excess grease into a tin can. Dispose of it in the garbage, never down a sink drain. Obstructions occur when grease or liquid fat is poured through a sink drain or washed through dishwasher. At first, the warm or hot water melts the grease and carries it through the piping. As soon as it reaches a cooler pipe, however, grease can solidify into a film that builds up and attracts other materials such as coffee grounds and small bits of food. Soon the pipe may become completely plugged.
- Avoid using sinks to hold paint cans, trash, or tools while you are redecorating or making repairs to surrounding wall or ceiling surfaces.
- Remember to caulk around the bases and other attached surfaces of toilets, bathtubs, and sinks. (See Figure 43-10.)

43-10. Bathtub and toilet seal caulking.

PLUMBING SYSTEM QUICK CHECKLIST

❑ Collect and keep the proper emergency tools and supplies handy. Include 24-hour phone numbers for at least two plumbers.

❑ Follow safety procedures such as draining hot water from fixtures, disconnecting electric power, and handling tools correctly. Be extremely careful with natural gas lines and appliances.

❑ Keep piping and traps cleaned out.

❑ Repair leaky piping, faucets, or appliances as soon as possible after detecting a problem.

❑ Repair and secure lines that experience water hammer.

❑ Prevent pipes, tanks, and fixtures from water freezing within them. Winterize plumbing where and when appropriate.

❑ Know where all plumbing shutoffs are. Label them and operate each valve several times a year to keep them in working order.

❑ Keep floor, sink, and appliance drains unplugged.

❑ Check your water meter at least once a year.

❑ Keep vent stacks open.

❑ Learn your faucet and toilet constructions before you have to repair them.

❑ Drain a few gallons of water from the water heater tank at least once a month. At the same time, check the tank's pressure valve.

❑ Keep the temperature of hot water between 140 and 150 degrees Fahrenheit.

❑ Service sump pumps regularly, and activate rarely used pumps to keep them in good condition.

❑ Keep water purifying filters and sediment screens clean.

❑ Keep grease and related food debris out of drains.

▪ All plumbing fixtures — tubs, shower stalls, sinks, basins, and toilets — should be free of cracks, rust, and other surface damage. Specialists can resurface or patch fixtures in your home. Stains may indicate that water treatment is necessary.

Water Wells

Where does your water come from? Some people haven't the foggiest idea. They know they are on either a public or private water system, or that they have a well. If they have a well, they will rarely know if it is shallow or deep, or what kind of pump has been installed. Since almost everything is below ground, well construction and operation remain a mystery to many homeowners.

Essentially, two things are important: the water's quality and quantity. Quality comes first. Ideally, the water should be clear, free of contaminants, and good-tasting. Quantity comes next. There should be enough water available from the well to supply the household dur-ing the driest parts of the year. Some water wells that cannot keep up with a household's demands require a storage tank to maintain a steady water supply.

WELL WATER INSPECTIONS

Well water should be tested at least twice a year by a local health department or private lab. Before taking a sample from a household faucet, hold a lit match beneath the spout to kill any bacteria present. Then let the water run through the faucet for two to five minutes before taking the sample.

The testing service will look for a variety of contaminants, some of them hazardous, such as lead, and some of them more irritating than dangerous, such as the presence of calcium or magnesium residues that cause "hard" water. A good source of corrective measures for any irritating water characteristics is a local water treatment company. The people there will possess knowledge and experience from encountering similar problems commonly found throughout your area. Usually, others living nearby will have the same type of water. Common water problems include:

- A cloudy, dirty appearance. This is usually caused by suspended particles of silt or mud. It can be corrected by installing a water purifying unit or sand filter.
- A yellowish tint accompanied by an unpleasant taste. This is usually caused by algae and other organic matter in the water. It can be cleared up

by filtering the water through activated charcoal, or by installing a chemical "feeder" unit at the well.
- High concentrations of calcium and magnesium. Again, the cause of "hard" water that leaves white, scaly deposits in faucets, spigots, and pipes. A solution here is the installation of an ion exchange water softener.
- High bacterial or coliform counts. These usually result from sewage contamination from a nearby septic system. It is an unhealthy situation that must be corrected at the source, which could be (and often is) the homeowner's own septic system. Shallow wells are most likely to become polluted, but deep wells can be affected too.
- High concentrations of lead, arsenic, mercury, or other hazardous contaminants. The testing service will highlight dangerous substances in a water sample, and can discuss corrective measures available.

Many factors can influence a water table from which drinking water is drawn. New construction in an area where additional septic systems are being installed can change the terrain and alter the water table, so that polluted water can reach nearby wells. Wetland locations can also adversely affect water supplies through flooding. Water tests are recommended after any nearby flooding.

Next, check for quantity. A well should be able to produce a minimum of 4 gallons per minute (at a steady stream) for at least 20 minutes before the water starts running out or muddied water starts coming out, which means that water is being drawn faster than it is being supplied by the well. If there is less flow than 4 gallons per minute, a special buffer or storage tank should be installed.

Inspect all well components located above ground or in a basement, garage, or utility area. Well water pumps (other than submersible units) are usually located in a basement or utility area alongside a pressurized storage tank, if needed. Pump motors should be periodically cleaned and oiled, as recommended by their instruction manuals. If the pump is belt-driven,

---

WATER WELL QUICK CHECKLIST

❑ Well water should be tested by a local health department or private lab at least twice per year.

❑ Water problems should be addressed by installing treatment equipment such as water softeners, filters, or purifying units, by correcting unhealthy conditions such as a leaking septic tank, or by drilling a new well in a different location.

❑ Maintain well pumps according to the manufacturer's instructions. Keep important spare parts on hand.

❑ Protect the well water lines from freezing.

❑ If you suspect the water has become polluted, stop drinking it until you have the problem corrected and the water tests clean again.

---

check the condition of the belt every three months. Keep a spare belt handy and replace the belt as soon as it shows signs of wear.

If you notice sand or silt in your toilet tanks, the pump screen may be damaged. If that is not the case, filters will have to be included within the plumbing to keep out the suspended particles.

In cold climate areas, above-ground pumps kept outdoors should be housed in insulated and heated pump house sheds to prevent the pump and water lines from freezing.

The well head should be tightly sealed or capped to prevent contamination.

A pipe that transports water from the well to the house should be protected from freezing temperatures. This is commonly done by routing the pipe below the frost line. Where this is impractical, the same effect can be achieved by wrapping it with insulation or attaching electrically heated wire or pipe heat tape. Frozen water pipes are expensive to thaw and can cause thousands of dollars worth of damages if they burst.

WATER WELL REPAIRS AND MAINTENANCE

Very few major well problems can be repaired by homeowners. When something as important as drinking water is at stake, you are better off calling professional service technicians who have the equipment and experience to diagnose and correct situations that could easily become hazardous to your health. Otherwise, keep above-ground components clean, insulated, and oiled when necessary.

WATER WELL SAFETY

If you discover that your water is polluted, stop using it for drinking and cooking. Use bottled water instead. Your local health department may be able to trace the source of contamination and get the problem corrected. It is either that, installing treatment equipment, or drilling a new well.

Septic Systems

A septic system is one of those hidden support systems that nobody thinks about until something goes wrong with it. To city dwellers who are used to the effortless convenience of sanitary sewers, septic systems are mysterious subterranean pipes and tanks that surely must take care of themselves.

Nothing could be further from the truth. Ask anyone who was raised on a farm. A septic tank system biologically breaks down household sanitary wastes. Bacteria within the system help decompose the solid wastes. As these tiny microorganisms grow, feed, and breed in the septic tank and lines, most of the wastes are rendered into liquids that are trickled or leached into the ground through a "leaching field" of perforated pipe laid in underground beds of gravel. Some of the waste-laden sewage water that leaches through the disposal lines is additionally decomposed or purified by natural bacteria found in the ground from 2 to 6 feet deep. Other wastes, however, remain inside the septic tank in the form of a sludge that gradually accumulates. A wide variety of factors can influence a septic system's operation.

SEPTIC SYSTEM INSPECTIONS

- Septic tanks that are filling with sludge. Remove the access cover or cap and measure the depth of sludge by inserting a long stick into the tank. When the total depth of solids exceeds one-third of the tank's capacity (certainly no more than one-half), it is time to have the tank pumped out and the solids removed. On many septic systems, if the sludge is allowed to accumulate, it will eventually fill the tank so there is no room for waste to enter from the house. If this happens, the tank may overflow and saturate the surrounding grounds with horrible-smelling raw sewage.
- Sluggish or plugged waste or sewer lines. When septic tanks are not functioning properly, a side effect is that lines running from the home's toilets are slow to convey wastes from the toilets to the septic tank. Solids and waste paper begin to settle and accumulate in the lines. Eventually the whole system could back up.

- Unusual foliage displays above leaching fields. Look at the grounds above and adjacent to the leaching field. Abnormal or luxuriant lawn conditions are an indication that the soil is being overloaded with waste-laden nutrients. Wet, soggy soil is another characteristic of failing absorption fields or clogged septic tanks. A good time to inspect leaching fields is during very wet weather. The size and composition of the leaching field should be sufficient to absorb household wastes and rainwater at the same time. If a heavy rain overloads the system and turns the leaching field into a swampy mess, improvements should be considered—perhaps adding more lengths of drainage pipe. Most problems are caused by the quality of soil around the leaching field. If there is a lot of clay in the soil, good drainage will be almost impossible to achieve.
- Trees and large shrubs growing on leaching fields. Roots can reach into the absorption beds and clog perforated piping. Make sure trees and large shrubs are not encroaching on or immediately adjacent to septic system leaching fields.

SEPTIC SYSTEM REPAIRS AND MAINTENANCE

Few individuals look forward to working on septic systems. Special tools and equipment such as heavy-duty pumps and vacuum units are often required.

1. Septic tanks should be cleaned periodically, or when they need it. Most should be checked twice, or at least once, a year to see that they are in working order. Typical septic tanks need cleaning about every two or three years. Ideally, the cleaning can be done in the spring. Because the waste material can give off noxious odors and may contain disease bacteria, and warm weather accelerates bacteria action, it is best to pump and get rid of the waste before hot weather sets in. Cleaning a septic tank is not recommended as a do-it-yourself project. There are qualified companies that specialize in working on septic, well, and similar plumbing systems. They will have the

knowledge and equipment, and they will also know where to get rid of the waste. It can't (by law) and shouldn't just be dumped anywhere.

2. Leaching fields should be kept free of trees and shrubs.

3. Avoid connecting non-essential home waste water streams to a septic system. Runoff from gutters should be channeled elsewhere, as should discharge water from swimming pools and sump pumps.

4. Review with other family members what household wastes should not be put into septic systems. If you have a kitchen garbage disposal, try not to grind and dispose of large amounts of vegetable and fruit matter. It is much better to dispose of them in an above-ground composting bin or pen, along with grass clippings, leaves, and similar vegetable and plant matter. Kitchen sink waste that is introduced to a septic system takes more time to be broken down by bacteria than do human wastes. If kitchen sink wastes are sent to the septic system, it will probably mean more frequent septic tank pumping and cleaning.

Avoid using drain cleaners and high-foaming detergents if the plumbing they go into is connected to the septic lines. Those substances will kill bacteria needed by the septic system to break down regular wastes. Low- and non-foaming detergents are fine to use, as are non-phosphate and biodegradable laundry soaps.

Never let petroleum products, paint thinners, solvents, cleaning fluids, dyes, cigarettes, plastics, or similar materials enter a septic system. Most are harmful to the bacteria that grows, feeds, and breeds in the septic tank.

Grease from cooking juices and related activities should be reduced as much as possible. Grease, animal fats, and related food particles tend to float and accumulate in the top layer of lighter-than-water scum and slime that is present in all septic tanks. It is usually pumped out during regular maintenance of the tank. Naturally, never pour grease down a kitchen sink. Instruct family members to scrape and wipe as much grease as possible from cooking pans before immersing the pans in soapy water.

Also avoid placing modern "flushable" sanitary napkins into a septic system. Naturally, that goes double for regular sanitary napkins as well.

NEW SEPTIC INSTALLATIONS

When planning a new septic system, the most critical factor is the type of soil. Soil with good drainage will make things easier. As a general rule, a three-bedroom house should have, at minimum, a 900-gallon septic tank. A four-bedroom dwelling should have a tank with at least 1,150-gallon capacity. Since the septic tank and system are so critical to the daily operation of a household, leave nothing to chance. Get professional help. Check with companies that have installed systems near your location. They will know what to look for and what to look out for as well. Also consider the following options.

In many areas, building codes insist that all toilets must be connected to a sanitary sewer or septic tank. These codes have not caught up with all the advances made by toilet manufacturers. There are composting toilets available that perform their own decomposing operations, channeling the waste (along with a very small amount of water) to relatively small tanks that are usually installed in a basement. These tanks need to be emptied as seldom as once per year. By then the waste has been broken down into a practically odorless material that can be used as a soil additive or fertilizer around the house. Composting toilets thus greatly reduce the amounts of solid wastes going to a septic tank, and the overall amount of water used in a bathroom.

A less radical option is one of a number of new toilets designed to use less water per flush. Since even now, new designs are on the drawing board, check with local plumbing supply houses for news on the most water-efficient models.

Another workable idea is to use two separate septic tanks: one for solid waste and the other for what is known as "gray water." Gray water is waste water that is not heavily laden with solids. It includes rinse and other water from washing machines, dishwashers, showers, bathtubs, and even sump pumps. The gray water can be routed through its own tank to the leaching field, so it won't overload the main septic tank.

NOTE: Large vehicles should not be allowed to drive over septic tanks or leaching fields. Be especially wary of heavy rigs such as concrete trucks, front-end loaders, bulldozers, drilling outfits, and the like.

SEPTIC SYSTEM QUICK CHECKLIST

❑ Clean out the septic tank when the total depth of solids within it exceeds one-third to one-half of the tank's capacity.

❑ Have the septic tank inspected at least once a year, typically during spring.

❑ Keep trees and large shrubs from growing over the system's leaching field.

❑ Avoid routing "gray" or non-sanitary waste water to the septic system.

❑ Keep kitchen wastes out of the septic tank. Same with petroleum products, paints, solvents, and similar materials.

❑ Don't use drain cleaners or high-foaming detergents if the plumbing they drain into is connected to a septic tank.

Natural Gas Wells and Fuel Tanks

During the years of the Arab oil embargoes, when the world was worrying about energy supplies, it became fashionable—as well as a sometime astute business decision—for homeowners to drill natural gas wells to reduce future dependency on oil and electricity. Individual wells, however, were always gambles. Some struck gas; others did not. Some wells struck gas reserves that would produce for decades; others tapped areas that dried up after a few years' (or even months') production. After the intense concern about energy supplies faded when the shortages disappeared, so did the interest in gas wells. Still, there are enough working wells to warrant a short section here. Oil and propane fuel tanks are also used by a considerable number of homeowners, in locations where natural gas is unavailable and in instances where electric heating systems are not selected.

GAS WELL AND FUEL TANK INSPECTIONS

Since gas wells are mostly below ground, there is not a lot you can inspect visually. But there is one very important step you can take. Maintain a yearly log of gas pressure readings. By recording pressures each January 15th and each June 15th, for instance, you can tell if the well is holding a constant pressure or if it is losing its ability to provide natural gas. When a well starts to fall in pressure, you can then consider possible remedial actions before the pressure drops too low to supply the household's requirements. Have the well's pressure gauge tested occasionally to make sure it is giving accurate readings.

If you smell or suspect natural gas (or propane) is leaking around well components, tanks, or supply lines, investigate immediately. Gas and other fuel leaks are among the most dangerous of household hazards. The easiest and safest way to check for gas leaks is with a solution of soapy water mixed in an ordinary spray bottle. Spray the soap solution over the pipe joints or locations you suspect to be leaking. If there is gas leaking, bubbles will immediately start to form at the leak.

Inspect fuel tanks and any lengths of piping visible. Look for corrosion and situations in which the pipes are in danger of being banged or otherwise damaged in a basement or garage.

Are oil or liquid propane (LP) tanks securely set in a firm base? Some outside tanks can be undermined by eroding soil. A winter frost or spring mud can move a tank around so it is in danger of breaking loose from its piping. (See Figure 46-1.)

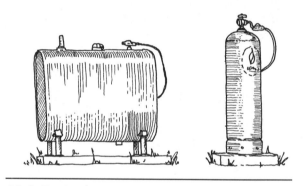

46-1. Fuel tanks.

GAS WELL AND FUEL TANK REPAIRS AND MAINTENANCE

1. One problem that could cause a marked decrease in pressure is that of water gradually filling up the well. A gas well company has the knowledge and resources to identify and correct such a situation. Water encroachment is probably one of the most frequent causes of gas well ailments.

2. Another pressure-related problem is simply that the well is weakening—there is not as much natural pressure as there once was. In that case, a gas well company can try to revive the well through the installation of a vacuum pump that will help draw additional gas from the ground. In some locations, there are fire codes or other laws that regulate how vacuum pumps can be used. A vacuum pump is not a cure-all for every case. It may work if the gas is there to be pulled out. If there

is simply no gas left, no amount of maneuvering will reactivate a failing supply.

3. Have a qualified plumber or pipe repair person correct any leaking pipes or connectors.

4. Corroded sections of a fuel pipe or tank should be sanded and touched up with rustproof paint. Rustproof paints are available in a variety of colors. A well-painted tank against a house or garage will not detract from the property's appearance. A sooty, grimy, rusted tank will.

5. Make sure oil or LP gas storage tanks are secured on their bases. If the weather isn't cooperating, make temporary repairs until a permanent arrangement can be undertaken.

6. Connecting fuel lines should be protected from rupturing if the tank moves. The lines should also be insulated, wrapped with electrical heat tape, or buried beneath the frost line.

7. Oil tanks can eventually rust through from the inside. Even if there isn't enough rust to breach the tank, enough corroded material could block the fuel line leading from the tank. Oil companies recommend adding an anti-condensation agent every time the tank is filled. Ask the oil company if such an agent can be purchased along with the oil. If not, hardware and builder's supply stores often carry cleaning and anti-condensation additives that come in liquid form. Just follow the manufacturer's instructions.

8. Another way to minimize condensation is to keep oil tanks full during the entire year. Condensation won't have a chance to form.

GAS WELL AND FUEL TANK QUICK CHECKLIST

❑ Maintain regular yearly logs of gas pressure readings.

❑ Test a gas well's pressure gauge occasionally to make sure it is giving accurate readings.

❑ Investigate and correct gas or other fuel leaks as quickly as possible.

❑ Make sure that fuel tanks are securely set and kept in like-new condition. Repair rust and corrosion as soon as they develop.

❑ Add anti-condensation agents to fuel oil, and keep the tank full during most of the year to prevent the tank from rusting from the inside.

Security

It is a shame that a section on security has to be included in a book on preventive maintenance, but it does. The times when people could leave their house unlocked while asleep or away are long gone. Nowadays, burglars will ransack your home while you sit in the backyard, entertaining guests. And if burglary is not bad enough, crimes against property can easily turn into crimes of violence if an intruder is discovered and confronted. The most important point stressed in this section is that burglars and other potential intruders will likely pass by a house that has good door and window locks and any number of features that will reveal or announce their presence, such as lighted entrances, wide-open spaces without encroaching shrubbery, and evidence of working security alarm systems.

LANDSCAPING

Shrubbery

A burglar's best friend is dark, dense foliage, from which he or she can safely work during the night. Hidden behind bushes or shrubs near a house, a burglar will feel comfortable casing the place or trying to pry open a window or door.

Illumination

Outside the house you should be able to see your way clearly from the street or garage to exterior doors. Entrances should be bright enough for you to identify callers before you open the door. Potential hiding places in the yard near the house should be illuminated or eliminated, and vegetation along the home should be kept low to the ground by regular trimmings. Ideally, the front door/porch, side entrances, rear entrances, garage/carport, driveway or breezeway, patios and decks, and part of the backyard could be illuminated.

Photo-sensitive floodlights and door lights can be installed that will respond to levels of daylight and turn themselves on at dusk and off at dawn. Or, one step beyond that, automatic floodlights are available that use infrared sensors to detect heat-emitting sources.

Anything warm—a car, person, deer, or dog, for example—triggers the light, which then remains on for a set period of time.

On the lower end of the scale, there are many ways to install regular flood and area lights, including fashionable lawn or gas lamps, outside wall mounts, pole mounts, and on-ground installations.

DOORS

Always lock your doors. Get into the habit, even when you are home during the day, of locking your doors. The safest doors are made of solid hardwood, or a combination wood and insulation clad with a metal skin.

Locks

In most cases, a burglar will first try a home's doors to see if they are unlocked. Why go to all the trouble of breaking in, when a simple handle could be turned instead? Outer entrance doors should be kept locked with deadbolts that are at least 1 inch long. (See Figure 47-1.) There are two basic types of deadbolt locks: single cylinder and double cylinder. A single-cylinder deadbolt lock is operated by a key from outside and by a thumb latch from the inside. However, if any glass panes close enough so a person could break the glass from the outside, reach in, and operate the thumb latch, the door is not safe enough. Either the glass

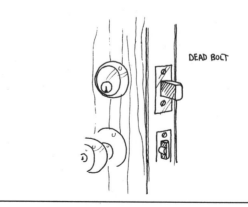

47-1. Deadbolt lock.

will have to be replaced with something more sturdy, or a double-cylinder lock will have to be installed. A double-cylinder lock has no thumb latch on the inside —it can only be opened by key from inside and outside the house. The double-cylinder lock is certainly more secure where windows are nearby. On the other hand, household members trying to escape from within a locked house for any reason would have to locate the key and operate the lock—which, in case of a fire or other emergency, could result in a costly delay.

In both types of deadbolt locks, the strike plate into which the deadbolt "throws" should be secured with 3-inch-long screws. The long screws are needed so they reach the underlying door framing stud.

Hinge Pins
Door hinge pins should be located on the inside of all doors leading to the outside. Otherwise, an intruder could merely pry up the pins with a screwdriver and lift the door up and out. Sounds too simple to be true, doesn't it? Unfortunately, many exterior doors are accidentally hung just that way—hinge sides out.

Peepholes
Peepholes should be installed in outside doors that afford no other view of callers. Plastic lenses tend to fog and scratch, and may be ruined within a short time. Quality glass peepholes offer a viewing field of 180 degrees, and permit you to see an entire front porch and as far as 6 or 8 feet away from the front door.

Sliding Glass Doors
Sliding glass doors can be secured with a good lock that is key operated from the inside or outside. (See Figure 47-2.) Also, a Charley bar, a device that prevents the glass door panels from being pried off their tracks, can be purchased from locksmiths and hardware stores. For the ultimate in glass door security, a

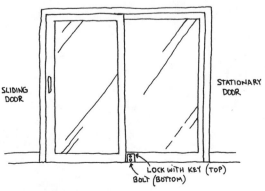

47-2. Sliding glass door lock.

cylinder deadbolt that locks from one door into the other is yet another security option.

WINDOWS
After doors, windows are a burglar's second most reliable means of illegal entry. Give extra attention to windows that lead to a fire escape, patio, or deck. Don't forget about second-story windows, too, especially if you or your neighbor conveniently store a long ladder in or behind a garage. Prune large tree limbs away from the house and prevent thick hedges and shrubs from encroaching on your windows.

Basement Windows
Basement windows are a favorite target. See that yours are secured with either sturdy grates or decorative wrought-iron bars. Another method is a bracket connected to the house sill. The bracket hangs down and blocks the window latch so the latch cannot be turned. (See Figure 47-3.)

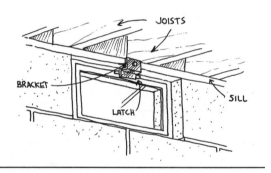

47-3. Basement window lock.

Double-Hung Windows
Double-hung windows can also be secured. When the window is closed, drill a neat hole through the top piece of the bottom window sash, at one side, all the way through and into the bottom part of the top sash. Then insert a metal bolt or pin. Windows fixed this way are almost impossible to open from the outside. Make sure the pin or bolt protrudes slightly from its hole so you can remove it easily in case of an emergency. During warm weather, to open a double-hung window partway while still keeping it secure, drill a few more holes into the top sash several inches above the first hole. The window can then be opened slightly, yet can remain securely fastened where it is.

Casement Windows
Casement windows are operated with a crank near

```
┌─────────────────────────────────────────┐
│         SECURITY QUICK CHECKLIST          │
├─────────────────────────────────────────┤
│  ❑  Trim foliage near all possible en-    │
│     trances, including doors and all      │
│     windows.                              │
│  ❑  Illuminate entranceways.              │
│  ❑  Use peepholes in exterior doors when  │
│     there is no other view of a caller.   │
│  ❑  Consider installing a security alarm  │
│     or purchasing a dog.                  │
│  ❑  Use deadbolt locks on exterior doors. │
│  ❑  Make sure exterior door hinge pins    │
│     are located on the inside of doors.   │
│  ❑  Use locking mechanisms on windows     │
│     and glass sliding doors.              │
│  ❑  Always keep your doors locked.        │
└─────────────────────────────────────────┘
```

their bottom. A latch locks the windows to a center post. For an additional measure of safety, remove the crank handles.

Sliding Glass Windows

Sliding glass windows can be secured by a special steel or wood bar available from locksmiths and hardware stores. The bar screws into place and locks the movable parts of the window.

Louvered Windows

Louvered windows can be locked with commercial locking devices. But on the whole, these windows are not very safe.

DOGS

These living security alarms, from yip-yippy miniature mutts to lumbering Golden Retrievers, are excellent burglar deterrents. The only requirement is a good, loud bark.

ALARM SYSTEMS

There are a number of different kinds of security alarms available. The most popular units operate with either electrical contacts on doors and windows (also called "wired" systems) or with "wireless" microwave, infrared, or ultrasonic technology that spans yard or room openings.

Practically any alarm system can be connected to a private central system that monitors individual home alarms around the clock. If your alarm goes off, the service calls your house. If someone answers with a code or password, the service knows it is a false alarm and nothing further is done. Otherwise, the police department is called.

Electrical Contact Systems

Electrical contact systems make effective, inexpensive, low maintenance security alarms. The contact system is easy to test and maintain. But because it is more obvious, it can be rather easily bypassed by an experienced burglar who detects the system in advance. Inexperienced burglars may also detect the system's presence, but they will probably be scared away by it.

Wireless Systems

Electric eyes operate via soundless electronic signals that establish a pattern of objects in a room or area, which is recognizable to the system. If this pattern is broken by the presence of an intruder, the alarm is activated. Electric eye and other motion systems require considerably more maintenance than do contact alarm systems. Infrared and ultrasonic motion systems can react to children heading toward the bathroom at night, and pets roaming around in the dark.

PART 6

Home Appliances & Accessories

Imagine a home without a refrigerator or an oven. Or without furniture or pictures on the walls. Or without any number of special equipment items you use every day. Televisions play important roles in our lives now, as do personal computers and telephone answering machines.

This section deals with various appliances and accessories found in many households. At the same time, they make our lives simpler and more complex. They serve, comfort, excite, teach, entertain, and provide modern conveniences for us.

On the other hand, they exact a definite amount of time in tending. Included here are sections on Ovens and Ranges; Refrigerators and Freezers; Dishwashers, Clothes Washers, and Dryers; Electronic Equipment; Furnishings; Furniture; and Fireplaces.

Ovens and Ranges

There are two main types of household cooking ovens/ranges: gas and electric. Which you have is a matter of cooking preference or fuel availability; some places don't have access to natural gas.

OVEN/RANGE INSPECTIONS

- A hood over a cooking range is usually equipped with an exhaust fan or a blower. Most hoods also have grease collectors that resemble a frame full of bright, coarse steel wool. A collector plugged with cumulative grease buildups will not allow air to be drawn through the steel filtering material.
- Does the hood vent to the outside, or does it merely recirculate cooking vapors, smoke, and fumes within itself? If it is not vented to the outdoors, there is usually a charcoal filter to purify cooking vapors. If so, is the filter clean or full of grease?
- How do the cooking spaces look? Rangetop burners, broilers, ovens, and surfaces between them should be kept free from buildups of grease and other spilled materials.
- On a gas range/oven do the flames burn a clear blue? If the flames are yellow, something is wrong with the combustion—perhaps the burner outlets are clogged.
- Check the back of the oven to see what kind of gas connection exists. The use of flexible piping is no longer legal in many communities. A better option is black pipe installed right up to an oven's main connection.
- Electric range/ovens should be installed with 50-amp fuses or circuit breakers on a No. 6 wire. Some community standards permit 40-amp circuits.
- Check the oven's clock, timer, and lights. These items may not seem important, but they contribute a lot toward efficient cooking. Periodically check the timer against your wristwatch or some other clock. If it is slow or fast, following recipes exactly will be difficult. If the oven light doesn't work, you will probably waste a considerable amount of energy by opening the door to check

on food as it is cooking. Doing so will also lengthen cooking times.
- Make sure that curtains, drapes, blinds, pot holders, aprons, napkins, and dishcloths are kept well away from burners. Never store any combustibles such as newspapers, magazines, or paper bags near a range/oven.
- Is there a charged fire extinguisher nearby?
- Are electrical cords free from insulation and plug cracks?

RANGE/OVEN REPAIRS

Ranges/ovens are durable appliances that rarely "break." Parts may eventually wear out and have to be replaced, but they are usually simple to take care of: a broken burner control knob or a bent door hinge, for example. On an electric range, if one of the top burners won't work, it could mean there is a loose connection or broken wire involved. In that case, disconnect the unit's main power at the fuse or circuit breaker and lift out the offending burner. If you see that wires are broken off at the terminal screws, just clean the wire ends with sandpaper and connect the ends back to the terminal screws.

Repair tasks that are more difficult should be left for qualified service technicians.

RANGE/OVEN MAINTENANCE

Remember to keep all range/oven records, including instruction booklets, operator's manuals, make and model numbers, sales receipts, warranties, repair histories, and service technician phone numbers.

1. Depending on how often you cook, and what types of cooking you do, clean exterior, interior, and hood filter and light surfaces regularly to prevent buildups of grease and other cooking residues. It is a fairly simple task to clean the hood, fan, and range and oven surfaces if they are not too greasy. Use a sponge and household cleaner. But if you wait until things get out of hand—until there are several layers of dried cooking grease

and tars adhering everywhere—it is a big, tough job that will take special non-flammable grease-cutting cleaners designed for blasting through heavy grease. Even if an oven is "self-cleaning," you should still wipe down its insides at least once a month.

On gas stoves, remove the burners and clean the individual gas outlets with pipe cleaners. When you have removed the burners, remember to clean pilot light orifices, too. If gas burners, broilers, or stoves fail to light, the pilot might be out. That problem is often directly related to clogged burners.

If there is an uneven gas flame, the burner ports may be clogged. Clean them with a pipe cleaner or straight pin. A yellow or noisy flame that cannot be corrected by cleaning the burners is probably due to an unbalanced air and gas mixture that needs to be adjusted by a qualified service technician.

2. Clean the oven door's sealing gasket.
3. Clean the rest of the outside of the range/oven with a non-abrasive cleaner such as baking soda on a damp sponge. Special appliance cleansers are available that will clean and protect against future stains. Never use abrasives on parts of a stove that are made of stainless steel. In fact, never use strong abrasives on any exterior surface.
4. Clean an oven's interior with a commercial oven cleaner, or place a bowl of household ammonia inside the oven overnight, with the oven vents closed and the oven's heat off. A damp cloth laid across the vent is usually enough to hold in the ammonia vapors. The vapors will soften the tars, greases, and accumulated food drippings. The following morning you should be able to scrub the buildups off relatively easily. Ammonia is a dangerous product, however, and children should be kept away while you are working with it. Use rubber gloves while handling ammonia, and make sure there is enough ventilation in the room so you don't breathe concentrated vapors. The key to clean ovens is not to let them get dirty in the first place. When something spills, clean it up before it gets baked onto the oven's surface.

PURCHASING RANGE/OVENS

When shopping for a new gas range/oven, favor units with automatic electronic ignition. Drip retainer tops —a rangetop with a raised lip on all sides—will prevent spills from running down the sides or front of the range. Lift-up cooktops will enable the otherwise hard-to-clean space beneath the burners to be cleaned

easily. A removable oven door provides better access for cleaning. Removable control knobs help make the oven front and the knobs themselves easier to clean. Porcelain enamel broiler pans and inserts are dishwasher safe and simple to keep clean. Porcelain drip bowls located under each surface burner or heating element are designed to catch spills and provide a certain amount of heat reflection to assist cooking.

OPERATING TIPS

■ Use flat-bottomed pans that closely match the size of your range burners. If pan bottoms and burners are mismatched, considerable energy will be wasted. Use lids on pans and baking dishes whenever possible, for the same reason.
■ Avoid using aluminum foil to line an oven. It can interfere with air circulation and reduce cooking efficiency.
■ Take advantage of aids such as meat thermometers, probes, and drip trays. Keep a time, temperature, and food chart handy for accurate cooking.
■ Try to plan oven and grill meals so more than one recipe at a time can be prepared. Cook more than the amount needed for a single meal and freeze part for later.

MICROWAVE OVENS

Microwave ovens are remarkable appliances. They cook quickly and cleanly and need almost no maintenance. Remember to keep the insides clean, the vents open, the door seal intact, and metal objects out of the cooking space. If a microwave oven is plugged into the same circuit as another major appliance, cooking times may have to be increased when both appliances are drawing power at the same time.

RANGE/OVEN SAFETY

■ Avoid storing food items on a rangetop, so children won't accidentally turn on the stove while reaching for items to eat.
■ Keep boiling/hot liquids and foodstuffs in pans with handles turned away from the edge of the rangetop. Whenever possible, use the rear burners.
■ Keep counters adjacent to rangetops clean and free from clutter. Store cardboard boxes, paper bags, paper towels, and similar flammables away from burners.
■ Instruct children never to touch electric rangetop burners. Electric burners may be hot without looking so.

OVEN/RANGE QUICK CHECKLIST

❑ Keep oven/range interior and exterior surfaces clean.

❑ Keep gas burner holes unplugged.

❑ Make sure oven door seals are intact.

❑ See that cooking aids such as timers, clocks, temperature probes, and oven lights are in good working order.

❑ Correctly match pot and pan sizes with equal-sized rangetop burners.

❑ Avoid storing food on a rangetop so children won't accidentally turn on the stove while reaching for a snack.

❑ Keep pot and pan handles turned away from the front edge of a rangetop.

❑ Avoid storing flammables such as paper towels, cardboard boxes, and related materials next to rangetops.

Refrigerators and Freezers

Refrigerators and freezers are reliable appliances that usually give years of service with very little maintenance. To avoid trouble, and to prevent a refrigerator or freezer full of spoiled food, here are some cold facts about refrigerator and freezer care.

REFRIGERATOR AND FREEZER INSPECTIONS

- Units placed in improper locations, near heat sources, in direct sunlight, or in tight areas having poor air circulation.
- Lint, dust, hair, and other debris plugging a refrigerator's or freezer's grill, coils, or condensers.
- A worn or damaged electrical cord.
- Loose, soiled, or deteriorated door seals. The efficiency of a refrigerator or freezer will be lowered if cold air can leak from the seam where the door closes against the frame. Open and close doors to see if the rubber seal is intact and if the doors fit tightly. Leakage can be caused by dirt buildups on the surface of a rubber-covered magnetic seal or gasket. The soil makes the seal weaker. The fit of a door and seal can be tested by closing the door over a piece of paper so the paper is half inside the door, and half outside. A tight seal should grab and hold the paper so the paper will tear before pulling out. If you can remove the paper easily, the gasket or seal should be cleaned (or if very old, replaced), and the door's alignment and latch may also need to be adjusted. Again, because a gasket replacement is done so infrequently, you are usually better off by having it done by a professional.
- Ice buildups of more than ¼ inch within a manually defrosted freezer.
- Temperature controls that are not responsive to various settings.
- Drawers that do not slide easily and non-working refrigerator lights.

REFRIGERATOR AND FREEZER REPAIRS

Other than simple mechanical adjustments and repairs to the doors, grills, shelves, racks, bins, and related components, leave the major operating system repairs for professionals. Repairs to or replacements of motors, compressors, and condensers are needed so infrequently that unless you are already trained in refrigeration repairs and safety or you have a burning desire to learn, it is far more efficient simply to call a qualified repair person. Another difficulty has recently been identified. Freon, a common chemical refrigerant present in many refrigerators and freezers, needs special handling techniques to protect both the handler and the environment. Laws have recently been passed to enforce its proper handling.

REFRIGERATOR AND FREEZER MAINTENANCE

1. Keep refrigerator and freezer grills, coils, and condensers clean. Vacuum them at least twice a year. Warm air is usually expelled through a grill at the base of a refrigerator or freezer. The grill should be removed periodically so dust and dirt accumulations behind it can be cleaned out. Excessive collections prevent proper air circulation and promote harmful heat buildup.

   Remove, empty, and clean the condensation tray that is usually positioned several inches off the floor, near the unit's bottom. Move the unit away from the walls to access the back panel. To prevent damage to the flooring, you can either permanently install rollers available at hardware or appliance stores, or tip the unit so a rug or heavy cloth can be slipped beneath the unit's "feet." Of course, because refrigerators and freezers are so heavy, enlist someone's help whenever these appliances must be handled.

   Remove vent panels from a unit's side or back, and using a plastic nozzle or crevice tool on a vacuum cleaner, gently vacuum dust and dirt from wherever you see it (a flashlight may help). Avoid using a metal vacuum tube or any sharp implement that could accidentally damage compressor coils. Where possible, clean grills with a soft brush that won't harm the heat-dispensing grids. Intake vents on a unit's back should also be brushed clean or vacuumed so heat generated by the compressor and fan motor doesn't get trapped, which, in turn, will decrease cooling efficiency. Remember to clean the fan and fan guard housing.

Different environments require different cleaning schedules. A household with several long-haired pets, for instance, should have refrigerator and freezer vents, grills, and tubing cleaned out every few months, while others could be done as few as one or two times per year. In homes with forced air heating systems, where a refrigerator is near or in the direct line of air flow from floor registers, dust and dirt can build up quickly.

2. Clean and polish the exterior and interior at least twice a year. In between major cleanings, wipe spills and remove food that has begun to spoil.

3. Keep an open box of baking soda on one of the shelves, to absorb food odors.

4. Keep all of the manufacturer's supporting documents and follow the operator manual's recommendations.

5. Manually defrosted units require regular maintenance. When layers of ice build up to thicknesses of more than ¼ inch, it is time to defrost and remove the ice.

6. Provide adequate space behind, above, and on the sides of a refrigerator or freezer for proper air circulation.

OPERATING TIPS

- Keep the temperature of the refrigerator between 38 and 40 degrees F.
- Make sure a refrigerator or freezer is standing level so the door closes and seals properly.
- Cover all foods, especially liquids. Food and liquids give off humidity, which causes frost buildup.
- Allow hot foods to cool partially before placing them in a refrigerator or freezer.
- Arrange food and drink items in an orderly manner to avoid having to keep the door open while looking for hard-to-find items.
- A refrigerator or freezer operates more efficiently when filled to capacity — with some space between items for air circulation.
- Refrigerator and freezer controls are sometimes accidentally moved to the off or defrost positions. If one of your units is malfunctioning, always check the controls first. Other troubleshooting suggestions include:

If a unit will not run, check the electrical service. Does an interior appliance light come on? If not, is the unit plugged in? If the interior light comes on, has the temperature control been turned off accidentally?

If a unit runs too long or too frequently, the condenser may need cleaning. Or the temperature control may be set too cold. It could also be because of prolonged or frequent door openings, or a loose seal that lets refrigerated air out. The outside temperature, too, has an effect on refrigerating capacities, as can large additions of warm food.

If the refrigerated section is too warm or too cold, adjust the setting, but avoid changing it more than one notch or number at a time. Allow about 24 hours for the temperature to stabilize before making another adjustment.

If a freezer compartment is too warm, readjust the freezer control according to the operator's manual. Check the door seal to make sure cold air is not escaping. Don't put hard-to-freeze items on the freezer door shelves; place them inside the main freezer compartment instead, where items will freeze more quickly. Check the condenser for dust and dirt build-ups. Avoid adding too much warm food at the same time. A general rule says that no more than 3 pounds of food per cubic foot of freezer space should be added to a freezer within a 24-hour period.

If an automatic icemaker does not make ice, make sure the ice stop arm is not in the "off" position. Has the water supply been turned off? Is the water pressure too low? Is the freezer being kept too warm?

PURCHASING A REFRIGERATOR OR FREEZER

Study your options. Manually defrosted freezers require regular maintenance. On the other hand, frost-free automatic defrosting units use as much as 60 percent more electricity while preventing frost accumulation on evaporator coils.

Energy-saving units are available, constructed with 2 to 4 inches of foam insulation instead of the conventional 1 to 2 inches of fiberglass. There are also independent freezer compartments and independent controls for heating elements beneath the refrigerator's outer "skin" that reduce surface condensation.

Probably the most important decision involves the correct size of a refrigerator or freezer. One that is too large will cool a space larger than you need. One that is too small will be jampacked with food placed too close together for proper circulation of air. Both cases will result in higher operating costs.

A refrigerator's or freezer's capacity is measured in cubic feet of storage space. If you live alone, rarely cook at home, have few visitors, and don't entertain

---

REFRIGERATOR/FREEZER QUICK CHECKLIST

❑ Avoid placing freezers and refrigerators near heat sources, in direct sunlight, or in locations with poor ventilation.

❑ Keep grills, coils, condensers, and all exterior surfaces free from dust, lint, pet hair, and other debris.

❑ Make sure that freezer or refrigerator door seals are clean and intact.

❑ On manually defrosted freezers, keep ice buildups from getting thicker than ¼ inch. Defrost the unit when necessary.

❑ Keep all interior surfaces clean.

❑ Call a qualified repair technician for major repairs and for performing servicing tasks that require refrigerant to be handled.

❑ Cover all foods to prevent liquid evaporation and high levels of humidity.

❑ Allow hot foods to cool partially before placing them in a refrigerator or freezer.

❑ Try to keep freezers and refrigerators filled to near capacity for maximum cooling and freezing efficiency.

---

much, a small refrigerator with between 8 and 10 cubic feet of capacity should be enough. Two-member households with similar lifestyles can probably be satisfied with a unit having 11 to 14 cubic feet of space. Larger families generally are best suited with units having between 15 and 20 cubic feet of storage. Depending on lifestyle and eating habits, those recommendations can be adjusted up or down.

Farm families or individuals who like to harvest vegetables, fruits, or large quantities of fish and game will need considerably more freezer space than a family that just needs a few ice cube trays and a handful of frozen dinners for weekends. The important thing is to match the needs with correctly sized refrigerators and freezers so the space is used wisely.

Dishwashers, Clothes Washers and Dryers

In the modern household, a dishwasher, a clothes washer, and a clothes dryer are standard equipment. With working schedules what they are, few individuals have time to contend with washing and drying dishes and clothes by hand. Enter the major appliances.

DISHWASHERS

Many makes and models of dishwashers are available. Some are "portable," meaning they can be moved from place to place, wherever they can be hooked up to water and plugged into an electrical outlet. Most, however, are permanently installed beneath a kitchen counter top, next to a sink. More and more units are appearing with water- and energy-saving features.

Inspections, Repairs, and Maintenance
- While running a full cycle, check a dishwasher for signs of water at the base. Periodically remove the dishwasher's bottom front panel to look for leaks beneath the unit. But never reach into the lower (or any) part of the washer while the machine is running.
- After the cycle stops, unplug the unit or shut off the electrical supply by throwing a breaker or pulling a fuse. Remove the strainer located at the base of the washer compartment below the spray arm. Flush it with tap water. Some units have a tap plug molded or fitted into their strainer so the plug can be removed and the unit flushed from the inside out. Clean food particles and other debris from the base of the spray arm spindle.
- The drain for the dishwasher is usually "trapped" beneath the kitchen sink. Periodically unscrew and remove the clean-out plug at the bottom of the piping trap and rinse out debris that may have accumulated in the trap.
- The door-latch fit on a dishwasher is important. A dishwasher will not run unless the door and latch are both completely closed.
- If you hear a loud humming sound, a piece of silverware, a pan handle, a piece of glass, or some other object could be jamming the impeller or spray arm. Shut off the electricity and remove the offending item.
- If a dishwasher won't drain, the kitchen sink could be clogged, or there could be a kink in the hose leading from the dishwasher to the sink piping.
- It is important to use the recommended dishwasher detergent. The wrong kind of soap could cause the unit to leak around its door.
- Watch the door. Don't let it slam open, and be careful not to drop heavy pans, pots, or sharp implements on its surface: ceramic will chip, and paint will scratch, baring steel to rust.
- Follow the loading instructions. Avoid jamming glasses into tight spots, and don't let pan handles and cooking implements jut through the grating or shelves toward the bottom where they can jam the washing and rinse arms.
- Unless you are familiar with plumbing and electrical repairs, you are usually better off to let a professional diagnose and complete repairs to a dishwasher. On the other hand, here are some troubleshooting guidelines you might try before calling in the experts.
- If a dishwasher won't start, see if it has power. If a portable unit, is it plugged in? Have fuses or circuit breakers been checked? Is the door latched properly? Try resetting the timer dial or cycle button.
- If a dishwasher won't fill with water, first check the power. Is the indicator light lit? See if the door is closed and latched all the way. On portable models, make sure the hot water faucet is turned on. If a dishwasher won't drain, make all of the usual electrical checks, then look at the household and dishwasher drainage system for a blockage.
- If the dishes are not clean and dry by the end of the cycle, check the water heater. For dishwashing purposes, the temperature is best set at about 140 degrees F.

CLOTHES WASHERS

Clothes washers have traditionally been located in basements. Recently, though, households have been setting up first-floor laundries near living areas to allow the clothes washing to be done (simultaneously with other activities) without having to climb up and down stairs frequently.

Inspections, Repairs, and Maintenance

▪ Run a full cycle with the clothes washer and check for signs of water at the base and back of the machine. Listen to the unit run. Are there any rattling, rocking back and forth, or grinding sounds?

▪ A washing machine should have fill hoses with brass fittings that are squeezed or crimped to prevent corrosion and leakage. If they're not crimped, have a service person crimp them for you.

▪ The washer should be cleaned and polished on the outside at least twice a year so corrosion won't cumulatively take hold. Appliance stores carry special cleaners, polishes, and waxes for modern finishes.

▪ Empty the lint trap regularly. Also, turn off the water supply; disconnect the hot and cold supply hoses at the washer inlets and clean built-up sediment from the hose screens. Depending on the condition of the water, sediment may have to be flushed as frequently as once a month (with "hard" water) or if considerable amounts of sediment have accumulated in your water heater. Although you may rarely need them, make sure the washing machine hot and cold water shutoff valves are in working order. A severe kink in a water hose will keep the washer from running, and a similar kink in the drain hose will prevent the water from draining. More often than not, a water problem can be traced back to a faucet or valve being closed instead of open.

▪ As with any appliance that runs with sudsy soaps, don't put too much detergent into a load. Too many suds will cause the washing machine motor to work harder.

▪ Follow the instruction booklet for washing clothes. Avoid always using the same setting. Vary the settings for lightly soiled clothes, moderately soiled clothes, and dirty work clothes.

Again, unless you are familiar with electrical and plumbing work, leave most repairs to professionals. Here, though, are some troubleshooting tips:

▪ If the washer won't run, check the electrical system. Is it dead on all cycles, or just one or two?

▪ If the washer won't fill or drain properly, check the faucets or drain.

▪ If the water in the washer is the wrong temperature, the hoses may be reversed at the washer or faucet connections, or one faucet may be turned down or off.

▪ If the washer won't agitate, see if it will operate on other cycles or parts of a cycle. If the motor is running but nothing else is happening, it is time to call for a service technician.

▪ If the washer won't spin and stops full of water, see if it can be restarted after raising and lowering the lid once. If it starts right up, chances are that the problem was an unbalanced load of clothes. Redistribute the clothing items more uniformly and start the cycle again.

Replacing a Clothes Washer

Many options now available on new clothes washers will help reduce the amount of maintenance needed, including:

▪ Quiet, direct-drive transmissions that eliminate the need for belts that can stretch and break.

▪ Sound-deadening insulation in the cabinet and around the moving parts especially helps when the laundry room is on a first floor, near living spaces.

▪ Various cycle selections to offer washing times and agitation and spin speeds for different fabrics, items, and degrees of soil.

▪ Programmable controls that allow you to delay the start of the wash until later, when you are asleep, for instance, to take advantage of lower electric rates.

CLOTHES DRYERS

These companion appliances to washing machines were once a rarity. Clothes were dried through hand rollers that squeezed most of the water out, then the damp items were hung outside or on lines strung through basements, utility rooms, and even attics. On the whole, dryers are remarkably reliable machines, considering the heavy use most households get from them.

Inspections, Repairs, and Maintenance

▪ A gas clothes dryer should have a tight-fitting natural gas or LPG (Liquid Propane Gas) supply line, complete with a working gas shutoff cock or valve. If there is no such shutoff cock or valve, consider that the entire gas supply will have to be interrupted and stopped each time the unit must be serviced, repaired, or moved. Building codes usually require ½-inch black or galvanized steel supply line.

▪ Make sure a dryer warms to temperatures referred to in the operator's manual. The efficiency of a dryer is affected by the position of the unit.

Clothes will take longer to dry within units installed in cold, damp areas such as some basements or unheated garages and utility rooms.

- Listen for any loud creaks, groans, or grinding noises. They could mean motor, belt, or bearing problems.
- A dryer's lint filter should be cleaned after each load or complete cycle. Also clean and vacuum air intake vents, exhaust vents, and flexible piping. Make sure any external vent hoods are working and free from dust and lint buildups. At least once a year, take the entire vent system apart, clean it, then reassemble it. Consider the purchase and installation of a heat-saver vent that can be used to vent the dryer's heat and humidity (minus the lint) into the house during times when the air is naturally dry and cold.
- A dryer's door must work properly. The latch also functions as a switch that can start or stop the drying action, depending on whether the door is open or closed.
- As with the two other appliances in this section, repairs are best left to professionals. Here are several troubleshooting guides:

If a dryer won't start, make a quick electrical check. Is it plugged in? Does the circuit work? If a dryer runs without heat, check the temperature select controls. If nothing looks wrong there, call a service technician. If uneven drying is a problem, the dryer may have been overloaded. In general, one washer load should equal one dryer load.

If the dryer takes too long to dry clothes, or runs too hot, or won't turn off, there could be something wrong with either the lint filter or the exhaust system. If the lint filter is completely blocked, air flow restrictions will cause the dryer to work harder than it should. Similarly, if exhaust ducting or tubing becomes plugged with lint, the earlier mentioned problems can arise. When installing exhaust ducting, the use of 4-inch aluminum material is recommended over that of flexible plastic tubing.

If the electrical cord is damaged or shows visible wear such as fraying or cracked insulation, have the cord replaced.

NOTE: Make sure the supporting information for these appliances is kept with your records. Instruction books, operator's manuals, warranties, sales receipts, service company phone numbers, and maintenance and repair records should be accessible and updated.

DISHWASHER, WASHER/DRYER QUICK CHECKLIST

- ❏ Watch for dishwasher and clothes washer water leaks.
- ❏ Use correct detergents and soaps.
- ❏ Keep dishwasher plumbing traps cleaned out.
- ❏ Treat a dishwasher door carefully. Avoid chipping or scratching its interior surface.
- ❏ Keep clothes washer exteriors clean. Detergent, bleach, and similar materials should be wiped from the top as soon as they are spilled.
- ❏ Empty lint traps regularly.
- ❏ Make sure there is a fuel line shutoff valve on a gas clothes dryer.

Electronics

Electronics. Name a home without them. Sure, there are people who do without television, but not many. And if they don't have TV, they most likely have something else—a sound system of some kind—a stereo to receive AM and FM stations. Or perhaps a tape deck, CD player, or turntable. With more and more people working from their homes, computers, printers, copiers, and fax machines are frequently being set up in basements, dens, and spare bedrooms.

On the whole, today's electronic recreational and business appliances are more durable and less likely to break down than their earlier cousins. Here are some guidelines to help keep your electronic equipment going strong.

Keep electronic equipment free from dust buildup. Dust can work its way onto and into computer keyboards, disk drives, stereo vents and seams, speaker fabric, television screens, computer monitors, turntables, tape decks—anywhere within a home's living or working spaces. While a small amount of dust may not affect performance, dust buildups will eventually cause a variety of problems, some of which can considerably reduce a unit's time until failure.

To remedy, dust or vacuum exposed surfaces regularly, preferably before dust collects to a point where it is noticeable when wiped away with a finger. Monitors can be cleaned with a lint-free cloth lightly sprayed with glass cleaner. Make sure you let the set cool before cleaning the face of the picture tube. As another safety precaution, always get into the habit of unplugging a piece of equipment before you start cleaning or working on it.

Avoid using liquids near electronic equipment. Water, ginger ale, coffee, and other drinks will not only damage inner electronic workings, but they can cause electrical shorts within the equipment's power supply, which could, in turn, result in electrical shock to an unsuspecting user. Except for lightly spraying the glass of a television or monitor screen, avoid spraying cleaners directly onto electronic equipment. You could damage the wiring or clog the ventilation or sound-producing holes. Instead, spray the cleaner onto a cloth first, then wipe the areas clean. Television cabinets are often made of plastic or wood veneer. A mild soap and warm water solution can be used in a cloth that is wrung nearly dry to prevent drips. To clean metal cabinets, chrome, or any other shiny trim, use a soft cloth moistened with a little rubbing alcohol, white vinegar, or window cleaner.

Occasionally refer to the operator's manual. Keep the operator's manuals for your electronic equipment in one place, so you always know where to find them. There are usually troubleshooting sections that can be consulted and simple checks that can be done before calling a repair person.

For example, on a television set, if there is no picture, sound, or light, make sure the set is plugged in. Then test the wall outlet with a lamp you know is working. If there is no power, replace the appropriate fuse or reset the corresponding circuit breaker in the home's main electrical panel. If there is a television circuit breaker on the back of the set, reset it. Check the power cord, the connections, and the wires. Examine the cord for signs of broken insulation, burn marks, or loose prongs at the plug.

If the picture is not correct, look for adjustment knobs and screws on the front, side, or rear panels. Most are for correcting picture problems and should be used as outlined in the owner's manual. Allow the set to warm up before making adjustments. If the picture appears grainy on a set with a mechanical channel selector and tuner, wiggle the channel selector knob. If the picture clears up right away, unplug the set and remove the channel selector knob. Purchase a spray can of "tuner cleaner" at an electronics supply store. Follow the can's instructions and spray some of the material through the knob opening. Replace the knob. After the television warms up again, the graininess will likely have disappeared.

Although cable television is rapidly spreading from area to area, wireless station reception could be poor due to a roof antenna or the connections between a roof antenna and the television. To investigate the possibilities, temporarily hook up a pair of "rabbit ears"—a portable antenna—for comparison. If the rabbit ears improve reception, you know that the main antenna system is the culprit. In that case, check the wire that connects the antenna to the television. Remove the connections at the set, then refasten them. Do the same to connections leading to a signal splitter, if you have an FM radio or a second television connected to the same system. Outside antenna wires sometimes become loose and stretched, and can be blown back and forth by the wind, causing the television picture to flip or lose color as the wires twist back and forth. Make sure the antenna wires and cables are securely fastened their entire length. (See Figures 51-1 and 51-2.)

Similar inspections and precautions can be used with other electronic equipment. Again, the owner's manuals provide maintenance reference instructions for each individual appliance.

Make sure the location is adequate. Most pieces of electronic equipment benefit from being positioned on a sturdy, level surface, where the temperature is consistently moderate (between 50 and 80 degrees F.), and where the humidity is not too high. Direct exposure to sunlight should be avoided, and the room should be well ventilated. Be careful of placing equipment in enclosed cabinets or similar homemade spaces. You should be able to get at the rear panels to clean and inspect things periodically.

Try to avoid frequent equipment moves. While electronic equipment is fairly durable, bounces and jarring motions can cause damage. Units designed to be moved from place to place—such as a portable CD player—are built extra tough. Many other units are not. If a piece of electronic equipment must be moved, use care during its transport.

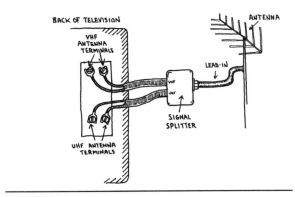

51-1. Antenna connections.

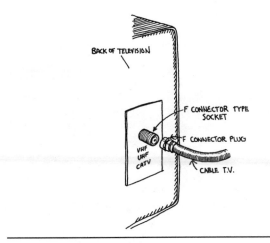

51-2. Cable connection.

ELECTRONICS SAFETY

Unless you are a skilled technician, never remove the back cover of a television, stereo receiver, or similar appliance. Noted exceptions are certain units such as computer consoles, where upgrades can be made per manufacturer's instructions. If you are not supposed to remove a cover, don't. You might make a dangerous mistake that could lead to radiation escaping or a severe buildup of heat. Touching interior parts could also cause an electrical shock; in some cases, even when the power cord is unplugged.

Always unplug a unit before you clean or work on it. Make sure the power cord is intact. Some sets have plugs containing one prong with a widened tip. The wide prong is meant to fit the wide, or neutral, slot of an outlet. Avoid jamming the wide prong into the small outlet slot.

Avoid blocking ventilation slots, and never position an electronic appliance near a heat source such as a fireplace, radiator, or hot-air duct.

If an appliance's cabinet gets damaged, there may be a possibility of a shock hazard. Have a certified repair technician examine and, if necessary, repair the set.

ELECTRONICS QUICK CHECKLIST

- ❑ Keep electronic equipment relatively dust-free.
- ❑ Avoid using liquids near electronic equipment.
- ❑ Periodically review and follow the operator's manuals' maintenance guidelines and instructions.
- ❑ Keep electronics out of direct sunlight and high humidity areas.
- ❑ Make sure there is adequate ventilation in the room.
- ❑ Try to avoid frequent equipment moves.
- ❑ Always unplug equipment before you clean or work on it.
- ❑ Make sure the power cord is intact.
- ❑ Attempt only repairs you are certain you can handle safely; refer others to qualified service technicians.

Furnishings

For our purpose, furnishings include items such as mirrors, curtains and drapes, pillows, comforters, other bedding, and similar kinds of decorative and functional home accessories. All told, they have a way of gradually getting soiled, worn, and damaged over long periods of time. To prevent cumulative deterioration, periodically inspect, repair, and clean them. While only a handful of furnishings are discussed here, their care is indicative of how other items can be maintained.

MIRRORS

Mirrors are generally positioned for two different purposes. One, so people can see their own reflections, and two, so certain living spaces will benefit from decorative mirrored surfaces. Mirrors tend to widen and heighten spaces, and intensify lighting effects. They can also hide wall blemishes. In any case, mirrors must be sturdily hung.

Hanging Plain Mirrors

If a mirror is unbacked and unframed or has only a lightweight frame, a simple, secure way to mount it on a wall or door is with J-shaped mirror clips on the bottom and Z-shaped mirror clips along the sides and top. The size and quantity of the clips needed depends on the size and weight of the mirror. If you are unsure about matching up the clips and mirror correctly, inquire at a glass specialty shop or hardware store.

To mount a plain, unframed mirror, first draw a horizontal, level line where the bottom of the mirror will be. Secure two or three J-clips along the line, spaced equally apart, using hollow wall fasteners or wall anchors, depending on the type of wall. Since these J-clips will support most of the mirror's weight, they must be securely fastened. If the clips are not padded, consider adding thin pieces of adhesive-backed felt to prevent the clips from scratching the mirror's surface.

Next, with a helper, gently lower the mirror into position. While the helper holds the mirror in place, install Z-clips at regular intervals around the sides and top so the mirror will hug the wall or door surface.

If desired, an acceptable option is to have a glass dealer drill holes through the mirror's corners. Mount the mirror with long screws sunk into wall anchors. Cover the screw heads with decorative rosettes.

Hanging Framed Mirrors or Framed Artwork

First, find out how much the mirror or artwork weighs. This is important because hardware stores and picture frame shops sell picture hooks in packages that indicate the safe maximum weights each hook will hold. If the mirror weighs less than five pounds, a simple sawtooth hanger can be fastened to the center of the back top part of the frame. The sawtooth hanger can then be hung on a sturdy nail, screw, or picture hanger that is correctly positioned and fastened to the wall. (See Figure 52-1.)

52-1. Sawtooth hanger.

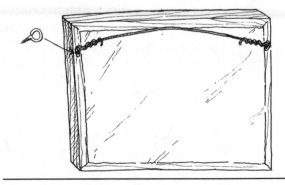

52-2. Picture wire hanger.

If the mirror weighs more than five pounds, attach screw eyes into both sides of the frame, about one-third of the way from the top on each side. Secure a strand of braided picture hanging wire between the eyes. (See Figure 52-2.) Hang the mirror on a sturdy wall hanger.

On large and extra-large mirrors, use heavier screw eyes and thicker picture wire. Two large picture hanger hooks should, if possible, be anchored into wall studs for extra holding power. Here are some guidelines for hanging extra large mirrors and artwork.

- Select large screw eyes and fasten them one into each side of the frame a third of the way down from the top.
- Cut a piece of heavy stranded picture wire 8 inches longer than the frame's width. Slip one end through an eye so that 4 inches of the end of the wire protrude. Slip the end through the same eye again, then twist the same end of the wire tightly around the main wire. Repeat with the other end and screw eye, drawing the hanging wire tight.
- Pull the taut wire's center toward the top center of the frame, and measure the distance from the wire's center to the top of the frame.
- Have someone hold the frame at its intended position against the wall. Mark the midpoint or center of the frame's top. Remove the frame, then measure down to where the hanging hook or hooks should meet the wire. Mark the spot.
- Crisscross masking tape over the marked spot. Fasten the hanging hooks to the wall.
- With help from a volunteer, position the frame in place, making sure the hanging wire catches on the hooks before letting go of the mirror or piece of artwork.

Cleaning Mirrors

Wipe mirrors with either a liquid glass cleaner and a "lintless" paper towel or use a solution of 2 tablespoons of vinegar, ammonia, or denatured alcohol mixed with one quart of warm water. Never allow any of the cleaner to touch the back of the mirror because it could discolor the mirror's reflective backing.

Remove spatters of paint by either rubbing the spots with extra fine—0000—steel wool, or by scraping them off with a razor blade in a holder.

To discourage fogging of mirrors, trail a soapy finger across the surface here and there, then shine with a lintless cloth.

To disguise a scratched or worn spot in the reflective backing of a mirror, insert a piece of uncrumpled aluminum foil between the mirror and its cardboard backing—the shiny side facing outward through the glass, away from the backside of the mirror.

CURTAINS AND DRAPES

Curtains and drapes are common window treatments that need regular maintenance to stay looking good. Old, shabby curtains and drapes, even if they are clean, should probably be replaced. Newer curtains and drapes in good condition should typically be cleaned once a year, depending on what they are made of and where they hang. Cotton drapes, for example, soil more quickly than nylon. Cleaning methods also depend on whether the curtains or drapes are sheer, lined, pleated, or textured.

Because curtains and drapes are cleaned so infrequently, consider having professionals do them. If you decide to handle all of your window treatments yourself, make sure that as you remove the hanging hooks, mark the places where hooks were inserted into the fabric. Either stitch several small loops of a colored thread at each hook position (knotting the ends so the thread won't come loose during the cleaning process), or dab small dots of a light-colored nail polish where the hooks are inserted. Another timesaver is to mark curtains or drapes in a similar way, with a scheme through which you will be able to tell which drape or curtain goes to which window, and in what order.

PILLOWS, COMFORTERS, AND MATTRESSES

A sunny day offers a perfect opportunity to air pillows, comforters, mattresses, and other "soft" furnishings. Mattresses should be vacuumed and turned —flipped over and reversed head end to foot end.

Most pillows, blankets, and comforters are simple to care for. Just wash them when they are soiled. Down pillows and comforters, on the other hand, need special care.

With normal use, down pillows need cleaning only once a year. To protect the outer shells from stains, keep pillows in a zippered, washable pillow protector, available in department store linen sections. Before washing or dry cleaning down pillows, repair any open seams or loose stitching. Pick a dry cleaner that is experienced with down products.

To wash down pillows or comforters in a home washing machine, use the gentle cycle, warm water, and a mild detergent soap — half the amount you would normally use. Start the washer's cycle without the pillows. When the water and soap are agitated, stop the cycle. Add a comforter or one or two pillows (no more than two) and a pair of clean white sneakers without laces to help keep the comforter or pillows moving. Continue the gentle washing cycle. When rinsing, repeat the rinse cycles until the rinse water runs clear. To dry comforters or pillows, set the dryer heat to low. Again, add the sneakers; their agitation will help fluff the down. In fact, whenever a down comforter or pillow loses much of its ability to trap air, try putting the item(s) in a low-temperature dryer setting along with the pair of sneakers or clean tennis balls. After about 10 minutes of tumbling, the down items should be back to their previous fluffy condition.

To prevent down comforters from soiling quickly, use an outside material shell made of a tightly woven washable cotton-polyester or similar blend. These materials let the down "breathe" properly, while trapping enough air and keeping the down from working out of the shell.

FURNISHINGS QUICK CHECKLIST

❏ Use correct-sized hangers to fasten mirrors and artwork to walls.

❏ Clean mirrors and pieces of artwork when they need it, before they become dusty.

❏ Clean curtains and drapes at least once a year. Mark them in some way so you know exactly how to rehang them.

❏ Periodically air pillows, comforters, mattresses, and other "soft" furnishings.

Furniture

Furniture gives a household character. In some dwellings, it is hardly used. In other homes, with young children, dogs, and cats, it takes a beating. This section consists of tips on how furniture can be kept in top condition.

WOOD FURNITURE

When household woodwork is inspected, be sure to add any wood furniture to the list. Older furniture may be fastened together by animal glues that become brittle with age and do not stand up well to heat and dry air. Blocks on the inside corners of tables, chairs, and cabinets can loosen, as can rungs on chairs and veneers on table tops and other surfaces.

The worst enemies of quality wood furniture are heat and dry air. Heat, when combined with dry air, causes wood to shrink and furniture joints to fail. To combat these ill effects, the atmosphere within the household should be kept at a humidity of about 40 percent, and the furniture should be positioned away from direct heat sources such as radiators and registers.

It is important to repair broken joints as quickly as possible. Furniture, especially fine wood furniture, is made of relatively lightweight pieces of wood. It is the combination or configuration of all the pieces that gives the piece its strength. As soon as one glued joint fails, it puts a strain on the other parts. If the broken chair, table, or other piece of furniture continues to be used, additional joints are likely to work loose or break.

Furniture glues have come a long way in the past few decades. It is often possible simply to glue a joint back together without taking the piece to a furniture repair shop. On fine or expensive pieces of wood furniture, resist the temptation to use screws or nails to tighten a joint. If you are not familiar with repairing furniture, you could easily make the situation worse by splitting a leg, rung, or other component.

Ultraviolet rays can damage clear finishes that are commonly found on wood furniture. If such pieces are kept near sunny windows, either pull the shades or drapes during the day, or apply sun-shielding film to the glass to filter out a high percentage of harmful rays.

Airborne particles that come in contact with fine wood finishes can act as abrasives that scratch and wear at furniture surfaces through everyday use. The best way to protect a finish from such damages is with application of a quality furniture paste wax. A good paste wax can be rubbed to a hard glossy finish that offers more protection than spray polishes will.

UPHOLSTERED FURNITURE

Your favorite couch or armchair may still be comfortable, but how does it look? Is it getting threadbare? Has it absorbed numerous food and drink stains? Have dust and soil been ground into its fibers? Has its color faded several shades lighter than when it was new?

To prevent dust and dirt from becoming embedded in the fabric, vacuum upholstered furniture weekly. Use a furniture brush attachment and vacuum the upholstery by moving the brush attachment slowly over all of the surfaces. Use the vacuum's crevice tool to reach "cracks" and difficult spots.

Sometimes cushions will absorb moisture and miscellaneous household odors during humid weather. During such times, they can smell dank and feel sticky. To remedy this, simply air them outdoors on a dry, breezy day. Place the cushions on a clean surface in the shade to prevent fading. Air them for several hours, turn them over, and let them air several more hours.

Even with regular vacuuming and airing, upholstered fabrics will eventually require a thorough cleaning. The method of cleaning depends on the fabric. Cottons and synthetics are often washable. They can be safely shampooed with a mild detergent or a commercial cleaning product. Natural fabrics other than cotton usually need to be professionally dry cleaned. Short of that, small soiled or stained areas can sometimes be spot cleaned with commercial solutions manufactured for removing spots from clothing. When applying spot removers, always wear rubber gloves and work in a well-ventilated place.

Before applying any spot cleaners or general cleaners on a large scale, test for colorfastness on a small hidden area, such as on the back zipper side of a cushion or low on an arm, next to a cushion. Let the cleaned or treated area dry to see if it alters the color or shrinks the fabric.

To clean many cotton or synthetic upholsteries, the suds from a homemade cleaning solution can be used. Avoid using the solution itself; use only the suds or foam.

1. Brush or vacuum the furniture to be shampooed.
2. Mix 2 tablespoons soap flakes and 2 tablespoons ammonia into a container of 1 quart hot water. With a wire whisk, whip the mixture until a mass of suds forms.
3. Rub suds into a small piece of the fabric in an out-of-sight spot. Let dry. If the area fades, discolors, or shrinks, call for professional cleaning help. If nothing happens other than a cleaner area, shampoo the rest of the fabric.
4. With a clean cloth, scoop enough foam or suds to cover a small area of the fabric. Gently rub the suds over the fabric. When the suds become soiled, scrape them off with a rubber or plastic scraper. Wipe the scraper clean on paper towels.
5. Wet another clean cloth in warm water. Wring excess water out and wipe the suds from the fabric, dampening the fabric slightly. Avoid soaking it.
6. Repeat this cleaning process, overlapping previously cleaned areas. Change the suds, rinse water, and cloths when they get dirty.
7. Set up an electric fan aimed directly at the cleaned, damp furniture piece.

BUYING FURNITURE

Much of the battle against furniture maintenance can be eliminated through the purchase of quality furniture that will last many years and will retain its appearance through normal use. Since you probably won't often shop for furniture, it is to your advantage to shop wisely. Here are some important points to consider.

Measure the area in which you plan to place furniture. And measure the widths of doorways or sliding-door entrances in your home. Horror stories abound of individuals who have purchased pieces of furniture only to find out the items wouldn't fit into the home. Take a measuring tape with you.

Match fabrics and wood types. If you intend to match other fabrics to those on existing upholstered furniture or window coverings, take a piece of the fabric in question to the store. If you don't have a piece of the fabric, use a photograph of the furniture piece.

Compare furniture from many stores and take notes. You might think you can remember details from one piece of furniture to another, but by the time you have spent a week in and out of a dozen stores, you will appreciate the convenience of keeping the facts straight in a notebook.

Once in a store, try out the furniture. See how it feels. Smell it. Is it noisy? Slippery? Easy to catch or snag the fabric? How does it fit? Put recliners through their paces.

Find out about the insides, too. What's beneath all that nice, plush upholstery? Upholstered furniture is generally manufactured in three parts: a frame, the filling or cushions, and the outer fabric. Salespeople should know what's inside. If they don't, ask for the manager. Find out what type of frame is under the fabric. If it is wood, ask if it is kiln-dried. Kiln-dried wood lasts longer and resists warping in humid conditions. Is the fabric weave tight or loose? Tight weaves hold up better. Are cushions reversible? That counts for a lot. If a child spills grape juice on one side, or the side gets otherwise damaged beyond cosmetic repairs, the ability simply to flip the cushion(s) over can save a considerable replacement expense.

Even if you don't smoke, ask if the furniture is flame retardant. Every year, people are horribly disfigured or killed when they fall asleep while smoking and let cigarette, cigar, or pipe ashes drop and ignite couches or easy chairs. A flame retardant designation doesn't mean that the piece won't burn. Practically no couch or easy chair is fireproof. It means that the piece will tend to smolder at first instead of bursting into flames. The fabric will resist flames longer when treated with a retardant.

Find out about delivery. If you have a truck or van and don't mind lugging furniture around, fine. Otherwise, ask if delivery (and perhaps removal of the old couch) can be included as part of the sale. If you plan to move a heavy piece yourself, make sure you get enough help and avoid damaging or soiling the piece in transit.

Find out how to care for the furniture. Make sure you understand how to maintain what you purchase. Inspect hang tags and insist on some manufacturer's instructions.

Buying Wood Furniture

Determine what kind or kinds of wood construction were used. "Solid Wood" means just that. Exposed surfaces should be made of the wood named, without any veneers or plywoods. Thus "Solid Cherry" means that a piece is constructed with solid cherry wood on any part of the piece that is typically exposed or seen. Other woods, however, may be used on parts that are not normally seen, such as drawer sides or unfinished rear panels of a desk that is expected to be positioned flush against a wall.

"Genuine Cherry" or oak, or any other type of wood, means that all exposed parts of the furniture piece can be made of a veneer of the named wood, in this case, a cherry veneer. Veneer is a result of a woodworking construction technique in which thin layers of fine hardwood are glued or bonded to other, less expensive plywood members.

"Wood" in its simplest term indicates that the piece of furniture has no major plastic, metal, or other non-wood components—except, of course, fasteners such as nails, screws, or hinges.

Manmade materials or "Oak Style" refer to plastic laminated panels or molded plastics imprinted to look like natural wood grains. When imitation wood laminates are involved, make sure the surface laminate is securely and smoothly bonded to the material underneath.

When shopping for fine wood furniture, watch out for imperfections in the finish such as streaks, bubbles, drips, lacquer runs, and excess finish material in corners. Be wary of finishes that are so thin as to be practically worthless. Consider that a painted or lacquered finish is easy to clean but hard to touch up if scratched or dented. One way to distinguish between quality and cheap finishes is that cheap, inexpensive finishes seem to coat rather than add to the appearance of the wood; quality finishes enhance the wood's appearance, and when clear, are very clear and deep. If the wood grain shows, the entire piece should appear to be uniform, with top, sides, legs, and arms all finished in the same tones. The wood's grain, too,

should be pleasantly matched.

If the piece has moving parts, move them. Open drawers, close doors, remove table leaves, and adjust any adjustable shelves. Do the hinges work crisply? Is everything lined up? Rub your hands along the finish. Is it smooth? Or are there rough areas that highlight inadequate sanding? Is everything sturdy? See that attached hardware—handles, knobs, hinges, and other components—are fastened securely from the inside. With drawers, look for center or side guides, as well as automatic stops that will prevent a drawer from being pulled all of the way out of its position, and possibly falling on your feet. Check interiors for areas that may snag clothing. Wood screws are superior to nails and standard staples.

Look at the joints. Are side and back panels fastened by sturdy, close-fitting dovetailed joints? Or are they mismatched and only loosely nailed together?

FURNITURE REPAIRS

There is no use trying to describe dozens of woodworking techniques that can be used to repair broken pieces of furniture. A few are mentioned in the section on lawn furniture, but that kind of furniture is a lot "rougher" than fine wood chairs and tables. Unless you are familiar with furniture construction and appearance is critical, you are probably better off having broken pieces repaired by professionals. There are probably small furniture upholstery and repair shops in your area that will perform quality work at a reasonable cost.

FURNITURE MAINTENANCE

Keep furniture out of direct sunlight, if possible, and away from sources of heat and moisture. Keep pets off furniture. Instruct small children to eat snacks in the kitchen or outside. Keep glasses or cups of hot or cold liquids off wood surfaces. Watch where cigarettes are placed. Shampoo upholstery when needed.

FURNITURE QUICK CHECKLIST

❑ Inspect wood furniture at the same time you inspect household woodwork.

❑ Keep fine wood furniture out of direct sunlight and sources of heat such as radiators and registers.

❑ Repair broken joints as quickly as possible.

❑ Polish fine wood furniture with a quality furniture paste wax.

❑ Vacuum upholstered furniture about once a week.

❑ Occasionally air cushions outdoors on dry, breezy days.

❑ When needed, shampoo cotton or synthetic upholsteries; have others professionally cleaned.

❑ When shopping for furniture, buy quality. Request flame retardant upholsteries when available. Understand the furniture's construction and obtain the manufacturer's care and maintenance instructions.

Fireplaces and Wood Stoves

Because of the nature of fireplaces and wood stoves, most of this entire section can be considered a safety discussion. Fireplaces and wood stoves — despite what their manufacturers or proponents might say — are more of a luxury than a necessity. A very few are installed to heat an entire house. Most are included with new homes for decoration and atmosphere. They add to a room in ways that excite our senses of sight, sound, smell, and touch. And there is something mystical about their flames — they crackle and pop as if calling from our ancient past when campfires provided heat, illumination, and a means to roast wild buffalo steaks. In short, any fireplace or wood stove should:

- Permit fuel combustion.
- Exhaust the by-products of combustion from the house.
- Deliver as much heat as possible into the house.
- Operate safely.
- Be positioned so as many people as possible can enjoy it.

FIREPLACE INSPECTIONS

For this section, refer to Figure 54-1.

- Dampers that do not work. Adjustable dampers limit the amount of warm air lost up the chimney to only that necessary to remove smoke. The damper should be able to be adjusted by increments, so air flow can be regulated when the fireplace is being used.
- A low chimney. A low chimney or a chimney that doesn't protrude much from the roof is a dangerous design feature. The chimney should extend at least 3 feet above a flat roof, and at least 2 feet above a roof ridge or raised part of a roof within 10 feet of a chimney.
- Flammable materials that are touching the chimney or fireplace. There should be at least a 2-inch space at all points except the firebox, where 4 inches is the rule, between the fireplace and chimney and wood or other flammable materials. This gap or space should be firestopped with non-combustible materials.
- No hearth extensions. A hearth should extend at

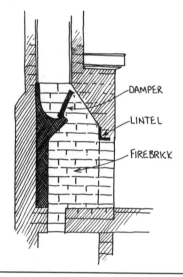

54-1. Fireplace.

least 20 to 24 inches into a room and at least 6 to 8 inches on both sides of the fireplace opening. This is so no sparks or embers land on wood, carpet, or other combustible floorings.
- No fireplace screens in use. Screens can be made of metal screening or tempered glass panes. They minimize the dangers from sparks and exploding embers, and keep young children from playing with flames.
- The fireplace smokes when burning wood. If smoke pours back into the room, even though the damper is properly set, there must either be something plugging the chimney, or there is a major design defect.
- Loose fireplace bricks or stones. If the mortar and masonry components are loose and falling apart, major repairs are probably needed. Cracks larger than ¼ inch wide, loose mortar, and loose or damaged bricks or stones should be repaired.
- Major structural problems. The lintel is a heavy piece of metal that supports the bricks or stones over a fireplace opening. Sometimes a lintel, due to age and corrosion, will start to sag. An indication of this is a wide crack developing between the lintel and its supported masonry. This is a situation that will need professional attention. Other

major problems can be obvious: large cracks elsewhere in the chimney; deteriorated supports in the floor beneath the fireplace; a disintegrating flue.

▪ A tar-like residue coats the inside and some of the outside of the chimney. Creosote is a gummy, flammable material that collects inside chimneys. Large amounts of creosote, when built up on the fireplace walls and flue, can start a chimney fire which could burn down the entire house.

FIREPLACE REPAIRS AND MAINTENANCE

Fireplace repairs are not to be taken lightly. Neither are design flaws. Both should be taken care of by masonry craftsmen. There is little sense in attempting to make one-time repairs on a home component that can result in disaster if repaired incorrectly.

Except for minor repairs and cleanings, leave the major tasks, from chimney sweeping on, to people who specialize in such work. Expend your efforts on proper and safe operation of the fireplace instead.

FIREPLACE OPERATION

▪ Avoid building a fire directly on the fireplace brick. Use the grate instead.

▪ Never burn trash, garbage, or large quantities of paper in a fireplace.

▪ Burn seasoned hardwood as fuel, or acceptable commercially manufactured substitutes. The wood should be dry, not "green" or freshly cut. Store firewood outside because it may harbor insects.

▪ Never use kerosene, gasoline, or other highly explosive liquids when starting a fire.

▪ Adding a handful of salt to the fire occasionally will help prevent the accumulation of soot and add colors to the flames.

▪ Use spark screens or glass doors in front of the fireplace opening to minimize spark dangers and to prevent children from playing with flames.

▪ Inspect chimneys frequently. Whenever ¼ inch of creosote has built up anywhere in the chimney system, it is time to call in a professional chimney sweep.

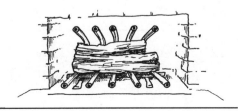

54-2. Hollow-tube grate.

▪ Because of the inefficiency of regular fireplaces, consider installing hollow tube grates (see Figure 54-2) which will help send additional heat out into a room. The C-shaped pipes point their open ends into the room near floor level. Logs rest on the tubes, which curve up the back of the firebox and back over the logs to face into the room. The heat from the fire creates a draft. Cool air enters the tubes on the bottom, becomes heated by the fire, and emerges from the top. Some models even employ an electric motor and fan to increase circulation.

▪ When using a fireplace without glass screens, close the doors to the room. Otherwise, the draft caused by the fire will pull heated air from other rooms up the chimney. If there are no doors to close, turn down the furnace thermostat to between 50 and 55 degrees Fahrenheit so the furnace won't be producing even more hot air for the fireplace to draw out of the house.

WOOD STOVES

Wood stoves are similar in design and function to fireplaces, but because they are simpler to install, and many are installed incorrectly by well-meaning homeowners, they bring greater fire hazards with their operation.

Again, because of the serious nature of this home heating appliance, it is important that you purchase a new stove from only an experienced, reliable dealer who will agree to install it in your home in a professional manner. Stoves need plenty of air space and fireproof material clearances. The purchase and installation of used stoves is not recommended.

Because many people who purchase wood stoves have very little experience with wood-stove operation, fires caused by faulty installation and misuse of the stoves are almost commonplace. Here are a few of the most frequent wood-stove fire causes:

▪ Heat radiation from hot stoves or pipes igniting adjacent combustible materials such as curtains, drapes, shades, furniture, wallpapers, carpeting, and items left leaning against or on top of the stoves.

▪ Sparks escaping into the house from the firebox, through the flue or stovepipe, or out the top of the flue, from the chimney top.

▪ Fire from creosote accumulation in the chimney.

Using and Maintaining Wood Stoves

▪ The chimney and stove connector pipes should, along with the entire setup, be inspected by a

---

FIREPLACE AND WOOD STOVE QUICK CHECKLIST

❑ Keep combustibles away from fireplaces and wood stoves.

❑ Keep fireplaces and wood stoves clean.

❑ Have them inspected at least once yearly by professionals. Make suggested repairs, if any are needed.

❑ Monitor creosote levels.

❑ Use mesh or glass screens or doors across fireplace openings.

❑ Make sure there is a working damper.

❑ Let professionals make major repairs.

❑ Make sure the chimney and flue are intact.

❑ Avoid burning trash, paper, and garbage. Burn only seasoned hardwood.

❑ Never use kerosene or gasoline to help start a fire.

❑ Closely supervise children who are in the same room as a working fireplace or wood stove.

❑ Have adequate fire extinguishers and smoke alarms on hand.

---

professional stove installer at least once a year, preferably at the start of the heating season, for possible defects that may have developed.

▪ Avoid storing dry wood beneath or directly adjacent to a stove.

▪ Favor short, hot fires rather than long, smoldering ones.

▪ Always be on the lookout for corrosion, holes, and cracks that embers could fall through. Make sure that all of the stove pipe lengths are securely fastened together with screws, so there is no chance of a pipe coming loose.

▪ Never leave children unattended in a room with a hot stove.

▪ Equip your home with adequate fire extinguishers and smoke detectors.

PART 7

Housekeeping

Many neighborhoods have one: a particular house that has gotten rundown. You know the kind—with rusted gutters, peeling paint, a boarded-up window half taped with plastic, a heaved sidewalk, a junked car in the garage, and worst of all, the yard.

The front yard is a sea of dandelions, unruly grass, and prickly weeds. Overgrown shrubs and trees threaten to engulf the front porch. In the backyard, you will find papers, junk, and garbage.

What happened? Well, maybe it was a stroke of bad luck that left the owners unable to care for the property. Or maybe the owners were simply irresponsible and lazy. Some people don't take pride in themselves or their homes.

Whatever the reason, the result is the same. The home loses its appearance and value long before its time. The owners move away, the bank repossesses, and the place sits vacant for months, subject to vandalism, fire hazards, encroaching vegetation, rodent infestation, and accidents involving neighborhood children who play on the abandoned site.

Contrast that property with a well cared for home, one the owners are proud of. There are no rusted gutters, no peeling paint, and no heaved sidewalks. No broken windows or junked car. Everything is in good working order, everything is in its place. The yard is free of weeds and clutter, neatly maintained and bordered by trimmed shrubs and trees. The property's appearance and value remains as high as can be.

What's the difference between the first house and the second? Good housekeeping. Housekeeping may not sound like much, but it is. It carries a lot of weight in our home lives. This section contains discussions of Storage Areas, Spring Cleaning, Special Metal Cleaning, Cleaning Equipment and Supplies, and Pet Proofing.

Storage Areas

If there is one thing home builders tend to skimp on, it is storage space. They usually put the minimum number of closets in a home—one per bedroom, a small closet near the front entrance, and perhaps a tiny pantry. Attics, in these days of modern truss roofs, are even scarcer still. This minimal closet space may work for single individuals or the single parent with one or two children, but what about the large family? Where do two adults and four children put all their clothes and belongings?

It is difficult to come up with rules of thumb that are acceptable to every situation, but a sound floor plan might well include a closet at least 4 feet wide by 2 feet deep for every family member, a linen closet large enough to hold extra bedding, bathroom closets for extra towels and washcloths, a roomy pantry closet, plus guest closets near the front door, and in cold climate areas, near the rear door as well.

CLOSETS

Closets are nice to have. They hide items that, if left in full view, would appear to clutter the home. Closets keep possessions out of sight and out of mind. They help organize belongings and provide continuity to storage systems.

Organizing Closets

Before reorganizing a closet, start afresh. Throw out or remove all excess items. If you haven't worn or used it within a year, ask yourself why it is still taking up valuable space. Chances are, you won't use it again.

Conventional closets are full of wasted space. They are generally spanned by a single rod situated below a single shelf. That is like building a full-size automobile with a single bucket seat in the middle. A single rod and a single shelf do not provide sufficient surface area for storage. They ignore the need for compartments, which are essential in combating clutter.

A simple way to plan the best closet storage scheme is to start with all of the items you want to keep there.

Hang coats, jackets, suits, dresses, blouses, shirts, and slacks so the longest items are at one end of the rod and the shortest are at the other. Next, place folded clothes such as sweaters and knitted items on the shelf. Then move back and study the area below and above the hanging and folded clothes. Open areas are spaces you can convert to additional productive storage.

One way to use the additional space is to fill it with free-standing shelves, some to fit beneath clothing that does not reach the floor, and some to fit above the clothing that is folded on the main shelf, almost up to the ceiling. Modular shelving can be purchased and suitably arranged, or you can make shelves yourself from $3/4$-inch plywood.

Another possibility is to install several additional clothes rods on which to hang clothes of different lengths. For instance, a second rod can be positioned halfway below the main rod, below shirts or blouses, for storing additional shirts or trousers that are doubled over on hangers. (See Figure 56-1.) Closet configurations where shelves at the top eliminate stooping, and clothes are hung in multiple rows, are the key to designing the most efficient storage layouts.

MOVEABLE SHOE RACK   LOUVERED POCKET DOOR

56-1. An efficiently planned clothes closet.

It can be helpful to plan a closet renovation on graph paper first. Begin by drawing a rectangle to scale, consisting of lines that represent your actual closet: the sides, top, and bottom. Pencil in the clothing where you want it and determine how best to fill in the rest of the space. Always take into account the size of the items you are planning to store. For example, a linen closet's shelves should be at least 16 inches wide and 12 inches deep to accommodate folded blankets. Shelves for sweaters need not be as large.

Plan for easy retrieval. Clothing you use every day should be stored at or near eye level. Items less frequently used can be kept on top shelves or on the floor. Shelves should not be too high. If you squeeze ten or twelve knitted sweaters together on top of one another on a single shelf, retrieving one from the bottom or middle of the pile can result in the rest of the sweaters being pulled out and unfolded along the way.

Consider ready-made systems available in hardware and builder's supply stores. These include ventilated shelves, wall racks and grid systems, undershelf accessories, stacking drawers and baskets, garment bags, shelf dividers, and other storage extras. Entire stores and mail order catalogs cater to people looking to squeeze every usable square inch of storage space from their homes. Most manufactured systems are simple to install.

In such a system, you may find fully adjustable shelves and rods, movable shoe racks that rest on the closet floor, and specialty hangers for ties, belts, hats, and trousers—where many items can be suspended from a single hanger.

Finishing touches to a closet can include replacing swing-out doors with folding or pocket doors, so you have a better view of the closet and easier access, and installing a closet light that turns on when the door is opened.

Closets used only by women benefit from the arrangement of inexpensive "cubbyholes," drawer units, and shelving—in addition to horizontal rods for hanging items. Shelves should be cut extra deep so shoes can be stored heel-to-heel. At the top of the closet, tall and narrow cubbyholes can hold handbags. The partitions between the cubbies can be removed to create another flat shelf if the need arises. In other words, everything should have a place. This can be accomplished through individual compartments that take advantage of every inch of available vertical space.

Children's closets are a different story. Home builders usually construct all of the closets to identical heights. With children, that can mean everything is way too high for their access. A child's closet needs to be scaled down. Children typically need more shelf and drawer space because their shirts and shorts and other individual items are often too small to hang efficiently. Perhaps the best way to make over a child's closet is by adding ventilated, movable wire shelves and drawers. Such accessories can also be expanded and changed as the child grows. Another advantage with the wire drawers is that they are see-through, so kids don't have to rifle through everything to find a favorite shirt. The highest shelf, at about 84 inches, can be reserved for storing out-of-season clothing. The lower one, at about 42 inches from the floor, is where a child can place clothes. Accessories can be easily organized with a wall grid for hanging belts and hats. For shoe storage, use small pocket hanging bags, narrow shelves, or shallow drawers.

Front entrance and rear entrance closets should not be filled with items other than coats, jackets, hats, and rain or winter apparel. Umbrellas, boots, shoes, and similar items that are removed once an individual enters the home also belong there. Although the family can keep their own outdoor clothing in the entrance closets, there should be room to spare so visitors can hang their coats and jackets before entering the living areas of the house.

Kitchen pantry and broom closets are nice amenities. In addition to the space provided by their shelves, more room can be created through a wall-mounted broom and mop organizer that will store a dustpan,

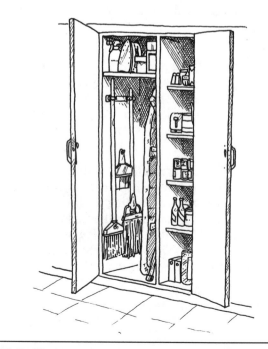

56-2. Kitchen pantry.

door to keep both the iron and ironing board tucked out of sight. (See Figure 56-2.) Special heat-resistant material makes the iron holder suitable for storing a hot iron. After you unplug the iron, just put it away. No cooling time is necessary.

DRESSERS AND OTHER FREE-STANDING STORAGE UNITS

How can you prevent items that are placed in dresser drawers from becoming all mixed up? To avoid the crushing and wrinkled tangle of clothing in the typical drawer, add separate compartments within each drawer. Store accessories in their own spaces within each drawer. Of course, you won't be able to store as much—jamming clothes in until no more will fit will no longer work. You won't be able to handle as much, but what's there can be kept neater. You will also be less likely to hang onto items you no longer wear. From any perspective, converting wide-open drawers to drawers full of carefully thought-out compartments will save considerable time in maintaining any wardrobe.

Free-standing storage units, or similar units designed to be placed inside closets, include compartments with door fronts, drawers, shelving, and garment rods. The units are available in beautiful contemporary colors and finishes that are durable and scratch resistant. Systems crafted from quality melamine laminated hardwood, with European-style hardware, can add both appearance and function to your storage scheme. Doors in see-through Plexiglas can be especially convenient in kitchens or laundry rooms to make a search for food or other supplies easier.

Storage drawers are opened and closed so frequently that they can require periodic adjustments and repairs. Typically, these repairs can be made with a screwdriver, sandpaper, and candle wax or paraffin.

1. For loose handles and knobs, simply tighten with a screwdriver from the inside of the drawer. You can purchase replacement knobs at hardware or builder's supply stores.
2. For sticking drawers, remove the drawer. Look for shiny places on the top or bottom edges or on the sides. Sand the shiny spots with sandpaper. Replace the drawer and try it again. Repeat the sanding if it still sticks. When you have it working easily, without sticking, the next step is to remove the drawer again and rub the drawer and frame (where they touch), with candle wax, paraffin, or even soap to make the drawer glide more easily. This is very important if the drawer

will be filled with heavy items.

If the drawer glides are badly worn, the drawer may not close all the way because the drawer is striking the frame. Such a drawer needs to be lifted. Remove it and insert two or three large smooth-head thumbtacks along the front of each glide.

WALL-HUNG SHELVES

Wall-hung shelves can be placed almost anywhere: in bedrooms, dining rooms, living rooms, bathrooms, basements, and garages — anywhere extra space is needed. You need to pay attention to three factors: the method of attaching them to the wall, the number of supports required to hold a shelf safely to prevent sagging, and the material the shelving consists of: does it clash with or complement the room or area where it is located?

Assuming that fastening screws are set into solid wood, a $3/4$-inch pine shelf on brackets spaced 12 inches apart will support over 650 pounds per square foot. That is a lot of strength. Take away some of the support brackets, though, and at 72 inches of spacing, that same pine shelf's load capacity drops down to less than 5 pounds per square foot. In general, the maximum safe bracket span for a heavily loaded $3/4$-inch wood shelf, with no support at the back edge, should not exceed 32 inches. Shelves in enclosed bookcases with back support can easily span up to 48 inches. Glass shelves of $1/4$-inch plate should not exceed 20 inches between support brackets. Go to a thicker glass plate, however, say $3/8$ inch, and the span can be doubled up to 40 inches.

Of course, even if you have a sufficient number of support brackets, that doesn't mean the entire shelf is sturdy enough. It depends on how well the brackets are fastened to the wall. Screws turned into thin wood

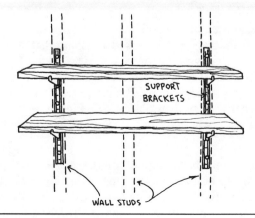

SUPPORT BRACKETS

WALL STUDS

56-3. Shelves.

paneling or bare plasterboard can easily pull loose. That is why, if possible, shelf brackets should be screwed into wall studs—2" x 4" or 2" x 6" boards positioned vertically within the walls, usually 16 inches apart. (See Figure 56-3.) You can then fasten support brackets exactly 32 inches apart from each other. This way the studs—not the wall surface—will support the load, so special wall anchors will not be needed. For long, lightly loaded shelves or shelves of heavier stock, you can go to every third stud.

But what if the studs don't cooperate? They can be hard to find, and they may not fall exactly where you want your shelf brackets. In that case, you will have to resort to wall anchors to achieve a strong bond between brackets and wall. On plasterboard and other hollow walls, the simplest anchors are plastic sleeves set or tapped into pre-drilled holes. As a screw is turned into the sleeve, it forces the sides of the plastic sleeve to expand and press against or wedge firmly into the wall.

Plastic anchors come in different sizes, and take screw sizes from number 6 to number 10. The larger the anchor, the more weight it will hold. Instructions on the package tell you which size screw to use with each anchor and what size hole you should drill in order to insert the sleeve into the wall. It is usually best to use as large an anchor as your shelf hardware will accept. The plastic sleeves work well with plasterboard and plaster walls, but they can't be used in masonry. In brick or stone walls you need lead sleeves called expansion shields, which are made especially for brick and concrete. Like plastic sleeves, these come in several sizes and work in the same fashion. A special drill tip and a star drill or carbide-tipped drill are needed to bore the pilot holes where the expansion shields will be inserted in the wall.

Sometimes whatever has to be fastened to a hollow wall is so heavy or bulky that plastic sleeves won't do the job. To suspend heavy loads from hollow walls, two different fasteners can be used: toggle bolts and expansion anchors. Both work by gripping the back side of the wall with a locked-in clamp that shouldn't pull loose. Toggle bolts have spring-loaded legs that compress as they are inserted into a pre-drilled pilot hole, then spring open behind the wall to lock their accompanying bolt in place. (See Figure 56-4.) They can be used wherever heavy supports are needed—on walls or ceilings.

One caution about toggle bolts is once they are installed, the bolts can't be removed or the back of the fastener—the toggle—will fall off inside the wall. You have to attach the bolt to the shelf bracket before inserting the toggle into the wall.

Expansion anchors, also called molly bolts, have a slotted sleeve that expands as the bolt is tightened. They form a clamp that looks like a bird claw behind the wall. Once installed, the expansion anchor bolts can be removed from the wall while the anchors stay in place, thus permitting the anchors to be installed before you attach the shelf brackets.

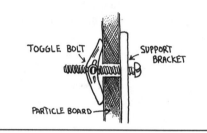

56-4. Toggle bolt.

OTHER STORAGE CONSIDERATIONS

A variety of plastic household products is available to help customize your storage abilities. Cabinet doors convert into storage areas with the installation of door-mounted organizers. Consolidate cleaning supplies by keeping all basic cleaners in a portable clean-up basket you can mount on a lower kitchen cabinet door. The basket or caddie slides off its mount and can be conveniently carried from room to room. (If you have small children, be sure the cabinet door locks.)

It is a waste of space to store trash baskets beneath sinks. The places toward the back of the sink cabinet go unused. Instead, place a step-on wastebasket of matching material/color near the kitchen side or rear entry. A tall-size kitchen step-on basket is easy to use and keeps the trash out of sight beneath its flip-up lid. Small bathroom-size step-on baskets are also available in similar decorative materials and colors.

Stackable storage bins can create additional storage where there is only room for one shelf. Pull-out trays fit nicely in lower cabinets where it is difficult to look and reach. The shelves glide out for easy access.

Additional kitchen space can be had by suspending cookware and lightweight plants from the ceiling, outside of traffic patterns, or by hanging shallow coated-wire bins from existing shelving. Tiered shelves can be installed in previously vacant corners.

Attics are ideal places to store certain items, as long as there is enough ventilation to prevent temperatures from skyrocketing during summer. Even when trusses make up the attic, the main part can be floored with plywood where headroom is the highest. In the off-season, outdoor maintenance and sports equipment (and similar items) can be kept safe until needed.

Garage and basement storage can reduce the pressure to store certain items in closets, under beds, and throughout the living areas of the home. No matter what size a garage is, many feet of relatively inactive space can be used for storage. One or more shelves 24 to 30 inches deep can be installed around the two sides and the back of the garage about 6 feet above the floor, attached by brackets fixed to the walls. (See Figure 56-5.) Other storage spaces can be salvaged from the area directly above each car bay. Horizontal racks can be hung there. If hung or constructed over a walking area, they should be at least 6½ feet high. Where they hang over the car bays, they can be dropped as low as 5 feet off the floor, depending on what kind of vehicle you park there. Remember that the more items you can keep elevated, the easier and faster you will be able to clean out the garage.

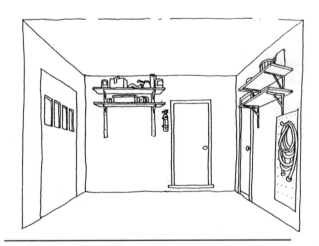

56-5. Garage shelves.

Pegboard is ideal for hanging all sorts of hand tools, garden tools, hoses, and many other items. If pegboard will be secured to finished walls, an air space must be left behind it so the pegs will be able to be inserted. This can be accomplished by using 2" x 2" wood studs between the wall and pegboard. (See Figure 56-6.)

Certain items, such as bicycles, ladders, lawn mowers, wheelbarrows, and other heavy or bulky objects can be hung from various storage hooks or brackets. Visit bike shops or gardening shops, hardware stores,

or other retail establishments to see how they display and hang those same items. What works for them will usually work for you.

A relatively new storage need for many households is space for separating and storing recyclable materials. Studies show that the key to successful recycling habits is setting up a system that blends in with your family's lifestyle and fits comfortably in your home. The most workable systems employ convenient and attractive or hidden sorting containers that lend a certain sense of stability to the program, so you are not doing it differently every week.

You may be required to separate newspapers, aluminum cans, steel cans, plastic containers, and three different colors of jars and other glass. That is seven different items. If you don't have room in your kitchen for enough stackable bins or containers, go to your garage with them. If you don't have a garage, they can be put outdoors, on a patio perhaps, or beneath a carport roof. For outdoor use, medium or large size bins are recommended in one of three nationally recognized colors: bright green, blue, or yellow. And make sure they have lids. If you have curbside recycling, buy a color to match what your community uses.

Unless you thoroughly understand the possibilities for recycling that are available in your community, it is a good idea to call your county or municipal solid waste office or sanitation department. Recycling is here to stay, and it is the right thing to do for our environment.

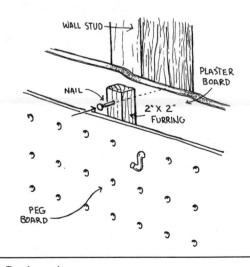

56-6. Pegboard.

STORAGE AREAS QUICK CHECKLIST

❑ Fill unused closet areas with shelves, clothes rods, and built-in compartments.

❑ Scale a child's closet down to the child's size.

❑ Weed out rarely used items from all "high rent" or convenient storage space within a home's living areas. Store infrequently used items out of the mainstream, in an attic, a basement, or a garage.

❑ Arrange compartments within drawers; avoid jamming things all together in drawers.

❑ Position free-standing storage units where there is not enough built-in storage space.

❑ Be sure to use the correct number of large enough fasteners of the proper type to hang heavy mirrors and artwork.

❑ Install enough well-fastened supports to hold shelving securely in place.

❑ Take advantage of specialty mail order catalogs to purchase low-cost clever storage items that will add more household storage a little at a time.

❑ Realize full storage use of basements, attics, and garages.

❑ Pay attention to retail store displays and storage methods; customize what you can for your own home.

❑ Set up a workable, usable recycling system.

Spring Cleaning

Does spring cleaning sound like something your grandmother used to do? If so, it was because she knew what needed to be done to prevent things from getting out of hand. No matter where you live or what you live in, your household will greatly benefit from yearly spring cleaning. It is a forced method of keeping things under control. It is cleaning up areas that you would otherwise bypass as "not needing it yet."

SPRING CLEANING SUPPLIES

Here is a list of items and supplies for a comprehensive spring cleaning campaign:

> Good upright bristle broom
> Dust pan and small whisk broom
> Vacuum cleaner with an empty bag
> Carpet shampooer or floor polisher/buffer, if needed (both can be rented)
> Mop and pail
> Good squeegee
> Rags, sponges, and paper towels
> Stepladder
> Toilet brush
> Shelf lining paper
> Household cleansers
> Glass cleaner
> Trash bags

A variety of proven cleaners should be kept handy. They include baking soda, liquid bleach, vinegar, ammonia, and plain old detergent soap. Beyond that are all kinds of homespun and gimmicky cleaning remedies such as hair sprays, art gum erasers, dry sponges, cornmeal, and even cat litter. Entire books have been written full of odd, specific cleaning hints. For instance: Purchase the cheapest brand of dishwashing liquid available, then add a few tablespoons of vinegar to the dishwater to cut grease and leave the dishes sparkling clean. Or: Club soda will quickly shine stainless steel sinks and cooking implements.

OUTSIDE CLEANING

When spring cleaning season arrives, don't forget the outside of your home. Lawns, driveways, garages, porches, decks, gutters, windows, siding, mailboxes, and lawn furniture can all be touched up and cleaned. Soiling problems vary according to local conditions. Sources of dirt that can mar the appearance of a home include dust, industrial pollution, smog, and debris from nearby trees. In some parts of the country, mildew discolors exterior walls. Mildew cannot be covered by paint and should not be hidden with siding. It must be removed before it causes more damage.

Rain will wash most dirt from siding, but that may not be good enough. A long-handled car brush or window cleaning brush that attaches to the end of a hose can be a helpful tool for giving a house a bath. If you live in an industrial area that is subject to heavy doses of grime and soot, a cleaning solution can be made by mixing $1/3$ cup household detergent to $2/3$ cup household cleaner in a gallon of water. Where mildew is a problem, mix the same amounts of detergent and cleaner with three quarts of water and one quart of bleach. To avoid streaking, start washing at the bottom of the wall and work your way up. Before you start, test some of the cleaner on an inconspicuous spot, to see if it has any undesirable side effects on the siding.

If your home has brick, stone, or wood siding, appropriate cleaners can be purchased at local hardware or builder's supply stores.

INSIDE CLEANING

Weather permitting, open all windows and air things out. Circulating air will help remove some of the dust you stir up and will keep it from settling while the spring cleaning is taking place.

Start from the top down, the top being the attic (if you have one). First throw out or get rid of any junk. In the rooms, clean light fixtures, replace burnt out bulbs as needed, sweep, wipe, or vacuum walls, window frames, and floor moldings first. Get rid of all the cobwebs. Clean windows, inside and out. Vacuum all exhaust fans. Swap storm windows for screens. Dry clean or wash draperies and curtains. Vacuum

---

SPRING CLEANING QUICK CHECKLIST

☐ Equip yourself with all the basic cleaning equipment and supplies.
☐ Clean up the grounds.
☐ Clean the home's exterior.
☐ Air out the home's interior.
☐ Clean the interior from the top down.
☐ Pay special attention to the kitchen and bathrooms.
☐ Clean out refrigerators and freezers.
☐ Clean the floors last.

---

and wipe down furniture. Reupholster furniture with worn out, threadbare surfaces. Treat wood moldings, cabinets, and other furnishings with a wood conditioner to replace oils that have evaporated throughout the year.

Check how well sink drains flow. If the traps have cleanout plugs, now is the time to clean them out.

Lift off bed mattresses and vacuum them. Then turn them over and rotate them so they wear evenly.

Pay special attention to the kitchen and bathrooms. Dirty ovens will be perhaps your toughest cleaning job. In addition to using ready manufactured oven cleaners, consider going with an all night ammonia bath: all you need are newspapers and a bottle of ammonia. Lightly soak the newspapers in ammonia and line the oven with the ammonia-soaked paper, making sure you block the vent in the back with the paper. Leave overnight. In the morning remove the paper and wash the oven with soapy water. Most of the crusty residues and stains can be removed in this manner. To keep the fumes to a minimum, keep a window cracked open or run exhaust fans available in the kitchen. Don't forget the exterior of the stove, the top broiler, the burners, the oven lights, and the filter from the exhaust fan, if present.

The refrigerator and freezers should receive attention too. Defrost freezers if necessary. Remove old food that is no longer good or wanted. Clean the inside shelves and compartments with warm soapy water. Rinse, dry, and replace. Vacuum the condenser coils on the back or the bottom of the refrigerator. It is usually best to move the entire unit out from the wall,

so the floor beneath can be cleaned. Clean the drip pan and wipe down the exterior. An application of appliance wax will make a world of difference to the appearance of any refrigerator or oven.

Give cabinets and drawers a thorough cleaning. Replace soiled or ripped shelf paper.

Bathrooms, although they should always be kept clean, will also benefit from intensive springtime cleaning. Hard water stains will respond to vinegar rubs. Fiberglass tubs and shower stalls can be cleaned with baking soda and then rinsed. Clean shower wall surfaces can be waxed to help water runoff, but do not wax bathtubs or shower bases. Mildew can be taken care of with a mixture of half bleach, half water put in a spray bottle and labeled accordingly. Spray on affected ceramic tile, grouting, or other surfaces. Let bleach mixture stand, then rinse well.

Scrub and disinfect toilet bowls and tanks, hand basins and faucets. Remove tub, shower, and sink water handles. Clean and replace them. If this isn't done periodically, the screws that hold the handles in place will corrode so badly that you won't be able to get the handles off without resorting to heroic methods, up to and including the services of a licensed plumber.

If grout or caulking around showers, bathtubs, or tile needs repair, now is the time to get it done.

The basement should receive some attention. Windows and sills should be cleaned. The ledges over the top of the walls should be wiped down. Vacuum along the walls and steps, where they meet the floor. Clean debris from outside basement window wells. Drain a few gallons of water from the water heater to remove calcium sediments. The furnace filter should be pulled and cleaned or replaced. Vacuum the accessible parts of the inside of the furnace to remove deposits of dirt and dust. The central air conditioner, if you have one, should have its outside screen housing removed and cleaned. All of the home's hot and cold return registers should be vacuumed and wiped to remove accumulated winter dirt and dust.

Clean the floors last. Go over carpeting for stains. Treat them. Vacuum all carpeting and rugs. Pay special attention to carpet edges and corners. Use a hand vacuum or crevice attachment. If carpeting is a little discolored, consider shampooing by a reputable contractor, or rent the equipment and do it yourself.

Special Metal Cleaning

Regular household cleansers are, for the most part, versatile enough to clean almost everything from floors to ceilings. But there are a number of special metals that from time to time need special cleaning care, including brass, copper, silver, and pewter.

In general, use one side of an old clean cotton sock to apply cleaner/polish, and the other side of the sock to buff. To avoid damage, use only polish made for the kind of metal you are cleaning. Be sure to buff away all cleaner or polish. Traces allowed to remain will hasten tarnishing.

BRASS AND COPPER

Brass and copper are frequently used in the manufacture of kitchen implements, pots and pans, door and cupboard hardware, fireplace tools, and a wide variety of decorative items.

If a piece of brass or copper is lacquered, and the actual metal is not exposed, wash the item in lukewarm sudsy water prepared with liquid dishwashing soap. Rinse, dry, and buff with a soft cloth.

Wash unlacquered pieces in hot sudsy water and rinse. Apply brass or copper polish with a soft cloth or brush. Let the polish dry thoroughly, then buff. Select copper/brass polishes that contain tarnish-retarding agents. Cleaners come in powder, paste, and liquid forms. Follow the instructions carefully. Apply with a sponge, cheesecloth, or piece of felt. Use an old toothbrush to reach irregular sections. Try to rub in a single direction to prevent making tiny scratches across the metal's grain.

If the metal is only slightly tarnished, make your own polish by mixing equal parts of salt, vinegar, and flour. Rub the paste on with a soft cloth. Wipe off excess paste. Rinse thoroughly before buffing.

Clear lacquers for copper and brass can be purchased in aerosol cans. Finishing with lacquer will usually keep the metal bright and shiny for months or years, depending on how the implement is used. Apply several thin layers, allowing plenty of time for each coat to dry before applying the next.

Another home remedy, when a soft luster is desired, is to rub with a paste made of rottenstone powder and salad oil or linseed oil. Rottenstone powder can be purchased at hardware stores or places that sell kitchen cabinet refinishing supplies.

SILVER

Some people think that fine silver serving trays, pitchers, and other serving pieces should only be brought out once or twice a year, for special occasions. Nothing could be further from the truth. To fully enjoy your silver, put it out for daily meals. Silver shouldn't be packed away somewhere. Believe it or not, frequent use can enhance silverware's beauty. It will keep the tarnish away and will also free up some storage space. Why not use your best implements, and maximize the enjoyment they can bring.

Wash silver flatware immediately after use in hot sudsy water. Rinse in clear hot water and dry immediately with a towel to avoid water-spotting. Although most silverware is dishwasher-safe, hot dishwasher temperatures have been known to loosen hollow handles and to dissolve decorative oxidized patterns.

Also be careful with dip polishes for silver. They can remove oxidized patterns as well as the tarnish. For oxidized silver cleaning and polish, stick with commercial creams or paste polishes instead.

Lean toward using dip polish with silver-plated flatware. Harsh rubbing with an abrasive polish can remove the soft outer layer of silver.

Because silver is tarnished by sulfur compounds in the air, wrap it in tarnish-inhibiting fabric or tarnish-proof tissue paper when storing.

Keep rubber bands and plastic food wrap away from silver. They can cause stains or corrosion, even if the piece is covered by several layers of tissue or cloth.

PEWTER

There are two main types of pewter: old and modern. Modern pewter, also called britannia metal, is an alloy

---

SPECIAL METAL CLEANING QUICK CHECKLIST

❑ Clean lacquered brass or copper in luke-warm sudsy water. Rinse, dry, and buff with a soft cloth.

❑ Clean unlacquered brass or copper with hot sudsy water. Rinse. Apply brass or copper polish. Let dry. Buff with a soft cloth.

❑ For a soft luster on brass or copper, apply a paste made of rottenstone powder and salad oil. Rub with a soft cloth. Wipe off excess paste. Rinse and buff.

❑ Wash silver flatware immediately after use in hot sudsy water. Rinse in clear hot water and dry as soon as possible.

❑ Use commercial creams or pastes on oxidized silver implements.

❑ Polish modern or old pewter with commercial cleaners. Match the correct types with shiny and dull matte finishes.

❑ Touch up stainless steel with very fine steel wool.

❑ Aluminum can be scoured with a powdered cleanser and fine steel wool. On polished aluminum surfaces, use nylon scouring pads instead of steel wool.

❑ Never use harsh, abrasive cleaners or polishes on fine metals.

❑ To prevent scratches, avoid rubbing or polishing against the metal's grain.

---

of tin, antimony, and copper. It resists tarnish and usually can be cleaned with a simple washing in warm, soapy water. Rinse well and dry thoroughly. Old pewter contains tin and lead that may cause a brown tarnish. A mixture of warm water and baking soda will help refresh old pewter. Remember not to eat or drink from old pewter implements because the metal can transfer lead to the food or drink.

Polish modern or old pewter with a commercial pewter cleaner as directed on the label. Or make your own modern pewter cleaner/polish with ingredients available in hardware stores. (1) For shiny pewter, use automobile polish or mix a paste of powdered whiting and denatured alcohol. Wash, rinse, and dry. (2) For pewter with a dull, matte finish, prepare a paste of pumice and water or pumice and vegetable oil. Apply with a soft cloth and rub gently. When dry, polish with a clean, soft cloth. Wash, rinse thoroughly, and dry.

To remove corrosion from pewter, rub with extra-fine steel wool dipped in vegetable oil.

OTHER METALS

Stainless steel can be smoothed and touched up with very fine steel wool rubbed in a single direction, with the steel's grain. Buffing with a dry cloth will remove watermarks and fingerprints. Although stainless steel will not rust, it is best kept clean by wiping it dry after each use. On highly polished stainless steel surfaces, use nylon-mesh scrubbing pads. Again, rub in the direction of the grain to prevent scratching.

Aluminum can be scoured with a powdered cleanser and steel wool. Go with the grain to prevent cross-grain scratches. On polished aluminum surfaces, use only nylon scouring pads.

Cleaning Equipment and Supplies

This section is about the cleaning equipment and supplies you will want to have on hand.

EQUIPMENT

Vacuums

For heavy sweeping chores including wall-to-wall carpeting, an upright vacuum is one of your most important cleaning aids. (See Figure 59-1). Go for a reputable make with at least a 6 amp motor and a 12-inch sweeping path. A bagful of attachments is nice but not necessary. A longer, commercial-size cord, however, is a definite asset.

59-1. Upright vacuum.

A canister vacuum or tote-along vacuum (see Figure 59-2) is powerful, small, and mobile. It is good for apartments or homes with low-pile rugs and bare floors and is easy to store in a small closet.

The power team vacuum is a combination upright/canister unit. It provides the strong, straight suction of a canister along with the motor-driven beater bar/brush of an upright. Newer models will switch from carpet to bare floor settings at the push of a button.

59-2. Canister vacuum.

You will also find lightweight vacuums or "electric brooms" and small rechargeable or electric hand vacuums. These come in handy for quick pickups and for cleaning items that are off the floor, but they are not intended for vacuuming large areas.

Central vacuum systems are easily installed at the time a house is being constructed, but can also be added later. Several times more powerful than leading portable uprights and canisters, built-ins make cleaning easier, more sanitary, and quieter. You simply attach a hose with a cleaning tool into convenient wall vacuum outlets that are located throughout the home. The power unit is positioned in an out-of-the-way place such as a basement or garage. Various attachments are available to clean carpeting, bare floors, stairs, draperies, and furniture. Vacuumed dirt particles and debris are filtered and trapped in a holding tank, which is emptied several times a year. Portable vacuums generally vent some dust back into a room. Central vacuum systems are recommended for people with allergies and breathing disorders because the system's filters do such a thorough job of removing impurities from the air.

Shampooers and Polishers

A carpet shampooer is probably more economical to rent, or you can contract carpet cleaning services when needed.

A floor polisher/buffer is another large, expensive piece of equipment that is probably impractical for the typical homeowner to own. It is better to rent one or contract floor polishing services when needed.

Hand Tools and Equipment

A squeegee for cleaning windows is a great tool. Get a brass or stainless steel one 10 or 12 inches long. Don't use it on anything other than windows or the rubber blade will lose its edge. Don't buy an inferior model. Stick with ones carried by janitorial supply houses. You will need several 1-quart spray bottles for applying diluted concentrates for spot-cleaning or window cleaning.

Get a lamb's wool duster. Feather dusters spread more dust than they pick up. For tables and other close dusting, try inexpensive disposable chemically treated paper dust cloths that dust will stick to. These are available at janitorial supply houses. A dust mop is great for cleaning hard floors. A small one will usually do the trick. Apply dust mop treatment for greater dirt adherence. Other necessities include:

> Set of screwdrivers
> Claw hammer
> Pliers
> Steel wool
> Various grit sizes of sandpaper
> Dust pan and whisk broom
> Good push broom for sweeping concrete surfaces
> Toilet brush
> New paintbrush, for dusting mini-blinds and louvered doors and shutters
> Several dry sponges for cleaning wallpaper and other wall and ceiling surfaces. Treated with chemicals and meant to be used dry, not wet. Available at paint stores and in paint departments at builders supply stores.

Old toothbrushes for scrubbing hard to reach places
Single-edge razor, for lifting or scraping anything stuck to window glass

SUPPLIES

On the supply side, consider keeping the following items on hand for all-purpose cleaning needs:

- Standard all-purpose household cleaner, without disinfectant. For use everywhere except bathrooms and showers. Can be purchased in concentrated form from janitorial supply houses.
- All-purpose household cleaner with disinfectant. For bathrooms and showers. Also available at janitorial supply houses in concentrated form.
- Window cleaner. Your local janitorial supplier will have it in concentrated form. Just follow the instructions when diluting.
- Ammonia, white vinegar, and bleach.
- Liquid clothes detergent.
- Furniture polish/treatment.
- Liquid drain opener.
- Masking tape, cellophane tape, duct tape, and electrical tape.
- Shelf paper.
- Assorted screws, nails, wall anchors, fasteners, and picture hooks.
- Lubricants such as WD-40 or "3 in 1", with spray nozzles.
- White liquid glue such as "Elmer's" and household cement or epoxy.
- Spot-remover kit.
- Extra light bulbs.
- Extra furnace or air-conditioning filters.
- Extra smoke alarm batteries.

NOTE: Always keep cleaning supplies and products out of children's reach.

Pet Proofing

Pets mean many things to many people. To some individuals, pets provide companionship and help stave off loneliness. To others, pets, when raised with children, help teach youngsters how to interact with nature respectfully. Pets serve as watchdogs, seeing-eye dogs, hunting dogs, and living mousetraps. Some birds will even talk back to their owners.

While people keep all sorts of mammals, birds, reptiles, and fish, the top of the concern list for homeowner pet maintenance has to be dogs and cats.

Cats are ... well, cats. On the whole, they can fend for themselves, despite being babied by homeowners. Give them a litter box, food and water, perhaps a few toys and a small basket bed, and they are set for life. Some cats are strictly house cats. Others spend part of their lives indoors and part outside.

Dogs, however, especially large dogs, require quite a bit of tending. Most benefit from spending time outdoors, but they may never attain the "street sense" that seems to come to cats so easily. Consequently, dogs must frequently be fenced in or tied to a long leash so they won't stray into a street where they might get struck by a passing car. To prevent dogs from venturing out into traffic, there are three basic solutions:

1. Training. Train the dog so well that it will never leave the yard, even if tempted by a 10-year-old child across the street who is waving a half-eaten hamburger in the air. Some dog owners have achieved such strict levels of training, but not many.
2. Conventional fences. Use a metal or wood fence. Because the typical dog is easily tempted off the property by other dogs, cats, or even people, a fence is a relatively foolproof deterrent. Hedges won't work; dogs will nose through them no matter how tightly the foliage is planted.

   The trouble with fences, however, is that they are expensive to install and bothersome to maintain. Wood requires painting or preserving. Metal fences also eventually require painting. Both need grass trimming or total vegetation control along their base.
3. Radio-signal fences. A third option is also a fence

—an invisible fence. This fence consists of a thin antenna wire buried 3/4 inch in the ground around the perimeter of the yard. The dog is fitted with a collar having a transistorized radio receiver. A separate radio transmitter is then placed in the basement or garage. The transmitter sends a pulsed radio signal through the buried wire.

If a dog comes within a specified distance of the energized wire while wearing the special collar, the collar will pick up the harmless radio signal and turn the signal into a beeping noise which will "tell" the dog not to go any farther.

The company marketing an invisible fence system will usually provide the initial training program with professional dog trainers. The dog will likely receive two or three warning corrections equivalent to the static shock you might encounter from walking on a carpet, before the warning beeps become effective and keep the dog within his boundaries. After that, the beeps alone will usually keep a dog in check.

An invisible fence costs three to four times less than a chain-link fence. Self-installed units are available. Owners who have invisible fences no longer have to worry about gates or doors being left open, cars speeding through their neighborhood, or animal control officers. They needn't walk their dogs in bad weather, and because dogs are no longer confined to a leash, the mutts receive more exercise and are healthier. From an aesthetic point of view, invisible fencing allows you to maintain the beauty of your home and property. It permits you to fence in a dog without fencing out the view.

Invisible fencing can also be customized to fit special needs. It can discourage a dog from entering a garden, pool, or patio area. You can shape it to any configuration you want, and you can take it with you when you move.

PET DOORS

Another time-saver is a pet door. (See Figure 61-1.) A pet door allows a dog or cat to enter and exit a house or garage without bothering you. It is simply a smaller door (sized in relation to your pet's height) installed in or near a rear or side entrance. Units are two way, self closing, silent, chew proof, insect proof, and energy efficient when fitted with a weather seal. They are also lockable.

61-1. Pet doors.

With a two-way pet door, you don't need to worry about heating or cooling the great outdoors by leaving a front or rear door propped open while you peer into the darkness and whistle for your pet to come home.

FURNITURE AND FURNISHINGS

Most dogs and cats are covered with hair, which they then shed. Your best bet in the war against pet hair, sharp claws, and curious snouts (after obedience training and meticulous grooming) is to outfit your home with furniture, flooring, and drapes that can withstand staining, snagging, hair removal, and other pet-inflicted damage.

Avoid loosely woven fabrics such as chenille or velvet. Favor tight weaves that a pet can't easily hook its claws into. Leather is also a no-no. When shopping for new upholstery, ask the salesperson how the fabric performs in abrasion and stain- and oil-repellency tests.

Color coordinate your furnishings and your pet. A black labrador will definitely clash with a houseful of white plush carpeting and sectionals. If you don't want an orange couch to match a cat of the same color, at least choose fabrics in the mid-range of colors, not too dark or too light. Plaids or tweeds are good. Solids, especially the light ones, tend to be the worst. Of course, a household full of black furniture is not practical if white cats and dogs are in residence; in that case, either the pets—or the furniture—should be changed.

Dogs and cats are creatures of habit. They like to sleep in the same places. To slow the constant wear

and soiling from a pet's snoozes, cover cushions with extra cushion covers, or toss an old afghan or towel on the floor or sofa, and train the pet to sleep there. For some pets, try telling them not to sleep where you want them to—then they will be sure to sleep there. Such reverse psychology has worked wonders for a sizable number of homeowners.

If your pet sleeps on your bed—which is considerably more common than people will admit—get a bedspread that will hold up to frequent cleaning. In fact, it is a good idea to get several bedspreads. Avoid fine linens or quilted blankets and comforters.

For general-purpose carpeting, avoid light or dark solids. Go for a mottled or tweedish pattern, preferably in a mix of colors.

Pet odors, particularly that of urine, can be a real problem in furniture or carpeting. Damp weather can reactivate old accidents. Even tiny, trace amounts of urine in furniture, carpeting, or drapes become detectable and can aggravate allergies. Surface cleaning won't work if the urine has seeped through the fabric into box springs or through carpet into a foam padding. Clean up any accidents as soon as possible to prevent penetration. If necessary, shampoo the furniture or carpet to remove stains and odors with special cleansers and "odor eaters" available in pet stores. Another option is to have carpet, drapes, and furniture professionally cleaned. After cleaning is completed, furnishings can be treated with fabric-protection sprays designed to make the carpet, drapes, and furniture more resistant to pet stains and odors.

Liquids and other substances can be applied to furniture to prevent dogs and cats from chewing. The substances are not detectable to humans, but they taste horrible to a pet.

FLEAS

Fleas are no fun. Most dogs and cats will run into them sometime during their lives. When brought into a home, fleas can settle in and multiply at a rate that puts rabbits to shame.

House treatments for fleas are available through veterinarians and pet supply stores. The treatments come in spray bottles. After removing all children and other pets from the dwelling, the treatment can be lightly misted or sprayed on carpets, rugs, upholstery, pet bedding, and anywhere else fleas are likely to live. Never spray the house treatments directly on pets or humans, and avoid overspraying near food preparation areas.

EFFECTIVE GROOMING

You can only be so meticulous when you live with a pet. But you can minimize the amount of hair a dog or cat sheds inside, and the quantity of dirt it tracks in.

A wire pet brush will remove shedding dog and cat hair. Another option is to vacuum the dog or cat— some animals grow to like vacuuming—on a regular basis, using the vacuum's crevice tool or upholstery brush.

Sharp nails can be filed or clipped, and in some cases, removed.

PET PROOFING QUICK CHECKLIST

❑ If desired, establish several pet-free areas in your house, such as a living room and formal dining room. Train your pet(s) to keep out of those rooms.

❑ Consider invisible fencing to keep dogs in the yard or away from pool or garden areas.

❑ A pet door in the garage or utility room will allow a dog or cat to enter and exit without bothering you.

❑ Favor furniture, flooring, and drapes that can withstand staining, snagging, hair removal, and soil.

❑ Try to color coordinate your furnishings with your pet.

❑ Guard your household against fleas.

PART 8

Financial Matters

True, money may not buy happiness, but it can help you lead a more comfortable and secure life. This section presents topics dealing with financial matters that affect the typical household. It discusses Insurance, Record Keeping, Energy Conservation, Water Conservation, Product Evaluation and Service Contracts, Repair Contractors, and Finding a Handy Person.

Some of these topics are important not only to your individual situation, but to the welfare of your community as well. Who can deny the importance of water and energy conservation? When looked at together, the points brought out in these sections can go a long way toward eliminating wasted resources and expenses that add up to major losses and costs throughout the life span of a household.

Insurance

Insurance is something people hate to buy but can't do without. Ideally, you want as much as you need, but as little as possible. How do you determine which coverage, and how much coverage, is best?

Many people go for years and years paying for homeowner's insurance they know practically nothing about. Plus they rarely, if ever, collect on it.

The best way to inspect your homeowner's insurance, if you already have it, is simply to pull out the policy and read the whole thing, including the fine print. In this day and age it is foolish not to protect yourself against a major loss. The amount of protection you have on your homeowner's policy in addition to the basics—theft, fire, and liability—depends on the type of policy you have. Some policies are more comprehensive than others. Some may cover items such as damage from frozen pipes, electrical surges, lightning, and wind-blown trees. To start you off, here are a handful of insurance terms and what they mean.

DEDUCTIBLES—This is the amount you will have to pay on each claim or accident before the insurance company will begin payment. Generally, the higher the deductible you select, the lower the cost or premium.

BURGLARY AND THEFT INSURANCE—This insures property against theft. Some policies include an off-premises clause that is active against theft of your possessions that may occur anywhere in the world.

FIRE INSURANCE—Fire insurance is just that. But besides covering full damages from fire and lightning, it should also cover miscellaneous related hazards such as water damage and vandalism.

LIABILITY INSURANCE—The Fuller Brush man slips on a patch of ice on your porch and decides to sue you. Under personal liability insurance, you are insured for up to a set amount of money if a visitor falls down your front steps, slips on your sidewalk, or is bitten by your dog. It also covers certain medical expenses if you or a member of your family accidentally injures someone or damages someone else's property.

PROPERTY INSURANCE — Property insurance is generally extended coverage against loss or damage to your property. It doesn't include personal liability. Property insurance can cover some of a home's contents, including furniture, clothing, books, electronics, and appliances. Additional supplements, floaters, or riders can be purchased to cover artwork, cameras, furs, jewelry, musical instruments, silverware, sports equipment, stamp and coin collections, and other valuable possessions. Keep in mind when applying for a floater policy to establish how much it would cost to *replace* the items you are having insured, not simply the amount you originally paid for them.

It is a good idea to make a list of possessions. Take an inventory of all appliances, pieces of furniture, and other items of value. Photographs are an excellent way to catalog your home's contents. Once you have made an inventory, put it in a safe place such as a bank deposit box or a fireproof container. Revise the inventory whenever you make significant changes. Most insurance companies have checklists or booklets to help prepare your inventory.

HOMEOWNER'S POLICY

A homeowner's policy is a package of theft, fire, and liability coverages. It should be reviewed annually because inflation, rising property values, and additional possessions you may have purchased will gradually add to your property's total value. Unless your policy has a built-in factor for inflation, you should consider raising your coverage to keep pace with the value of your property and possessions.

NOTE: If you are a renter, don't assume that any of your losses due to fire or theft will be covered. Find out. You may elect to purchase your own coverages.

Here are a number of ways you can cut homeowner insurance expenses:

- If your home is protected by approved fire or burglar alarm systems, you may be eligible for a 5 to 10 percent discount, depending on whether the system automatically notifies the fire or police department.

- Newer homes sometimes qualify for discounts up to 16 percent of the total homeowner's insurance cost.
- Using the same insurance company for auto, life, and homeowner's may save between 2 and 15 percent of the total cost.
- Consider using higher deductibles. Again, as a rule of thumb, the higher the deductible, the lower the premium.

Record Keeping

Part of any good maintenance program is accurate record keeping. As mentioned in the Introduction, keeping records will tell when inspections were last done and when they are due again. Records include pertinent backup such as appliance operating manuals, parts lists, servicing and repair histories, warranty and cost information, plus vendor names, phone numbers, and addresses.

Some problems will occur so infrequently that you will need to jog your memory as to a solution. What did you do the last time the flame from the gas clothes dryer went out? Was it three years ago when you installed the new water heater, or five? Is it still covered by the warranty? And where is the warranty? Did you throw it out with your old high school papers? Or was it in the boxful of papers you kept in the garage—the one the field mice chewed to smithereens when they constructed their nest in it last winter.

Reasons to develop good record-keeping habits are many. The most important are:

1. For your convenience. It is much more convenient to keep everything together in a house file: all the documents you obtained from a previous owner or a builder, plus all of the written information you have accumulated since taking over. Exactly how you organize the material is nowhere near as important as the fact that all house construction, ownership, and maintenance-related materials can be found in the same place.
2. For your income taxes. You never know when your home could turn into investment property. What if you decide to sell, but nobody wants to buy? So you rent your home for a summer, and make other living arrangements for yourself. A year passes. The renters renew their lease and suddenly you drop the idea of selling and plan instead to handle it as a long-term rental income property. Once that happens, you need to track capital or long-range improvements you make in the property. Maintenance expenditures become tax deductible. Even if you never rent your home, it is still important to keep track of all home-related costs. It will help you budget for future expenses, and you can better plan repair jobs when needed.
3. To save money. If your builder or contractor needs to be approached about warranty work, it is important to have organized information to fall back on. Most problems are taken care of by reputable construction or repair companies. If a non-routine situation comes up, you should follow certain procedures to have something corrected. (1) Check to see if the problem is covered under the builder's or contractor's warranty. (2) Identify the exact nature of the problem in a letter to the builder or contractor. Include your name, address, and work phone number. Type the letter if possible. Typed letters are considered to be more official. They get faster and more serious results. Make the letter brief and to the point, but include all relevant details. State exactly what you want done, and how soon you expect the problem to be resolved. Be reasonable. Don't ask for anything beyond what is covered in the warranty. Include copies of all documents regarding the problem. Keep a copy of the letter for your records. If you have an insured warranty, send a copy of your letter to the warranty company as well as to the builder or contractor.

Having readily accessible home documents and records can make life much easier. If you already have a house file, a cold February day is the time to update it.

Energy Conservation

Energy conservation. Who could possibly be against it? Even utility companies are telling their customers how to use less energy. It is good for the environment and for your financial well-being. The less energy used to run a household, the less costly the household will be to run. It is simple economics.

Here is a grab-bag of tips to help you reduce your energy consumption. Naturally, you won't be able to take advantage of all of them. Pick out whatever items fit your situation, and give them a try.

HOUSEHOLD HEATING AND COOLING

Set thermostats at 68 degrees Fahrenheit during cool/cold weather, and 78 degrees Fahrenheit in warm/hot weather.

If possible, replace old inefficient heating and cooling units. Purchase a gas furnace with a seasonal efficiency rating of better than 90 percent. Purchase an oil furnace with a seasonal efficiency rating of better than 80 percent. On window air conditioning units, select models with Energy Efficiency Ratios (EERs) of 8 or greater. An Energy Efficiency Ratio is the British Thermal Unit (BTU) ratio divided by the appliance's wattage. For example, a 12,000 BTU unit that uses 1,500 watts has an EER of 8.0.

Keep your attic or top-floor crawlspace vented. These spaces can reach very hot temperatures during summer. If necessary, add an attic vent fan to remove hot air from the house. (See Figure 65-1.) Another possible location for a ventilating fan is an upstairs window.

65-1. Attic fan.

Check your roof insulation to see if it is adequate. Insulation quality is often expressed in "R-values," numerical representations of the ability of any material to resist the passage of heat. For example, a fiberglass batt or blanket 9½ to 10 inches thick has an R-value of approximately 30. Adding two or three more inches of fiberglass brings the R-value to about 38. The greater the R-value number, the greater the material's resistance to the passage of heat or cold, and the better its insulation value.

Conservative recommended insulation values for the typical house are walls, R-20, and ceilings, R-40. Because heat rises, the area with the greatest potential for heat loss is the roof. Pay particular attention to the insulation laid in an attic or crawlspaces. If more could be added, it is money and effort well spent.

Another insulation tip is to insulate cover plates on electrical outlets and wall light switches located in exterior walls. Inexpensive outlet and switch gasket kits are available, consisting of foam backing that can be placed behind the outlet or light switchplate.

Caulk or seal exterior gaps where different building materials meet. Common trouble spots include where exterior siding meets windows and doors, along the roof and foundation lines, around chimneys, and where pipes protrude through the walls or roof.

Apply duct tape to gaps in hot and cold air furnace ducts, and insulate all ductwork in unheated areas. Check ductwork for air leaks at least once a year if you have a forced air system.

Heat register openings should be dust-free and unobstructed by furniture, drapes, and rugs. Dust or vacuum registers or radiators frequently. Shut off air vents and close doors to rooms that aren't used during winter months.

Consider adding air deflectors to heating or cooling registers or vents. (See Figure 65-2.) These are simple adjustable devices that magnetically snap onto any vent. Often vents are inefficiently placed, and misdirected heated or cooled air travels against a ceiling or behind drapes or furniture. Deflectors can aim the system's conditioned air where you want it.

65-2. Register deflector.

Consider adding radiator reflectors behind radiators. Heat reflectors will bounce heat off a wall and into the room, where it can be put to better use. Reflectors are made of rigid plastic foam covered with metal foil on one side. The foam insulates the wall, while the foil reflects the heat outward. Otherwise, too much of the radiator's energy goes toward heating the outside wall to which the radiator is fastened.

Consider replacing an existing thermostat with a timer thermostat that can turn down the heat (or reduce air conditioning) when you are asleep and when you are not home. This can result in savings of 10 to 15 percent. A single-setback timer can automatically lower the temperature at night; a double one can adjust the temperature during the day as well—for people who leave the house for work.

Operating a boiler at a constant temperature wastes fuel. Consider installing a boiler modulating control. It can reduce heating energy consumption by as much as 25 percent.

The pilot light on a gas furnace accounts for between 5 and 10 percent of total gas consumption and should be shut off completely for the summer or off-season months.

Fossil-fuel and wood heating equipment should be cleaned at least once per year. The cleaning can save approximately 5 percent of fuel consumption.

Dirty air filters in a forced-air system cause improper air flow and wasted fuel. Furnace filters are cheap. Try changing them once a month or installing an electronic air cleaner. Either can save 5 to 10 percent in fuel costs.

Extremely dry air is difficult to heat. A humidifier can

add optimum amounts of moisture to the air within a house, and enables the heating system to heat that air at less cost. Deciduous plants also add moisture to the air, and help the furnace during dry air spells throughout the year.

A fireplace should have a damper that is kept closed when the fireplace is not being used. Glass doors on the fireplace's front will also keep heated air from escaping to the great outdoors.

When air conditioning is running, turn off as many lights as possible in the house. The air conditioning has to work that much harder to cool off heat generated by individual light bulbs. It is also a good idea to keep shades and drapes closed as much as possible when using air conditioning.

When not in use, cover outdoor air conditioning units and seal the edges of the covers with weatherproof tape.

If you can, take advantage of savings offered for making early payments to utility companies. Avoid making late payments on utility bills. Some people automatically pay their utility bills without understanding what the charges are. They may, in fact, be so used to paying late fees that the fees are considered normal.

WINDOWS AND DOORS

Add more layers of glass to your windows if the windows are single-paned. Storm sashes or panels and Plexiglas inserts will help weatherproof an inadequate older window. If you don't already have them, installing storm windows and doors should be high on your priority list.

Seal cracks around glass, sashes, and window frames to prevent air infiltration. Apply adhesive-backed foam weatherstrips to top and bottom window rails. Nail felt weatherstripping where window sashes and frames make contact. (See Figure 65-3.)

Cracked window panes in low-profile locations can be repaired with transparent sealing tape. Leaky joints where window panes are set into frames can be sealed with press-on glaze compounds.

The installation of movable shutters or closures on the exterior of a window can trap an additional layer of insulating air next to the glass. The installation of similar shutters, shades, or heavy drapes on the inside will also trap another layer of air next to the glass. These devices can block out the sun on hot days, and hold in the heat during cold nights. Insulated drapes and curtains are available that equal the performance of storm windows, especially if the drapes or curtains are sealed to the sides of the window casing. Another energy effective window treatment is a roll-down shade or blind with a "space-age" blanket attached to the backside. Tightly fitted against the window casing, such an arrangement has excellent cold-weather insulating properties, and will also keep heat out of the home during summer.

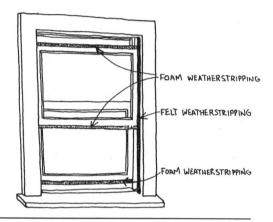

65-3. Window weatherstripping.

LIGHTING

When a choice can be made, fluorescent bulbs will out-perform incandescents. Favor the former for kitchens, for reading, and for workshops.

Use bulbs with the smallest possible wattage when re-lamping light fixtures. Rely on the more efficient reflector bulbs for task and accent lighting. Reflector bulbs focus light forward, as opposed to general bulbs that emit light in all directions. Opt for task lighting whenever you can—lighting that illuminates only the part of the room in which you are working.

Wherever possible, use adjustable dimmer switches to match lighting levels to different activities appropriately and for a variety of effects. Use photoelectric cells on timers to turn outdoor lights on and off automatically.

Instruct children to turn off lights when they leave a room.

WATER HEATING

Insulate your water heater. If it feels warm to the touch, you are losing valuable heat that should be kept inside the tank, keeping your water hot. Standby heat loss can account for as much as 33 percent of your water heating costs. To prevent this, wrap your

tank with a blanket of insulation. You can purchase insulating kits at hardware or builders supply stores, or you can do the insulating yourself with a roll of fiberglass insulation, a pair of heavy-duty scissors, and a roll of duct tape.

Sediment that collects at the bottom of a hot water tank retards heat transfer and can make any unit operate less efficiently. Sediment can be periodically removed by drawing a few gallons of water from the tank's bottom drain cock. Once the discolored water ceases to come out, the sediment has been flushed out.

For every 10 degrees you lower the temperature on a water heater, you can save up to 6 percent of the energy it uses. Experts say you can comfortably lower it to 130 or even 120 degrees Fahrenheit.

Replace old gas water heaters with modern, energy efficient models having electronic ignition and flue dampers.

Electric water heating equipment can be situated almost anywhere. That means instead of running long pipelines that allow hot water to cool off while traveling, the electric hot water supply can be located as close as possible to the point of most frequent hot water use.

Insulate hot water supply lines. To prevent heat loss through hot water pipes, insulate the lines with preformed pipe wrap or insulation, or with fiberglass or urethane insulation you wrap around the pipes. Protect water pipes that travel through unheated basements or crawlspaces by insulating them as above, or by wrapping them with electric heat tape.

Repair leaky hot water faucets and showers.

Take advantage of time-of-day rates offered by electric utility companies. Off-hour use of electricity to heat water will lower your overall electric bill. The installation of automatic timers allows water to be heated during non-peak hours for use throughout the day. Large water heater tanks can provide enough water to meet round-the-clock needs.

REFRIGERATORS AND FREEZERS

Go for the most efficient units you can find, even if the initial investment is on the high end of the pricing scale.

Keep freezers defrosted. Ice buildup means the freezing unit will have to work harder to achieve desired temperatures. At the same time, remember that self-defrosting units use up to 50 percent more energy than those requiring manual defrosting.

Set freezers at 5 degrees F. for normal use, or 0 degrees F. for long-term storage. Set the refrigerator so the temperature stays between 38 and 40 degrees F.

OVENS

Gas stoves should have pilotless or electronic ignition.

Believe it or not, the oven section of a stove is often more efficient for cooking than the top range burners are. The oven stores heat well, while the burners give off a greater percentage of heat than is stored or used.

Rely on the oven door window and light for checking a recipe's progress, instead of opening the oven door. Replace burned out oven lights.

The seal around an oven door prevents heat loss and conserves energy. Too often a seal will fray or otherwise wear out, and the owner will not repair or replace it. Any appliance repair store can solve this problem.

DISHWASHING

There is no need to rinse dishes with hot water before placing them in a modern dishwasher. If you must rinse them, use cold water.

The most energy efficient dishwashers will have a no-heat drying cycle, a light-wash cycle for dishes that are not heavily soiled, and a delay-start control that could wait until non-peak hours for electricity use. For maximum savings, you could run a light-wash cycle and a no-heat drying cycle, timed for the middle of the night, when everyone is asleep and electricity is available at reduced rates. Avoid running a dishwasher with partial loads.

Get in the habit of rinsing dishes with cold water immediately after use, so food residues will not dry onto plates and silverware. An alternative is to store dirty dishes in a sinkful of cold water until time to wash.

When operating a disposal unit, use only cold water. Warm or hot water will melt particles of fat, which will then pass through the drain. When the fat cools farther down the pipe, it will collect and eventually cause a blockage. Remove grease and fat from dishes and pans before they are washed.

CLOTHES WASHING AND DRYING

Most laundry can be washed with warm or cold wa-

ter. Cold water rinsing is a good way to conserve energy. Rinsing is merely a dilution process, and a cold water rinse, for most purposes, is just as effective as a warm one.

Automatic presoak cycles—for soaking heavily soiled clothes such as work clothes or diapers prior to the wash cycle—will improve the cleaning results. Some washers provide a presoak that automatically advances into the wash cycle. This is both convenient and energy saving since only one tub of water is used. The soak cycle can help remove stubborn stains, which might otherwise require a second washing.

Use the water-level control on your automatic washer. If no control is available, wait until you have a full load.

Make sure the clothes dryer is vented to the great outdoors. To recycle the moisture during winter, install a dryer heat-saving unit. It will vent the heat and moisture into the home's air while leaving the lint trapped for collection and disposal. Use a clothesline as frequently as possible.

BATHING

Showers generally use less water than baths. But if you take a bath during winter, let its water cool afterwards to help heat the room and moisturize the home's air.

Install low-flow shower heads. These save both energy and water. In fact, they can reduce the amount of shower water you use by 50 percent without reducing the quality of washing. Time your showers. Try to keep them short.

Install water aerators on spigots. These act as a flow restriction and can reduce amounts of hot and cold water used.

Use bathroom vent fans sparingly during times of heating or cooling the home. A constantly running bathroom (or kitchen) fan can displace a household full of warm air to the outside within an hour.

NOTE: The individual ways of saving energy may not sound like much when considered one at a time, but taken together, they can add up to considerable energy savings. And whenever there is a choice, why not use less? It is a way of becoming involved with your ecology while putting extra dollars into your pocket as well.

ENERGY CONSERVATION
QUICK CHECKLIST

❑ Set heating system thermostats to 68 degrees F. during cool/cold weather. Set cooling system thermostats to 78 degrees F. in warm/hot weather.

❑ See that furnaces and other heating units are inspected, cleaned, tuned, and fitted with new filters, if needed, at the beginning of every heating season.

❑ When replacing heating or cooling systems, select energy-saving models. The same goes for replacing appliances such as dishwashers, clothes washers, dryers, freezers, refrigerators, and ranges.

❑ Make sure that roof and side-wall insulation is adequate.

❑ Insulate your water heater/tank and hot water supply lines.

❑ See that your attic or top-floor space below the roof is vented.

❑ Caulk exterior gaps, seams, and cracks.

❑ Make sure you have and use storm doors and windows.

❑ When a choice is available, favor fluorescent light bulbs over incandescents.

Water Conservation

There are several good reasons water should not be wasted. First of all, it is a precious natural resource drawn from supplies that are, in effect, limited. By far, most of the Earth's water is salt water. Fresh water, both above and below the surface, makes up an extremely small proportion of our world's total water supply. Second, wasting water costs money that could be saved or better spent on other things. Even in communities that still don't meter their water and charge flat quarterly fees, overuse of water is reflected in municipal costs: pumping, storing, treating, maintaining the equipment and lines take labor, supplies, and capital dollars.

Water conservation is the way to go. Here are some points to consider.

DRIPPING FAUCETS

A dripping faucet can waste 20 gallons per day, or 7,300 gallons per year. Faucets can be divided into two types: those with washers and those without washers. The more modern washerless faucets are tough for a novice to repair because their various nuts, screws, and inner workings are difficult to access—hidden under snap caps and exterior parts.

Faucet drips usually originate from one of three locations. If water drips out of the spout no matter how hard you turn the tap or handle, a washer or its seat is worn. If water leaks out of the base of the handle, the packing nut is loose or its washer or packing material is worn. If water appears at the base of the faucet, the coupling nut that connects the plumbing to the faucet beneath the sink is defective.

Without access to a basin wrench, it is difficult to repair the last type of leak. Since an effective repair may involve removing the pipe in order to replace washers or packing, this job is best left to a plumber. The other two types of leaks can be tackled by a novice with a few tools in hand: probably a screwdriver and an adjustable wrench. There are numerous illustrated pamphlets and articles that discuss minor repairs to faucets. Many are available, free of charge, at plumbing stores or builder's supply stores that sell replacement parts to contractors and homeowners.

In a nutshell, the pamphlets will tell you first to turn off the fixture's water supply. Remove the tap or handle (the screw that holds the handle on may be visible, or may be hidden beneath a decorative cap that can be gently popped out with a screwdriver). Next, possibly also hidden under a decorative housing, is the packing nut. (See Figure 66-1.) If this is the source of the leak, tightening it may cure the problem. If not, then a new washer is probably needed. When replacing a washer, be sure to use one exactly the same size.

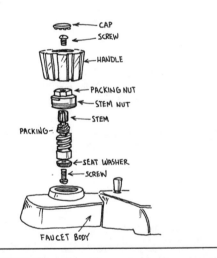

66-1. Faucet parts.

When it comes time to replace a faucet, lots of innovative designs have been introduced. Consider one that operates from an infrared beam. The faucet turns on and off depending on when the beam is broken. Because water flows only when needed, water savings during certain activities can be as high as 80 percent. The beam shoots straight down from the spout, so it is triggered when anything is placed beneath the faucet. The depth can be adjusted so you could still have a colander of washed lettuce in a kitchen sink without triggering the faucet. It could mean no more wasted water running down the drain while you are brushing your teeth, and no more wasted water while you are rinsing dishes to go into the dishwasher. If you need the water to run continuously, there is a flow button for that purpose. The only drawback to such a system is that the faucet sensors are operated by electricity, so a power failure would knock them out of commission.

TOILETS

Toilets can also waste water. The most common problem with toilets is when they refuse to stop running. The telltale whining sound of water coursing through the toilet tank usually means a malfunctioning inlet valve or a faulty float ball or plastic float. (See Figure 66-2.)

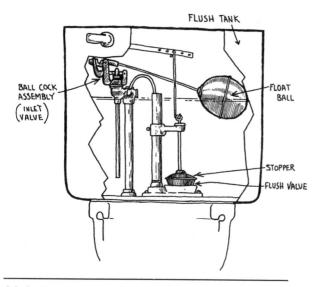

FLUSH TANK

BALL COCK ASSEMBLY (INLET VALVE)

FLOAT BALL

STOPPER

FLUSH VALVE

66-2. Toilet tank cutaway.

The inlet valve is opened when the tank is flushed. It closes when the float is raised as water refills the tank. If the float does not rise high enough, it will not shut off the inlet valve, and water will continue to run. Newer floats that malfunction will probably need to be replaced. The older ball-style floats attached to a flexible rod can sometimes be bent slightly downward so they shut off the inlet valve when a lower level of water is reached within the tank.

When a toilet is flushed, a trip lever moves a device that controls the entry of water from the tank into the bowl. This device is usually either a plastic flapper or a rubber ball on the end of a rod or chain. As replacement water flows into the tank, these devices should settle back over the bowl inlet and completely seal it, so water can once again build up to the proper level in the tank. If the ball or flapper is misaligned or worn out, water will continually flow into the bowl from the tank, and the tank will not fill up enough to shut off the inlet valve. This situation will be apparent

by ripples on the surface of the water in the bowl and the same whining or singing of the water as it attempts to refill the tank. Misalignment can likely be fixed by simply bending a wire or guide rod for a better fit, but worn parts must be replaced.

Beyond purchasing a water-saving model, regular toilets can be modified with the addition of capacity limiters in the tanks. Adding several bricks to the tank, for example, can often save that much water per flush without seriously impeding the flushing action. (Clean the bricks thoroughly first.)

DRAINS

Try to minimize the amount of water that runs down through drains. Some people believe water that disappears down a drain is somehow miraculously "recaptured" to be used again. Not so. It goes somewhere, of course, back into the environment, but it is not simply recycled as clean water within whatever water system delivered it. While lawns, laundry, and bathrooms are among the average household's heaviest water users, kitchen faucets draw thousands of water gallons per home, per year. Much of it could be prevented or reused within the home. Many small savings can be accomplished with common sense and a mind tuned to water conservation.

- Recycle cooking water. Use vegetable and pasta cooking water for soups, sauces, or stews.
- Carefully measure water for recipes. For example, if one cup of raw rice requires about two cups of water for good results, avoid haphazardly pouring three or four cups of water into the pan and later dumping out the excess.
- Adjust icemakers. Many individuals routinely freeze and then discard binfuls of mechanically produced ice that become tainted with food odors from sitting unused in the freezer. Instead, keep a few trays full of ice and turn off the automatic icemaker until you need another batch.
- Water used with a food disposal depends on how long and how often you run the disposal. Manufacturers say that cold water should run full force while a disposal is in operation. Make sure the faucet aerator insert is in place to reduce the amount of water while still permitting a strong flow.
- Try to run water into a container, not just down a drain. If you turn on the hot water tap and wait for the water to come out hot, you will waste between 100 to 300 gallons a month of water that is not yet hot enough. Same thing with running water to let it get cold. Want hot water? Let it pour directly into a saucepan or teapot, then heat

it on the range. Need cold water? Keep a jug in the refrigerator or use ice cubes, but avoid letting water run until it gets cold. If you must run the water, let it run into a stopped sink or into a watering can, pan, or other container. Use water in the sink for soaking dirty dishes. Water houseplants, a shrub, a garden, or a small section of grass with water saved in containers.

- Wash vegetables and fruits in a container. Loosen soil in the standing water, then give a quick rinse under the tap. Trap that water for garden or houseplant use.
- Use the dishwasher. By running full loads on a regular cycle in an efficient dishwasher, you can save an average of 8 to 12 gallons of water per load over hand washing the same amount.
- When hand washing dishes, stack them efficiently in the sink. By nesting pots and dishes together, you can fit more in a sink to soak. Don't scrape and scrub them under running water. Instead, add enough hot water to wash everything, then transfer the washed dishes to a sink full of clear cool water for rinsing. When you need to rinse an item, use the spray device with quick blasts of water rather than a long steady stream from the faucet.
- The shortest wash-rinse cycle of a dishwasher is designed to use the least amount of water, averaging about 9 gallons per load. The normal cycles average about 11 gallons per load.

OTHER TIPS

- Water lawns, landscaping, and gardens only when necessary. For the most part, trust in Mother Nature. When watering is necessary, avoid doing it during the hottest parts of the day, when much of the water evaporates or becomes too hot for plants to use safely.
- A typical clothes washer uses about 24 gallons per load, with the water level set at the lowest setting. Large capacity machines run on maximum water settings will use over 40 gallons per load.
- Select low-sudsing cleansers. Mopping floors can require several buckets of water. With low suds detergents, you will minimize rinsing. Mop least-soiled floors first, moving to heavier soiled areas before returning to rinse.
- Take quick showers instead of baths. Use water-efficient shower heads. Shortening your shower by just two minutes—turning off the tap while you scrub—could save up to 700 gallons a month.
- While shaving, close the spigot between blade rinses and save three gallons per shave.

There are many more ways that water can be conserved. To be successful at it, a person needs only to think of alternatives in each situation involving water.

WATER CONSERVATION QUICK CHECKLIST

❑ Repair dripping faucets.
❑ Install water-saving components such as faucet aerators and modern shower heads.
❑ When replacing appliances and fixtures such as dishwashers, clothes washers, and toilets, select water-saving models.
❑ Minimize the amount of water that runs down drains. Recycle cooking water and don't let kitchen faucets run while waiting for tap water to get hot or cold.
❑ While washing or rinsing dishes, avoid letting the water run full blast.
❑ Favor quick showers instead of baths.
❑ Water lawns, landscaping, and gardens only when necessary.

Product Evaluation and Service Contracts

PRODUCT EVALUATION

Product evaluation is your first and strongest line of offense and defense against inferior products. Product evaluations comprise ninety-five percent of finding and purchasing the best values for your dollars.

Here are some guidelines that have worked well for consumers:

1. Unless compelling reasons exist to the contrary, favor established, reputable, local retailers. They have reputations to maintain, and they want repeat business. They know their appliance lines well, and they are willing to stand behind their products to ensure a customer's satisfaction.
2. Select appliances and other items with established brand names known for quality and dependability. Unfamiliar makes can be difficult and expensive to repair. Choose a model that best suits your requirements. It needn't be the least or most expensive model.
3. If possible, ask for a demonstration so you can see the item in action and learn how to operate it.
4. If the item will be replacing another you own, ask if you will be allowed any credit on a trade-in. If it is not worth anything, will it at least be removed from your home when the new item is installed? Understand exactly what is included in the quoted price. Free delivery? Installation? Free service for a certain "break-in" period? These "extras" could help sway your buying decision from one dealer to another.
5. Find out the availability of competent service technicians and spare parts. How quickly can a service call be arranged?
6. Read the warranty or guarantee made by the manufacturer. Resolve any questions before the purchase.
7. If you consider paying for an item on credit, realize what must be given in exchange of that credit. Can installment plans be paid off in advance? Are there any up-front credit costs?

SERVICE CONTRACTS OR EXTENDED WARRANTIES

It is becoming standard procedure. Walk into any appliance store, electronics shop, automobile dealership, or real estate firm. Purchase the item offered, and some salesperson will invariably inquire if you also want to include, at extra cost, a service contract.

A service contract is really a form of insurance. Consider that no company in its right mind would offer an insurance policy—or a service contract—without fully understanding the possible outcomes based on known mathematical probabilities, and without making sure that those probable outcomes favor the company—not the consumer. For example, a two-year service contract on a new clothes dryer might cost $120. You can be sure that the manufacturer arrived at that price based on the knowledge that average repairs on the unit in question during the first two years of a typical owner's use will cost considerably less than $120. Well, if that is the case, why would you ever consider or want a service contract?

There are reasons. Perhaps you are planning to use the appliance more frequently than the typical user does. What if you are the designated uniform washer for a grade school soccer team? You know that for the next few years — during your stint as uniform washer—you are really going to put ten years' worth of use into your new dryer. In that case, the service contract could likely be of real benefit.

Another reason could crop up with the purchase of an older home. Perhaps the circumstances are such that you cannot test all of the home's components. You wonder about the roof, for instance. Because it hasn't rained during the past four weeks, and there is no rain in sight, you can't see for yourself if it leaks or not. If you suspect there is something major wrong, and you aren't prepared or willing to accept the worst, a home buyer's warranty may be worth the peace of mind.

In any event, purchasing a service contract or an extended warranty is a gamble. It is in your best interest to see that the odds are tipped at least as far as possible toward an outcome that will be favorable to you. If you simply feel more comfortable with and can afford service contracts and extended warranties whenever they are offered, so be it. You are well covered, and you will be unlikely to experience any major repairs. But unless you plan to use those items much more frequently than most other individuals do, you will probably be paying a premium for the coverage.

For those purchases that will be used for routine service, do your homework before you buy. Find out which makes and models have the fewest problems, are the least expensive to run and own, and are superior performers. If you buy the best-value items to begin with, and if no special or extenuating circumstances exist, you aren't likely to need a service contract. Before you go for any repair type service contracts, you must have a clear understanding of what is being promised in all of the fine print, and you must do a thorough evaluation of your own needs and how you will be using the item in question. Here are some additional considerations.

- Is the contract already covered, in full or in part, by a manufacturer's warranty? This happens. A manufacturer will warrant their product and another company — a different company offering extended or other warranties — will accept payments for the same protection.
- What does the contract include? Labor? Labor and parts? Must you pay for the repair person's travel time? Some contracts cover only certain components, such as the motor in a washing machine, or the heating elements on an electric range, or the picture tube on a television.
- What if the repair is needed at night or on a weekend? A water heater that fails on a freezing Friday night in February needs to be fixed before Monday morning. If the service contract doesn't specify repair service seven days a week, a costly overtime charge could result.
- Does the cost of the service contract rise as the item ages? It probably will. Naturally, expected repair costs are minimal during the early life of most appliances and major components. Ask about maintaining the contract in the third, fourth, fifth, or later years.
- Never take a salesperson's word for what a contract covers. He or she may forget important details or may misunderstand the terms. Find out what a contract includes and excludes by reading it yourself. Where will the product be serviced? In your home? In a repair shop? In a manufacturer's service center? Is the contract transferable if you sell the item? How much time do you have

to decide if you want the service contract?
- Find out who is offering the service contract: the retailer or dealer you are buying the item from, the manufacturer, or an independent third party?
- Find out who will be doing, or who you can have do the repairs. Regarding appliances or individually manufactured units, will repairs be made by technicians trained to service your product?
- To check on the reputation of a company offering service contracts, contact the Better Business Bureau or your local consumer protection office.
- If you are shopping for a new or used home, you will probably notice that most home builders and real estate companies offer home warranties providing certain repair coverage for about ten years with rates based on the selling price of the home. Most of these warranties cover major home components and systems such as heating, air conditioning, plumbing, electrical, and major appliances. But some things can be left out of the existing house warranty, such as structural or roof problems or termite damages.

Although a warranty can be a good safeguard for an older dwelling, it should not take the place of an evaluation by an impartial house inspector who will provide a complete report on the dwelling in question. Such a knowledgeable inspection should reveal any major defects before the sale is approved by both parties, and will give buyers a chance to change their mind or renegotiate if major problems are foreseen.

PRODUCT EVALUATION QUICK CHECKLIST

- ❑ Prepare before you buy. Compare and evaluate products and services.
- ❑ If reasonable, favor established, reputable, local retailers.
- ❑ Buy quality. Generally, select appliances and other items with established brand names.
- ❑ Always ask for a demonstration.
- ❑ Ask about parts and service availability.
- ❑ Favor service contracts (or "repair insurance") if you plan to give unusually rough use to whatever you are buying, or if you feel that something such as a furnace in an older home is ready to fail.
- ❑ When purchasing items for normal use, buy models offering superior performance and maintenance records, and you won't need a service contract.

Selecting & Working with Repair Contractors

When warranty work is involved, there may be no choice but to use a particular manufacturer's or dealer's representative for making repairs, and that is generally fine. When warranty work is not involved, perhaps there is only one company in your area with technicians qualified to repair a particular make or brand of appliances or components. In other cases, however, you will usually have a choice of repair contractors to select from.

SELECTING CONTRACTORS

If possible, first try to use the dealer or contractor who was involved with the initial construction, sale, or repair in question. Unless that person or company has left town or become otherwise unavailable, such a person or company usually wants to keep customers satisfied to get repeat business.

When circumstances require that you select a repair contractor you have never dealt with before, and major repairs must be undertaken, here are some guidelines to consider.

First, qualify the contractors from whom you plan to solicit bids. Select at least three contractors for bids.

- See the section on finding a good handy person. If you have found someone to take care of numerous home maintenance and repair tasks, ask him or her which contractors you should approach when major repairs are needed.
- Ask friends, coworkers, and relatives who they have used in the past.
- Inquire at appliance stores or wherever the item in question is sold new, if possible. Building supply companies can be another good source of referrals.
- Check with the Better Business Bureau in your area to see if potential contractors have been charged with unusually large numbers of consumer complaints. This will also indicate if the contractor follows up on complaints made after the work is finished.
- See if the contractor advertises in the local phone directory. How long has the contractor been in

business? It usually takes at least five years to establish a financially sound organization. If the contractor does not have a permanent place of business with a business telephone number, be wary. Anyone can paint a business name on the side of a pickup truck. Also consider if the contractor is likely to be in business throughout the life of warranties he or she may provide. In other words, if you read that the contractor is entering bankruptcy, it is time to question whether any warranties provided by the contractor would remain in service.

- Ask the prospective contractors to supply you with several names and phone numbers of individuals for whom they have recently worked. Check out the references.
- Find out if any potential contractor has connections that can give him or her advantages over competitors. Does he or she own a lumber supply store, or any other building supply companies? If so, you might be able to obtain lumber, windows, insulation, fixtures, siding, and roofing at very close to cost.
- Do the contractors have state contractor licenses and tax identification numbers?
- Are the contractors fully insured, bonded, and willing to show you their credentials if asked?

Danger signals to watch out for when hiring contractors:

- You can't verify the name, address, and telephone number of the contractor's business.
- A salesperson approaches you door-to-door or by phone and tries to pressure you into signing a contract through scare tactics, threats, or intimidation.
- A company or salesperson says your home will be used for advertising purposes—as a model job or show home — and that their sign will be displayed—all in return for you receiving a "cut-rate discount" on services rendered.
- A contractor tells you it is a special price available "Only if you sign the contract *today*."
- The contractor does not follow through on your request for references.

- You are unable to verify that the contractor has adequate insurance coverage.
- You are asked to pay for the entire job in advance, or to pay cash to a salesperson instead of a check or money order to the company itself.

PROVIDING BID REQUEST INFORMATION

Be sure to provide all of the information to each contractor selected to bid. Prepare three separate bid requests and write down what you want the contractors to provide. But leave it open-ended enough for them to suggest alternate materials or solutions based on their experience and resources. On major jobs, state that you will want product and labor warranties in writing. Ask if the warranties must be acted upon, who will be responsible for handling the claims? Find out if the warranties are transferable to future owners, and if the contractors have emergency phone numbers during off hours and weekends. Once you receive the written proposals back, evaluate them and select the best one.

APPLIANCE REPAIRS

First, read the unit's operating instructions, especially the troubleshooting section. Next, read the warranty or your service contract.

If you forgot to mail the owner's registration card, you can still get the warranty service if you kept a sales receipt or a cancelled check—either can prove the date of purchase. Although you are not required to return a warranty card, you need to if you want to receive any safety notices the manufacturer may eventually send to product owners.

If your warranty or service contract requires that you use an authorized service center, call for a list of acceptable repair companies. Be careful if you just skim through the yellow pages. The appearance of a manufacturer's logo or trademark does not always mean the business is currently authorized to make warranty repairs.

If your service contract allows you to choose a repair service, ask if the potential contractor has technicians trained to service your product brand, if they charge for a diagnosis and estimate in addition to a house call, and is the labor charge by the hour or a flat rate. Can you get a total or not-to-exceed price before the work is started? What are the warranties on the repairs?

Before you take an appliance to a service center, call and talk to a competent service technician. Describe the problem. The technician may recognize something simple to try that could eliminate a repair trip entirely. At least the technician can be better prepared to solve the problem at his or her shop or in your home.

Give the technician clear, complete information on the problem, including any unusual sounds, smells, or other conditions. If possible, also provide the model and serial numbers and the approximate purchase date on the initial call.

If you can take the appliance to a service shop, you will save on a service call. Here's what you should get from the repair company after you drop the item off: (1) A claim check that shows the date your product went into the shop for repairs. It will have the service center's name, address, and phone number on it. It should describe your product by brand, model, and serial number. (2) A signature of the technician or counter clerk along with a written description of what is to be done. Are known repairs to be made? Or is the item in the shop for inspection and evaluation? If the cause of the problem is unknown, leave a phone number where you can be reached so the condition report and expected repair costs can be relayed to you.

REPAIR OR SERVICE CONTRACTS

After selecting the contractor you want, the next step is to draw up an agreement or a contract. This may mean simply signing the original written bid proposal. In any event, this agreement, along with any accompanying plans, drawings, and specifications, will act as a guideline for your relationship with the contractor. The agreement must be signed by both parties before any work can be done. It should cover most of the concerns either party could have, yet it can be changed, or parts added or deleted, with the approval of both parties.

The contract should address the scope of work involved, expected time for completion, and—in cases of long, involved projects—list reasons for legitimate delays. It may state the inability of the builder to assign his responsibilities to others. It should describe all contract documents, explain insurance particulars, present procedures for arranging alterations or extra work, and discuss housekeeping and trash removal from the work site. It should cover compliance with local ordinances and statutes, arbitration in the event of any disputes, plus what constitutes your acceptance of the completed work. It should also provide a schedule by which the contractor is paid and a description of all warranties involved.

REPAIR CONTRACTOR QUICK CHECKLIST

❑ Avoid violating warranties by using repair contractors other than those specified by the warranty, as long as the warranty is in force.
❑ Ask at least three qualified contractors to bid repair work. Check out their references.
❑ Provide all pertinent information to each contractor selected to bid.
❑ When possible, take appliances to repair shops to save on service call charges.
❑ Request a written bid or estimate on all repair work.
❑ Never pay in advance.

The contract should be slowly reviewed, section by section, with the contractor before signing. Question anything that isn't crystal clear. Here are some additional points to consider.

Will the contractor put in writing "Satisfaction guaranteed, or your money back"?

The contract should include everything that was discussed. If you don't get it in writing, you might not get it at all. The language should be in terms you or anyone else can clearly understand. It should include a complete description of materials and installation procedures that will be used, including models or brands, size, quality, quantity, colors, weights, or any other specification details that are important. The details will change for each kind of job. For example, if painting is the task, then the make and name of the paints should be specified, as well as the number of coats that will be applied. The quality of the finished job should also be written into the agreement. (Professional painters usually offer three grades of paint jobs: premium, standard, and minimum.) Changes in the contract should be made in writing and should be agreed to and initialed by both parties.

If all of this sounds more elaborate than what you are used to, realize that many people do business in a far more informal manner. If you personally know the contractor in question, and you have had a number of good experiences with that contractor, you can probably continue to do business with him or her in similar fashion. It is with the unknown contractors, and with very expensive and complex projects, that extra caution is needed.

REPAIR WORK INSPECTIONS AND PAYMENT

You should have the right to review and approve the work at various stages if the job involves several major steps.

One rule of thumb is never to pay in advance. Reputable contractors don't need an advance to purchase supplies because they have already established good credit with vendors. The payment terms should be spelled out in the contract.

Before the entire bill is paid, if any questions have arisen about the financial condition of the contractor, make sure that no supplier or contractor has placed a materialman's lien or mechanic's lien against your property because of failure to pay for materials or equipment used on your repairs. Although it is not usually needed with established, reputable contractors, the best way to protect yourself from marginal or inept contractors is to include a clause in the contract that says the final payment will not be made until any and all mechanic's or materialman's liens are released. Of course, if you suspect that you will need such a clause, you are better off simply not dealing with such a contractor in the first place.

Finding a Good Handyperson

Notice the difference in terminology here? In the previous section, we *selected* contractors from individuals and companies known to the open market. In this case we are *looking* for someone special, someone who most likely is already part of an underground network of "informal" or unofficial contractors. We are trying to find a jack-of-many-trades who can tackle a wide variety of jobs around the house: replacing a screen door, installing a new sink and faucets, running a few receptacles and a basement light fixture, installing a garage door opener, and so on. Such a person should be even-tempered and reliable. He or she should be qualified for the type of work, and should accept only work that he or she can complete safely and correctly. This person must be able to do or arrange for the entire job, get help when needed, and should be doing it not only for additional or supplemental income, but also for the love of the work. Be wary of "informal" contractors or handypersons who are trying to support a family solely through their moonlighting efforts.

Where can such a person be found? You have to ask around. Inquire of friends, coworkers, and casual acquaintances. Who do they use? Finding a good handyperson is part luck and part persistence. It is not easy, but the effort will pay off if successful.

You will save a great deal of money, time, and aggravation over the years if you find a good handyperson who will help you with routine and emergency jobs. Often he or she, though not able to tackle a particular task, will come up with options and provide help deciding which avenue is best.

Unfortunately, good handypersons are a dying breed. Most maintenance people these days are specialists—plumbing, electrical, concrete, roofs, framing.

If you find a good general, all-seasons handyperson, a person who is available at practically any time, who does quality work at reasonable cost, who cleans up after every job, who of all possible solutions, and who has a wealth of household repair knowledge, treat him or her well. In return you will get peace of mind, slimmer repair outlays, and an ongoing friendship that is frequently lacking with many homeowner-contractor relationships.

When more specialized help is needed, for putting in a new driveway or a patio, for example, an alternative to hiring a large concrete or paving contractor is to ask someone who works in a plant or an organization that frequently uses the services of paving contractors if any paving contractor employees do driveways or patios on the side. Often the same skilled labor available through higher-priced companies can be obtained at considerably less cost on weekends and during evening hours for anyone who learns how to make the contacts and arrangements.

PART 9

Home Safety

Everyone is safe in his or her own home, right? Not quite. Spend a night in your local hospital emergency room and you would be surprised at how many serious accidents occur to people at home. And why not? We spend most of our time in our homes performing a wide range of activities, many of them dangerous.

This section presents discussions of Fire Protection, Slips, Trips, and Falls, Electrical Safety, Poisons, and Environmental Issues. We have already said enough about maintaining the home. This is preventive maintenance for the household members.

Fire Prevention

FIRE PREVENTION INSPECTIONS

Fires are far simpler to prevent than to put out. Here's how.

Electrical Hazards

Read the section on Electrical Safety. Of the main electrical fire hazards, the worst are:

- Overloaded fuses, circuits, motors, and outlets.
- Wiring with frayed or worn insulation.
- Loose ground connections.
- Lights or machinery coming in contact with combustible materials.

Good Housekeeping

Read Part 7, on housekeeping. Are items haphazardly piled up in the attic, basement, and garage? Are gasoline and other highly combustible materials stored properly? Are old boxes, rags, newspapers, magazines, and similar materials disposed of periodically? Or have they collected to a point where they have become fire hazards?

Avoid Careless Smoking

Never smoke in bed or while reclining on a couch where the possibility of falling asleep exists. Be careful when and where ashtrays are emptied. Use ashtrays that are noncombustible, large, deep, and heavy. Douse ashes and cigarette butts with water and make sure they are completely out before disposing of them. Never leave cigarettes, cigars, pipes, or candles burning unattended.

Close the cover of a matchbook every time before lighting a match. Store matches out of children's reach, in covered metal containers. Do so even if you don't have children; it is just a good habit. Discard matches carefully. Make sure they are cold before you throw them away. Never use matches to search in dark attics, closets, or other closed places. Teach children to give matches they may find to an adult.

Heating Equipment Fire Hazards

Read the section on Fireplaces and Wood Stoves. Is the chimney sound and clean? Is all heating equipment checked and cleaned regularly? Has a wood stove been properly installed and inspected by professionals? Are combustibles such as drapes, curtains, and carpets kept away from heating equipment? Here are some additional points to consider.

- Burn only dry, seasoned hardwood such as hickory or oak. Burn coal only in heating appliances designed for that use.
- Have separate flues for each major wood-burning appliance.
- Inspect the chimney for creosote buildup, and have the chimney cleaned regularly.
- Never burn trash, plastic, or large amounts of paper in a wood-burning appliance or fireplace.
- Burn smaller, hotter fires. Add fuel often instead of packing the firebox full of wood.
- Never use lighter fluid, gasoline, or kerosene to start a fire.
- Store wood and other combustibles at least 3 feet away from the firebox.
- Use a metal fire screen or glass doors in front of fireplace or wood stove open fireboxes at all times.
- Make sure a fire is out before you leave the house or go to bed.
- Keep a multi-purpose ABC fire extinguisher handy.

Bedrooms

- No smoking in bed.
- Keep lamp, radio, television cords in good condition.
- Don't overload outlets.
- Make sure windows and screens are not blocked and are easy to open.
- Have a working smoke detector present, at least in the outside hallway.

Living and Family Rooms

- Make sure all electrical cords are in good condition.
- Don't run cords beneath a rug or furniture.
- Allow enough space for air circulation and ventilation around stereo, television, and other electronic

equipment.
- Don't overload outlets.
- Use safe ashtrays. Check rooms after smokers leave to make sure no smoldering ashes were left on carpet or furniture.

Kitchens
- Store matches, lighters, and candles out of children's reach.
- Keep range, oven, and vent fan clean and grease-free.
- Keep flammables away from range and oven.
- Maintain small appliances clean, in good repair, and unplugged when not being used.
- Keep curtains, towels, and bathrobe sleeves away from burners. Take cooking grease off the stove when it is not being used. Turn pot handles toward the side or back so small children aren't attracted to them. Have a household fire extinguisher available just in case.
- Install a smoke detector in or just outside the kitchen, away from the cooking area.

Attics
- Don't keep boxes and boxes of old clothes, newspapers, magazines, and similar items. Throw them out or donate them to charity.
- Keep the attic stairs clear. Don't store anything on them.
- Evaluate the condition of an attic on a routine basis. Attics will slowly become depositories for junk that will never be used again. Be ruthless. Weed things out and get rid of them.

Basements
- Inspect the heating system. Flue pipes should be the right size, as short as possible, well supported, tightly connected, and free of rust or weak spots. Uninsulated flue pipes should be at least 18 inches away from any combustibles. Along the same line, combustibles such as newspapers, trash, wood, paint, and other items should be stored away from the furnace. It is best to keep as few of those items as possible anywhere in the basement.
- All heating equipment should be cleaned and inspected at least once a year.

Garage and Yard
- Make sure electrical equipment and lighting have weatherproof cords, outlets, and other components.
- Keep power tools and gas-motor units clean and in good repair.

- Avoid starting charcoal fires near buildings, fences, or trees. Never add lighter fluid, kerosene, or gasoline to a charcoal fire. Use starting fluids *only* to help start a charcoal fire, per the manufacturer's instructions. Never use starting fluids to quicken an already lit fire. Don't wear loose clothing around charcoal fires, and make sure the briquettes are completely out before leaving them.
- Keep gasoline and flammable liquids stored in the garage or yard in approved safety containers, out of direct sunlight, away from all heat sources, in secure, adequately ventilated areas. The most common liquids to be careful of are paints, thinners, strippers, adhesives, gasoline, kerosene, and acetone. If possible, limit the supply to small amounts and keep them on hand only if they are absolutely necessary. Consider getting rid of flammable liquids you haven't used in a long time. Nothing should be stored in glass jars. For flammables kept in metal containers, make sure the containers are marked so anyone can determine the contents at a glance.
- Refuel equipment such as gasoline lawn mowers after the engine has cooled. Always refuel outside, never indoors.
- Regularly collect and get rid of debris such as dried grass clippings, leaves, branches, and weeds.

SMOKE DETECTORS

Smoke detectors are the last line of defense against the ravaging effects of fires. There are several basic designs—those that are battery operated, and those that rely on the house electricity. The battery-powered models are simple to install and are operable as long as a charged battery is in place. Naturally, the batteries need regular checking and replacement. The unfortunate truth is that of all battery-operated smoke alarms in place, about a third of them are inoperable at any given time because of worn-out batteries or batteries that had been removed to stop the annoying warning signal that some detectors have built in to let people know the batteries are about to fail. Household current models — the ones installed directly to the home's electric system—need to be put in place by an electrician and need far less attention once they are set up. On the other hand, they may fail in case of a blackout without battery backup. Beyond that choice, here are some other points to consider about smoke detectors.

- Purchase only models that carry a testing laboratory seal of approval.

- The alarm must be loud enough to wake a sleeping person behind a closed door.
- Try to purchase detectors with five-year manufacturer's warranties.
- There should be a malfunction signal on the unit. It will warn when batteries or bulbs need replacement.
- Maintaining and cleaning the detector should be a simple task, not requiring a lot of tools or complete removal.
- Sleeping areas need the most protection. A single detector in a typical hallway outside bedrooms is usually adequate. But take the individuals' physical health characteristics into account as well. If the people sleeping in a bedroom do not hear well, perhaps a single detector directly outside of each bedroom door is necessary.
- Bedroom hallways longer than 30 feet should have a smoke detector at each end.
- For maximum protection, sleep with doors closed and install detectors in each bedroom, as well as in the hallway.
- Place a smoke detector at the top of each stairwell and at the end of a long hallway. Smoke rises easily through stairwells.
- Smoke detectors positioned in living areas should be kept away from fireplaces and wood stoves to avoid frequent false alarms, which could lull a family into a false sense of security during a real fire. Kitchen and dining area detectors should be kept away from cooking ranges and ovens for the same reason.
- In basements, mount a smoke detector close to the stairway but not at the top of the stairway or near the furnace exhaust. On the ceiling above the bottom step is a good place.
- Battery-powered detectors are simple to install, but those connected to household wiring should have their own separate circuit and should be installed by a professional electrician.
- Ceiling mounts should be kept at least 4 inches away from the dead air space near walls and corners. It is best to install detectors as close to the center of a room as possible.
- Wall mounts should be placed 4 to 12 inches below the ceiling and away from corners. Keep detectors high on a wall because smoke rises.
- Avoid placing smoke detectors near air supply registers. Keep them at least 3 feet away, or the register could prevent smoke from reaching the detector.
- Avoid installing smoke detectors on uninsulated exterior walls or ceilings. Temperature extremes can affect batteries, and temperature differences

could keep smoke from reaching a detector.
- Replace smoke detector batteries at least every year, or as needed. Keep spare batteries on hand. Some people like to change batteries whenever daylight savings time comes around.
- Replace bulbs every three years, or as needed. Keep extras handy.
- Replace damaged parts as soon as they break.
- Check the alarm on a smoke detector every 30 days by pushing the test button or releasing smoke in the detector's vicinity. Also test the device if you have been away from home more than a few days.
- Clean a detector's face and grillwork at least once a month to remove dust and grease. Use a vacuum cleaner tool to get rid of dust and cobwebs that could impair a detector's sensitivity.

FIRE EXTINGUISHER USE

Fire extinguishers look easy to use, but during a real emergency, things happen fast. Household members should read the instructions on how to use an extinguisher *before* the extinguisher is needed. Here are some points to consider about fire extinguisher use.

- If only one extinguisher will be purchased, it should probably be a multi-purpose ABC dry chemical extinguisher, to cover the possibility of all types of fires.
- Use the extinguisher only if everyone else is out of the area and the fire is still small. If there is any doubt, get out and call the fire department.
- Never let the fire get between you and the escape route.
- Aim the extinguisher nozzle at the base of the flames, and use a sweeping motion from about 6 to 8 feet away from the fire.
- Inspect fire extinguishers every few months. Keep records of the inspections by fastening a durable tag showing dates of inspections and any recharges that may have been necessary. Look at the pressure gauge to make sure the extinguisher hasn't developed a slow leak which has partially discharged the tank. Lift the extinguisher off its bracket to check its overall condition and to make sure it is easy to remove in case of an emergency. Weigh carbon dioxide extinguishers every six months to see if the contents are leaking. Don't expel contents of regular or multi-purpose dry chemical extinguishers in an effort to check them. Once any amount has been used, they should be recharged. If repairs or adjustments are needed, have them made by a professional fire equipment company.
- Place fire extinguishers so there is at least one per

FIRE PREVENTION QUICK CHECKLIST

❑ See that no electrical hazards are present.

❑ Maintain good housekeeping.

❑ Avoid careless smoking habits. Never smoke in bed or while reclining.

❑ Follow all safety procedures when using heating equipment such as furnaces, fireplaces, space heaters, and wood stoves.

❑ Keep multi-purpose ABC fire extinguishers near high-risk areas such as kitchens. Make sure that you and all family members know how to use the extinguishers.

❑ Have enough smoke alarms installed. Maintain their batteries or other power source.

❑ Keep matches, candles, and lighters out of children's reach.

❑ Regularly inspect fireplace and other flues and chimneys.

❑ Develop a household fire escape plan. Practice the plan until each family member knows what to do.

❑ Make sure bedroom windows unlock and open easily.

❑ Keep all escape routes such as doors, windows, stairways, and hallways clear.

❑ Post the fire department phone number at every phone in the house.

❑ Teach children how to warn others, leave the house, and call for help.

---

floor, near exits and in full view so they can be reached quickly and easily. Consider placing extinguishers in the garage, in the basement at the head of the stairs, near the kitchen, and near any wood-burning appliances and portable heating units that are put into service.

FIRE ESCAPE PLANNING

Despite the best prevention efforts, an accidental fire is still possible. Household members should discuss what to do in case of a fire—how everyone will escape.

- Rooms should ideally have at least two escape routes.
- Windows should unlock and open easily.
- Escape ladders may be needed upstairs if there is no nearby roof. Store them near the windows or under beds. Practice using them.
- Remember that smoke and poisonous gases rise with hot air from the flames. Instruct family members to crawl along the floor where smoke and fume concentrations are the lightest.
- In the event of a fire, bedroom doors should be closed to prevent the flames from spreading. Avoid opening a door that feels unusually warm or hot to the touch.
- Escape routes such as doors, windows, stairways, and hallways must be kept clear. People might need to negotiate them in the dark. Never paint windows shut so they can't be opened.
- Decide on a meeting place outside where every household member knows to gather. Hold several practice fire drills.
- Teach children how to warn others, leave the house, and call for help if a fire occurs.
- The fire department phone number should be posted at every phone in the house.

Slips, Trips, and Falls

Charlie Chaplin. Laurel and Hardy. Red Skelton. The Three Stooges. Jerry Lewis. Benny Hill. Peter Sellers. Chevy Chase. Cartoon roadrunners and coyotes. They are all characters who have employed slipping, tripping, and falling down as an art.

Sounds funny, doesn't it? People slipping, tripping, and falling down. It may sound comical, but it is not. In fact, every year falls kill about 13,000 people. Over half those fatalities occur at home; the rest, at work or in public places. And on top of that, every year about 14 million others are injured enough to receive medical care.

Most of these accidents are not dramatic "fall off a bridge" kinds of incidents. Most of the falls that injure people result from slips and trips that happen at or near floor level.

COMMON CAUSES OF SLIPS, TRIPS, AND FALLS

Slips can be caused by a wide variety of conditions, including:

- Tile and vinyl flooring, wet or waxed.
- Carpets or rugs that aren't fastened down.
- Bathtub and shower surfaces.
- Icy patches on flat and sloped surfaces.
- Oily or greasy spots.
- Changes that occur to familiar walking surfaces.

For example, for years and years the steep attic stairs in a ninety-year-old home are covered with dark brown rubber treads to provide a measure of safety for occupants who carry items to and from the attic. One day the rubber tread on the third step from the top works loose from its nails. The homeowner removes the tread entirely and forgets to install a replacement. (See Figure 71-1.)

Weeks later, he goes up to the attic in his stocking feet to retrieve a box of Christmas decorations. He grabs the box and starts down the stairs. When his foot hits the third step from the top, it slips out from under him on the slick painted step. Airborne, he crashes to his back on the steep stairway. He slides,

still on his back, still clutching the box, to the bottom of the steps, where, in excruciating pain, he hopes he hasn't injured himself for life.

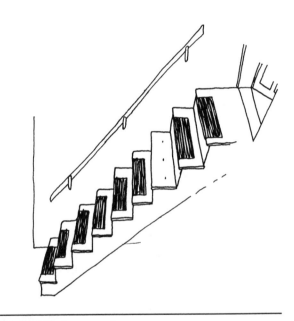

71-1. Missing tread.

Trips also contribute heavily to accidental falls. Some causes include:

- Poor housekeeping, with materials stored in walkways.
- Furniture placed in odd positions.
- Electrical cords not properly secured.
- Carrying too heavy a load.
- Poorly lit staircases with items stored on the steps.
- Irregular steps and uneven walkways.
- Cracked or loose flooring.
- Toys and other items left on floors.

PREVENTING SLIPS, TRIPS, AND FALLS

To prevent slips, trips, and falls, attention is needed to five key concerns: footwear, walking surfaces, activities, surroundings, and preoccupations.

Footwear

Shoes should have non-skid soles. Low-profile models are best. High heels are notorious trippers. Heels should be made of rubber, not leather. Use snow shoes and boots for wintry weather.

Long baggy pants with cuffs dragging on the ground may have suited Charlie Chaplin, but they are dangerous around the house. Keep pant and skirt lengths at proper heights to prevent catching a heel.

Walking Surface

- Is the ground or floor flat? Free from clutter and slippery materials? Is there enough light to see where you are going?
- Any rug, large or small, that has not been tacked down or does not have a rubber backing or mat beneath it, may slip when stepped on. Keep all loose rugs away from the head and foot of stairways.
- Use non-skid mats for bathtub, shower, and bathroom floors.
- Loose or uneven flooring should be repaired or replaced. Loose tiles, floorboards, bricks, and flagstones come to mind. Worn or ripped carpeting or tile floorings should be replaced.
- Make sure all spilled water or other liquid is quickly cleaned up. When mopping floors, take up excessive water so the surface will dry faster.
- If you have floors that require waxing, remove excess wax with a floor buffer.
- Have rags, sawdust, or absorbent materials or cleansers ready wherever oily substances are used or kept. Don't let grease accumulate on a garage or basement workshop floor. Clean spills as soon as they occur.
- Handrails or grab handles should be present for use at all stairs, showers, and bathtubs.
- Never store materials on a stairway or in a hallway. Keep items tucked away in closets and cabinets.
- Small loose items, when left on a floor, can cause big falls. A pencil, spool of thread, or golf ball at the bottom of a stairway could lead to a serious fall.
- Check for stair treads that are cracked or worn. Non-skid treads or mats provide an extra measure of safety.
- Always keep drawers closed, even when you think it is unlikely that someone will bump into them.
- Arrange furniture to avoid building obstacle courses in walking paths throughout the house.
- When carrying items through the house, make sure you can see where you are going. Maintain adequate lighting in stairways and halls. Place bedroom lights so they can be turned on from bed.
- Maintain adequate outside lighting at all entrances and walkway steps.
- Don't allow toys, tools, and equipment to be left in driveways or walkways.
- Icy spots in driveways and walkways should be sprinkled with sand, salt, or chemical de-icers.

Activities

- Do you have to carry a heavy object? Get help or use a mechanical lifting or carrying device such as a dolly or hand cart. Don't try to carry everything at once. Make several trips.
- Allow yourself enough time. Don't rush.
- Concentrate on keeping your balance.
- Use safety equipment such as gloves, safety goggles, or hard-toe work shoes when corresponding hazards exist.
- Never stand or jump from an elevated platform such as a picnic table, patio, counter, or bed. Lower yourself instead.
- Avoid leaning back in a chair so the chair's front legs are lifted off the floor.
- Use a stepladder for all hard-to-reach and out-of-reach items and projects. Don't substitute a stack of furniture or boxes for a sturdy, properly balanced ladder.
- When using a ladder, check the condition of the steps or rungs periodically. Spread the legs of a stepladder to their limit and check the locking mechanism. Avoid turning or twisting while on a ladder. Don't climb onto the top two steps. Always use both hands to climb. Wear a tool belt or rope to pull materials up after you have positioned yourself on the ladder. It is a wise practice to have someone hold the bottom of an extension or straight ladder to make sure it doesn't slide or tip, and so no one accidentally bumps into it while you are up there.

Surroundings

Are there other activities in the area that could interrupt or distract you? Children underfoot? Pets lying down behind you? Cars speeding by? Loud, startling noises? Equipment in motion? Pay attention to your surroundings.

Preoccupations

Be alert. Watch where you are going and what you are doing. Anticipate problems and take care of them ... before they take care of you. Naturally, no one *expects* to slip, trip, or fall ... unless, of course, he or she is a real comedian.

SLIPS AND TRIPS QUICK CHECKLIST

❑ Wear good shoes with non-skid soles. The lower the profile, the better. High heels and leather heels are dangerous.

❑ Use a ladder, not a stack of boxes or a swivel chair to reach high places. Know how to use ladders safely.

❑ Allow yourself plenty of time to get places so you won't have to hurry.

❑ Be alert. Watch where you are going and what you are doing. Anticipate slippery and difficult conditions, such as:

- slippery linoleum, tile, or wood flooring
- rugs that aren't fastened down
- bathtub and shower surfaces
- wet, icy, oily, and greasy surfaces
- poor housekeeping
- crowded storage areas
- poorly lit staircases
- furniture placed in odd positions
- electrical cords not positioned securely
- toys and other items on floors and steps

Electrical Safety

Electricity is invisible. Unless sparks are flying or smoke is coming from somewhere it shouldn't, an electrically charged wire, component, or piece of equipment can appear to be harmless. Because electricity is such a common, everyday part of life, people tend to forget how dangerous it really is.

Electricity can kill. When someone gets a shock, that means electric current is passing through his body. When an electrical switch is turned on, it completes a circuit that allows electricity to move from a charged outlet or generating station to the light, tool, or piece of equipment that was just turned on. The wires the electricity moves through are called conductors. They are enclosed in plastic or rubber materials that insulate or keep the electricity from traveling to other conductors that could touch the wire along the way. Electrical equipment and wires must be "grounded" —connected to the ground through contact with a ground wire in a three-pronged plug, or, as many clothes washers have, a wire that acts as a ground by being fastened to a copper cold-water plumbing line. The grounding helps prevent electricity from taking a shortcut through a person who touches the wire or appliance.

When someone gets shocked, that usually means an electric current is taking a shortcut because the circuit is exposed or has defective insulation. The longer the current is in contact with someone, the greater the risk, especially if the current enters the body near the heart. A common misconception is that "normal" electricity, the kind available at typical household outlets, is not very dangerous. Nothing could be further from the truth. *All electricity should be considered dangerous*. It doesn't take much electricity to kill someone. The amps —the amount of power in the circuit — rather than the amount of voltage are the important factor. The effects of electric shock can range from a tingly feeling to death. In between, it can cause varying degrees of damage to nerves, muscles, and tissues. It can cause internal bleeding. It can burn internal or external parts of the body.

WIRING

Wiring should be installed and inspected by qualified electricians. All of it should meet local and national codes. The home's main electrical panel or box should be rated for at least 100 amps. If the box or panel isn't clearly labeled, or if the household power is delivered through ungrounded outlets designed for the older style of two-pronged plugs, the wiring system should be upgraded or replaced. Additional signs of inadequate wiring include:

- Knob-and-tube wiring.
- Lights that flicker or dim.
- Electric motors that change speeds when an appliance is turned on.
- Heat-producing appliances that are slow to heat up, such as stoves, toasters, irons.
- A general lack of wall outlets.

Another important electrical feature in the wiring is the presence of ground-fault circuit interrupters. These devices detect electrical leaks, then quickly shut down power to prevent accidental shocks. They should protect locations where water can pose serious electrical hazards, such as bathrooms, kitchens, and near swimming pools. Consider installing them if they are not already included in the household wiring.

FUSES AND CIRCUIT BREAKERS

If an electrical panel's fuse blows, take the following steps to correct the situation.

- Unplug the appliance that caused the problem.
- Stand on a dry surface and shut off the main power switch on the fuse panel or box.
- Replace the burned fuse, using a fuse with the correct rating. Never use a higher-rated fuse, or stop-gap measures such as a penny or aluminum foil.
- Turn the main power switch back on.
- Make sure a flashlight and spare fuses are kept on hand.

If a circuit breaker trips (1) unplug whatever appliance caused the problem; and (2) reset the circuit breaker according to the instructions. That usually means simply flipping the switch back to "on." If the circuit breaker trips again right away, and you can't tell why, call an electrician. In any event, the cause of the tripped breaker should be determined. It could be a defective appliance, a faulty electrical cord, or simply an overloaded circuit — too many electrical appliances plugged into a circuit and operating at the same time. To prevent a repeat occurrence, fix damaged appliances. If overloading is the problem, contact a qualified electrician.

ELECTRICAL APPLIANCES

All electrical appliances, including units wired directly into a household's electrical system, such as water heaters and furnaces, should display a seal from a certified testing laboratory. One commonly found testing laboratory symbol is UL, representing Underwriter's Laboratories. (See Figure 72-1.) Here are a number of important safety tips for using electrical appliances.

72-1. Underwriter's Laboratories Seal of Approval.

- Avoid using extension cords. If one must be used, don't exceed its recommended rating. Avoid stringing multiple extension cords together. Choose the right type of cord: a heavy-duty cord for power tools, a weather-resistant cord for outdoor use, and a three-wire cord with a three-prong plug for tools and appliances that require grounding. (See Figure 72-2.) Never remove the third prong to create a two-prong plug, and avoid using an adapter. Handle the cord with care. Avoid stretching it taut, kinking it, twisting it, or crushing it while in use or in storage. Pull the plug, not the cord, to disengage the plug from an outlet. Pick a safe location to lay the cord. Keep it away from places it is likely to be walked or ridden on. Keep it away from heat sources and water. Don't rely on extension cords for permanent installations; if you need another outlet to run a freezer, refrigerator, dehumidifier, or other stationary appliance, have a new one installed where it is needed. Always unplug the cord from the appliance and the wall outlet between uses. Perform frequent inspections of extension and appliance cords and replace

place damaged cords. Naturally, teach children not to play with cords or wall outlets.

72-2. Three-pronged plug.

- Never operate electrical appliances while touching metal objects (especially plumbing), while standing on a wet surface, or with wet hands.
- If an appliance smokes, smells, sparks, or gives a shock at any time, unplug it, then have it inspected and repaired or replaced, if necessary.
- Keep electric motors free from buildups of dust, dirt, lint, and lubricating oil.
- Space heaters, toasters, irons, and other heat-producing electrical appliances and components require extra care to minimize fire hazards. Never place combustibles such as paper, drapes, or furniture near them. Keep them clean, in proper condition, and out of high-traffic areas. Unplug these appliances after each use. Let them cool before storing them in a safe place.
- When using power tools, the operator should dress properly. Rubber-soled shoes and rubber gloves should be worn when working in wet areas. Avoid loose-fitting clothes that could become entangled in rotating equipment. Remove rings, bracelets, wristwatches, and other jewelry while operating power tools. Clean the area regularly. Sawdust, shavings, rags, and other debris should be kept from piling up where they could create a fire hazard or damage tools.
- Always unplug appliances before cleaning, repairing, removing parts, or adjusting internal components in any way.

CHILDREN

Children may not understand how hazardous electricity can be. Most efforts in this direction should go toward teaching and making sure the opportunities for accidents are reduced.

- Instruct children to stay away from electrical outlets.
- Cover unused outlets with plastic safety caps.
- Have ground-fault interrupters installed in bathrooms, kitchens, and anywhere else water is present, such as near swimming pools.
- Keep electrical appliances such as hair dryers, curling irons, and radios out of reach.

ELECTRICAL SAFETY QUICK CHECKLIST

❑ Inspect electrical equipment and wires before they are used. Make sure they are insulated and properly grounded, and that their electrical connections are tight.

❑ Disconnect the power source or unplug the unit before cleaning, repairing, or adjusting internal components on electrical equipment.

❑ Avoid using extension cords whenever possible. If extension cords are required, use the correct size and type of cord: an outdoor cord for outside tasks and a heavy-duty cord for power tools. Don't leave cords tangled, crushed, or lying across where people walk or drive.

❑ Make sure your hands are dry before handling anything electric. Water and sweat turn your skin into an efficient electrical conductor.

❑ Teach children to respect electricity. Correct conditions potentially hazardous to children.

❑ If a piece of electrical equipment sparks, smells, smokes, or gives shocks, don't use it. Have a professional inspect it before trying to use it again.

❑ Don't let grease, oil, dust, dirt, or lint build up on electrical machinery.

❑ Don't touch a person who has been shocked. Instead, call for professional medical help. If you can safely turn off the power that is causing the problem, do so. If not, attempt to use a piece of lumber or a stick to try to push a person away from the wire or other source of the shock.

❑ Never use water on an electrical fire. Notify firefighters immediately. If it can be done safely, turn off or unplug the current. If a fire is small, a type C, or multipurpose ABC extinguisher, or baking soda could be used to douse the flames.

▪ Store clothes irons out of reach, and make sure they are kept away from places children frequent. Avoid a situation where a child could pull an electrical cord and yank a hot iron down from an ironing board.

OUTDOOR ELECTRICAL SAFETY

Follow these guidelines for outdoor electrical use.

▪ Make sure outdoor electrical outlets are weatherproof and protected by ground-fault circuit interrupters.

▪ Make sure lighting fixtures, extension cords, and other accessories are designed for outdoor use.

▪ Keep away from power lines, especially when performing tasks in which equipment could come into contact with electrical lines, such as working with ladders, dump trucks, roofs, gutters, and antennas.

▪ Avoid using electric lawn mowers or other tools during wet conditions, if possible. It is best to wear rubber-soled shoes whenever power tools are used outdoor.

▪ Turn off circuits or unplug extension cords before hanging or adjusting outdoor lighting fixtures and decorations.

▪ Antennas should be properly grounded and wired to lightning arrestors. Homes in locations subject to frequent electrical storms should have lightning rods professionally installed.

ELECTRICAL EMERGENCY PRECAUTIONS

For electrical fires:

▪ Use only fire extinguishers rated for electrical class C fires. Never try to quench an electrical fire with water—the water could cause an electric shock.

▪ If a fire is confined to a small spot near an appliance such as an iron, a space heater, or a microwave oven, try to unplug the appliance or turn off the electricity.

▪ Call the fire department if you think the fire is too large to be put out by family members. Make sure everyone leaves the house.

For downed outdoor power lines:

▪ Never touch them.
▪ Keep away from water the lines may be touching.
▪ Warn others to stay away.
▪ Call the electric company and police if necessary.

Poisons

Poison. The very word conjures up images of rattlesnake fangs, of curare-tipped African pygmy darts, of jealous spouses and arsenic, of fumes from out-of-control chemical fires, and a whole range of deadly and exotic substances.

That may have been true a century ago, but today—more than ever—products we purchase at supermarkets, hardware stores, and gas stations, products we handle every day in our homes, can be classified as hazardous—especially when used and stored without the proper safety procedures. The dangers of household poisoning are directly related to the fact that more and more people are likely to come in contact with one or more of an ever-increasing number of chemical products that have worked their way into our way of life.

Unfortunately, the greatest poisoning toll is taken on the very young. Children, unaware of the danger, may swallow a toxic poison at any time. It takes only seconds. And there are other ways to be affected. Inhalation, particularly of gases and vapors, can result in drastic reactions. Skin contact can also cause harm.

To put things in perspective, a conservative estimate of the number of poisonings that occur in the United States during a typical year is about 145,000. Of those, about 70,000 can be ascribed to medicines—medicines used in the wrong manner: too much taken at one time, or taken by the wrong people, or by people taking the wrong medicine by accident. About 18,000 poisonings result from cleaning materials, 13,000 from vegetable products, 11,000 from cosmetics, 8,000 from pesticides, 6,000 from paints, and 4,000 from petroleum derivative products such as gasoline, kerosene, motor oil, and anti-freeze. Of every 145,000 total incidents, about 90,000 involve children less than five years old.

Due to preventive measures taken in the workplace, very few poisonings occur there. Most poisonings happen at home. Again, most of those happen to children less than five years old.

What happens when a poisoning occurs? For a physician to make a reasonable diagnosis, he or she will need to know:

- The precise identity of the suspected material.
- Its form and formulation.
- How the exposure occurred (swallowed, breathed, skin contact, etc.).
- How toxic the material is.
- What visual and physiological effects resulted.

Because many poisons are fast-acting, a phone call is frequently the initial contact with medical help. The more information that can be provided to a physician, the better.

POISON CONTROL INSPECTION

Here is a list by area of products that could be harmful, especially to children:

Kitchens
- Polishes (furniture, floor, silver)
- Detergents
- Dishwasher detergent
- Drain cleaner—*very dangerous*
- Oven cleaner—*very dangerous*
- Ammonia
- All-purpose cleaners
- Glue
- Alcohol
- Medicines
- Vitamins

Bathrooms
- Disinfectants
- Rubbing alcohol
- Mouthwash and fluoride mouth rinses
- Cosmetics
- Hair care products
- Toilet bowl cleaners
- Medicines, both prescription and over-the-counter

Bedrooms
- Sprays (hair, deodorant)
- Cosmetics
- Medicines

- Perfumes, colognes, aftershaves
- Mothballs

Laundry Area
- Fabric care products
- Bleach—*very dangerous*
- Dyes
- Stain or spot removers
- Detergents and soaps

Basements and Attics
- Insect traps
- Rodent poisons
- Hobby and craft supplies
- Ink, glue, and other adhesives

Garage and Outdoor Storage
- Pool supplies, such as chlorine
- Gasoline, kerosene, and other petroleum and automotive products
- Garden products such as herbicides, pesticides, and fertilizers
- Paints, thinners, solvents

House General
- Some house plants and some outdoor plants are highly toxic to people and pets. It is difficult to determine which ones are and which are not. Books and pamphlets are available through pediatricians and poison control centers. The best policy is simply to prevent very young children from having unsupervised access to house plants.
- For a long time the medical community did not realize how dangerous lead (from paint chips, painted toys, imported ceramic ware) could be to our health. High levels of lead in a person's system can cause coma, convulsions, and death. Lower levels may result in stomach aches, cramps, irritability, fatigue, frequent vomiting, and constipation. If that isn't bad enough, small amounts of lead can also bring on headaches, sleep disorders, and poor appetite. Lead can interfere with the growth process, damage the nervous system, result in hearing loss, lower IQ scores, and cause excitability and inability to concentrate.

How do you know if lead is a problem at your house? The only way is to have soil, water, paint, and any other suspected material tested by a reputable laboratory. Children under six years old should be screened. Get further information for testing at your public health department or at your family doctor's office. The sources of lead include:

- Soil contamination—chips and dust from exterior paint; lead-based insecticides; highway pollution.
- Water contamination—lead water pipes; plumbing fittings made out of brass or bronze; lead solder used to connect plumbing.
- Food contamination—grown or raised near heavily traveled roads or other sources of lead pollution; stored or baked in poorly glazed pottery; prepared by someone with lead dust on his or her hands; packaged in cans with lead seams; stored in leaded crystal for prolonged periods.

Other Sources
- Battery casings.
- Antique pewter.
- Some folk medicines and cosmetics.
- Some porcelain and pottery.
- Dust or fumes from hobbies that use lead, such as stained glass, fishing sinker making, and shotgun lead shot reloading.
- Dust from renovation of your own or a neighbor's house.

Lead Poisoning Prevention
- Use lead-free paint on walls, furniture, toys, and other household items.
- Make sure children and others wash their hands before eating.
- Have your tap water checked for lead. Draw drinking and cooking water from only the cold tap, after allowing water to run a few minutes.
- An older home should be tested for lead paint.
- Store food in glass, plastic, or stainless steel containers, not in open original packaging cans.
- Unless pottery was designed to be used for foodstuffs, with lead-free glaze, use it for display only. If you are not positive, use it for display only.
- Don't allow children to eat snow.

POISON CONTROL MAINTENANCE

1. Restrict access to poisonous products to only those individuals trained in the product's use. Keep products out of children's reach. It is better to have products out of reach and out of sight, than in supposedly child-resistant containers that are kept out in the open. Some children view child-resistant containers as a personal challenge to their intelligence, and try even harder to open them.

2. Keep products in their original containers, or mark them legibly. If you don't, confusion can result. For example, photographic darkrooms use chemicals for preparing liquid developers and stop baths. Some of these liquids are a yellowish

clear, honey color. A photographer was using clear glass ½-gallon apple juice containers to store his developing solutions. The solutions looked exactly like apple juice. They were in jars that said apple juice. And they were kept in a basement, a few feet away from a food cabinet which contained several jars of—you guessed it —real apple juice. That is a condition ripe for tragedy.

3. Store food and non-food items separately, so there is no confusion possible.

4. Alcoholic beverages are best stored locked up.

5. Use products that offer safety packaging whenever you can.

6. Clean storage areas regularly. If a product's expiration date has passed, toss it out, especially if it is a medicine. (Medicines should be flushed down the toilet, not thrown in the trash.)

7. Get into the habit of returning products to safe storage as soon as you finish using them. Replace covers tightly. Don't allow children in an area when a dangerous product is being used.

8. Teach children about the dangers of poisons. Start instructing them as early as possible. It is better to explain that something is dangerous or potentially painful, than to tell a child that it is "just against the rules" to touch.

9. Read directions and follow them. Always turn on a light and read the fine print on medicine containers before taking any yourself or before giving them to a sick child. Never give a person someone else's prescription. Never leave medicines by a bedside; it is easy to take medication while drowsy without realizing it.

10. Have your local family physician's phone number and the number of your Poison Control Center written on or near your phones.

POISON QUICK CHECKLIST

❑ Review the lists of common household poisons in this section, then go through your household room by room, identifying potential problem materials.

❑ Keep young children away from house plants.

❑ Have the household water, paints, and other possibly contaminated materials tested for lead content.

❑ Place all poisonous materials in locked cabinets or out of children's reach, including alcoholic beverages and medicines.

❑ Keep products in their original containers, or mark them legibly.

❑ Store food and non-food items separately, so there is no confusion.

❑ Use products that offer safety packaging whenever possible.

❑ Get into the habit of returning dangerous products to safe storage as soon as you finish using them.

❑ Teach children about the dangers of poison.

❑ Have your family physician's phone number and the number of your Poison Control Center posted near every phone in the house.

Environmental Factors

For lack of a better title, this section is called "Environmental Factors." Referring, of course, to *your* home environment. It is concerned with water, an integral part of any household, and a number of other substances you are better off without: radon, asbestos, and lead-based paint.

WATER

Water. The elixir of life. Everyone needs it. We drink water, cook with water, clean with water, and maintain our lawns, cars, and many other possessions with water.

But not all water is pure. Not all water is fit to drink, or even fit for use in a water heater or washing machine. If water from the tap develops any of the following symptoms, it is time to have it analyzed:

- Cloudy water (not just air bubbles that disappear in moments).
- Laundry that comes out stained.
- Fixtures that corrode quickly.
- Awful-tasting water.
- Awful-smelling water.
- Soapy scum buildups.
- Rust deposits.

Both municipal and private water systems and wells can develop water problems. No matter where your supply is from, it is a good idea to have it checked every other year or so. One approach is to keep the water line inactive for about six hours, then take a sample to be tested by your local health department office. Laboratory testing of a sample is really the only way to determine if a water supply is contaminated.

If lead levels are present in dangerous concentrations, they can be caused when old plumbing fixtures, pipes, and solder corrode and leach their components into the water. In those cases, lead levels in the home will be substantially higher than those in water before it enters the house. Copper water pipes connected with lead-based solder can also result in high levels of lead in drinking water. These situations frequently exist in older homes. The only way to achieve a safer water supply is to replace the offending plumbing with lines that cannot leach lead into the system.

Groundwater contamination can occur when chemical wastes, pesticides, herbicides, fertilizers, or other substances seep through the soil into underground water tables and supplies.

Faulty private septic systems that have been improperly installed or managed can also contribute to groundwater contamination. If such problems are found, it is time to contact health department officials. Usually it won't just be your problem. Contaminated water will probably affect an entire area. It is likely to be a community concern that will demand community action.

Some areas, particularly those with certain types of soil, have "hard" water, or water that may look or taste a bit odd. Even if it is not harmful to your health, it could still cause rust-staining or corrosion, or you just might not like the taste. A variety of water conditioning systems are available to remove impurities so the water is more to your liking. Contact water-treatment experts in your area. They will be familiar with local conditions and will know how to rectify them.

RADON

Radon is a radioactive gas that is given off by the decomposition of radium, an element that occurs naturally within the ground in varying (usually very small) concentrations. Evidence that radon exposure is hazardous to humans came to light years ago when high percentages of workers in German and Czechoslovakian mines developed lung cancer while working in areas having high concentrations of radon.

How Radon Enters a House
Radon can enter a house in a number of ways:

- Through cracks and voids in basement side walls, foundations, and floors, or in openings around drains, sump pumps, joints, and pipes.
- Through dirt-floor basements.

- Through areas left unfinished by the builder.
- Water drawn from a private well may contain radon that subsequently gets released into the house.
- Low air pressure can increase radon levels. Low air pressure can be caused by large appliances such as a furnace or clothes dryer that draw air into the house, by a warm indoor temperature during cold weather, and through kitchen and other exhaust fans, and chimneys.

Testing for Radon

Since radon gas is heavier than air, it tends to settle to the bottom areas in any dwelling in which it is found. Winter is generally the best time to test, because windows and doors are kept closed for long periods of time.

A preliminary screening can be done with a tester called a charcoal canister. It may be available through your health department. The results will tell you if there is nothing to worry about or if further tests are needed.

Results from radon tests should be read by health department officials. They will help you decide if steps should be taken to try to reduce radon levels in your home.

Radon Preventive Measures

The most effective method of reducing radon infiltration is to make a dwelling more airtight in those areas radon has been entering. This can mean:

1. Improving natural ventilation. Windows, doors, and vents can be opened to allow radon concentrations to dilute and escape, so radon won't collect in a basement or lower living area.
2. Using forced-air fans to blow air into a house, increasing the natural air exchange and reducing the amount of radon drawn in.
3. Sealing cracks and voids where radon enters, such as in the basement floor, openings around utility pipes, gaps between floors and walls, and holes at the top of concrete block walls and foundations.
4. Covering exposed earth in crawlspaces, storage areas, drainage areas, and the open part of a basement sump system.
5. Other methods include providing alternative air supplies for furnaces and clothes dryers, ventilat-

ing foundations, block walls, and drainage lines, and even supplying a pressurized atmosphere inside the house.

ASBESTOS

Asbestos is nasty stuff. Its tiny particles can be inhaled and retained in the lungs indefinitely. Years ago asbestos was frequently used as insulation, and to manufacture house siding and shingles. Children used to peel threads of it from samples included in mineral collections. Now you need a moon suit just to get near it. If you live in an older home, you might have asbestos in the attic, around your furnace or water heater, or in your siding.

It is difficult to identify asbestos on sight. The trained eye will even have problems distinguishing it from certain fiberglass and similar materials. If there is any doubt, your best bet is to hire a qualified professional to survey your home. He or she will know where to look, how to take samples, and what corrective actions are necessary, if any.

Never try to remove asbestos yourself. It is too hazardous. You might not get it all, and you will possibly inhale some during the task. Plus it is illegal to dispose of such a hazardous substance at your local sanitary landfill. There are strict rules that apply. Environmental Protection Agency regional asbestos coordinators are available to provide information on removal and disposal.

LEAD-BASED PAINT

Lead-based paint is another hazardous material that was once commonly applied to the inside of homes, to toys, and to innumerable items with which we come in contact.

The only accurate way to determine if paint in a home contains lead is to remove a sample of the paint and have it analyzed at a certified laboratory. If you suspect there could be lead paint in your home, contact your local health department office for a laboratory referral and more information.

Preventive measures include painting over the dangerous layer with different paint, or covering it with wallpaper, paneling, or some other building material so children do not disturb or accidentally ingest any of the hazardous lead paint.

**ENVIRONMENTAL FACTORS
QUICK CHECKLIST**

❑ Have your household water tested for dangerous substances, including lead.

❑ Test any suspected materials and items for lead-based paint.

❑ Test basement and lower living areas for radon infiltration.

❑ On older homes, inspect for asbestos insulation, shingles, and other materials.

PART 10

Your Custom PM Schedule

As mentioned in the Introduction, many inspections, cleanings, and repairs are associated with specific seasons. Depending on your location, and the components your home contains, each season should be used to spread a number of inspections out over its three months, so no particular month's maintenance tasks become overwhelming.

By putting together your own custom preventive maintenance schedule, the inspections and related maintenance tasks will require only brief investments of time each week.

Referring to the sample Master Schedule, note the areas that will apply to your personal schedule. (You have already made notes based on the text you just read, right?) Spread out the inspection and maintenance chores you will need to do, according to how you would like to schedule them.

After you have completed your Master PM Schedule, make copies of the blank Monthly PM Schedules. For these, either photocopy page 279, or copy it from the book as a template. Below is a sample Monthly PM Schedule.

MONTHLY PM SCHEDULE	August 1993
Inspection Items	**Repairs, Services, Comments**
1. Gutters /downspouts	OK
2. Caulking	Touch up windows on east side
3. Foundation walls	OK
4. Chimneys	Call chimney sweep for cleaning
5. Energy conservation	OK
6. Water conservation	Install low-flow shower head
7.	
8.	
9.	
10.	

MONTHLY PM SCHEDULE	
Inspection Items	**Repairs, Services, Comments**
1.	
2.	
3.	
4.	
5.	
6.	
7.	
8.	
9.	
10.	

MASTER SCHEDULE: *1993*

OUTDOORS FEATURES	Dec	Jan	Feb	Mar	Apr	May	Jun	Jul	Aug	Sep	Oct	Nov
Driveway		X						X				
Sidewalk								X				
Front patio								X				
Back patio								X				
Chain-link fence					X							
Landscaping — lawn				X			X			X		
Landscaping — trees				X			X			X		
Landscaping — garden				X			X				X	
Landscaping equip.			X								X	
Lawn furniture			X								X	
EXTERIOR SHELL												
Doors				X								
Windows/screens				X								
Siding							X					
Flashing/trim							X					
Roofs							X					
Gutters/downspouts				X					X			
Caulking									X			
Foundation walls									X			
Chimneys									X			
Pests						X						
INTERIOR SHELL												
Walls	X											
Ceilings	X											
Recessed lighting	X											
Interior doors								X				
Wood trim								X				
Carpeting		X										
Tile flooring		X										
Basement floor								X				
Garage floor								X				
UTILITY SPACE												
Staircases/steps		X										
Basement		X										

MASTER SCHEDULE: 1993

UTILITY SPACE	Dec	Jan	Feb	Mar	Apr	May	Jun	Jul	Aug	Sep	Oct	Nov
Garage		X										
Workshop		X										
MAJOR SYSTEMS												
Electrical	X			X			X			X		
Heating								X				
Plumbing					X					X		
Security						X						X
HOME APPLIANCES												
Ovens			X									
Refrig./freezers			X									
Clothes washer/dryer			X									
Computers			X									
Fireplace/wood stove			X								X	
Furniture											X	
HOUSEKEEPING												
Storage areas					X							
Spring cleaning					X							
Cleaning equip.						X						
Pet proofing				X								
FINANCIAL MATTERS												
Insurance	X											
Recordkeeping		X										
Energy conserv.									X			
Water conserv.									X			
HOME SAFETY												
Fire safety	X									X		
Slips/trips/falls	X				X							X
Electrical safety	X						X					
Poisons		X										
Environmental			X									X

MASTER SCHEDULE:

OUTDOORS FEATURES	Dec	Jan	Feb	Mar	Apr	May	Jun	Jul	Aug	Sep	Oct	Nov
Driveway												
Sidewalk												
Front patio												
Back patio												
Chain-link fence												
Landscaping — lawn												
Landscaping — trees												
Landscaping — garden												
Landscaping equip.												
Lawn furniture												
EXTERIOR SHELL												
Doors												
Windows/screens												
Siding												
Flashing/trim												
Roofs												
Gutters/downspouts												
Caulking												
Foundation walls												
Chimneys												
Pests												
INTERIOR SHELL												
Walls												
Ceilings												
Recessed lighting												
Interior doors												
Wood trim												
Carpeting												
Tile flooring												
Basement floor												
Garage floor												
UTILITY SPACE												
Staircases/steps												
Basement												

MASTER SCHEDULE:

UTILITY SPACE	Dec	Jan	Feb	Mar	Apr	May	Jun	Jul	Aug	Sep	Oct	Nov
Garage												
Workshop												
MAJOR SYSTEMS												
Electrical												
Heating												
Plumbing												
Security												
HOME APPLIANCES												
Ovens												
Refrig./freezers												
Clothes washer/dryer												
Computers												
Fireplace/wood stove												
Furniture												
HOUSEKEEPING												
Storage areas												
Spring cleaning												
Cleaning equip.												
Pet proofing												
FINANCIAL MATTERS												
Insurance												
Recordkeeping												
Energy conserv.												
Water conserv.												
HOME SAFETY												
Fire safety												
Slips/trips/falls												
Electrical safety												
Poisons												
Environmental												

PART 11

Keeping It Up

There is not much more to be said. The reasons for keeping up your maintenance inspections? They are the same ones that were discussed earlier.

Everything in your home will last longer and stay nicer, too. It will be safer. Equipment will function as it should. You won't be as inconvenienced. Surprise failures will be greatly reduced. You will protect your investments because your home and belongings will be worth more if you decide to sell or bequeath them. Most important, you will enjoy greater peace of mind, with less psychological, financial, and physical stress just by knowing that things are in good working order.

If you fall off the "maintenance wagon" once in a while, don't worry. Just start again where you left off. Rest assured that you are far ahead of the typical home owner who does no preventive maintenance — who simply reacts when repairs must be made. There is a lot of material in this book. Don't let it overwhelm you. No one household can use every idea of every section. Be selective. Depending on the condition of your home and the number of major components it contains, you might want to start slowly the first year, and gradually increase the items you are inspecting as the rest of the house comes under control.

The most important thing is to keep at it. Don't let months and months go by without doing *something* for your home's preventive maintenance. It is easy to set aside ten minutes of time here and twenty minutes there. You just have to get into the habit.

Now let's get on with the homework!

Index